TELEVISION

A BIOGRAPHY

DAVID THOMSON

ISION

A BIOGRAPHY

Thames & Hudson

First published in the United States of America in 2016 by
Thames & Hudson Inc., 500 Fifth Avenue, New York, NY 10110

thamesandhudsonusa.com

Published in the United Kingdom in 2016 by
Thames & Hudson Ltd, 181A High Holborn, London WC1V 7QX

www.thamesandhudson.com

Library of Congress Catalogue Number
2016932145

British Library Cataloguing-in-Publication Data:
A catalogue record of this book is available from the British Library.

ISBN: 978-0-500-51916-5

DESIGN: BTDNYC

Printed and bound in China.

FOR MARK FEENEY

Ordinary life was touching still, but science-fiction was happening.
You could call that technology. But an oven of fiction, a virtual reality,
had opened. And we wanted to be in it.

CONTENTS

The invisibility to posterity has always been television's difficulty. Many programs are intended to be disposable, to disintegrate even as you look at them.

MARK LAWSON

It's an incredible gauge of the generic. If we want to know what American normality is— i. e. what Americans want to regard as normal— we can trust television. For television's whole raison is reflecting what people want to see. It's a mirror. Not the Stendhalian mirror that reflects the blue sky and the mudpuddle. More like the overlit bathroom mirror before which the teenager monitors his biceps and determines his better profile. This kind of window on nervous American self-perception is simply invaluable in terms of writing fiction.

DAVID FOSTER WALLACE

THE ELEPHANT IN
THE ROOM?

IT'S OLDER THAN MOST OF US, parental yet uncritical, if not unconcerned. It poses as some kind of comfort, but you can't kid yourself it cares. So when did you start to think about television?

I admit "thinking" may be an inadequate word for what happened between you and this medium. So much that is formative in television has to do with the loose textures of ease or unthinking—"I'll go home and I'll watch…and then I'll feel all right." As if you hadn't felt all right out in the world. How could you, with that horizon getting grimmer from 1914 onward? But television's magic has always embraced safety, the possibility of "useful" intimate company, and the thought of time elapsing restfully but constructively. It's the sofa as church. Or rather, it is church reduced to the soft status of a sofa, minus guilt, redemption, or moral purpose.

There is this added, rueful comfort: Whenever you started thinking, it was too late. For the thing we used to call television doesn't quite exist now. The sacred fixed altar (the set) has given up its central place of worship and is now just one screen among so many, like the dinner table kept for state occasions in a life of snacking. The appointment times of TV have eroded; the possibility of a unified audience (or a purposeful society) has been put aside. In the dire 2015–16 presidential election campaign, it was obvious that the thing—the talent show—had found the frenzy of other game shows, with drastic but meaningless dialogue and monstrous celebrity better suited to daytime soap operas. As a democratic process it was not just shaming; there was the portent of worse to come, even a fear that "the vote" might be buried in some instant TV feedback derived from *American Idol*. "You like to vote—let's do it all the time." Could such a game show go on…forever? Because the media fed on it and felt some deranged fulfillment. The more debates, the less subjects were debated. Journalists were alive with jittery, spinning self-importance. They said the election was the most important ever—that sweet dream. We knew it was just a nightmare show our trance had allowed.

‖‖‖‖‖‖‖‖‖‖‖‖‖‖‖‖‖‖‖‖‖‖‖

TELEVISION WASN'T ALWAYS "ON" OR THERE. It had no place in the settled order of things. There was an ancient time, BT, after which the new word sounded rather sci-fi or gimmicky—like plastic, the bikini, or the atom bomb. In other words, people wondered if the craze could last—but then it spread, like weather.

The invention, or the quaint piece of furniture, wandered into our life in the 1940s, as a primitive plaything, a clever if awkward addition to the household. It was expensive, unreliable, and a bit of an invalid. "Reception" was so vexed and frustrating we laughed and scolded ourselves for being idiots. If we couldn't get its image to stay still, how could we foresee that it would devour us? We're hardly to blame, are we? We were used to movies and radios, which came on like shows and performances—versions of theater. Television would try that for a while, putting a stress on schedules and neurotic start times. But that was a ruse to hide the deeper import—that it was simply on or off. As with sex, reception gave way to absorption. Some shows flopped while others soared, but some people were content with the test card. Watching, criticism, judgment, meaning—all those esteemed procedures—were on the way out.

The household pet of once upon a time became a strange, placid being—the elephant in the room, if you like—not a monster that attacked us and beat its Kong chest in triumph but an impassive force that quietly commandeered so much of what we thought was our attention, our consciousness, or our intelligence. Television wasn't just an elephant in the room. It became the room, the house, and the world.

You can respond to this with alarm if you wish. (In theory, alarm is still available.) But the deepest nature of television is to be reassuring. That may be the most frightening thing about it.

I know, that doesn't seem to fit: How can reassurance be a source of anxiety? But doesn't one spur the other? We are selling our complex experience short if we don't take note of the modern pressure for impossible simplicity, like stopping fossil fuels or carpet bombing ISIS. In the course of this book, I will refer to screens having done so much to organize our experience—I mean our making our way by watching screens, or by having them on, hardly aware of how the television screen has trained us for the computer screen, the iPad, the iPhone, or even the iI (coming so soon I wish I had invested), and the assumption that because information is carried in those ways so knowledge must exist there.

Some rejoice at this. They say it is the highest proof of universality and prospects of the global village, which brightened for a moment when the glimpse of "world action" lit up Paris in December 2015 in the PR war against… call it global warming.

There was once a British news show, *World in Action* (1963–98), that never sought to question the titular confidence that news happened in an orderly, televisual way. It was an appealing concept, and one that spoke to the relatively tidy problems that dominated the postwar world, like "beating fascism"—or *Licking Hitler*, to use the title of a brilliant TV play written by David Hare in 1978. Adolf was licked, but just because the war was won didn't guarantee the death of fascism. The disconcerting mix of dread and desire in that ism still waits on problems we know are not for licking. But the passive imprint of screens does exist, and sometimes we can be forgiven for wondering if their secret intent is to be the only thing that exists—not a server for the world so much as a replacement.

At one point, I thought of calling this book *The Elephant in the Room*. For a jacket, I saw a desolate, droughty rural scape (with the teeth of an urban horizon behind it: think *True Detective*, Series 1—don't go past Series 1). In the foreground of that wasteland, along with an abandoned television set—a fussy antique from the fifties or sixties—you could see an elephant, perched on its hind legs, like Babar in a circus, twirling his trunk at us in a mood that might be teasing, saying "Hi, there," or sending a warning.

But the more I thought about books and television, the more this approach felt like an ominous relic from the sixties and seventies—and there were books then, stunned by television and its threat. The most striking of them was Jerry Mander's inspired and irrefutable *Four Arguments for the Elimination of Television* (1978). But it's too late for that doomsday spirit. We are never going to resist our future or doubt a technology. The world's not going to end. *We* may make a hurried exit, but the global village or its desert, not to mention the intersidereal vastness, will linger and wait for cell scum to re-form so that people can invent television again.

The last time I saw a version of that alarmist classic *Invasion of the Body Snatchers*, it occurred to me that the takeover of our valiant, vivid selves by pod people had become comic and antiquated as a threat. Hasn't so much of it happened already? There we are, identifying with those decent liberal resistance fighters—Kevin McCarthy (1956) or Donald Sutherland (1978)—when truly we are the new occupying pods.

Those heroic resistance figures in *Body Snatchers* are striving to stay free, to be themselves: unique, independent, critical spirits—to this day our education still recites those admirable homilies. But FDR had the secret in 1941 in identifying the value of freedom *from* things (want and fear) as much as freedoms *of* speech and worship. So much freedom is a vast negative capability: Keep me free from cancer and Alzheimer's (and death, too, while we're on the subject). Put shock absorbers on the big ones, the San Andreas Fault or the Cascadia Subduction Zone. Do not rerun the calamities revealed at Fukushima, or permit the onset of thermonuclear war, *terrorist attack!*, bad breath, the creeping tide of oceans driven by climate change, or days like that when Secretary of the Treasury Hank Paulson threw up because the whisper of the fiscal abyss was so scary. (It was William Hurt on TV, in *Too Big to Fail*—there's a title from elephant culture.)

Grant me those freedom-froms and I'll be a well-behaved, politically correct, fully insured soldier of order. I'll behave. It's old-hat optimism to think that fascists only come wearing brown shirts, beating people up, and having a concentration camp at the end of the lane. They may be obedient, anxious citizens. Like us.

Another consequence is that our "living room" has altered in disconcerting ways. We like to think that a living room (don't we live in *all* the rooms? If not, what are we up to in the *living* room? Does it mean that room is alive?) is a part of the scheme called "home," the way we buy or rent a place that is ours, secure, private, and nurturing. It's so nice to come home to home, isn't it?

But is that mood turning archaic? Already, the tableau of the family gathered at the hearth called television is an emblem of nostalgia like Dickensian tableaux of Christmas. We've known for our lifetime that any home can be disappeared: It is vulnerable to destructive blast, to bombs, drones, and occupation. One of the abiding images of television (on the News, in fiction) is the devastated home—is it a poetic corrective to the neurotic domesticity in commercials? Are those footsteps on the stairs coming to dispossess us? We have new fears of weather, and there is a fresh open-mindedness in the market over repossession and the next big short. There may be a derelict sleeping on the street outside who views our home with a mix of envy and vengeance close to illness or ideology. Home means more and more in that world, for it is the last refuge. But that attachment is also a source of such vulnerability—not least because the on/off function, that sweet switch, will be dead. Imagine your screen if it doesn't come on.

WE ARE NEVER GOING TO RESIST OUR FUTURE OR DOUBT A TECHNOLOGY.

THE ELEPHANT FIRST AMBLED INTO MY THOUGHTS on seeing Michael Almereyda's movie *Experimenter* (2015), a dramatization of the research done by Stanley Milgram at Yale in the early 1960s. As a social psychologist, Milgram ran tests or experiments to study the human habit of obedience. He was Jewish, of Rumanian and Hungarian descent, and he felt prompted by the 1961 televised trial of Adolf Eichmann, an accused who said he had only done as he was told. Eichmann sat in a glass box in the Jerusalem court; like that, he resembled the people Milgram was using in his experiments, but he also dramatized the weird condition of being on television.

The setup at Yale required two spaces or rooms linked by sound: A "teacher" sat in one room and asked questions of the "learner" next door. If the answers were incorrect, the teacher was to administer an electric shock to the learner. The voltage strength of these shocks increased with every wrong answer. A few teachers resisted the situation, horrified at the sounds of distress they heard from next door when the jolts were delivered. But the great majority went to the limit in obediently punishing the groaning people in the other room. They had been told to do it by those running the experiment.

In truth, the teacher was the stooge while the learner was part of the plot, acting out the pain. The shocks existed only in the mind of the unaware teacher and in the prerecorded grunts of agony.

It was what is called an elegant experiment, and it's hard to resist its implications when so many have followed orders beyond the point of pain, even as far as genocide or the enlightened management of others' poverty, which can still seem academic or chilly to the poor. That line of consequence is an elephant in our room. There is a moment in *Experimenter* where Milgram (Peter Sarsgaard) is seen walking in a corridor of the building where he works. All of a sudden, a young elephant falls in behind him and ambles along in benign, if not obedient, pursuit of Stanley. You might guess that we would worry over some threat to the experimenter; instead, the elephant seems a whimsical or tolerant companion in the same space. Milgram smiles gently, like a man fond of such creatures and able to hear their tread.

Experimenter is as unsettling as it is charming. Milgram's test points to the potential for a modern fascism that has learned to trot along with the discreet charm of the decent middle class. It is not Eichmannesque or dressed up in SS black; it is not deliberately cruel or crushing. It knows the instinct for conformity in most of us, and understands that fascism feeds on the spirit of nullity. Fascism is not just a movie about Nazis torturing people—it is what happens when we the people withdraw from our participation and responsibility and give authority its head.

So "the elephant in the room" also suggests something ominous if one believes television may be suited to passive acquiescence or turning a blind eye. That notion of "a room" is especially pointed in considering television, because for most of us TV was born in domesticity. It promised to be fun, controllable, like a pet—a puppy maybe. Then it grew.

So the elephant felt like a proper signpost for a book that wanted to be a provocative biography of what I will call the television era, which began to be surpassed and explained by Internet screens that recast our habits and our experience.

Years after the medium had been "invented" or "demonstrated" in the 1930s, the first mass-produced television sets went on sale in the United States in 1946. The medium seemed so ramshackle and foolish, you could hardly call it a medium. But it was the dawn of an empire

and an unobtrusive passivity that beggars those waves of ism that rushed over the surface of modern history. By 2015, according to very rough, childlike calculation (mine), if you wanted to play *everything* that has been on *all* the channels of American television *all* the hours of *every* day, that playing would take *5,000 years*, give or take a century or so. Except that by the end of 5,000 years there would be a new number of accumulated hours to play, so enormous that it is wearying to contemplate (and worthy of Carl Sagan's wide-voiced adoration of "billions and billions").

The *stuff* is growing at a demented pace, as if "the wasteland"—once a lofty put-down of television—were actually a rampant jungle. Maybe the only one on Earth that is still growing? Where is television going, and can it be guided or redirected? Are those questions folly or topics for the Aspen Institute? Is there any reason to think we are in charge of the landslide? Tell me the large technologies humans have stopped, diverted, or put a brake on.

HOW DIFFERENT IS THE "ELECTRONIC SYSTEM" FROM THAT LIGHT YOU TURN ON?

Is it cynical or irrational to suppose that television has already, for decades, been organized to calm and quell unease in a mass society that could turn to panic? Is it possible that in societies such as the United States it has been a steady promoter of the marketplace and what is sometimes called "the economy" by those who prefer to ignore the damage made by poverty? Or is the system simply very practical? One can argue that television is the product of corporations, talents, and urges toward profit as well as entertainment. Throughout this book, I'll address the efforts of such individuals and business enterprises to make something good and new on television.

But consider the possibility that all that ordinary greed and creative ambition distract us from a kind of authority that requires order and obedience. The mechanical process, the medium, is a helpless bearer of political connotations and the chance of meaning (or its diminution) in a mass society. Look at a basic definition of television, and its value-free implication is clear: "an electronic system of transmitting transient images of fixed or moving objects together with sound over a wire or through space."

Think about some of those words.

Electronic: Generated by electricity, which is explicable but is also magic in that you cannot see it happening.

Transmitting: That calls for some generating source—a factory, a government, or even you or me sending out the stuff.

Transient: They're moving, they won't last, or both? Must have something to do with time.

Images: Things you can see, rendered appearances, like photographic records? But do they have to be lifelike, or can they be like lives you've never seen?

Fixed or moving objects: Stuff? Nature? Us?

With sound: So you can hear and see at the same time? So much of television doesn't insist on being seen: the News, comedy, commercials. Synchronicity? Or can you only hear what you're seeing?

A wire: A live wire that carries current?

Through space: So the transmission goes from here to there? But how far?

Think of the definition in terms of electric light. That's an image, or an illumination, lasting in time—or it's a force that permits all images. It needs a wire. It comes through space. It doesn't have sound—yet, if you listen very carefully, I think an "on" thing does have a low level of sound, or being, or tone, or presence. Electric light doesn't do fixed or moving objects? Perhaps, but the light is fixed and objects move in it. And electric light makes you notice time: When it gets light enough outside, you can turn off the lights inside. So how different is this "electronic system" from that light you turn on, and leave on, when you enter a room?

As a kid, I went to the movies for the light on the screen. The story was sweet, the people were desirable, but so often it was the same story: good guys beating bad guys and getting the pretty woman. I went in for the spill of light, not caring what the story was. In other words, TV can be a light (or a light therapy), a service and a possibility, without any pressing messages. The novel thinking in "the medium is the message" may have taught us not to bother so much with messages. The shape of this book—the Medium and its Messages—suggests a struggle in which our most ardent and honorable hopes for meaning may be eclipsed by the passive persistence of the thing itself.

Think about this small confession. At about ten o'clock every evening, I used to take the dog for its last walk around the houses. Often enough at that time, the television was on, and I noticed that I did not turn it off for the fifteen minutes or so we'd be away. I left the lights on, too. It was irrational and uneconomic, but I did it. Was that to make the house welcoming when I returned and to save the few seconds it took to turn the set back on again? Was it a neurotic habit, a weird way of saying the house *needed* these things on to be alive—or did I need this contact while I was "away"? Was I comforted if it stayed on? [Pocket assignment: Write a paragraph about how you feel when you turn a TV off. It will help you with this book. A short paragraph will suffice.]

As the book goes along, and we consider the impact of electricity, screens, and being "on," I'm going to say that television isn't just its own golden ages of shows and stories and personalities. It's the harbinger of the computer screen, the Internet, your smartphone, the thumbnail that is tracking the Dow, not to mention the chip in your head that one day will play Mahler, observe the daily life of the ocelot, or teach you Hungarian. Not to mention the screens to come in the next 5,000 years.

||||||||||||||||||||||||||

WHEN *DID* YOU START THINKING ABOUT TELEVISION? That's a pointed question because so much about the medium encouraged a contrary notion: "Oh, you don't need to *think* about it—any more than you do when you turn on the light." But forces we don't think about can still map our brain, like breathing, heartbeats, looking at the light, and living with an elephant.

I got into thinking about movies at the age of four, as I realized that the show I loved was also sending me into terror so bad I often had to be taken out of the theater. What I was afraid of was the awesome reality that did and didn't exist. Reality is daunting enough at four, but it's more confounding if you feel it may not exist. And I could not pin down whether there was a magic footpath by which I might enter the screen's chamber. Or was its world beyond reach, just a mirage? Well, I converted my terror into the idea of being told a story. I then made it something to write about and teach, and soon I was devout in feeling a movie could be a work of art. But sometimes "a work of art" is itself a brand that gets in the way of thinking. Naming *Citizen Kane* the best film ever for fifty years didn't help our open-minded experience of it.

I was teaching film studies at Dartmouth in the late 1970s, and enjoying it. Students easily assumed that Orson Welles, Howard Hawks, or Luis Buñuel might be as valid as Milton, Mozart, or Velázquez—but more charming or cool (they were alive still in 1977). There was one student who nosed around my office, eager to talk. He was doing a film class on documentary: He made a cinema verité doc about hazing in his fraternity. It was crude, awkwardly shot, but a local sensation.

As I got to know him, I realized that film struck him as quaint or archaic. He was so far ahead of me, yet he reminded me of my childhood and the way I once let screen light wash over me before I discovered "directors." As a teacher or an author, by 1978 I was devoted to the idea that certain

POCKET ASSIGNMENT: WRITE A PARAGRAPH ABOUT HOW YOU FEEL WHEN YOU TURN A TV OFF.

people—"auteurs"—made films and were subjects for seminars or books, the scaffolding for making a living. But this kid had a wiser intuition: He guessed that a machine made television as a kind of air or Muzak pumped into our room. Television was his obsession, his nervous system. And he knew much more about American shows than I did (I was only lately arrived from England): He could recount entire episode arcs of *My Three Sons* (1960–72) and *Hawaii Five-0* (1968–80). But if I asked him which shows he favored, he would smile and say it didn't much matter. He liked them all; he liked television. (People had, and have, a similar attitude to the United States.)

He was rather boring in a friendly way, but quite amazing (that's a hint about TV), and one day I asked him how many hours a day he watched. Now, he was a serious student with a major in economics; he was passing his courses, and he was part of a fraternity. He had a life; he laughed a lot. Yet he told me, without any attempt at irony, "Oh, I hardly ever watch more than seven hours a day."

That was more amazing than boring. Or was it alarming? I had colleagues in the Dartmouth community—liberal intellectuals, bookstore veterans—who refused to have a television set in the house because of the distraction it would be for their young children, or for them. There was still a worry that television undermined a discriminating, humanist culture. But it had been part of my message in teaching "cinema" that moving film had been a challenging marvel of the twentieth century whereby young people saw movies (I saw three a week in my teens) without any attempt by their educational system to assess the nature of shots, close-ups, editing, movie stars, cinematic information, lifelike dreams, and so on. Three movies a week meant six or seven hours—what this Dartmouth student was logging on television every day.

I introduced the first class in television at Dartmouth College—An Introduction to Television—in 1979. Twenty years late, I felt I was breaking ground. But you couldn't just do that on a whim. A new course had to secure the approval of the Committee on Instruction. So I took a full description, an argument, a reading list, work requirements, and suggestions on viewing to the committee, and opened myself up to their examination. I was determined to be serious with an issue some academics found frivolous or trivial. (The idea that triviality was a key to America was only just dawning.)

One member of the committee was Leonard Rieser, provost of the college and so exceptional a physicist that he had been enlisted in the Manhattan Project when only twenty-two. I knew Leonard a little: We were neighbors in Norwich, Vermont, a beautiful place, little changed in two centuries. You could not feel television's imprint there—though in just a few years it would be the setting for *Newhart* (1982–90), the place where the characters Dick and Joanna Loudon would take over and reopen the Norwich Inn (not that the real place had closed).

Our relationship made the talk on the committee amiable. At one point, striving for significance, I said something like, "Television may be the most powerful cultural force in our students' lives." Leonard smiled magnanimously and said he was of the opinion that the existence of nuclear weapons was more potent.

That was 1979, which was a lot safer than 1945 or 1962. In practice, people were worrying less about the Bomb by then. So I replied, "Well, you're right in an important way. But while the Bomb hovers overhead, oppressing our sense of destiny or possibility, six or seven hours a day, every day, some kids are wrestling with *Charlie's Angels* and *Fantasy Island*." (People will say anything at committee meetings.) From his look, I guessed that Leonard had not faced those threats. To his credit, he was much involved with the Doomsday Clock project (at present, that estimate of our future stands at three minutes to midnight).

The course was approved, and I taught it, and even then I wondered if movies were coming to an end as TV advanced on its 5,000-year empire. But that was an innocent age of TV still: No one would exult over *Charlie's Angels* or Farrah's hair now, when we can get years of pudding-whipped porn. I have written books about movies, and they will surely influence this one, but I think I began to feel the prospect of the book you are holding now in 1979. (Perhaps you're reading it on a screen.)

||||||||||||||||||||||||||||

SO HOW DOES ONE tell "the story" of the television era? I had approached this book as a history that tracked the spread of the medium. But the more I thought about that (and tried to find a structure), the more I felt confounded. Almost any biographical account is persuaded by the passage of time that one thing happens after another, as a kind of consequence. But this history doesn't necessarily work in that obedient way anymore. Once upon a time, TV had such restricted choices to make that choice seemed vital: three networks in the United States and just one in Britain. But if you look at your TV now, the range is effectively infinite: All these things are going on at the same time. It's impossible to keep faith with the principles of choice, attention, and understanding. So sometimes we yield to the chaos just by keeping the thing *on* and trying to stay on ourselves. It's really not far-fetched to think we could become screens.

Put it this way: If you're watching *The Affair* tonight on Showtime (and trying to decide whether you *believe* in it or you are just being patient with a sex show acting intellectual), you know there is also a Spanish shopping channel going on, reruns of *Friends*, the Warriors playing the Rockets, swirling weather maps, a preacher preaching, elephants ignoring hyenas, Cary Grant about to say something, and maybe five hundred other channels, all at the same time. That's how we amass our 5,000 years. That's the unconfined untidiness of the stuff. There is no control, anywhere, beyond the stuff being all crammed on one screen, and that is a richness as well as a challenge.

TELEVISION (OR SOMETHING LIKE IT) WILL OUTLAST US.

I tried starting at the beginning, but it went against the grain of being lost. How can you say, "In January 1950, these shows were playing… Then in February…But in March…"? That led to the trap of feeling bound to mention every program ever made, not just the ones worth remembering. That can't be done without making the book a list or some ponderous *TV Guide*. And it's not just the good shows that matter. So much of TV has been forgettable, or worse: Some has been so ghastly we cannot forget it, and most of us admit that we spend hours and years watching "rubbish" on TV. "There's nothing on!" we lament. Does that mean we're mad, or could it be that our definition of "watching" has shifted?

So I arrived at this structure: a book of two parts, the Medium and its Messages. In chapters 1 through 9, I will try to explore the climate of TV, the things that are always there. Then in chapters 10 through 21, I will take themes or messages—the News, drama, live TV, police shows, comedies, documentary, and so on—and describe how they have developed over the decades, not just *here* in the United States, but over *there*, in Britain, which was once my *here* and which has offered some exciting alternatives to American directions.

Early on in Part One, I'm going to look at a couple of formulaic shows, just because they stand for that era when TV was moving from novel craze to complacent habit: *The Fugitive* (1963–67) and *The Donna Reed Show* (1958–66). I could have chosen many other shows, just as this book has to omit so much television you might think of, and which you liked. In Part Two I move on to consider shows that (in my opinion) were good, even important. But bear in mind, "opinion" and "important" may be old-fashioned thinking. We don't believe that the electric light is better or more significant than it was the night before last.

There's another reason why the historical approach is misleading or cumbersome. It wants to believe in positive development. A similar fallacy exists in treating the larger thing we call history as an arc of progressive narrative. It's as easy to see it the other way around, as a process that has witnessed decline, entropy, and even a narrowing of human aspiration. So the sea or the river has its current, but it can no more understand its direction than alter it. We'd best reconcile ourselves to a scheme in which television (or something like it) will outlast us and become not just a window on the world but the entire house where we live. This is going to be a book about the cultural atmosphere our several small screens have made, and how we have little power over their momentum beyond the on/off switch. It is less a straight line ahead than a plan of rooms in a house. It is the house we live in, busy but helpless, untidy but structured—and it has had strange effects on how we live.

Perhaps television and all the smaller screens it has made are a chance to come to terms with our experience, be overwhelmed by our insignificance, or find some radical structure for controlling it—I mean a political discipline or a survival system, even a scheme for reassessing ourselves as warm, soft technologies, that will pacify some of the doubt or pain attached to being alive. One disconcerting consequence of small screens is how they offer a way of bypassing real, complicated experience, even to a point where that "real" seems archaic and elderly. More than I knew with the Dartmouth Committee on Instruction in 1979, television has redesigned us. The age of humanism may be burning off. Are we even a society (that's a rose-colored word)? Or are we a jittery mass, identified in demography, purchasing habits, digital fingerprints, virtual participation, and fantasy response instead of through real individual behavior?

You can put that questioning down to my age and personal history. Someone younger may see it as all working out for the best, so why bother? I'm never sure. Writing about movies, I reckoned to be clear or decisive—or even "right," as if experience and history could be controlled by aesthetic judgments. With TV, I lack that certainty. Instead of watching stories that might be art, I feel we're witnessing a world past caring, a world that is profuse, wonderful, scary, and as heedless as time. Don't go away.

TELEVISION HAS REDESIGNED US.

PART ONE THE MEDIUM

BUY THE NUMBERS

EVERY HOTEL ROOM HAS ONE; there's one by your hospital bed. So many threats of solitude or loneliness have a set at hand, like oxygen  or the morphine button in that hospital. You get on a plane and the screen is embedded in the back of the seat in front of you. In prisons, cells have screens. (Why not in solitary?) Isn't the screen now a measure of a necessary impacted solitude? People going places on the street are studying their hand screens. Grown-up children wander from room to room carrying their iPads; it is like an IV, and seems to be life-supporting. You see cardboard and tent cities under freeway ramps where "derelicts" have a set and the community has a battery to power it. At public arenas, big ball games on the road are put up on huge screens for thousands of home fans. In some bedrooms, archival footage of prior (youthful) couplings may be watched as older lovers try again.

And sometimes the set, "the telly," plays forever, like surveillance in an underground parking lot, waiting for a terrorist or Deep Throat, but quite content with calm nullity. In January 2006, the remains of Joyce Vincent were found in her Wood Green rented room in north London. She was said to be a busy and gregarious person, but no one had reported her missing. She had apparently died in December 2003, and nothing was left of her but the skeleton and strands of dried tissue. Her television was still playing.

This is the medium central to modern experience, yet so embedded we do not always notice it. Its centrality emerges most clearly in any comparison with movies, the form that it was infamous for replacing, although that is not quite what happened in those years after 1945 when moviegoing reached its peak in popularity. An assumption of competition covered that overlap in the late forties and early fifties as one audience declined and another soared. But the overlap, and the way some of the same people were involved in both media, were incidental to the enormity of the technological shift and the alteration in focus.

We went out to the movies, as if going to a stage play, a concert, a sporting event, or a religious service. It would happen at one public place at one announced moment. Even if a film had many showings, we had to be there on time to see it. The atmosphere was auspicious— quite simply, there *was* atmosphere. The screen was enormous and the light was as bright as attendant darkness could make it. We had to watch the faces and follow the images while listening to what was said. From the outset, a movie show seemed miraculous, but in fact audiences quickly worked it out. They appreciated the list of essential elements: a white screen, a projector with its light, and reels of celluloid. The viewer might not know how to load a projector or repair it in an emergency, but the process was understood even if the matters of identification and fantasy remained mysterious.

TELEVISION SUGGESTED IT WAS THE OLD MESSAGE IN A NEW FORM.

Television suggested it was the old message in a new form. But the atmosphere was domestic, commonplace, and automatic. People could watch unshowered, unshaved, undressed; they could accommodate all manner of interruptions. They didn't actually have to watch; they often behaved as if they were not quite there as an audience.

A sweet inattention dawned, a mix of boredom, liberty and futility. Shows played at set times, but the thing itself—the medium, the presence, the on-ness—persisted for as long as it had anything to show. Some of us gazed at the test card, or watched the last dot of light vanish.

The screen was small, shabby, and its picture and sound were unlovely. No one noticed or complained—reception could be as precious but hazy as Admiral Byrd's voice from the South Pole. Hardly anyone understood how the set worked. For years, the TV was the least reliable appliance in the house, at a moment when America was falling in love with durable goods. The mechanics of television involved pesky receiver aerials attached to the roof, or antennae sitting on top of the set and in need of endless adjustment. For a generation, cities were forests of those H-shapes, as if in secret warning of the hydrogen bomb. It was enough to have a set (and it was called "a set," suggesting bulk and complexity)—if you could afford it: In 1938, a 12-inch set cost $445, more than $7,000 in 2015 dollars. By 1949, with the medium on the move, the Sears, Roebuck catalog offered a TV set for the first time—it was a cabinet surrounding and seeking to domesticate a 9-inch screen—at $149.95 (more than 10 percent of the average annual salary in the United States). About 3 million households had a set then, well under 10-percent coverage.

You put those sets on and you got just a few channels, to be found by turning another switch or dial on the set. Nothing is that simple now. We have hundreds of channels and on/off devices and remote switches that require our cable carrier to have hotlines for emergency helplessness. My household has known the comic crisis when the kids leave for college, taking with them the last chance of making the set work like a reliable household item.

We might be frustrated by that, because we are paying for it. But we suffer and endure, because that is part of our curious participation, and the strongest link television has with cinema. Neither medium knows we are there, anonymous and existentially unknown numbers in the mass medium. We are in our own home, yet displaced—no one planned or understood that possibility, yet it has occurred. The set and the screen sometimes control the house; it is as if so many domestic pastimes have been undermined. We are used to claiming that our precious privacy is being betrayed in so many *external* ways. But there is a more sinister dismay: that *domestic* privacy is being erased. I don't mean "sinister" in the old sense, for no Big Brother is doing this. It is we who are letting slip that unobserved solitude in which thought may occur. Like the screens, we risk being always "on" without the need for thought, or critical alertness. Of course television can pacify loneliness. It was said to be a medium for the young, but it has had no greater beneficiaries than the elderly and the sick, who may feel part of the world again—if they are prepared to accept the branding of "elderly" or "sick."

It was said for decades that television was a service: It covered live events, news reportage, and the commodity all too easily encoded as entertainment or fun. It also encouraged us to buy certain goods and hold dear some "correct" ideas and ideologies (many of them connected to purchase). Those functions still operate, despite enormous shifts in technology. But the medium had another role, all the more powerful because it was never intended or organized: It promoted the principle that it was sufficient for the world to be witnessed, or to have it pass by. It did not require the effort of understanding or criticism. Its "on-ness" was paramount, just as our participation began to be offset. This was a new solitude, not just that of living alone: You could be in a crowd, but you might not matter.

Nothing in this is new (even if the impact of the idea may be unsettling). In the first age of television use, there were some prescient visions. In Canada, Marshall McLuhan published *The Mechanical Bride* in 1951, a series of essays and commentaries on various phenomena in advertising and media. He was a decade or so away from saying "the medium is the message," but he was feeling his way toward that at a time when it was widely believed that media were innocent, obliging forms that simply delivered entertainment and information. Two years before *The Mechanical Bride*, a novel had felt the possibility that some device or service could be introduced into households that was not just a means of surveillance but a radical reorganization of our place in modern times. The novel was *Nineteen Eighty-Four* by George Orwell. It is usually claimed that Orwell was inspired, and alarmed enough, to create Big Brother because of a

figure he had seen on advertising billboards. There is no evidence that Orwell had a television set of his own in England. Still, the telescreen that exists in his world of Oceania is not just a screen for fun and diversion; it is an eye that sees and hears citizens in their private places.

Television did not yet have the surveillance power that frightened Orwell, though it would introduce a piece of technology into the household that was based on a cable system that could, in theory, send information in both directions. More immediately, the economics of television broadcasting depended on measured audience response, to which the messages could be calibrated. The medium was often paid for by advertising, and the payment would be invalid or frustrated if the commercials did not work. So the medium was always a crude social survey in those territories where it was funded by advertising.

The contract with advertising was based on a ratings system. Arthur Charles Nielsen (1897–1980) was of Danish descent, born in Chicago. His A. C. Nielsen company began by doing market reports on advertising, and in 1942 he established a system for reporting the number of people listening to radio shows, with a view to helping advertisers decide whether they were getting their money's worth. It was in 1950 that Nielsen initiated a television ratings service. To this day, that service is instrumental in the overall economy of television, no matter that its surveys now have only a feeble relationship with what happens in our homes with that light box. Far from certain in what it reports, Nielsen has been oil to the engine of television. That only helps show how poor or incomplete our understanding of the medium is.

Nielsen has had two ways of judging how many people are watching: It gave out diaries that members of a household were required to fill out accurately on their viewing; or it installed meter systems that recorded how long a set was on and what channel it was tuned to. Sometimes there were on-the-street interviews asking what people had seen last night.

It's likely that in the first novelty of public opinion polls, people answered or filled in their diary honestly. But by now we have been polled beyond patience or faith. Many of us reject opinion polls as soon as we realize what they are—and that scorn can extend to politics itself. Because we hate polls, we sometimes offer absurd answers just to screw up their system. As for metering, it was designed for households that gathered as obedient units in front of TVs with limited options. Yet even in the sixties it was clear that some households (usually the most potent in terms of purchasing power) had several sets going at once. All of them might be on yet unattended—playing in an empty room. Similarly, the meters were inept at dealing with situations—college common rooms, hospitals, institutions of various kinds—where groups might be watching one set. Then throw in the fact that, with remote control and channel surfing, the medium was being watched, or it was "on," without the clickers settling on one program.

Take all of those conditions together and add them to our developed tendency to mock or ignore ads, and the principle of the ratings becomes very uncertain. The numbers thrown around as a measure of success apparently still sustain a large economy of the medium: The more people watch a sponsored show and see its ads, the better the advertised products will do in the marketplace. But it's reasonable now to say **WE LIVE WITH A SITUATION WHERE TELEVISION IS WATCHING US.** that the most involved watching—that for long-form series on cable—cannot be linked to viewership or product sales. Indeed, the audience numbers on our famous cable series have long been very modest compared with those the networks claim for their hit shows.

Later on, I will refer to the decline in the audience for the Oscars, even though the rates charged for ads on that show have risen. It doesn't make sense, and in general, rational systems should pay attention when that charge arises. We do more and more irrational things because technology, statistics, and feebleness have made a modern marriage. In 2015, Congress improved its education service—it was upgraded from "No Child Left Behind" to "Every Student Succeeds," despite mounting evidence that students were failing at impressive new rates, while some children were so tragically left behind that the branding had to be beefed up. Less than 40 percent of graduating high-school seniors are "ready" for college—so college moderates its levels.

Some books are called "best sellers," reflecting actual numbers sold. But books are for reading, not just selling. The experience and the impact of reading involve the way words can change us or offer us new possibilities. Books as a whole reach a tiny fraction of the population, but some books have had a disproportionate influence on the readers that take them in. Thus, the ratings system (which I will use often enough in this book in an attempt to measure the effectiveness of a program) is unsound. It misses the way TV is like the light, on but unnoticed, and the way inattention can shape our minds. You know this is true: Television is not for attention; the ads trained us in not watching. But the ratings system is a self-serving code of success, and it instills the notion that the more people watch, the better, because that empowers capitalism. But the ratings cheat on the possibility that television may play programs that are not for everyone, that are actually intended for a few. Television has seldom liked to offer the prospect that it might go "off." So the mainstream of the medium clung to the idea that everyone can understand everything—but that can slip into the delusion that no one needs to understand anything.

So we live with a situation where television is watching us. A modest lifetime after 1949, that surveillance is so much more sophisticated, with your most precious screens—the computer, your phone, your iPad—the most far-reaching versions of television. At present. You can see most programs there if you are so inclined, just as you use them as a means of letter writing and reading, a library of information, a means of purchase that can come close to eliminating conventional shopping and its journeys—we are big travelers still, but technology is in place that could cancel out the urge to go anywhere. It follows that we realize our words, our tastes, and so many of our choices may be known to those allegedly eternal forces in the world— our government; commercial operations of all sorts—and that information could be used to make us malleable and predictable. Maybe gravest of all, we are not sure how much those entities know about us or how steadily we are being observed. Much of this scrutiny is done in the name of security, order, and control, when you can sense the fear, the panic, of a world losing control. A very frightening prospect in a culture of electronic screens is the power going *off*, depriving us of all those comforting services in on-ness. How long would such a breakdown last before panic set in?

Somehow we have to find a way of believing that the process is straightforward and benevolent, even if it feels alienating as it assesses us and converts us into statistics. Will a time come when we need to surrender precious human feelings just to be orderly and identifiable, the end product of *Invasion of the Body Snatchers*? Will terrorism realize that turning everything off could be its coup?

This is a book about the possibility that technology can take control by offering a feeble imitation of contact. And few things are more likely to trade on our solitude. Let's now pursue an example: *The Fugitive*, a great favorite of the sixties, seemingly a show about a man in the desperate position of being hunted, but secretly a celebration of being unattached, free, and led on by desire.

WHERE ARE YOU GOING, FUGITIVE?

I'M GOING TO WRITE THIS DOWN, but words on the page are not sufficient. I would prefer to *hear* this introduction as narration from the

voice of actor William Conrad in his end-of-human-history growl, and the first four slamming notes of the theme music beneath him. I require the terrific bogus certainty of that voice and the flourish of that Pete Rugolo music, echoing through the house, summoning us to the sofa:

This is January 5, 1965, on ABC at 10:00 P.M. It is one day after President Lyndon Johnson's State of the Union address, in which he has announced a new series, "The Great Society." That one will run forever. In the next two months *The Sound of Music*, the movie, will open; the Bloody Sunday march will take place in Selma, Alabama; and the first 3,500 combat Marines will land in Vietnam. But this is

January 5 still, episode 16 in the second season of *The Fugitive*, where "an innocent victim of blind justice," Dr. Richard Kimble, is making his uneasy, tentative but yearning way across the anthology of America…a QM Production!

Kimble then appears in slacks and a windbreaker. He is a dapper vagrant, calling himself "Ben Horton" for this week's episode. His name can change from week to week, so it's natural to think of him as David Janssen, an actor out of Naponee, Nebraska (pop. 106), who had come to Los Angeles and a career of disappointment, until he found himself as this lost soul, this fugitive, Dr. Richard Kimble. So many people shared that dream: We agonized for Kimble the fugitive, but we admired his courage, envied his strange liberty, his escape from reality, and the odd ease of his on-the-run existence with fresh people every week. He seemed an outcast, but as you felt your way into his ghostly shyness you understood how far he lived up to D. H. Lawrence's lesson from America: "That's why most people have come to America and still do come. To get away from everything they are and have been." Thus TV was a new home for the uprooted.

Where is Kimble this time? It's a seaside town in Southern California, with a pier and a few tourist attractions. Ben has these off-the-rack clothes, laundered but anonymous, and that widow's peak hair. I still wonder if it was a toupee. So, without money, driver's license, or a Social Security card, without a cell phone or passwords, with his constant need to be unnoticed, somehow Kimble has crisp, wind-resistant hair on top of his rugged, sleepy-voiced attractiveness. He's looking for a life, or an episode, and he has won the attention of the nation. Some of those first 3,500 Marines dream about Kimble and wonder if they'll be home in time to catch the end of his story. Guys who think of going AWOL have a tender spot for Kimble and being on the run. Fifty years later, I wonder whether, deeper down than Quinn Martin Productions ever guessed, *The Fugitive* was a parable about America trying to find a haven for an outcast hunk. The question was never asked at the time, but decades later I wonder: Was Kimble gay?

He is running for his life: Convicted of murdering his own beloved wife, he escaped death row in the confusion of a train wreck, and now he is loose, pursued by detective Philip Gerard (Barry Morse) and searching for the one-armed man (Bill Raisch) he saw leaving the scene of his wife's murder. There, I did it in one sentence. This cockamamie routine was the inspiration of Roy Huggins, the "creator" of *The Fugitive* (and many other shows). In his office he kept a photograph of himself, smiling. "Here," he had called out to his wife, "take my picture—I just had the greatest idea." His brainwave was *The Fugitive*. Do you have a photo like that? (Take one anyway, and wait for inspiration to come along.)

I suppose Kimble has a bus pass, the kind kept for neat derelicts and yearning episodics. But he is only marginally more rootless than

"OH, KID, DO WE NEED AN EPISODE!"

so many television characters. Every now and then, someone is plainly embedded in life and battered by context (think of Marty in the Paddy Chayefsky play, Tony Soprano, or Philip Marlow in *The Singing Detective*). But most of the flimsy, good-looking people are unattached, oblivious of money worries, health issues, friends, or relatives. Decades of such people (think of them as body-snatched) have fostered a similar feeling in audiences.

Here is this week's idea on *The Fugitive*, with Kimble arriving in the seaside town, looking for a job and somewhere to rest at night, somewhere he can turn himself off. He is directed to a mediocre gift store, and that's when it happens. He walks in and there's this needy woman at the counter who wants to know if she can help him. Her name is Norma Sessions (romance trapped in routine). But she's Angie Dickinson, too, in her prime, not richly wardrobed (it's a J. C. Penney world) but she fills the clothes tidily, and her hair is done in that up-swept way she had. The merest dramatic gesture will establish her as a lonesome, wistful spinster in this dead-end gift store, having to look after a crippled brother but waiting and hoping for some great guy to come by. She is an actress, and all she needs is a part, a line, a shot, the chance to throw a glance. And when she and David Janssen look at each other, it's not so much chemistry or the intimation of sex (this was still ABC in 1965, subject to standards and practices) as a silent, shared exchange, "Oh, kid, do we need an episode!" That easily matched the longing in the audience—they wanted an episode, and a cigarette, too. The endlessly fleeing Valjean in Richard Kimble had become a vagrant, yet mobile, strong, and sensitive, roaming the country not with huckster home remedies or dubious life-insurance schemes, but with 52-minute episodes and escape acts.

Kimble's plight is not much addressed in this episode, called "Brass Ring." It's enough that he is on the run and available, with no strings attached. But he has drifted into a situation. Norma Sessions has this brother in the back room behind the gift store, still and baleful in a recliner wheelchair, paralyzed or something, with hollowed-out haunted eyes that stare at his own bleak condition—plus he looks like Robert Duvall only two years after his Boo Radley in *To Kill a Mockingbird*. Ben Horton is hired on the spot to take care of Leslie Sessions—the Sessionses were called Norma and Leslie after Norma Shearer and Leslie Howard! (Google them: At forty-three and thirty-four, they played Romeo and Juliet in the terrible 1936 movie.)

It *is* Robert Duvall and he is harsh, bitter, and intense over Leslie's fate: He was hurt in a car accident, and his resentment was not eased by a suitcase of compensation money. Then Dr. Richard Kimble lays healing hands on the supine Leslie and brings the wreck back to life, or to scenes where Duvall can move a bit and start to *act* frenzied. Norma watches this with…well, mixed feelings, and Dickinson could seem spring-fed by mixed feelings. By then, she and Ben are on the beach at night, kissing a little and being doused in ocean spray (Angie laughs as if some stagehand really was getting her wet). She recounts her dream of wanting to be taken away by a knight, not just for a night. Now, Norma does have a boyfriend in town, Lars (John Ericson), but he's nasty, envious, and bad news. Ben and Norma are the episode. Until, one day, Leslie is discovered stiff in his wheelchair. A relapse? No, he's been murdered, and that is awkward for Ben because it guarantees police involvement.

THE FUGITIVE WAS SELLING A ROMANCE OF DANGEROUS LIBERTY ON THE OPEN ROAD.

Norma has a moment of treachery to come, followed by sublime sacrifice and a look of anguished love for Kimble as she's led away to prison. That last look suggests what Dickinson might have done in a career if anyone had found the anxiety of compromise within her glamour. But by the close of Act IV and the epilogue, Dr. Richard Kimble is off and away again, with little but his windbreaker, and episodes to go before he sleeps. The regard for dramatic plausibility has been nonexistent: We never discover where Ben was living, let alone what he does for money. But so many people on television never have cash—they are like the British royal family. And they never need the bathroom.

The episode is directed by Abner Biberman, and whenever it gets to a real building with an odd outside staircase, he shoots it prettily, as if thoughts of a movie came into his head. But this story is more delivered than told; it's UPS, not mise-en-scène. The actors are immense but impassive presences, defying the need for background or revealing dialogue. Yet the inner urging—the idea of a romantic episode with a fateful outcome, the longing to escape—matches the way in our free society we all long to get away into an unstressed commercial for looking like Janssen and Dickinson, where suspect hair meets a loaded 35C. Those urges are profound, if shaming, and *The Fugitive* was selling a romance of dangerous liberty on the open road, as if Kimble might be journeying on the frontier of 1750.

The Fugitive is in aspic now, and a measure of how no "Great Society" project had a chance of saving us from irrational desire. But the series was vital to millions of people from 1963 to 1967—including me, in England, where it was part of the screen known as America. When this episode played, *The Fugitive* was number 5 in the US ratings, between *The Andy Griffith Show* and *The Red Skelton Show*. Eventually, in a two-hour finale, in color, Richard Kimble was cleared so that his life could resume; the one-armed man was killed and Lt. Gerard shook hands with his quarry. That was August 29, 1967, when justice was done on *The Fugitive* with a 72 share of all television viewers watching. It was the day before Thurgood Marshall was confirmed on the Supreme Court; *Bonnie and Clyde* had opened two weeks earlier. Even in its heyday, *The Fugitive* was from a dreamy past, oblivious to the real America.

But that 72 share (over 27 million households) was a record that lasted until *Dallas* broke the truth on who shot J. R. That was November 21, 1980, and it got an 80. (But do you even remember the truth about J. R.? Why should you even know who J. R. was? I asked two young men—twenty-five and twenty—and drew a blank. And they are my sons.)

3
NORMA'S SESSIONS

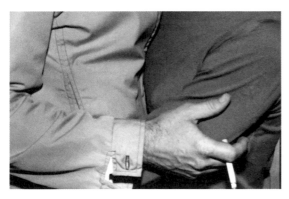

HERE'S THE REST OF THE STORY. In this small town on the shore, Norma Sessions has been rotting away, running a sad gift shop and trying to care for her self-pitying and overacting brother. She and that boyfriend, Lars, have devised a plan to kill the brother, Leslie, and take his suitcase of money. How will they do that? Well, one day along comes this providential Ben Horton, constitutionally unattached, but a man who can handle himself. Click: The plot falls into place. Ben will be hired to look after Leslie. He will be the more eager for that because Norma has given him the longing eye. Then the murder can be pinned on this available drifter.

Granted the format is fifty-two minutes, the plot goes pretty well. Ben takes the job. He starts to help Leslie—and there's a hint that the brother's crippled state may just be part of his overacting. And Ben and Norma…? Well, they darn well fall for each other in the way people did on television then, even those who weren't David Janssen and Angie Dickinson. But the attractiveness of the characters is inseparable from the sheen and bearing of the stars. So Norma begins to become intriguing and tortured—she's a would-be fratricide, a conniving devil—but she's slipping into love (in an age when she couldn't have sex on screen). Pretty women on television then were made to be in love—so they had to be pretty. The same fallacy prevails still in every ad that needs a cute girl. So every product has this grotesque aura of pretty lovability as torment to a world in which people drive battered cars with homely mates. But it hardly mattered in the age of *The Fugitive*: Norma was raised to the level of a gift-store Magdalene.

Leslie is killed, and the cops assume Ben is the murderer. Norma lets this happen, and Ben realizes the dark truth about her—deep down in the fineness of Richard Kimble he feels it, because he loves her. And she is torn. There is a scene in her upstairs apartment where he tells her what arrest will mean for him. She does nothing in response, except kiss him desperately—and then she turns him in. The moment is electric: The fanciful episode has found life. But as Ben is led away down that odd outside staircase, Norma changes her mind. She tells the police that she and Lars did the killing. Ben is innocent. She will be doomed, but she *is* going to get away.

But she has saved Kimble. There are crosscut shots—Ben and Norma, Janssen and Dickinson. It's not that they "act" or soup it up. But the situation of pain and longing has been established, and the rootless charm of *The Fugitive* has been relocated. These two might have been perfect, or happy…for a while, if only in our imagination. And in their faces, lovelorn and sad, there is the look that was always like our faces watching a brief screen encounter. That silly story might have been us. It is the nature of television acting not to act but to be the flawless window through which our desire joins that of this undecided Norma Sessions. That's how the ads work.

You may be saying to yourself, "I *have* to find that episode, and *watch* it!" You can, and I don't think you'll be disappointed. On the other hand, I'm not sure you need to: It is in the nature of television that its jeweled moments pass away time, wind, and the light erode the gems the way videotape can be wiped. There are so many moments from television history as arresting, and as superfluous. I could just as easily have fixed my attention on the Robert Duvall character. After all, Duvall is a very good actor, or even a Great Actor, as is certainly threatened in "Brass Ring." More than that, I'd say he could have been arrested—for "acting" in public.

Dickinson was at a delicate point in her career. She was thirty-four in 1965 and she had worked a lot, big screen and small. It had been a breakthrough when she was cast as Feathers in Howard Hawks's *Rio Bravo* (1959). Her part of that film could have been made yesterday: She is pretty, mischievous, sexy, intelligent, unstable, a nervous wreck, and utterly modern without betraying the straight-faced joke of the film being a Western.

There must have been times when men and productions, in life as well as on the screen, told Dickinson just to be a great doll and shut up. And she seemed pliant or amiable, if never quite obedient. Her career drifted, though she was memorable in a made-for-TV movie of *The Killers* (co-starring with John Cassavetes, Lee Marvin, and Ronald Reagan—all in one life), in *The Chase* and *Point Blank*, as well as in those closing minutes in "Brass Ring." But she was not generally regarded as an actress in the way, from the outset, Meryl Streep let it be known, with Thatcherite firmness, "Look, I'm an actress." When Angie Dickinson did her Norma Sessions in 1965, there may have been appreciative murmurs about "good work…nice job," but no one would have considered that Ms. Sessions was awards material or other than a pretty woman on TV, an adjunct to the male gaze.

Not that television knew what it felt about acting, or presence on the box. The awards we call the Emmys assumed television was about people. From the outset, talking heads were the medium's most frequent shot, and the most easily identified in the blur or speckled granola, the pixels and the lines. But were those people real or fictional? In the awards presented in 1950, there were prizes for "most outstanding live personality" (Ed Wynn) and "most outstanding kinescope personality" (Milton Berle). In effect, those two guys did the same thing: They stood up and made us laugh. This raises an endless riddle: While it seems clear that Bryan Cranston is acting in *Breaking Bad*, what do we make of David Letterman or Jon Stewart "being themselves" night after night—except to say that television has always favored the sly, hip presentation of self, as opposed to the studious playing of Great Roles. Heavy-duty acting can look as silly on television as very serious and important sex. The terminology fluctuated for years: By 1952, "best actor" and "best actress" were Sid Caesar and Imogene Coca in *Your Show of Shows*. Next year, those awards went to Thomas Mitchell and Helen Hayes (he won for his Mr. Antrobus in a version of *The Skin of Our Teeth* and she got it as Harriet Beecher Stowe in *Battle Hymn*). Imogene Coca and then Helen Hayes? By 1955, act-

"THE MOST SUCCESSFUL CELEBRITIES ARE PRODUCTS." —GEORGE S. S. TROW

ing Emmys went to Robert Cummings in the first iteration of *Twelve Angry Men* and to Judith Anderson for a Lady Macbeth, but best actor and actress in a regular series were Danny Thomas in *Make Room for Daddy* and Loretta Young in…*The Loretta Young Show*.

Loretta Young had been a movie star since the late 1920s. She was very beautiful, very gracious, groomed, and very saved, in the Roman Catholic sense. That assurance may have been spurred by her guilt about the way, in 1935, she had gone on location at Mount Shuksan, in the Washington Cascades, with Clark Gable for the movie *The Call of the Wild*, and felt a call. More likely in a warm ski lodge than in a snowbound tent, they had coupled, and in time she had gone away and then, a while later, she said, "Oh, look, I have a lovely adopted daughter!" If every actor requires a secret, she had hers. You can't quite be saved (as she hoped to be) without awareness of some burning sin—this is close to the spirit of advertising, where beauty will wash away acne and commonness.

As television came into being, she heard that call, too, which was unusual among movie players. By instinct or professional advice, most of them shrank from the small screen, and believed their careers would be over if they appeared on it. So television became a field of work for players who had not quite made it in movies: Lucille Ball is the most celebrated example of that, but the list reaches down to the generation of David Janssen, James Arness, Andy Griffith, and Carroll O'Connor, and even as far as Jon Hamm, James Gandolfini, and Claire Danes.

Loretta Young was remarked on as an authentic movie star bringing prestige to early television. Even so, an Emmy? *The Loretta Young Show* (1953–61) was a half-hour anthology series on NBC. Every episode was a small play or movie that began with Young, lovely in a full gown, coming through an elaborate door to announce the show. She was back at the end, with a moral that frequently reminded us of Catholic lessons. Many of the episodes were alleged to have been based on viewers' letters, in a stew of glamour and implausibility that went largely unremarked. Anyone and everyone acted in the stories, and Young appeared in about half of them. The theme appeared to be acting out as a way to ethical improvement, and it's unnerving to consider how that cockeyed intent persists—surely Oprah always wants a better world. Young was earning $5,000 a week, and she would win the best actress Emmy *three* times. (She was the first actress to get both an Oscar and an Emmy.)

The show owed its business identity to Young's husband, Tom Lewis. When they married in 1940, he was a rising figure at the advertising agency Young & Rubicam. When the television venture seemed

A CONCEPT HAD TO BE SHAPED TO ATTRACT NOT JUST A NETWORK BUT A SPONSOR.

a possibility, Loretta was eager for the challenge. She said she wanted to be in people's homes: It was like a mission. But it was Lewis who saw that a concept had to be shaped to attract not just a network but a sponsor, too— that proved to be Procter & Gamble. The term "soap opera" came from the many shows Procter & Gamble backed, most of them aimed at housewives anxious to be clean. The product was the message. Tom Lewis is but one example of an advertising executive who would have more power over a show than its writers and directors. As had never happened in movies, product placement infiltrated narrative content. (Hasn't there always been a fraudulent suggestion that advertised products are good for society? If King Lear had a Mercedes and Viagra, perhaps Cordelia would not have to die.)

Lewis had a theme memo worked out: "What do we have to sell here? Mostly the star. We have to sell beauty—a woman's beauty, a woman noted for wearing clothes. Setting styles. And we have something more. We have a substantial woman. A mother. A civic-minded woman. A major motion picture star and a versatile actress." Young herself took pride in the show's on-air ads, for which she would introduce the presenter or announcer—often George Fenneman, who would serve as the lulling baritone voice on many shows. The actress also loved to make a bold turn at such moments, skirts aswirl, showing off the back of her lavish dress as well as the front—Young understood that female viewers were eager for fashion hints.

Tom Lewis would be executive producer on the show until the strains of that work broke up their marriage. Some said the actress was driven to take charge and resented Lewis's power. The show was also such hard work that she liked to live in her dressing room, a cottage built to match her emotional needs and cultivate her inspired benign vision. Lewis said Loretta had pushed him to resign from their company, and he eventually sued her for "dishonesty, mismanagement and unfairness." (Alas, that viewer's letter never made it as an episode.)

Tom and Loretta had had two children and a hit show, an institutional tribute to her ladylike virtue and Catholic integrity. Procter & Gamble backed out because the actress had objected to a toothpaste ad that described bacteria in the mouth. "It isn't dignified," she said. "It isn't me." Loretta's teeth were battlements. She went off the air while hailing the loyalty of her following. Compared with movie fame, she said, "There's a closer, perhaps a more affectionate—even more possessive quality about the friendliness of [television] viewers and a sort of 'member of the family' quality when they don't like something."

That figurehead glow of Loretta Young in the fifties is more interesting now than her show. But she was one of the people who shaped the public's notion of an actress and a woman on television. Angie Dickinson in "Brass Ring" seems far more modern than just ten years after Young's heyday. But surely Dickinson heeded the older actress's example. In the sixties, Angie Dickinson was known, and sometimes very good, but she was also obliged to do what an actress had to do. One of her best films is John Boorman's *Point Blank* (1967), where she plays a lost soul, a woman who sleeps with gangsters. She has great things in that film—notably a surreal explosion of advertised kitchenware in which she tries to break the impassive armor of Lee Marvin's character by turning on every electrical device in a plush Los Angeles home—but there is also a scene where her character has to take off her clothes. Few people did that better than Dickinson, but you understand that if she had declined, then someone else would have been cast.

So she took the deal to play Sergeant "Pepper" Anderson in *Police Woman* (1974–78), not a noble show but an effective compromise that won her some security. She earned $40,000 per episode and there were ninety-one episodes. Pepper was always going undercover, which gave the show the opportunity to dress her up in provocative Las Vegas rags. It was the first major action series centered on a woman, and apparently it led to an increase in applications from women to the LAPD. Business flows and society rolls over in the sleep of forgettable shows.

I can't do justice to all the performances as striking as Angie Dickinson's in the last few moments of one episode of *The Fugitive*. No one will watch that archive again. But she has another item of enduring value, a moment from the years of *The Tonight Show* when Angie was one of Johnny Carson's guests. The moment is not just casual, it's ephemeral, but it would play still, while Norma Sessions seems fabricated.

Angie comes through the curtains. They embrace: Television made that kissing a new American habit. But you could tell they liked each other. She sits on the sofa (and she sat well). She plays with her hair, as if unable to forget shampoo ads. Then Johnny starts to kid around with her, to tell her she's a knockout and to flirt a little in ways that were never going to upset standards and practices, not after 11:30. And she laughs. It's her own laughter—not that of Norma Sessions or Pepper Anderson—and she had a melodious, appealing laugh. But what is most endearing about it is the attitude, the wife's way of pretending surprise: "Oh wow, John, that's funny, and I never guessed you were going to make me laugh."

Of course, she knew. She had been on *The Tonight Show* many times before. She knew the artifice of impromptu talk, and she understood Johnny well enough to realize that his unbreachable uneasiness always led him to try to make people laugh. She laughed in a sweet, natural way that was a testament to television existence. It may not have been a conscious thought, but her nature intuited that being on television as her own smooth self was part of her act.

She was with the master and the source. Johnny Carson was on television more than anyone else in his time. He was on so much he was the spirit of "on" and was never regarded as an actor, not even when he did Carnac the Magnificent. Every night he played Johnny Carson, just to let you know you were never going to get him, or find out his secret or the magic. Being on television was the act. It still is. David Letterman (a disciple of Carson) played a similar game for over thirty years. He knew it was the only way not to be boring, of which there have been crushing late-night examples. Gore Vidal claimed that

once you started on television, you had to be on it as often as possible to stay current. (That's a drab secret to the presidency. When Vladimir Putin "went missing" for a week in 2015, it was rumored that he might not be just off, but offed.) Another Vidal credo was to have sexual intercourse whenever it came in sight (though probably not on television).

That restraint may drop one day: The wicked Channel 4 series *Black Mirror* (2011–) launched with a story where a British prime minister was blackmailed into having sex with a pig, live, on the air. This was to save the life of a favorite British princess who had been kidnapped by a performance artist intent on demonstrating the public's addiction to screen life—the ingredients of fairy tale and media terrorism sat side-by-side. The prime minister was horrified and humiliated by the grim deal, but he did it. That meant he lost the love of his wife, but his approval ratings rose.

OH, DONNA!

HER NAME IS DONNA STONE but she looks so like Donna Reed it's uncanny. She is married to a pediatrician, Dr. Alex Stone (Carl Betz),

and they have two children, Mary and Jeff. They live in a place called Hilldale; it seems to be a small country town where the pediatrician still makes house calls. Nearly every show begins in the morning. Donna is there to cook breakfast in a flowing A-line dress, a perfectly waved hairstyle, a single row of pearls, and high-heel shoes. She packs the family off for the day, with brown-bag lunches for the kids.

At the door, as her husband goes off, preoccupied but good-looking in a manly late-fifties way, he sometimes forgets to give her a good-bye kiss. Then he collects himself, comes back, and delivers a regular network peck. She stands there for an instant before the story begins, one hand on her hip and a serene smile on her face, as if to say, "Aren't husbands the darnedest guys?" In truth, Alex is not in the least darnedest: He has no secret life—he has no inner life. He is the fixture of Donna's dream.

This show ran on ABC from 1958 to 1966, with 275 25-minute episodes, sponsored by Campbell's Soup. After early uncertainty, it pushed itself into the top 25 for a while. Reed won a Golden Globe and was sometimes nominated for an Emmy. Later in life, when *The Donna Reed Show* was over and being reappraised by critical feminists, she defended it and said, "It was a realistic show about a strong woman—with a comic twist."

I have only sampled *The Donna Reed Show*. It did not come to Britain; its lacquered portrait of a wife and mother at home could have seemed offensive in a country slowly extricating itself from the mood and rationing of war. The Stone house is so large and bright; it's like a bank of polished fruit in a supermarket—hard, pretty, and presumably sweet and nourishing, yet most itself as an image and a promise. You feel that if you took one apple from that castle, it might come tumbling down, and *The Donna Reed Show* has a similar feeling of a perfection not to be probed. That's why this sitcom is as much an endless commercial as a development of drama, or story. It's hard to see now without remaking it or Pythonizing it in your mind. But its situation, lovely and numbing, is what helped shape people who are dear to me. (I daresay we are now as devoted to shows that will look just as awful.)

So I'd like to see an episode of *The Donna Reed Show* where the family follow the Cuba crisis of 1962, or come home from seeing *Rebel Without a Cause*…or *Psycho*. "Gee, Mom," you can hear one of the kids saying, "don't you dare do a Mrs. Bates on us!" And Donna will radiate that lovely Donna Reed smile and rock with laughter so maybe one wave of her hair stirs and drops on her brow, enough to hint at the discreet wanton. And then her husband looks at her as if to say, "My God, Donna, you're a very attractive woman, and sometimes I just wish I wasn't out all the time looking after other people's children."

Donna makes the breakfast and the lunches; she sends the family off and welcomes them back; she keeps a sweet, tidy home—she is a homemaker and she's proud of the two Picasso prints (blue and pink periods) on the walls. They are part of the Stone situation, where the

kids are dutiful, cheerful, and regular, and honestly unable to comprehend the torments felt by James Dean, Sal Mineo, and Natalie Wood
in that rueful Southern California of *Rebel Without a Cause*. In fact,
this Eisenhower-like show actually ran over into assassinations, civil
rights, drugs, and Vietnam. It had a lot to ignore. But it had ABC,
Campbell's Soup, and its producer, Tony Owen (he was also Mr.
Donna Reed), telling Donna that this was the way to go to make a
sane, wholesome, and decent America. So Donna Stone must get up
at 4:00 A.M. to iron her dress, do her hair, her make-up, and get the
eggs to scramble.

And in those small hours does Donna ever recall Lorene? In the
book and the film of Reed's great role, *From Here to Eternity*, Lorene
is a whore in wartime Honolulu, the snobby
girl in the cathouse, saving her self-esteem and **YOU'VE BEEN DOING SCENARIOS**
her meatloaf recipe and going back home to **ALL THE TIME.**
somewhere like Hilldale, a doctor to marry,
and respectability, and where only once in her life she might meet a
middle-aged alcoholic veteran with a tin leg who remembers the lewd
tricks she turned at the New Congress Club.

I was going to say that none of this is in *The Donna Reed Show*,
that mine is simply the perverse response of a viewer in 2015 who is
watching old episodes of the show to find something that could match
the awe in his wife's voice when she sees what he's doing. But it's not
as simple or Golden Delicious as that. In the several episodes I watched,
I saw the beginning of a strange syndrome.

In one episode, Donna and Alex are just dreaming of a simple
weekend getaway together. Nothing is said directly, but if you were so
disposed you could believe they're thinking of some kind of sexual
splendor free from the children. Or maybe they'll find an agreeable
couple at the hotel and play canasta. The plan hovers, until Alex realizes that he has to be a witness in a silly minor trial involving a friend,
their banker. At which point, Donna goes to see the banker, and her
loveliness falls away to disclose the shadow of Lorene, a cunning,
manipulative woman who will persuade the banker that this court
case could damage his reputation. And if he drops the case, the Stones'
canasta weekend is clear. This does the trick, and Donna's face flashes

in triumph: She loved being the liar and the schemer. She really is a tethered demon. (Could she have turned into Joan Crawford?)

In another episode, she wants to persuade two married friends to stay together instead of divorcing. This couple have no children, she explains to Alex. That is what's missing from their life and their club membership. So Alex brings home a baby up for adoption, and another plot hurries through its twenty-five minutes. Donna gazes on the newborn, and she says, "If they don't adopt him, I'm going to." It is a generous, addled thought, but it has madness in it, too. And in just a year, looking for fresh life for the series, the Stones did adopt another child for themselves! In the same spirit, their two teenage children introduced songs into the show to make it seem up-to-date. The daughter (Shelley Fabares) did "Johnny Angel" (it hit number one on the *Billboard* chart), and her brother sang "My Dad."

You and Tony Owen could chide me for being unduly suspicious. Donna's not like that; she's not a suspect. She just wants to do the best for everyone and act on the principle that if you can smooth away a few rough corners, then the bigger issues may take care of themselves.

In its golden age, television proposed that any American dilemma was just a set of soluble narrative difficulties, the solving of which led to purchase and the blithe assumption that that would take care of the nation. With the right husband and a good Westinghouse, you would be set—and, ideally, both were under guarantee. Plus, Donna has time on her hands, but not mind enough to wonder about "feminism." I'll guess that she'd have said such ideology was not "feminine." Watching old television can drive you crazy or awaken your buried child. It's a curious way of coming face-to-face with your own situation. And mine was one in which my father and mother never talked about anything, including the way he was living with another woman on the far side of London. (Good series material, I think, but not done.) And yet my mother did everything to keep calm and assure me that everything was all right.

Carrie Mathison in Homeland: Mom out of control

So I dream over an unmade episode of *The Donna Reed Show* in which Donna sends everyone off to school or the office, retrieves her secret bottle of vodka, gazes in the looking glass, and strips off her A-line dress so that she can get down on the vacuumed carpet under the Christmas tree (the Stones keep it up all year because Christmas is the time and the situation when people are nicest to one another) and make love with the gardener who arrives to tend her garden and whose love of fragrance and roses has awoken her romanticism. That's not too different from the Todd Haynes movie *Far from Heaven*, where a Connecticut housewife played by Julianne Moore realizes the fraud in her magazine life and starts to fall in love with her gardener (played by Dennis Haysbert, a fine actor now best known for his Allstate commercials).

Of course, that was 2002, but *Psycho* was 1960, and there was a movie that exulted in the surreal riot of American domesticity. So *The Donna Reed Show* (and so many other family series) now looks like a rearguard action more determined and desperate than Vietnam or any "just say no to drugs" campaign to secure that endangered American situation in which the dream was cracking up. "Are you in good hands?" Haysbert keeps asking.

Sixty years later, *The Donna Reed Show* seems fatuously locked in genre attitudes of the late fifties and a bizarre role-model code for being "ladylike" that feared feminism. But maybe television always relies on getting some "now" feeling. In 2075, will the innovative *Transparent* feel as stale and absurd? That question seems shocking now: Streaming on Amazon, *Transparent* (2014–) was a breakthrough in TV delivery, as well as a purveyor of social revolution. Conceived and controlled by Jill Soloway, it is the portrait of an elderly man (played by Jeffrey Tambor) who becomes transgender. The show is funny and daring—so much so that Ms. Soloway rather hid its coming from her own transgender father. It won awards and an audience, and feels so much more enlightened and "useful" than *The Donna Reed Show*.

As an exercise while waiting, you might like to draft a one-act play in which the old Donna meets Jeffrey Tambor's Morton/Maura Pfefferman. These figures live on the same screen, and they mingle in our cultural consciousness, so why should they not meet? You may say you're not a writer, but there on the sofa you've been doing scenarios all the time.

GENTLY "ON": A NEW AGE OF TELEVISION PEOPLE

SOMEWHERE BETWEEN THE ICONS in commercials and characters in a story, a new species was appearing—television people. Often, they were the names from the movies, playing characters familiar from that prior medium. But they were there, more or less, all the time, and that quietly shattered the old splendor and authority of "movie acting" and film fame. These figures were sometimes like ghosts or spirits, but ever-present, like shadows. They appeared every week, or every day. We felt we had to keep up with them. And sometimes we hated that: A friend who used to be on television a lot still recalls astonishing letters from out of the blue—"I hate everything about you, your nose, your eyes, mouth, hair…!"

If you worked in the movie business in 1945, you had reasons to be cheerful. The gossip reckoned that movies were coming back as families reunited and felt ready to face romance and story together again. It was a new world of victory, wasn't it? Surely the golden empire of movies from the late 1930s could be resumed? For a moment the world played along with that dream, no matter the real tension and insecurity of the peace. For two years, well into 1947, moviegoing stayed a boom business in the United States. In some weeks as many as 100 million tickets were sold, when that number was more than half the national population. A few old-timers in the business believed happiness was back.

The reality was so much more complicated. The public could never again be as foolish or blithe as they had been in 1939. Progress is the constant erasure of our own foolishness. It took constitutional blindness to misunderstand what had happened in the

EVEN IN VICTORY, ABSURD PARANOID SCENARIOS COULD BE SOLD TO THE PUBLIC.

Holocaust, what was possible after Hiroshima and Nagasaki, and how the several million displaced persons in Europe undermined conventional ideas of nationhood, home, or well-being. Even in victory, absurd paranoid scenarios could be sold to the public—like domestic Communism being a dire menace, spread on the religiously conservative parables of Hollywood movies!

The Holocaust asked us to digest not just six million deaths, but the way a larger number had acquiesced in it and carried it out. (That would prompt Stanley Milgram's obedience experiments, discussed earlier.) Imagine if Donna's husband had been in the war and was masking some ugly betrayal of honor and manly duty. There was a movie like that, in 1948: *Act of Violence*, too abrasive to get on TV and a failure in theaters. It was directed by Fred Zinnemann, who had left Austria in time but whose parents stayed and died in the camps. He never shed that "survivor guilt"—decades later, he made *Julia* about the same subject.

A new kind of war had begun as the old one ended. The sudden fear and loathing of the USSR and the surge in US prosperity helped hide survivor guilt and the realization of how obedience had led to horror. This was called a Cold War, and people would have to learn what that meant. There was a new class of young working families and the middle class that believed the war had been a deal made for new prosperity or comfort. It was more practical than dreamy and, with a speed that shook Hollywood, a lot of those people started staying home, looking after new spouses and babies, redecorating the home, and eventually sitting round a new piece of furniture, an ornate and fussy cabinet—walnut or even plastic—with this bowed gray screen and rotten reception.

By the late forties, the movie boom was shutting down, and it's important to separate it from the spread of television as a habit. Audiences were giving up on movies *before* they had the alternative of television. But the idea of staying home did a lot to ease insecurities. After all, said the new medium, we can cater to you all the time, we can take care of you—it's going to be all right, no matter the millions in the world outraged, starving, vanished, and so easily forgotten. You're safe, sitting on your couch, watching but letting life go on. Governments often stressed a new order and prosperity, but the people clung to safety. So the stupid commercials (the stunning new TV genre) were a way of seeming "all right."

Careers took off in unexpected directions. Karl Freund had been born in Königinhof in Bohemia in 1890. Early work as a movie projectionist led him into film production, and in a few years he was recognized as one of the great cinematographers in the school of German expressionism. He would shoot *The Last Laugh* for F. W. Murnau, *Varieté* for E. A. Dupont, and the landmark film of that era, *Metropolis*, for Fritz Lang. This work was in black-and-white, but it specialized in deep shadow, low-key lighting, and highly subjective emotional atmospheres. In 1929, Freund decided to take a chance on America, and his German reputation led him to photograph several key works in early sound horror: *Dracula* and *Murders in the Rue Morgue*. But he went on to be a prized craftsman in a wider range of films, especially at MGM, where he shot *The Good Earth* (for which he won the Oscar) and *Pride and Prejudice* (with Laurence Olivier and Greer Garson). In 1946, he did a small film at MGM, *Two Smart People*, a noir romance that starred Lucille Ball.

That had been Ball's last film under her MGM contract; people at all levels in movie production were not being renewed by 1946–47. Ball had been ten years in pictures, and she had done good work as both comedienne and straight actress, but she knew she hadn't quite made it. She'd been married six years by then to Desiderio Alberto Arnaz y de Acha III, the son of a wealthy Cuban, who had become a Latin bandleader and a wild and unreliable husband. People called him Desi. The couple had furious ups and downs but were about to become the first television model of enduring and endearing family life.

By 1949, Ball had been driven into radio, and she was playing on air with Richard Denning in a series called *My Favorite Husband*. But Jess Oppenheimer, a writer and the producer on the radio show, wondered if so agile a clown as Ball might flourish on this new medium, television. Lucy and Desi were excited by the prospect, and Desi began to function as a businessman—though he wanted to play the husband, too. Eyebrows were raised: a Cuban and an American girl from Jamestown, New York? A couple as nearly out of control as Lucy and Desi?

(She was six years older than Desi and was frantic over his appetite for younger women.) They had never been given this sort of chance in a movie, where mixed marriages were less common than mixed drinks.

The genius of their show was in capturing yet reversing the desperation in the real couple; so it's a series about a crazy wife with a husband trying to keep control of her. Notice the subtle shift in titles from radio to television, and the way it places Desi (or Ricky Ricardo) as the figure of frustrated control and reason. It's that situation (or "sit") that lets Ball run riot, and the domestic upheaval needed some sense of Desi's fond keeper restoring order. But mayhem had a technological rationale that was of the utmost importance to the new business.

Lucy and Desi hired Karl Freund to be director of photography on the show. Thus, the master of shadow and expressionist dread created a glaring high-key look that made the Ricardos' New York apartment as bright as Southern California, like ads for the postwar life. That steady, cheerful illumination would be copied in hundreds of shows, and it meant that banks of lights could hang on a studio soundstage and never be altered. All you had to do was turn them on. Even nocturnal scenes had their own lighting, "day for night."

At that time, October 1951, a live show needed or was expected to be shot in New York and then passed down the line. But Lucy and Desi insisted on living in LA. So the idea arose to film the show, cut it, and then send it out. To that end, Freund devised a system of live filming of the story with three cameras going at the same time. He used the rehearsal days to work out the best vantages. He marked up the studio floor and he had run-throughs as a test. He was soon able to shoot the fragments of a 23-minute episode in no more than an hour—with live laughter from the studio audience. It could be cut quickly. Film cost more, and that's where Arnaz the executive producer gambled. Kinescopes—the standard form available for television—looked rough and were not expected to last. But film could be trusted—and thus for decades *I Love Lucy* could be syndicated and make a fortune not just for CBS and for Philip Morris (the first sponsor), but also for this new enterprise, Desilu. The three-camera system has never been surpassed, and it is the decisive imprint on sitcom television, on newscasts, and on most dramas. The Ricardo household was usually close to chaos, but the camera triangulation gave it order.

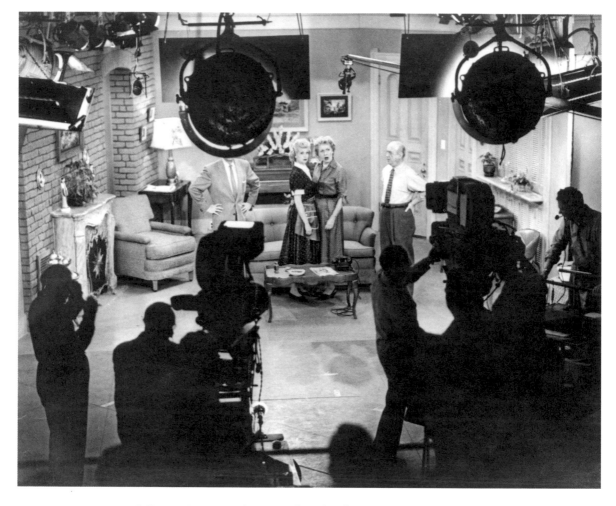

I Love Lucy took immediately, from its debut on October 15, 1951: It started out at 9:00 P.M. (there were some fears), but then it was brought forward because children loved the couple. It went to number 3 in its first season, and then it was tops for three years in a row, with ratings of 67.3, 58.8, and 49.3. It won the best sitcom and best comedienne Emmys for 1953. In January 1953, when President Eisenhower was sworn in, he was watched by 29 million on television. The previous day, in an episode in which the pregnant Lucy went to the hospital to give birth, she had 44 million viewers. (Both Lucy and Lucille were pregnant—it was a reality show.)

Lucy and Desi would last longer on screen than in life. She filed for divorce in 1960, for the second time: She had made a move in 1944 and been talked out of it. But by 1957, Desilu purchased outright, for

$6 million, the RKO studio lot, one of several production companies that had once doubted Ball as a movie star. The new company went powering ahead with a wide range of shows: *Our Miss Brooks*, *The Life and Legend of Wyatt Earp*, *The Real McCoys*, *The Untouchables*, *The Andy Griffith Show*, *My Three Sons*, *The Dick Van Dyke Show*, *Hogan's Heroes*, *Mission: Impossible*, *Star Trek*, and many others. There were sequels to *I Love Lucy* (without Desi), and many of them are still playing somewhere. Karl Freund shot 148 episodes and then he retired, a visionary of dread who had become a pillar of the Establishment.

Lucille Ball had been forty in 1951, and her realistic hopes as a movie star could not have lasted much longer. Bette Davis was forty-three and she had just had one of her biggest successes in *All About Eve*, but she had reached a point where movies were more comfortable with her as a villain, a spinster, or even a gargoyle than as a figure deserving romance or passion. Should she be ready to do television? There were warnings current in the film business at a time when its attitude to

LUCY AND DESI WOULD LAST LONGER ON SCREEN THAN IN LIFE.

the usurper was belligerent and dismissive. The small screen would never take over. Movies should not even show television screens in American interiors.

Male stars were especially shy, or aloof. Gary Cooper never did a thing for television; neither did Clark Gable, James Stewart (until his last years), Spencer Tracy, or Cary Grant. Others did cameos for friends—John Wayne played General Sherman in an episode of *Wagon Train*; Bogart redid *The Petrified Forest* with Henry Fonda and Lauren Bacall; Cagney did one play, "Soldier from the War Returning," for *Robert Montgomery Presents*. Some actors—like Paul Newman and Rod Steiger—did a lot of TV when young and then stopped dead once the movies took them up. Warren Beatty appeared as Milton Armitage in *The Many Loves of Dobie Gillis* in 1959–60, often with Tuesday Weld as Thalia Menninger. But then his film career took off and he never looked back—the movie with Weld that they and the world deserved never transpired. (They could still play geriatric outlaws on the lam—just a thought.)

It was understandable in the late forties that a new era of stars reading the first postwar box-office numbers—Burt Lancaster, Kirk Douglas, William Holden—should ask themselves, "Why would I do television?" The picture quality was humiliating, the money was negligible, the audience was tiny. It was easier, and more inviting, to do radio, which still had close marketing links to the movies and where sound-track versions of hit pictures often played with stars. Whereas, if you ventured onto television, you might find yourself standing next to that weird TV fellow, Milton Berle.

The technical difficulty of getting television to work was so great that sometimes no one had enough time to think of how to fill the shaky air. So there were scenes of peaceful meadows, the cute behavior of pet animals, flower-arranging contests, sermons (a ready-made half hour, unlikely to offend), shows on home maintenance, and maybe the cameraman's uncle telling a few jokes— "Keep 'em clean, Uncle Miltie!" Born Mendel Berlinger at a West 118th Street apartment in New York, Milton Berle had been a child actor, a comic in vaudeville and on the radio, and a guy who had been in a few movies. He was known as the radio host on *Stop Me If You've Heard This One*, where a panel of comedians finished off jokes sent in by listeners. In 1947–48, he was doing *The Milton Berle Show* on NBC radio, but it was clear that he was several notches below other radio comics of that time—Jack Benny, Bob Hope, Groucho Marx, Abbott and Costello. He sounded as insecure as he deserved to be.

But in September 1948, when fewer than two million American households had television reception, Berle took advantage of the raw medium, like a domineering comic taking over an amateur show. He told jokes, he interrupted other acts, he wore silly clothes, he did slapstick routines—he did anything he could think of. He had a gang of writers, one of them a kid named Neil Simon. And the America that was also experiencing the arrival of Norman Mailer, the vaulting solos of Charlie Parker, and the nervy paint trails of Jackson Pollock, as well as the diffrent dances of George Balanchine and Sugar Ray Robinson, thought Uncle Miltie was the cat's whiskers. He acquired that nickname by stepping up to the camera and telling the kids to go to bed like their Uncle Miltie was telling them. This was the moment George Orwell published *Nineteen Eighty-Four*, and you might have seen Berle as a farcical Big Uncle figure.

How did Berle do it? In part, it was just a lifelong carnival barker sniffing a break. He had no theory of television but a lot of nervous energy, desperate cheerfulness, and an instinct that this curious toy mattered. He had a performer's confidence in the tumult, and faith that his caprice would work. Over the years, a similar charm or instinct could be observed in Allen Funt, Chuck Barris, Ronald Reagan, or Bill O'Reilly. There really was very little defense for them, or explanation, beyond their getting on television.

Berle's reputation spread by word of mouth. This guy was kinda amusing, but not good-looking. Lucille Ball had been close to "beautiful" in movies, but on TV she gave up on that cruel discipline and let ordinariness in. What mattered then was the witnessing of a surprise in your own living room. If you had played the *Texaco Star Theater* in movie houses, you might have emptied them. Many people started watching television for the novelty and because of Berle. It was reckoned that he sometimes commanded 80 percent of those watching, and proved that an amiable or nonthreatening personality made the new machine friendly. By 1951, *Texaco Star Theater* was really the Milton Berle show, and it had a 61.6 rating. Berle had a $1-million-a-year contract and people called him "Mr. Television." By 1950 there were four million TV households—and in 1951 the number had risen to ten million. Naturally, the reasons behind that shift were complex and transcultural, but no one had a better claim than Uncle Miltie that he had done it. Stores selling sets knew that Berle was their big huckster; water companies across the country reported a bathroom rush at the end of his show.

Berle's own kingdom didn't last, but his lesson was clear. The pantheon of great movie stars might feel disdainful of television, or threatened by it, but the field was open for players who had never flourished in movies. Lucy and Desi were the classic escape artists. But wherever you looked, you were seeing them. Jack Webb had been a mediocre small-part actor on the big screen, and then he became an imitation act for kids of all ages because of *Dragnet* (begun in 1951). Eve Arden had been a tart, witty presence in many movies, without impressing the business that she was beautiful or dreamable enough to be a star. But the funny schoolteacher in *Our Miss Brooks* (1952–56), adapted from another radio show, made her a household name and let her be a spokesperson for teachers—she was given honorary membership of the National Education Association. Her show was frequently in the top 20, and Brooks won an Emmy as best female star in a regular series.

Arden got Miss Brooks at the urging of her friend Lucille Ball (it was a Desilu show). There is another notable act of generosity in early television history. In the mid-1950s, CBS wanted to turn a hit radio show of theirs into a TV show: It was the story of a true-blue frontier marshal, Matt Dillon, called *Gunsmoke*. In fact, the creators of the radio show, Norman Macdonnell and John Meston, preferred to keep it on radio. But CBS ignored them. In television then, producer geniuses were appearing at the infant networks.

CBS offered the role of Dillon to John Wayne for partial ownership in the show and $2 million up front, an unprecedented sum for movies, let alone television. Wayne had that elitist feeling, and maybe he had heard about the ruinous workload on a hit TV series. So he proposed an actor he had under contract, James Arness, six foot seven and seemingly made of rock, but just as solid as an actor and too tall for kissing scenes. Arness was cast, and on September 10, 1955, the first night of *Gunsmoke*, there was Wayne on camera to introduce his buddy:

"Good evening. My name's Wayne. Some of you may have seen me before…I've made a lot of pictures out here—all kinds, and some of them have been Westerns. And that's what I'm here to tell you about tonight: a Western…No, I'm not in it—I wish I were though, because I think it's the best thing of its kind that's come along, and I hope you'll agree with me. It's honest, it's adult, it's realistic."

It is a core of conservatism to have no doubt about what is realistic, and to regard it as honest. *Gunsmoke* was terse, unequivocal, and functional, but it faltered badly at first before becoming the top show in the country from 1957 to 1961. CBS head William Paley, who enjoyed movie moguls like David O. Selznick, and entertained the thought of taking over from them, loved the show and kept it playing through bad years.

Gunsmoke was a Western, to be sure, but it was a police show, too, founded on the airy notion that Dodge City could be civilized. What that seemed to require was prowess with a gun, height, power, moral authority, and a weekly tradition of doing nothing risqué with Miss Kitty (Amanda Blake), who might be a Dodge whore—well, she wasn't a school-teacher; she was there, running the saloon. Some people behind the show thought of marrying her off to Dillon, but maybe many guys watching *Gunsmoke* liked Westerns just because the heroes were *not* married. And no one

seemed to notice Dillon's chastity or wonder how it might affect his aim. Arness did it for 635 episodes. There's no way Wayne could have been as patient or self-effacing. But by not playing Dillon, he found the opportunity of his life in being Ethan Edwards in John Ford's *The Searchers*.

The heroic aloneness of the Western archetype isn't casual. If nothing else, the cult of the very independent male lead was a way of saying women were not as active or significant, or not operating at the same level. *Gunsmoke* led an era of Westerns in which the men might have passing romances without yielding to marriage or commitment. You have to see the appeal of the Western myth as needing that independence or male fear of women. Shane (1953) comes to the homestead. He observes the family and likes them all. He may feel for the wife. But it is his duty to win their range war and then move on—like Richard Kimble.

That is prelude to another Western, and a new kind of Mr. Television, so much more interesting than Milton Berle or James Arness. Roy Huggins was a recurring figure in the innocent heyday of television. He was born in 1914; he was a Communist briefly in his youth—he named names later; and he hoped to be a novelist. But he drifted into movies and wrote a couple of routine Westerns, and then the impressive *Pushover* (1954), a thriller about voyeurist attraction, with Kim Novak and Fred MacMurray. For television, he wrote a few episodes of *Cheyenne*, a Western that had Clint Walker as a wandering hero, until the actor walked out on the show.

Something in Huggins wanted novelty—he prided himself on unusual story angles, and he had the instinct of a producer, or a creator for shows that might run and run (like *The Fugitive*). He conceived a Western about a more ambiguous figure—a gambler, perhaps—call

THE HEROIC ALONENESS OF THE WESTERN ARCHETYPE ISN'T CASUAL.

him Bret Maverick. Looking around to cast the lead, Huggins noticed James Garner (born Bumgarner in Norman, Oklahoma, in 1928). The actor had done a few episodes of *Cheyenne* and he had been promising in support of Marlon Brando in the movie *Sayonara*. He got the part, found the smartest wardrobe yet for a TV Western, and one way or another—was it from Huggins or from within himself?—he began to make a little fun of Westerns. Garner was a natural comedic actor; he was very good at perplexed double takes or cheeky eyebrow-raising. By every account, it was Garner's persona and leisurely mischief that tilted *Maverick* (1957–62) in a direction that whispered to the audience, "Haven't you seen an awful lot of Westerns by now? And do you still take them seriously?"

Bret Maverick was a gambler and a chancer. He was someone Matt Dillon would have urged out of town. But how could that marshal even talk to Maverick? Bret could fight and use a gun if he had to. But there were playful hints that he was actually shy about violence—or was it timid? William T. Orr produced the show. Huggins was around most of the time. He produced fifty-four episodes and wrote eight. Budd Boetticher, a master of small Western movies, directed three. Robert Altman did one. You couldn't exactly call *Maverick* a satire, but it wasn't set in adobe and solemnity, either. By 1958–59 it was rated number 6. At which point, Garner dropped out of the show in a mix of boredom and some suspicion that he was being screwed financially. It was the sort of conclusion Bret Maverick might have reached.

"I DON'T WANT MY PRESIDENT TO BE A TV STAR." —BILL MAHER

Garner headed off to the movies, as if that was a sensible course. He did well enough, in hits like *The Great Escape* and worthy failures such as *36 Hours* and *The Americanization of Emily*. But he had dud roles, too, like *Mister Buddwing*, where he seemed unable to push his humor into the story. He was a dour Wyatt Earp in *Hour of the Gun*. He did *Grand Prix*. The audience rated him very popular, but stardom wasn't happening. He wasn't himself. It was as if a television series where he had a few minutes here and there just being Jim was the field where Garner could play.

He was drawn back to the small screen by Roy Huggins again, who offered him *The Rockford Files*, about a private detective who had had a spell in prison from a wrongful conviction but who had learned about life there. It was actually a conventional series about a contented maverick (he lived in a trailer on a Malibu beach, with a trendy car and one of the new phone-answering machines). He was smart, wry, funny, a little world-weary, with a real girlfriend, even if they didn't do too much on-screen, and resilient. In fact, Garner was beginning to feel pain from the effects of war wounds and injuries incurred in filming. We might regret the distress, but it helped his stance and his sensibility. Stephen Cannell (a very productive screenwriter) was co-creator and the lead writer on the show at NBC, and it ran from 1974 to 1980. Among its other valued writers and producers was David Chase, just twenty-nine in 1974. *Rockford* was his education in television (leading to *The Sopranos*). By its second season, *The Rockford Files* was at number 6. It fell off, but never lost a cult following or flagged in its clever construction and witty dialogue. In 1977, Garner won the Emmy for lead actor in a drama series—Carroll O'Connor won that same year for comedy in *All in the Family*, when you could make a case that O'Connor was the drama and Garner the comedy.

Jim Rockford was a good guy, all the more appealing for being a sturdy loner in an increasingly bureaucratic world. He wasn't that far from Richard Kimble, except that he saw the joke in what he was doing. He could right modest wrongs if they came to him in an intriguing anecdotal form. You could hang a set of liberal hopes on his rugged good looks and his sentimental pragmatism. So a case might mean having to prove that Lindsay Wagner's friend hadn't committed suicide. But Rockford was never challenged by a family being evicted from a wretched home in Bakersfield because they'd signed a cruel mortgage deal in ignorance. He didn't have to sort out the single mother who had her driver's license suspended for two years because she'd been unable to pay a couple of routine parking tickets. The mundane strains of American life didn't get into the Rockford files.

Nor did the show think to devote the time to a substantial litigious issue in the way James Garner and his Cherokee Productions would eventually sue Universal for misdirection of funds due to him from his one-third ownership in profits, in what was called a case of "creative accounting." This matter was eventually settled out of court, with no one allowed to mention the monies involved. But Garner won and his audience cheered at his extra wealth and the stoicism with which he bore up under it. Everyone in the business knew the likelihood of being screwed on those deals, but few were stubborn enough to pursue the matter.

This is not an attack on Garner—I am volunteering him as a deserving candidate for "Mr. Television," and his best is still to come. But I am trying to untangle the knot of identification that an audience makes with a hero, and to understand how the whole process stresses one kind of problem at the neglect of others. So, the business says, well, the case of the single mother who loses her car and then her house is not really entertaining or constructive. Understood, but then ask yourself carefully about the honesty or

I AM TRYING TO UNTANGLE THE KNOT OF IDENTIFICATION THAT AN AUDIENCE MAKES WITH A HERO.

responsibility in offering other, fanciful stories for *her* entertainment (in the halfway house, if she's lucky). And then recognize how deeply this kind of entertainment is bound up with the economy that has turned this woman into a victim, simply by virtue of the advertising that sustains the shows. Yes, we are expected to separate the one from the other, but how are we to do that without enforcing unreal divisions in our own experience?

There was a battle going on in America over what were called "instant cameras." It seems quaint now, because those devices are scrapheap material and the pictures were never instant. The iPhone has taught us that. But Polaroid and Kodak were fighting over the instant camera and who owned the rights to it. So Polaroid devised a campaign of television commercials and looked for a figurehead to appear on camera. They liked the Jim Rockford type, reliable yet tricky, a clear star but folksy, too. Then an idea came along that the campaign would work well if Jim had a female companion—she was a wife, plainly, though that was not spelled out and children were not seen (except in pictures). You could tell that not just from their thorough awareness of each other, but in their banter, which could shift into barbs and eye-rolling. They seemed in love, for sure, but an actual love that made trust or credulity an everyday challenge.

Mariette Hartley was twelve years younger than Garner, but she often came off more grown-up in their sparring partnership. She had studied acting with John Houseman; and for a while she became a cohost on CBS's *The Morning Program*. Nothing she would do as an actress matched the impact of the Polaroid commercials that started in 1977 and ran for seven years, until the campaign had accumulated close to three hundred thirty-second ads.

Just as *Maverick* had teased the Western, so these spots kidded the earnestness of advertising on television—the medium was learning that one of its necessary charms was to admit its own absurdity. Of course, many stars were nervous about "selling out" for these ads—or getting enough money for them. They did ads for foreign markets; they might let their voices be used; but talking on camera, being yourself and pushing a product, was an edgy decision. Garner seemed to enjoy it, and it's unlikely that he really needed the money. He was on $100,000 an episode of *Rockford*, and there would be 123—before he gathered the disputed profits from the show. What he got for the ads is also private information. But if you have time for a small game, guess what portion of his x Ms. Hartley received.

The couple were seen in cozy domestic situations, dressed nicely and casually. There was an air of improvised talk, as if to say, "Well, I have a moment spare, so let me tell you about this cute camera gadget." In one of them, he tells her he has a great Christmas present for her. She tries to guess what it is, but can't get the answer. He reveals the Polaroid OneStep, and she tells him, "But you get those free!" It's a small joke, but smart, and it's very tidily written and shot, with the players giving a credible if shallow portrait of marriage. Viewers started looking for the new Polaroid commercials. Instant camera sales doubled from 1976 to 1978.

As a rule, she was more discerning, truthful, and down-to-earth than he was. This was a comedy of marital subterfuge, and probably someone wondered about doing a married sitcom with the two of them. Why bother? In bite sizes, these ads deconstructed half of television and put it back in a witty, abbreviated package. Hartley was poised and perfect—which is all a commercial requires. But Garner was discovering his element. These ads let one realize he might be Cary Grant if someone had Katharine Hepburn and a script for him. But who needed that whole show anymore—why not let a running series of ads be a sitcom? In hindsight, the ads are all the more alive and shining in their fond awe over a photo device that we regard as archaic. It's in those tiny technological shifts—from a few seconds of photo paper emerging from the OneStep to what your iPhone can do—that we see human discourse altering faster than we will ever keep up.

In any time capsule left for aliens, there should be a few minutes of these Polaroid ads, with Mariette looking at Jim as if he's having an affair with the OneStep. That wasn't quite possible then, but by now many *are* co-responding with a small screen. (How long before *I Love Selfie*—the series?)

The idea of "television people," or contenders for "Mr. Television," is not dealt with fully yet. The stars in movies had been large, beautiful, and emphatic; from today, they feel overdone as well as antique. The archetypes of television were not so bold. I am fond of James Garner, but anyone could tell how reluctant he was to be emphatic—if he tried that, he started acting badly. No one rated James Arness as an actor, or Milton Berle as a comic. These figures were doorkeepers who helped us into their world while we remained in our room.

All its life, television has sought such men. Newscasters have to be that way; you won't be trusted with the news if you're too vivid or adventurous. The talk-show host has been equally calming. He can be as funny as Carson or as sharp as Dick Cavett. He is also a go-between of such deferential skills that you don't notice him too much. Merv Griffin (1925–2007) was such a case. He had been a big-band singer who did a few movies. But by the sixties, he was hosting his own television talk show (1962–86). In time, he would be a creator of game shows that we have never given up on—*Jeopardy!* and *Wheel of Fortune* are the two most famous, with over 6,000 episodes each. What made Merv so likeable was his enthusiasm for talking to show business people and being their friend for fifteen minutes. (He was especially good with Orson Welles—that great man's last gig was doing conjuring tricks in mid-afternoon on the Griffin show.)

Yet there was little to Griffin beyond his gloss of charm and eagerness, and the way he drew us into the box. Television has had so many vital figures like that, all famous for a certain devitalization or ease: Mr. Rogers; sports commentators like Bob Costas and

Al Michaels; Ed Sullivan—glaringly wrong for his long-lasting hit show, but unremovable; Dick Clark, that benign, boyish, very safe guide to the disruptive energies of rock and roll; Dean Martin on his celebrity roasts, as bland and ingratiating as Don Rickles was caustic and alarming; Alistair Cooke most of the time when introducing *Masterpiece Theatre*.

It was as if somehow the medium sensed its enormous reach and its profound influence on us, and said, "Let's play that down, let's be charming, rather self-effacing, somewhere between expert and obliging house servants and reassuring docents at a museum. Let's be gently 'on.'" These figures should be an illumination in which the bulb never burns out. They were "cool" in the McLuhan sense—Don Rickles is one of the few who were "hot" and aggressive, and survived. Television goes on and on, like an unending sports season, and it's the perpetuity that matters most, the easygoing constancy more than the melodrama of particular games. So there's an implicit admission in these figures—"It's all right," they say. Bill Cosby signaled that once.

Maybe this theory seems vague, or even ungenerous to the people I've mentioned. But then ask yourself how many women there have ever been serving the same function. Barbara Walters is one, and her special status is testament to her many skills and ambition. But the case of Joan Rivers shows the strains on a woman of genuine wit and risky ideas trying to be our tranquil host and our friend. There have been women newscasters and talk-show anchors, but it's hard to put them in the company of Dick Clark, Merv Griffin, or Mr. Rogers. Or is that just a stuffy male point of view? There have been women hosts cherished by the public, from Dinah Shore to Martha Stewart and Oprah. Since its start in 2003, *The Ellen DeGeneres Show* has been a mainstay of syndicated daytime shows, with an audience close to four million, and with 13 Emmys for Ellen herself. She is liked, trusted and followed; she has been a pioneer spokesperson for new ideas on gender; she is a cool, wry institution. But I hold to the opinion that, one way or another, she has refused magic or mystery. Perhaps she reckons that those qualities are silly male fetishes.

But I wonder how easily television can function without its mysterious Misters? Fred Rogers was one of the most sincere uncle figures, and without our realizing it, his "neighborhood" became our notion of our children's world.

You say Mr. Rogers was just for children? But many anxious parents watched him and were soothed. Perhaps you underestimate how far we are all kids with TV, or how close he came to being Valium.

THE SIT AND
THE SITUATION

TWO CUBES CONFRONT EACH OTHER: dream and domesticity. The one is "the box," containing a standing set and an infinity of shows;

the other is the box in which we live, our room, but another set. The two boxes are uncertain about their relationship, and there is this oddity: In the right light, and with benefit of reflection, it can look as if we are in the box with its ghosts. But each box—the one for the actors and the characters, and the one for us—believes it is real and primary. We call the boxed life we are looking at the "sit" (as in a sitcom), while we are part of a larger "situation," sometimes known as the world.

The "sit" in TV is the location and the social arrangement in a regular and long-running show, usually a comedy where part of the fun resides in this endless place, shabby but beloved. It is that Boston bar in *Cheers* (though Barstow, California, and Kansas City were first thoughts, until Beacon Street won out); the household in *All in the*

Family at 704 Hauser Street in Corona, Queens; and that Mobile Army Surgical Hospital in *M*A*S*H*—except that the latter never seemed especially mobile, or quite Korea. Instead, it felt like an effective, cut-price combination of a stage on the Twentieth Century Fox lot and a piece of ranch at Calabasas, up in the Malibu hills. The latter was a natural choice, for it had been used already for Robert Altman's 1970 movie of the same name. It was convenient, too, because all the actors lived or were stationed in LA. In time, and because of the TV show, the Smithsonian asked to have a few of the movie's venerable props, and set dressings that had been lingering on the ranch, for they had become part of folklore.

The "situation" is harder to describe. It should cover the world in which a show exists, even if the show may do everything it can to rise above that context. More than that, the situation should extend to the larger world in which the audience is living, and to the hope that the one might reflect on the other. So *M*A*S*H* claimed it was set close to the front lines of the war in Korea, which lasted three years, 1950–53; yet the show played with famous success from 1972 to 1983, a span of time that witnessed the conclusion to the Vietnam War and its bitter retrospective. There is still argument over which war the show was referring to, or was against, but folklore tends to forget that discussion. We take it for granted now that *M*A*S*H*'s real purpose was not to disapprove of war but to be a successful television show, even the most beloved we have ever had. There are some who regard it as a model of network television, just as *Gone with the Wind* is still hailed as the spirit of Hollywood in its golden age. In hindsight, the United States seems to have been coming apart during *M*A*S*H,* but the show bound it up, just like decent medical care.

Richard Hornberger had been a surgeon during the Korean War. Years later, with the aid of a sportswriter, W. C. Heinz, he wrote a novel based on his experiences. It was called *MASH*, and was published under the name Richard Hooker. The book was well reviewed. The screenwriter Ring Lardner Jr. was sent a galley for a jacket quote. He obliged and passed the galley on to his ex-agent, Ingo Preminger, saying it might make a movie. Preminger agreed, and took the novel to Fox, where he had a production deal. The studio bought the rights to the novel for a modest sum. Lardner wrote a script that was widely admired, but it proved hard to find a director who wanted to do it. The search ended with Robert Altman, who had then made only a few, unsuccessful films.

Altman was compelled to accept a flat-fee contract of $75,000, without points or residual interest. The film that resulted was controversial and very successful. It was bloody, irreverent, very funny, jazzy, unpredictable, cruel in some ways but sentimental in others. Far from being antiwar, it seemed to say, "Look, if you're going to have a war, this is the way guys are going to behave"—and it was largely guys. "They'll crack cynical jokes while they're doing bloodbath surgery;

"WHERE EVERYBODY KNOWS YOUR NAME."

—THEME SONG FOR *CHEERS*

they lust after nurses, pretty or not; they screw the system and authority for all they can; and they act smart and nonchalant to show how little they care, or are afraid. In short, they're going to have a hell of a time, if they survive." The film was the work of someone who had been there: At nineteen, Altman had enlisted in the Army and fought in the Pacific with the Army Air Forces.

Twentieth Century Fox loved *M*A*S*H*. The film won the Palme d'Or at Cannes and was voted best film by the National Society of Film Critics; it won a Golden Globe as best musical or comedy, and it received five Oscar nominations, winning for Lardner. On a budget of $3 million, the studio earned rental income of $40 million. So a boisterous, bawdy, risky picture had done very tidily.

It was unusual for network television to recognize the chance for a series in a movie—though *Wagon Train* was loosely derived from a film Ward Bond had made with John Ford, *Wagon Master* (1950). But Fox liked the idea of *M*A*S*H*, and they assigned the development process to Larry Gelbart and Gene Reynolds. Gelbart was such a pro as a comedy writer, he had actually started out while in high school. His career had been hit-and-miss, though he wrote for top comics and was part of the writing team on Sid Caesar's *Your Show of Shows* (1950–54), which included Mel Brooks, Neil Simon, and Woody Allen. But he would never have another hit like *M*A*S*H*. In outline, the show seemed promising: It had a clear-cut sit, where all the characters were away from home and fancy-free; it was a study in comradeship; it had a hit movie behind it; and it was material for comedy. *M*A*S*H* was going to be a sitcom, not a drama or a war story, but a kind of overgrown school story for wild, crazy, but likeable people who didn't want to be at war, or admit that sometimes they were having a ball.

The TV show is a gelded version of the Altman film, and that speaks to a day when bold movies were still far ahead of what television would dare. The language of the film and its nudity were toned down for network decorum. On the small screen, "Hot Lips" (Loretta Swit) turned into an amiable figure, who relaxed as the series went on—she became her real name, Margaret. Whereas in the movie (with Sally Kellerman), she was so nearly deranged that the final public-shower humiliation of her was hostile and gleeful—we wonder why we're watching but can't help laughing. The TV show had dark episodes, to be sure, and characters killed off, but it never had the irritable whiplash air of an Altman, who might do something nasty on the spur of a moment. On TV, we were spared the blood of the film's operating theater—and the insolent indifference of Altman's lead surgeons, Hawkeye and Trapper (Donald Sutherland and Elliott Gould). The TV flinched from showing servicemen with so little respect for the service—yet that kind of contempt had been current in fiction since James Jones's *From Here to Eternity*, and it had been given a new thrust by Joseph Heller's *Catch-22* (1961). That's a novel about the organized madness of war, and the TV show was afraid to handle that open blade or question why "we" were there.

Instead, on television, with eleven seasons and 256 episodes, *M*A*S*H* went on more than three times as long as the Korean War, with the network pushing Fox and the actors to keep going. The sit smothered any situation. At such points in TV, the setup of the show becomes its own persistence (and profitability), and any imperative of necessary drama is compromised by the desired continuity. It becomes more an institution than a story, and so it's awkward for war to end while money is being made. Our familiarity and comradeship with the actors can bury the narrative need of the characters.

Not that the countless fans of *M*A*S*H* felt the characters were diminished. As with most regular TV shows, putting aside the humor, the suspense, or the poignancy, it is the characters themselves that hold us. Sometimes that involves very little in the way of dramatics or narrative. It is their loyalty to us and our life together that we love; it is their way of doing something that is essentially Edith, or Joey, or even Carrie Mathison. But some numbing alchemy falls on these people, and it affects our situation, for it is our watching that alters them.

So we have to talk about Alan Alda, who was more identified with *M*A*S*H* on television than anyone. Alda was Captain Benjamin Franklin Pierce, or Hawkeye, from start to finish. Wayne Rogers was his Trapper John for three seasons, until Rogers argued over his deal and was replaced with Mike Farrell. That meant that the original pairing was subtly diffused and defused, and the applied sweetness of Alda (I was never happy with it) became the life-force or the placebo. Go back to the movie, and the abrasive charm in Sutherland and Gould is their not caring whether they were liked. They were outrageous, where the guys in the TV show were trained for longevity. Deep down, they knew the war might go on forever, and rather welcomed it. Yet real acting and catharsis depend on danger and the prospect of closure.

That is the source of the film's disconcerting edge. Whereas, I don't think anyone could ever accuse Alan Alda of being less than available for us, ingratiating and anxious to be liked. Alda has done movies, of course, and done quite well in them as a supporting player. But he does not have the confidence to be a lead, and so—in the way of television—Alda's Hawkeye doesn't achieve the resolute privacy of great movie characters. He doesn't persuade us he's there for just the *now* of the story—he has taken a drug that whispers, "You're forever, baby."

So he was institutionalized. Alda was nominated for the best-actor-in-a-comedy-series Emmy eight times, and won twice. He also won Emmys for writing and directing on the show. It became a feature of *M*A*S*H* that actors were given the chance to write and direct, and that's a measure of its family identity: The actors often knew best what their roles should do and say. Alda directed thirty-one episodes and wrote nineteen. He was as much a shaping force as Larry Gelbart, and in its final seasons it was Alda's often reluctant participation that kept the show going. Over the years, that meant a lot—and made him less than the most popular man in the outfit. But being ingratiating can lead to that. He had earned $10,000 for the pilot, and by the time of the final episode—a two-and-a-half-hour movie—he was at $365,000.

Alda was godfather to the mood and the story sense, if not in command of the 4077th Mobile Army Surgical Hospital. Which means that he, Gelbart, and Gene Reynolds (and a legion of other writers and directors) share the credit for a simply crafted show, ready to take risks and departures, and certainly mindful of the reality of war. It was a great show when it played—and that is all TV requires. But that raises intriguing points. *M*A*S*H* was not an immediate hit, despite the momentum of the movie. In its first season, 1972–73, it was ranked 46, and there was talk of cancelation—and cancelation is more decisive for a character than the risks he takes in a story. But

then the on-air status of *M*A*S*H* was changed. It had been scheduled that first season on Sunday nights at 8:00 P.M., playing against *The Wonderful World of Disney* and *The FBI*. That note of archaic institutions and their wonders is as much of a time warp as the realization that 1972 was also the year of incidents at the Watergate Hotel, the shattered Olympiad in Munich, and *The Godfather*. That ongoing Disney celebration on NBC and the endorsement of the FBI on ABC (with Efrem Zimbalist Jr.—still more likely as an anagram than an actor) are impossible to conceive playing now. In turn, that says something about *M*A*S*H,* and may place it in the league of belated entertainments about military camaraderie in the Second World War, as opposed to wars from the modern age of terror.

But CBS adjusted (the network was then headed by Fred Silverman, a dynamic young executive, the green-lighter for many shows and trends, especially when he moved over to ABC in 1975). For the 1973–74 season, Silverman shifted *M*A*S*H* to Saturday night, and placed it between *All in the Family* and *The Mary Tyler Moore Show* (rated 1 and 7 in that season). The rest of the evening was *The Bob Newhart Show* (16) and *The Carol Burnett Show* (22). So CBS owned Saturday nights—in retreat, the two other networks generally ran movies, and in those days "new" movies were still an attraction in their television debuts. The result for *M*A*S*H* was immediate: It rose to number 4 in the ratings and had an audience of over 17 million households. For years it would stay in the top 10, with 17–20 million households watching. Or with the sets on. The question of a happy slot has to do with the habit-forming nature of television. In the early seventies, the three networks were still the main players in the game (like a czar, a kaiser, and a king), and it was widely understood that many sets remained tuned after a popular show had ended. "Don't go away" was a mantra in an insecure business, especially one that interrupted itself at least four times an hour for commercials.

Equally, "Don't go away" was a plea in the hearts of many viewers when *M*A*S*H* came to its close at last. (It's a condition of TV—something in the atmosphere—that loyalty and persistence do not want it to end. The on-ness becomes desirable in itself.) So a finale is definitely a return to looking, and in this case the facts are so famous that they say more about television than they could about *M*A*S*H*.

The show concluded on February 28, 1983. (Congress had just issued a report critical of the internment of Japanese Americans during the war, and President Reagan was about to launch his Strategic Defense Initiative.) This last, 256th episode of *M*A*S*H* was a movie of 135 minutes. It had nearly a dozen writers, and Alan Alda was its director. The episode had Hawkeye in a mental hospital after a breakdown, and his scattered memories were a structure for a series of farewells that greeted the official end of the war in Korea. Of course, the Korean conflict was not and is not over—some wars do not end tidily, but find their own syndication—but the episode had talk of some of its soldiers being sent to the "new" Indochina war. The finale was profoundly accomplished, a trigger for tears, but done with tact and taste,

SOME WARS DO NOT END TIDILY BUT FIND THEIR OWN SYNDICATION.

regret and congratulation, and perky humor. Nearly every viewer remarked on how it felt like a last, fond party for a group of actors and crew people.

The buildup had been so organized that CBS was charging $450,000 for a 30-second commercial. (So Alda's pay was covered in 24 seconds.) It is reckoned that 121 million people in the United States watched some of the episode. To this day, that is the greatest number of viewers for the finale of any show. It is also a lot more than generally watch all the channels on modern television on any night now. Coming on the eve of so many disruptions in the technology of television-watching, *M*A*S*H* seems increasingly like a homage to the close gatherings of Americans that network television once generated. The huddle in the show—its camp life—is a model of the idea of us gathered in our room, even if the meaning of "camp" shifts as time passes.

In commentaries on the show and how many people were there for the finale (about six times the number who had watched preceding episodes), there was much comparison with live telecasts of a Super Bowl. This is not just a numerical affinity. Many of us watch every

Super Bowl over the years, with more or less need. The San Francisco 49ers began to win that prize in 1981, and that city was part of my situation. Thus I watched "our" victories over several years, but I have no desire or patience to see them again. The essence of a sporting event—and always one of the most potent heartbeats in television—is to be there for a live event, when the outcome is at issue, and only then.

Nothing sustains sports viewership more than that uncertainty, which also affects whether the 49ers would beat the Bengals, what the verdict would be in the O. J. Simpson trial, or whether Fukushima might go so toxic that the cameras had to be abandoned. I saw the finale of *M*A*S*H* in February 1983, and I was happily appreciative of it. I tried to watch it again for the purposes of this book and I couldn't endure it. As to re-viewing the complete 256 episodes, that prospect is outlandish. It's not that the show wasn't good, or well done, or one of the best sitcoms ever made. But the viewing situation was being alive and there for that moment. That's how television finds its best nature: not as some kind of particular entertainment or information to please us, but as a reflection of our unique and momentary existence.

But if *M*A*S*H* had its own time slip, between Korea and Indochina, artfully finessed by the show, imagine one more. Take Alda, Mike Farrell, Loretta Swit, Jamie Farr, Harry Morgan, and all the others left at the end, and shift them forward to a twenty-first-century military base in Kandahar or Falluja. The shock is startling, for all of a sudden the *M*A*S*H* boys look middle-aged, antique, comically white and genteel, and possessed of a view of war that is embedded in the virtue and justice felt in 1941–45. There were right-wingers in the United States who sometimes grumbled about *M*A*S*H* being liberal but never realized how lucky they were, for its liberalism was one that FDR would have found quite comfortable forty years earlier.

In short, the 4077th was staffed with colorful and largely likeable white actors. Klinger (Jamie Farr) had been a maverick figure for years: He seemed Jewish (yet actually he was Lebanese), and he was a cross-dresser. That was more to escape the Army than to realize his sexual status: Larry Gelbart said the character had been loosely based on Lenny Bruce's desperate efforts to get out of the service. Klinger had been accepted as an oddball—not gay—and in the final episode he had come unstuck by electing to marry a sweet Korean woman, Soon-Lee. So the prospect of gay life and gay repression in the military was put on a shelf with a pretty ribbon wrapping. And the absence of black men of war, guys who were there because it was one of the only natural ways for them to proceed in Americana, simply made the show more palatable. The show lacked boredom, narcotics, foul language, natural cowardice, amazing courage, self-sacrifice, the spirituality in weapons, technology as a religion, casual racism, sweeping political ignorance—the nature of modern military situations.

There were even times when *M*A*S*H*—more modern, more hip, and much more talented—could still give you a flash memory of *Hogan's Heroes* (1965–71, Vietnam years), that fun-filled fairy tale about life in a German prison camp in which every Nazi was a knockabout idiot and the camp became a cool hotel for the guys. If you had dared rerun *M*A*S*H* in Kandahar (where soldiers were playing Xbox combat games on their screens), it would have been for an audience of ill-educated kids, many of them black or nonwhite, some of them deranged by the experience and turning to drugs—and some of them women.

There really were not women at the battlefront in Korea, so Altman's *M*A*S*H* could have been excused, but the film had still liked two types of women: the shrill, officious, and stupid Hot Lips, or nurses named Dish and Storch—cute, available, and uncritical, the type of nurse guys could dream of. When the situation reached TV, the nurses were a little less complacent and a lot less difficult. They were there for their guys, and in fact the credits often referred to "various nurses," with actresses shifting from one to another, without identity, backstory, or identifiable problems. You have only to think of the changed attitudes in a movie like *Courage Under Fire* (1996, with Meg Ryan leading a downed chopper crew in Iraq), to see how far audiences had become ready for a military living out most of our social problems, but under more intense pressure. Nevertheless, television has not given us a military show since *China Beach* (1988–91). The community of guards, interrogators, translators, dog handlers, and CIA observers at Abu Ghraib, or some of the other unknown enhanced-interrogation sites, has not interested network comedy. You can learn a lot about the overall situation of your nation from the forbidden sits or the blind spots in public entertainment.

You may say it's a low blow to propose a sitcom in Abu Ghraib, or the dark thought may help you explore the odd nature of the sit and a situation. Here's more prompting. When CBS saw the first series of M*A*S*H, they identified it as a comedy, sure enough. So shouldn't it have laughs? After all, a great deal of early television had a live audience at its filming, and those people were encouraged, cued, and even trained to laugh, because that signal had a Pavlovian effect on the home audience. Of course that's unfair, too…I doubt your dog never laughed at M*A*S*H.

It happened that the first time I saw Altman's M*A*S*H was in Tours in France. It was playing dubbed into French, and that language enhancement was not kind to a picture so full of overlapping, idiomatic wit, and insult. The French dub never got the jokes in the camp speaker system. But a young Tours audience laughed, as if they felt they'd never seen a film with such needle or unexpectedness. This film didn't salute its own institutions (it was made in the same year as *Patton*, which beat it for Best Picture). The laughter was infectious and authentic. But television laugh tracks, such as CBS wanted for M*A*S*H, are fabricated, edited, tonally adjusted, wiped for offensiveness or idiosyncrasy. It's syrup laughter to help us swallow, a commercial for its own show as well as an editing device, an understanding enhancer, like music and cutting. If comedy depends on surprise, then a laugh track is anxiety-resistant.

Nevertheless, Larry Gelbart fought the laugh track. He said the real Korean War hadn't had one, which was a good wisecrack but not really practical television. The argument went on, but the network was sure the audience needed to be placed and permitted to have a good time: Their situation required definition and comfort. So a compromise was reached, and the show had a modified laugh track.

That comfort verges on instruction. In January 1975, Kenneth Tynan observed:

Nobody—on TV—has to be funny any more. All laughter is canned, pre-recorded, *fixed*: the art of comedy is in the hands of backroom engineers, matching laughter tracks with jokes: and so infectious is laughter that home audiences laugh along with the mechanised euphoria. This is perhaps the most hateful thing about TV: that it removes from the audience its great prerogative of deciding which performers are good and which are not. So subtle is the manipulation that when the comic pauses, the engineer will dub in a tiny audience cough to indicate that the pay-off line has not yet arrived.

That was written (for Tynan's diary) forty years ago, and the point about the providential cough is still acute criticism. But the malaise Tynan was addressing has swept on and done so much damage to our "great prerogative of deciding." For as screens are desperate to keep our attention, so their anxiety dismays real concentration. Television programming has yielded to superscripts to tell us what's coming next, along with musical cues that indicate "importance," "sensation," or "novelty" as much as silent-movie musical accompaniment captioned (but hurt) the sentiments in a story. On the www, these intrusions can be so gross and strident, so much a matter of fraudulent headlines and insipid stories, that we are torn between following the crude bait and despising the entire process of watching. Our lack of value is brutally taken for granted.

For every hysterical insistence that we keep watching, that we pay attention, because this is about us *and* US, the heedless momentum of television—its own sit, its pressure—tells us that our useful deciding has been slipping away for several decades. So we may witness something called the "Presidential Election" on our box, and the din of TV's self-hype says this is really *happening*, that it is *important*, and history before our eyes—the state or the situation of the nation. Yet one deadly and very acute TV campaigner took it for granted that the whole thing was only a show, a sit, in which he could hire and fire people, ideas, and semblances of reality.

7 COMMERCIALS

THIS TRUTH IS EASILY MISSED, but the ads are the staple programming of television and still the formative element on our diverse screens. The programs are there to break up the ads; the news, the jokes, the wardrobe malfunctions, the lists, whatever's online are there to sustain "monetization." Often, per second, these grabbers have had the most money spent on them, and the most creative agonizing—using that term in a generous but not satiric vein. They persist for weeks and months at a time, the most familiar things on television and the most loathed; they are the tunes, the chants, and the flagrant lies we cannot forget. They remind us always that we have a culture of fraud in which pretty pictures and plain statements are always offset. They are the shows that strengthen our resolve to hate the medium and ourselves for persevering with it. Yet sometimes they are as delightful as a new kitten— until we see that the young charmer can toy with an old sparrow that looks like us. They are advertisements, and their desperation that we keep watching is as intense as that of the sparrow.

We tell ourselves that we can't put the new stuff back in the old bottle, whether it is elixir or poison, Coke or strontium-90. So it's not possible for science or progress to "forget" how to make a nuclear weapon or a sweet, peppy beverage. Our past actions do not give us up, not even when we hardly noticed we had taken a decision over them. Having commercials was never put to a vote, and it is too late now to reform the constitution and stifle them at birth. Stuff happens.

There is no more striking demonstration of the proximity and the gulf between a sit and the situation than a TV commercial. In thirty seconds, one of life's problems and its sad sit are "solved": Discontent and deprivation turn into satisfaction. But in the larger situation that surrounds this facile miracle—call it the domain of politics and philosophy—the bargain between buying and feeling better is put to the test. It would be a sit if a derelict sleeping on the street got a new, ultra-easy comb-in shampoo—but then suppose he howled to the moon, "I have no comb! And neither do the million others!" At that point you're into a politico-social-economic crisis. It's a situation in which, just for peace of mind, either the derelicts go or we go.

The ads may be the most damning and damnable things on television. They are a curse that can never be exorcised. They may be our most damaging invention. Still, we have our favorites.

It is 1979, and we are in the tunnel that leads away from an NFL playing field. There are a few people standing at the end of the tunnel against the white light of the arena, the game, and its roaring crowd. You feel it must be a set, but in fact it was shot at a stadium in New Rochelle. A tall black man is coming down the ramp, hobbling from an injury and likely defeat, his shirt tossed over his right shoulder. It is Joe Greene of the Pittsburgh Steelers, "Mean Joe" Greene, a defensive tackle, anchor to the Pittsburgh "Steel Curtain" defense, who played on four winning Super Bowl sides. Perhaps he hurt so much already he did not have to act the hobble. Greene was not the first choice for the ad. Roger Staubach, the white quarterback for the Dallas Cowboys, had been nominated, as well as Tony Dorsett, Ed "Too Tall" Jones, and Jack Lambert, another Steeler. But

FLAGRANT LIES WE CANNOT FORGET.

McCann Erickson, the agency making the ad, decided on Joe Greene, and maybe it was the label "Mean" that swayed them.

The ad is a minute long and it consists largely of two camera setups, edited together to make a bond. A white boy appears (the actor was nine) holding an open bottle of Coca-Cola. He tells Greene that he is "the best ever," but that doesn't ease the player's pain. Then the kid offers his Coke. Greene stops his retreat to the dressing room, takes the bottle, and drinks it down in one gulp. The kid is pleased, but he feels his moment is over. He turns away to leave. But Greene calls him back; he takes that playing shirt from his shoulder, says, "Hey kid, catch!" and tosses it to him. This Mean Joe seems like a gladiator, yet he is becoming a role model. The deal is paradise for the boy, and the sense of well-being is lifted higher by a jingle that began as Greene started to drink. A printed slogan appears on the screen, "Have a Coke and a smile," and, in the corner of the screen, "Coke adds life."

GREENE APPARENTLY DRANK EIGHTEEN BOTTLES OF COKE IN ONE DAY.

The shot of Greene is from the level of the boy's gaze, looking up at this six-foot-four linebacker, while the shot of the kid (his name was Tommy Okon) is from slightly below his eyes. They probably tried other angles on what was a three-day shoot for that one minute. If you worked that hard on a 150-minute motion picture, you'd require a shoot of 450 days.

The time and care spent (Greene apparently drank eighteen bottles of Coke in one day) pays off in the most immediate sense. What can I say? Is it a "beautiful" little movie? Is it simply judged to a fraction of a second? Is it plain cute? I watched the ad whenever I could; I sometimes turned to sporting events on television to catch the ad again; I think it has not gone quite stale, no matter that it is candidly manipulative baloney. I never drank Coke before the ad, and I only did once afterwards. I hated the insipid sweetness.

Greene would say later that he felt the ad helped people (especially white people) to like him, or talk to him. Without subtlety or shame, the ad urges and indicates a specious chance of better race relations in America. It sees a paradise where white kids and black athletes might be buddies, bound by an equitable social contract.

Coca-Cola had already run ads that taught the whole world to sing. Could that sweet drink be a unifying force? If you're captured by ISIS, make sure you have a chilled Coke handy to cool their temper? That may seem a fatuous aside, but ads are always making extravagant hints at larger, insane well-being. So they deserve darker underlinings, too. That leaves one angrier at the diverting project of advertising, and being a sucker for it. We are watching reckless lies or false assertions, and they come in the midst of the News, a great baseball game, *Mad Men*, or so many other things that have some claim on our reality and our life. The News fears unreliability in its anchors, but doesn't it hear the dishonor that sets them up?

How many ads have we seen in all our years, and how many do we remember? I have picked out the Joe Greene Coca-Cola ad. But over the decades there have been others (like James Garner and Mariette Hartley for Polaroid) that amused me or pleased my eye, and more still that I have forgotten but which, on seeing again, would make me smile and say, "Oh yes, I remember that one." There are also hundreds of thousands of ads I loathe. Just try calculating the total you've seen. Assume ten an hour, and allow that you have seen three hours of TV a day for forty years: The answer is 438,000 ads.

That's not just startling or ghastly, with the folly held in abeyance by passing cuteness. It's a kind of brain death, where the damage is irreversible. And we say we are against brain death. If I urged you, "Drink this tasty, destructive draft every **438,000 ADS.** day—better still, I'll slip it in your water supply, where it will account for x brain cells, or $100x$," you would be outraged. You can't put advertisese back in the bottle, any more than we can forget nuclear fission, methods of torture, or how to run a tidy concentration camp. Now advertising is exerting its grip on the small screens of the Internet and your iPad. And so television and the Internet, once hailed as available, neutral forms of discourse to make knowledge more accessible and the world more united, have been made into a travesty. It may seem silly to raise such a settled matter. But even if we have ruined ourselves, that is no reason not to explore the damage. After all, there may be worse to come, and we should know how the process works.

This did not have to happen—it does not happen everywhere. Television and the airwaves are easily regarded as assets that government should administer on our behalf. Aircraft carriers and public decency work that way. There are some Americans who flinch at the thought of government control, yet they expect an American army, and the reach of a secure state to cover all kinds of policing. In a pinch, the NRA would likely support state provision of at least one free gun

ONE OF THE UNIVERSAL LANGUAGES WE ALL LIVE WITH.

for every person (ammo to be negotiated). We say we believe in state education, and are coming to understand the value of a national health policy. Americans all drive on the right-hand side of the road in a scheme of interstate highways, and expect a coherent system of air traffic control when they board a plane (even if it is their own plane). There is a federal tax authority, a Federal Bureau of Investigation, and we generally adopt the function of the English language while paying lip service to minority tongues. Always open, we have nearly 1,700 Denny's. We say we believe all men are equal, from a black man on death row in Texas to Warren Buffett. But some of us dislike "government."

America did not welcome the notion of television administered as a national service. But look at how it worked in the United Kingdom. In 1946, after the delaying war, television was in the hands of the British Broadcasting Corporation (the BBC; the C stood for "Company" originally), which had begun with radio in 1922 and operated under a royal charter from 1927 onward. The charter and the foundation of the BBC have a large and challenging ideal: that government and the people will fund the BBC, with its board of governors suffering no government interference. In many countries that say they have state-authorized broadcasting, that has not worked out and the media have become distorting instruments of propaganda, or worse. This has not happened in Britain, despite anxieties and pressure from people as varied as Prime Minister Margaret Thatcher and Rupert Murdoch, who felt the system was "unfair."

So in 1946 the BBC began to charge a license fee to all individuals and institutions that received TV. It was £2 pounds at the outset, and at present it has risen to £145.50 (about $210). In 2013–14, that gave the BBC revenue of just over £5 billion, the money that paid for programs, infrastructure, and employees. By now, the board of governors has been replaced by what is called the BBC Trust, operating with what we hope is the old independence.

The first director-general of the BBC, from 1927 to 1938, was John Reith, the son of a Scottish Presbyterian minister in the United Free Church of Scotland. He was morally austere and culturally enlightened. He believed the BBC's chief purpose was not just to uphold British life and its virtues, and to represent Britain to the world, but to launch a process of public education and challenge. He was not overflowing with humor or insight: He ordered that radio newsreaders should wear evening dress, and he took it for granted that his Britain was a superior being in the world. Reith also approved in his

John Reith

diary of the way Hitler was "cleaning up" Germany in the 1930s. No one is perfect, not even those with large educational ideas.

Reith's attitude to the BBC was that of a missionary, a harsh benefactor, and a polite authoritarian. He did enormous good work, yet he is very hard to stomach now. This is a lesson in how naive we are when we lay hands on new technologies. We do not know what we are doing. I am a child of the BBC, through radio first, who learned about the world through broadcasting. Long before I read the book, in a radio serialisation, I had been frightened by the sound of the wind and Cathy's cry in a radio serialization of *Wuthering Heights*. The BBC could be staid and provincial (it still can), but it overflows with altruistic, unexpected ideas in programming and with shows designed for just a few people. A lot of its entertainment is rubbish, and it has always relished shows that can't go outside the country—*Dad's Army* (1968–77), written by

Jimmy Perry and David Croft, concerned the comic shambles of a provincial Home Guard unit (at the fictional resort of Warmington-on-Sea) during the Second World War. It had a sublime cast that included Arthur Lowe, John Le Mesurier, Clive Dunn, and John Laurie, and I think it was tender and hilarious, though I'm not going back to make sure. Nostalgia can be too precious to be put to the test.

On the other hand, paid for out of the license fee, and without commercials, the BBC promoted many things that have pleased American audiences, and some that may have seemed too local for export: the Nature unit; the career of David Attenborough; the great run of plays that fed into the lengthy literary adaptations that have been a part of the diet of what America calls *Masterpiece Theatre*, and include *The Forsyte Saga*, *The Six Wives of Henry VIII*, and *I, Claudius* (all glimpses into how naughty the upper classes can be), to say nothing of programs from *That Was the Week That Was*, *Monty Python's Flying Circus*, *Not Only…But Also* (with Peter Cook and Dudley Moore), *Fawlty Towers*, and *The Singing Detective*, to the polemical documentaries by Adam Curtis, *The Fall*, and *Peaky Blinders*—all calculated risks such as few countries in the world would have dared. And many of them incurred domestic complaints about misuse of the license fee, all of which were politely ignored. And don't let's overlook the steady use by American News of BBC and ITN reporters, on the spot, since British broadcasting still has foreign correspondents in a way America finds it harder to support.

ITN is the news broadcasting arm of Independent Television—which signifies being other than the BBC more than any pronounced independence of attitude. The BBC monopoly of television ended in 1954 with the foundation of the Independent Television Authority, a network that would show commercials in the American way. Yet even in its origination there was heavy-handed advice that it not become so American

Prunella Scales as Sybil in **Fawlty Towers**

as to be offensive. ITV was a single station (it is called Channel 3 now), contributed to by a number of separate broadcasting companies: The leading parts were London Weekend, Associated-Rediffusion, Granada, Thames, and Scottish Television.

Many in Britain felt that ITV was a vulgar intrusion. Its coming was greeted with a streak of the schoolboy cheekiness that the BBC has never abandoned: Commercial television began transmitting in Britain on September 22, 1955, but to upstage its debut, on that very day, BBC radio had its popular evening serial *The Archers* devastated by the sudden death by fire of a beloved character, Grace Fairbrother Archer (and I can still recall the name of the actress, Ysanne Churchman). Grace had an added luster, vivid for 1955—she was the daughter of gentry who had married a farmer's son. The shock at her death was genuine and ridiculous, so fewer people had space in their agog heads to notice that television with advertising was doing quite different levels of damage. *The Archers* started in January 1951, and it still plays regularly.

There were more than enough viewers frustrated by the solemn excellence of the BBC and its grave pursuit of minority tastes to make ITV work. The ads, unsurprisingly, were in the American pattern— for advertising is one of the universal languages we all live with. On the whole, British ads tended to be more ironic than American ads, as if to admit, well, advertising really is rather foolish, so let's have fun with it. ITV never gained any part of the license fee. But it quickly became profitable. Roy Thomson, a media tycoon born in Canada of Scots descent, and a founder of Scottish Television, once said that "running a commercial television station is like having a permit to print money."

That was blunt but candid, and a forecast of what Rupert Murdoch would do with Sky, effectively the first cable network in Britain, launched in 1989, notable for its winning away of many sports from the BBC monopoly. Of course, Britain deserved an alternative, and today the BBC still retains about a 30 percent share of total viewership. But ITV created immense new wealth in the fifties and sixties, a time of economic expansion and escape from the austerity that lasted

THE BBC HAS A LARGE AND CHALLENGING IDEAL.

for over a decade after the war. For a while, Britain had just two BBC channels and ITV. But in 1982, Channel 4 was introduced, funded by advertising but owned by the public. The ingenious compromise in 4 was signaled on its opening night, when the featured offering was *Walter*, a play or a movie about a mentally handicapped man who becomes alone in his world. Written by David Cook and directed by Stephen Frears, with Ian McKellen as Walter, it was one of the most searching and depressing things ever seen on television, as if in defiance of its own cheerier ads.

THE BRITISH IMAGINATION LOVED CHEEKY, WITTY COMMERCIALS.

The British imagination loved cheeky, witty commercials, and with movie directors as diverse as Joseph Losey and then Ridley and Tony Scott working on them, the marketing profession soon created awards for its own excellence. If commercials were mini-movies, then they were work opportunities and a training ground for would-be movie auteurs. Thus, the mise-en-scène of movies began to be affected by the gloss and speed of commercials. That helps explain the retreat of personal style in moviemaking.

There's a striking example of what these mixed impulses could lead to. In 1973, at a record-breaking cost of £900,000 (about $1.3 million), Thames Television mounted a twenty-six-part documentary, *The World at War* (about the Second World War). This was spurred by BBC series like *Civilisation*, in which Kenneth Clark had led a tour through Art History in which the audience never had to move. *The World at War* was produced by Jeremy Isaacs, who scoured newsreel archives all over the world and got interviews with those who had fought, from generals to privates. Carl Davis wrote a somber score and Laurence Olivier narrated the series. The corps of writers included Peter Batty, Angus Calder, and Neal Ascherson. Again, the audience stayed still as their past flowed by. Naturally, the show played with ads.

But when this history reached the concentration camps, in the episode called "Genocide" (written by Charles Bloomberg and directed by Michael Darlow), it was announced that "out of respect" it would play without commercials.

It was an eerie moment, exposing much more than tact, for it seemed to acknowledge that there were some filmed events, or some moments in a show, too grim or too serious to handle the instant adjustment to the battle against drab hair or forlorn automobiles. But the longer you thought about it, the sillier the compromise became, and the more surely it signaled the betraying nature of commercials. It was possible that the "Genocide" episode covered more deaths than any other in the series. But carnage and casualties had been plentiful in other episodes: the German invasion of Russia; the firebombing of German cities; and "The Bomb" all played with commercials.

Was there a tacit admission that ads were at odds with intellectual respect and our attempt at attention and understanding? Was there even implied consent that commercial breaks were against the grain of intelligence and being a part of the world that always faces the threat of disasters? Is a comb-free shampoo the derelict's most pressing need? Could a beverage save a lineman from concussion?

Look at it another way, one that may seem foolish or impossibly belated. Imagine you are at the movies, watching anything from *Rear Window* to *Ida*, and every fifteen or twenty minutes the sequence of the movie is broken in on by two minutes of ads. Or suppose that the book you are reading has a couple of ads after every sixteen-page section—most newspapers and magazines have had that kind of flexibility for decades. Consider a CD of a Mahler symphony where the luster of the latest Mercedes-Benz or the efficacy of a new drug separated one movement from another. Suppose you are searching out the background to the news on the Internet and every lead is prefaced by an ad for insurance, penile enlargement, and extra insurance against any penile enlargement that lasts longer than four hours. I hope you're laughing, but can the humor forget a pit of horror in the joke?

Go a step further: Your children are at school, and they are learning to read. A couple of times during the lesson, the teacher steps away from that script and does a short, jolly act to recommend whiffle puffs and Skola in the lunch break just ahead. The teacher may object (cling to that hope) because he or she relies on the absolute trust of the children. But schools need funding, and some administrator may say,

"Don't worry too much. The last ones to notice this 'outrage' will be the kids, because they are born and raised to ads in everything."

This test is not quite over: You are having sex with someone you like. It is going very happily. But just as climax may be anticipated, he or she backs out of an embrace and asks, "What's in your wallet?"

It's not just the claptrap can't-get-it-out-of-your-head idiocy of the ads, it's their function as interruption and the way they stain everything else on the screen. When we have children, we ask them not to interrupt our wise words (we need confidence) on how to live life, and we try to listen faithfully to their halting account of what they did today. When we urge reading on them as a habit and plea-sure, it is because we believe in the dividends of concentration and the sense of going deeper into *Madame Bovary* or Stephen King— plus we point out the foolishness of our son complaining, "Well, the French book is all about *a woman*!" If you take a teenager to see *Long Day's Journey into Night* or the Ring cycle, you tell them to be patient and let the work build in their head—just take care not to doze yourself.

But in practice, ever since the arrival of commercial television, we have adopted a structure of calculated interruption. This is violently apparent on the Internet, where items are preempted by ads and we are looking at a panorama of alternative links, so that we sometimes drift and click from one to another, without quite admitting that we are going nowhere and failing to stop following grabber headlines that are not just crude but fraudulent, but which come and go so fast there is no chance of regulation. So we have an extension of television that is simply filling our time. Without hope of value, we go to it several times an hour. And our children go there quicker and with more thrill than we can muster. We have even identified a malady that legitimizes their scattered attitude. We call it attention-deficit/hyperactivity disor-der. Today's news on the Net is that 7 percent of children worldwide suffer from it; it raises the odds of premature death and the risk of self-harm and suicide. There are medications prescribed for it, chiefly methylphenidate hydrochloride, generally known as Ritalin. That is marketed by a Swiss company, Novartis International, which has an annual revenue of $58 billion.

I'm sure that Ritalin "works" sometimes, according to the children taking it and the parents paying for it—of course, the medicine is actually prescribed to adults. So maybe you give the kid a new Xbox game as a reward. In other words, a culture of mounting disorder or interruption is fostered in which the haphazard attention of us all is not just taken for granted and but relied on.

This stress on jaggedness in the mind can affect so many attitudes in life. And if we are consenting to a medium so spasmodic or self-fractured, we are encouraging the sensibility of "Nothing can be done about this." Look at the News, so intruded on by ads, and wonder whether that organized disarray isn't the start of an excuse for feeling futile. The very nature of thought is at issue here, and the damage extends far beyond attention problems for a few children.

So the business of television works hard to maintain the integrity of certain figureheads. A Brian Williams, no matter that he looked so good, spoke so well, and was a dreamer and a fantasist like us all, had to be relied on for authority. O. J. Simpson ran through airports for Hertz rental cars, and his grin seemed impeccable. But then he got in a tangle and he was unwilling to own up to the Bruno Magli shoes we could see him wearing. If he ever gets out of

THE VERY NATURE OF THOUGHT IS AT ISSUE HERE.

Lovelock Correctional Center, he won't get a spot, not even for sleep aids and forgetting. He will be one of the most known people we have ever had, but what was once his brittle and untested authority is forever shot.

It can happen, even if the meanness of Joe Greene faded away with his ad. So he lives now in Flower Mound, a comfortable suburb of Dallas where the white population is 83.9 percent. There is celebrity in ads, but it is double-edged, as if it understood how swiftly such fame can get its guillotine. By the late nineties, at Indiana University, Jared Fogle weighed 425 pounds. He avoided people, until he started eating at Subway and somehow translated himself into a bright-eyed, amiable nerd, less than half his old weight, who could become a spokesman for those six-inch-long sandwiches, which might help you, especially if you stripped out the cheese, the dressing, and even the bread. Fogle shot over three hundred ads, and Subway business rose from $3 billion to $11.5 billion a year in the first decade of this century. He became nationally famous, with a net worth of around $15 million. But he was also into pornography and seeking sex with minors.

The charges against him were not the gravest possible—they were nothing like as ugly as those leveled at the British television personality Jimmy Savile after his death. It was not fully clear how far others had been hurt. But a plea deal was set up for Fogle, and Subway dropped him—an announcement offered on Twitter. A scandal consumed Fogle such as waits for so many figures made on television and the Internet. That process is instant, mindless, and vicious, and it has no intention of examining or curtailing its ads.

Subway won't be hurt too badly, I think. Fogle had helped reposition it in the marketplace, and the sight of the diminished Fogle means more than the loss of his authority. Cockeyed self-help remains viable.

All of which helps recover another fundamental question that seldom gets asked: Do television commercials work, and if so how? It's one of the premises of *Mad Men* that the driven characters, often on the brink of disorder, are doing what they do to promote certain products. But *Mad Men* is set in the late fifties through to the early seventies, the first era of television, when some campaigns gave a spectacular boost to the sales of Revlon or Chrysler or Westinghouse, no matter that most of those ads seem very feeble if seen now. At the outset, commercials were so novel that an avid and innocent audience was swayed by them enough to make a purchase. But many ads have now fallen into an ironic or camp attitude, while some are simply cynical, with the persuasive power of an ad replaced by its constant reiteration of the brand, so that it becomes a cliché imprinted in our minds. Thus taglines from ads, or even the name of the product itself, have turned recognition into a kind of dismal prayer. You advertise not to say Coca-Cola is a nutritious or reviving drink, a pleasure, but to assert that it "adds life." The stable, lasting products of our lifetime do not add anything much; their name just needs to be impressed in our pulpy brains over and over again. They are no longer products, but role models for consumption.

In 1954, there was a fascinating movie, *It Should Happen to You*. It was written by Garson Kanin and directed by George Cukor, with Judy Holliday playing a young woman who is an odd mix of dumbness and cunning. She wants to make it in New York, but how, when she has no credentials or talent? Then technology comes to her aid. One day she sees an empty billboard on Columbus Circle with a notice saying the space is for rent.

Her name is Gladys Glover and she rakes together the money to lease the space, where she puts up no more or less than GLADYS GLOVER in lights. The city starts wondering who this person can be. On a deal, she trades that one spot for six others. She begins to become a celebrity, without the credentials still, except for the means of broadcasting her name as a brand for nothing.

The numbers and the content mean less than analysts would have us believe. The 2015 Oscars broadcast, on ABC as always, took a hit. The previous year its watching audience had been 43.7 million. For 2015 it was down by 16 percent to 37.3 million. Yet the ads for 2015 had been charged at $1.9 million for thirty seconds, as opposed to $1.76 million for the previous year. Where is the market economics in this? It's a superstition that "Oscar" is a potent brand—it's

DO TELEVISION COMMERCIALS WORK, AND IF SO HOW?

like saying "Gladys Glover," no matter that the Oscar awards have lost contact with the history that made them an institution. So nowadays, young people are beginning to ask "Why do we have Oscars?" ABC pays $75 million a year for the show—it was three hours forty minutes in 2015 (which is a lot of commercial time) to celebrate the votes of about 6,200 members. In a democracy, there may be no other club decision that gets more public attention. In advance of the 2016 awards, the Academy suddenly took fright over what a select club of old white guys it had always been.

The median age of that audience was fifty-three, and a survey disclosed that a fifth of those viewers felt they were "three times more likely to purchase from an ad," a significantly greater percentage than that of the Super Bowl's audience. Little of which seems like a guarantee, though a director at one advertising agency said that the Oscars were "sort of the Super Bowl for women."

On these figures, the Oscar show as we know it can hardly last, though many other more significant things may have vanished before then. But the Academy depends on that show for its life. That funding supports its many functions, including the library, which is one of the most valuable research facilities in the world of film. But there's a widening gulf between that gathering of historical data and its faith in knowledge and the ongoing flimsiness of the Academy Awards in the face of the vanishing habit of theatrical moviegoing. What screens are urging now in all their slipperiness is that it hardly matters whether we keep records. Why treasure Cary Grant if we are forgetting FDR?

You're right, I fear, this situation won't be reformed. But don't let that lead you into forgetting that the BBC has flourished in television for seventy years. Without any strain, some of its shows force their way into this book and abide in the history of the medium. Then consider this: *Breaking Bad* played on television on AMC, which uses commercials. The show held its place despite that, for five seasons and many awards. It worked; it was very good television. But you can buy or rent a boxed set of the whole of *Breaking Bad* and watch it without

WHY TREASURE CARY GRANT IF WE ARE FORGETTING FDR?

commercials. In that process—well worth trying—a hit show becomes what is sometimes called "a novel for television" (though it doesn't actually stimulate reading). Attention and concentration have to be in our hands. Most of us do not need medication.

Meanwhile, a pattern of public service television operates, often on license fees or government funding, in other countries: Japan, the Czech Republic, Denmark, France, Germany, Italy, the Netherlands, Poland, Spain, Australia, and Brazil. Already, though, whether they like it or not, those countries have been covered by the crazy quilt of the Internet.

The advertising on television has always been at war with the optimistic thrust of a new information medium. It's not just that the ads are a way of advising us, "Well, you don't really need to watch or listen to everything." Another danger, less clear but nearly infinite, is that the methodology, the thrust, and the cinematic imagery of commercials have invaded the texture of "regular" entertainment programs. Their goal is a sense of necessary and desirable well-being that itself promotes the products being advertised. The house in *The Donna Reed Show* might be inane and out of reach, but the desirability factor in TV was to suggest that such domestic facilities, such space and light, such appliances and good nature, could be brought within reach. It's surely the case that the tone and sheen of American TV have helped make the United States more attractive as a destination for poor people in remote countries and desperate conditions. But don't forget the same impact on American audiences. The world displayed on TV has been a different country from the one we inhabit.

It was always the most intriguing aspect of *Mad Men* that it gave promise of assessing that gap. By the time the show ended in May 2015, it was widely praised for outstanding quality and significance. That was the end of its seventh season and ninety-second episode. It had won the Emmy for outstanding drama series in its first four seasons. But it nearly didn't happen.

In 2000, Matthew Weiner had done a pilot script on spec. It went nowhere, but David Chase saw it and was so impressed he enlisted Weiner as a part of the *Sopranos* team. Weiner kept trying with his project, but both HBO and Showtime turned it down before AMC took it on and began showing it in 2007. The idea was to make a sit out of a leading advertising agency in New York, starting off in about 1960. The title referred to men at work on Madison Avenue. But a deeper meaning was how far advertising and its lifestyle accompanied dysfunction in its practitioners. The show opened with graphics of a man falling into a skyscraper canyon, as if a suicide or a fallen soul, no matter that the flourishing ad business was a success story.

Its central figure, Don Draper (Jon Hamm), was one of the most interesting characters ever created by television. He was handsome in a blank-faced male-model way. It helped Don that Hamm had a quality of being unoccupied or vacant. He was expert at his job and the psychological insights required in advertising. And he was a thorough mess—a womanizer, an adulterer, a manipulator subject to addictions and depressions—in so many ways, he was the ideal jittery target of his own ads, a man looking for magic. But as the show progressed, darker things were revealed about Don. These were not just matters of bad behavior—and smoking. His real name had been Richard Whitman (and there was a Whitman shadow behind Walter White on another AMC hit, *Breaking Bad*). "Don Draper" was the name of a soldier killed in the Korean War, an action "Whitman" had seen and taken advantage of. He sought to escape his humble rural background, his prostitute mother, and his alcoholic father by reinventing himself as Draper. That recasting of his own life was an ambition at the core of most advertising.

Early on in the show, Don Draper said, "Advertising is based on one thing: happiness. And you know what happiness is? Happiness is the smell of a new car. It's freedom from fear. It's a billboard on the side of the road that screams with reassurance that whatever you are doing, it's OK." It was the strength of the show that it made that brilliant speech a series of incriminating lies and the recipe for Don's toxicity. But could *Mad Men* rip its own room to pieces—and keep us happy?

Placed on AMC, and eventually obliged to have ads, could *Mad Men* live up to the creative daring in its opportunity—could it let the modern ads on our show be the ones Don and the others were working on?

Weiner ran the show, rather like an advertising executive keeping secret campaigns to himself. But he was encouraging to his writers and directors, and it was quickly apparent that there was a care for detail, in décor and the passage of time, as the story got into the seventies, along with exceptional writing and devoted use of an ensemble. *Mad Men* had a welcome openness to women. Thus Peggy (Elisabeth Moss)

"ADVERTISING IS BASED ON ONE THING: HAPPINESS . . . ."

began as a secretary trying to prove herself as a copywriter and an executive. She made it, and Weiner had a writing staff in which women often outnumbered the men. At the same time, with Moss, January Jones, Jessica Paré, and Christina Hendricks, the show was well stocked with attractive, "cinematic" women, and arcs of sexual intrigue at the agency. The resemblance was not stressed, but the partner-swapping and the casual betrayal of others bespoke a culture of lust and opportunism, as if the people in life were often treated as the audience for a campaign. Advertising was seen as a way of acting or self-presentation that had become second nature, so deft that its ugliness got a pass.

Mad Men was what we think of as a great show, reviewed and reported on beyond its actual viewing figures. It took four seasons to build to an average audience of 2 million an episode; even its heavily promoted finale had only 3.3 million. Many people on the show complained that the pay was modest, and it's not that *Mad Men* made a lot of money at first—its payoff is likely to come with boxed sets and streaming reruns as it takes on a "classic" status.

But *Mad Men* played on AMC, eventually with commercials. The show was full of inside knowledge on how Madison Avenue had operated. The key agency in the story was Sterling Cooper, but the real McCann Erickson was talked about a lot, and several historical campaigns were referred to in the story line. *Mad Men* was an autopsy on the sort of people who had flourished in the ad business, as well as the millions who had absorbed its messages, from cute to toxic, without protest. It reveled in its own darkness, with Draper struggling to persuade us and himself that he might be likeable. The show was often on the point of a grim, inescapable verdict. But how could *Mad Men* be so "great" or "classic," let alone so bold, as to make its own commercial breaks part of the show?

I can think of a *Mad Men* in which the creators saw the logic of making their own commercials—some of them bland affirmations of the process, and some so savage and satirical they could not mask contempt for the audience. Imagine the show written by a novelist like

Dreiser, Bellow, or David Foster Wallace; or envisage it as made by Billy Wilder or Preston Sturges, by Luis Buñuel or the collective personality of Monty Python. In short, entertain the idea of a *Mad Men* in which the structure of the show was wrestling with its own fraudulent profession. *Mad Men* did make fun of ads, and their masking, but it could not invent the space to step back and level the culture of AMC.

It couldn't happen, you say, because that would have been self-defeating for Matthew Weiner, for AMC, or for Lionsgate, the chief production company behind *Mad Men*. That would have exploded its tenuous budget and its possible profit, just as it would have mocked the two or three million following an ordeal over the years. The actual ending was a very effective escape, in which Draper, the man without qualities set on a course of breakdown, was allowed to get away to an Esalen-like retreat and "see the light." This is how Jon Hamm explained it to the *New York Times*:

> My take is that…he wakes up in this beautiful place, and has this serene moment of understanding, and realizes who he is. And who he is, is an advertising man. And so, this thing comes to him. There's a way to see it in a completely cynical way, and say, "Wow, that's awful." But I think that for Don, it represents some kind of understanding and comfort in this incredibly unquiet, uncomfortable life that he has led.

So, truly, actors shouldn't be trusted to make up what their characters say. They are role models who have no more responsibility for what they say than admen have for their products. Meanwhile, Matthew Weiner was curiously defensive and defiant, a showman sticking by the show:

> I hate to say it: I don't really feel like I owe anybody anything. I've been lucky to have them invite us into their home, but we have held up our end of the bargain so far. We really have, and we've made such a painstaking effort to surprise and delight and move machinery that tells the story?

In its last moments, the show went from a close-up of Don in a meditative rapture with the Pacific behind him to the celebrated "Hilltop" ad made for Coca-Cola in 1971—"I'd like to buy the world a Coke and keep it company." There wasn't a definite narrative link, but it was as if Don had repaired himself and overcome his likely breakdown by coming up with that ad campaign. So *Mad Men* concluded, but Don could have gone on forever.

In history, that jingle had been written by Bill Backer. He regarded the ad not so much as an endorsement of a drink, "but as a tiny bit of commonality between all peoples, a universally liked formula that would help to keep them company for a few minutes."

Among the Internet comments following Weiner's *Rolling Stone* interview, one reader took a positive line and thought Don and Joan might still end up together. To which a "Kevin Spencer" replied:

> w[hat] t[he] h[eck] are you talking about? you're just saying what you WANT to happen. Pretty clear how it ends, joan picks career over relationship, her and don were never to hook up, betty does die, don doesn't actually change, he uses his yoga retreat and the people there to make a commercial to sell pop instead of to make himself better.

"You're just saying what you WANT to happen." It's the tagline from our eternal commercial for advertising. In the end, the ads have one simple but lethal duty: to be on. I cannot shrug off the charm of some ads. I know how wounding that cuteness can be. In the early seventies, I gave a college lecture on John Berger's *Ways of Seeing* (a television program and then a book), in the course of which he describes the treachery in most ads as the betrayal of reality. I thought I had done a good job. This hope was encouraged when, after the class, a young man came up to thank me. He was profuse and he seemed honest. His life had been changed, he said, and he was alive with joy. He had been a drifting soul, uncertain what to do. But now he had eyes that could see. He knew what he must do.

"Yes?" I said, breathlessly. A teacher likes to feel he's changed someone for life.

"I'm going to go into advertising!"

8
WASTELAND

YOU ARE ALONE WITH YOUR TELEVISION SET—there are other people in the room but, as on the subway or in the hospital waiting room, that does not repair the solitude.

You know you have several hundred channels or numbers to choose from. It can seem like the bounty of choice, liberty, and America, but it's an imponderable set of alternatives. So the remote is the best Xanax to quell the melancholy at what the receiver offers. More and more windows may only persuade you that there's more you don't want to see. Some dank nights you clutch the remote and wonder if the last chance of having a soul to save might be throwing the television out on the street as a prize for derelicts sleeping there. But these days the set is so embedded in the wall it does not make for easy ripping or removal. You can turn it off and see your pale self in the black mirror hanging on the wall like a vulture in the trees.

Or you can blunder into *The Jerry Springer Show* (1991 and onward; 3,891 episodes so far). In that night when you're alone, as you stagger through the numbers, you're likely to get a flash of Jerry and his raucous show. The format is blunt and ugly. The warring members of what may be called a family or "a commonality" are brought together in a studio with an audience who sometimes seem to be auditioning for the featured spots on the show. Those cases have a grievance, involving infidelity, children without a known father, or financial disputes. Very often the family is of color; although there are bouncer types around to restrain impulsive attack, the chance of violence is constantly provoked. It is there already in foul language that is steadily bleeped. Jerry is the woeful referee—he will produce the blood-test report to settle paternity; he runs the hypocritical routines about soothing these contrived passions. Springer seems upset by the chaos and the hostility, but he soldiers on because he is making a lot of money out of it (personal net worth, $45 million). You will have other pet hates, but this is one of the more distressing things on television and I despise myself every time I stay with it for more than a few seconds.

But I have lingered long enough to see that the show is preposterous and contrived, while generating a subtext of disapproval toward ill-educated people of color and near poverty. So you click the remote, and you're into an automatic montage that feels like a grinding process. I get a Chinese newscast next, always slightly out of focus; a shaking, complaining fragment of *The Simpsons*; desultory basketball between Virginia and Virginia Tech; balloon-like heads talking about the day's movement on the Dow and "the long-term prospects," with numbers flickering at their feet; a panel of ex-players discussing the upcoming season in the tough, halting language they have learned for TV; a domestic catastrophe where that scatterbrained Lucy seems likely to explode; some after-echo music from *Law & Order*, and "In the judic…"; a shopping channel where florid fossil jewelry is being fondled in its close-up; an erect penis about to be sucked—or is it aimed at Mars?; a Southern sermon by a preacher who looks like an escapee from *SmackDown*, the wrestling show—he tells us God is watching; the scene in *Casino* where Robert De Niro retrieves his pants, hanging in an office closet, and puts them on for a visitor; golfers crouched on a Day-Glo green, like prospectors for gold; a weather channel where the background maps oscillate with snow, another foot of white stuff in Haverhill, Massachusetts—"they're up to thirteen"— and the weatherman tries to look sympathetic, though he loves excess; an unexplained scene of lions prowling toward the camera—are they going to do a pet trick?; and ads forever… If you play this game with your remote, you'll find yourself in the middle of an ad every sixth or seventh channel you hit; then, couched in the same lush photographic style as the ads, a glimpse of Robert Redford

THERE IS SOMETHING LIKE BEAUTY IN THE SURREAL LINKAGE OF ALIEN THINGS IN THE MONTAGE.

in *The Way He Was*; and Jaye P. Morgan snarling like a Burbank Cleopatra at the dithery, dissolute hosting of Chuck Barris on *The Gong Show*.

Such spasms of montage could go on forever, because of the sweet and cool power your remote has over television. Moreover, while you have had a conscientious horror of the pulse of interruption in the medium, there is something like beauty in the surreal linkage of alien things in the montage. You can have a pretty good time for thirty minutes, and it occurs to you that this may be the natural way of watching television. Do what the technology allows. When you stop, having found no program to watch, go back to the beginning, because a set of different shows will have begun.

But there are deeper oddities in this game. I have a good library of movies on DVD; I have access to streaming Netflix and several other systems. There are even times when my haphazard watching falls upon an old movie that I already have in my library. But something in me prefers to watch it on television. I may dislike ninety-nine of the hundred channels I flick through, or the full hundred. I could turn off the set and read—or even write—a book. But I do that all day, and somehow I abide by the patterns that tell me I'm tired by the evening so I want to be served. My passivity in front of the set (even with unabated disapproval of what it offers) is hard to overcome. Is this torture from Abu Ghraib—"they're up to thirteen now," a guard is saying—oh, I've never seen that before. Television—that foolish, wasteful, inept medium—has its own authority. If I think about it too deeply, I may realize that I'm in a kind of wasteland, but one that I accept.

"Wasteland" is not one of our pleasant, homey words, no matter that a GLADYS GLOVER sign may still be pink-and-green neon amid the scarred bomb sites. When T. S. Eliot published his poem in 1922, the title seemed to refer to the desolation of a destroyed culture, or a battlefield landscape after the Great War. It was not a travel brochure: "I will show you fear in a handful of dust." With television, however, the "wasteland" has a particular meaning.

On May 9, 1961, Newton Minow, then chairman of the Federal Communications Commission, gave a speech to the convention of the National Association of Broadcasters. This was a time when *Gunsmoke*, *Wagon Train*, and *Have Gun—Will Travel* were the most popular shows, with television schedules dominated by just three networks. So the wasteland Minow conjured up was smaller and far tidier than it would be now. But Minow spoke in a way that attracted immediate attention and controversy:

> When television is good, nothing—not the theater, not the magazines or newspapers—nothing is better.
>
> But when television is bad, nothing is worse. I invite each of you to sit down in front of your own television set when your station goes on the air and stay there, for a day, without a book, without a magazine, without a newspaper, without a profit-and-loss sheet or a rating book to distract you. Keep your eyes glued to that set until the station signs off. I can assure you that what you will observe is a vast wasteland.
>
> You will see a procession of game shows, formula comedies about totally unbelievable families, blood and thunder, mayhem, violence, sadism, murder, western bad men, western good men, private eyes, gangsters, more violence, and cartoons. And endlessly, commercials—many screaming, cajoling, and offending.

One understands why Minow named no programs, but it's fascinating to wonder what he regarded as "nothing...better." There is a faintly paternalistic tone in his speech, which is the stranger for coming from the government agency supposed to regulate television but acting helpless. His faith in magazines and newspapers has dated badly; cartoons are more sophisticated now, and far more pointed as social commentary. We don't do Westerns as 1961 did. Our violence is far more graphic; and so is the sex. But you know what he's getting at. In 1995, J. G. Ballard deplored nothing less than "the pre-empting of any original response to experience by the television screen," and had little faith in anyone being unsullied.

Newton Minow was on good terms with the Kennedys and he must have known what they were doing to make what Ballard called "politics conducted as a branch of advertising." Even for 1961, it is hard to conceive of anyone active in politics, journalism, education, the law, or the arts who did not have a television. Today it would amount to an aberration, or willful un-Americanness. So if we're all in the wasteland, and that term is merited, and we're doing our best to get along, is there any point in putting up a WASTELAND signpost, like the signs that say THE LONELIEST ROAD IN AMERICA on Route 50 in Nevada? I think there is.

There were charges straightaway that Minow was an airy elitist. By 1961, 89 percent of American households had television; they were watching as much as they could, which seemed to imply enjoyment; they were being given what they wanted, said the system—wasn't that obvious? A mass medium has to reach out to everyone; and the medium had been a spur to business across the nation—who was the chairman of the FCC to say this was wrong, wasteful, or a source of cultural danger? That response took many forms. On *Gilligan's Island* (1964–67), created by Sherwood Schwartz, the castaways on the island came from the shipwreck of a charter boat named the *SS Minnow*.

That may be the best joke from *Gilligan's Island*. (It's proper in a book like this to admit there have been some worthless programs, and some that were shameful, but we need to be generous in a medium where popular acclaim dates as fast as the shows themselves.) I was always a prude with movies: They had to be good (if not great). But snobbery melted away with television, and worthlessness became entirely acceptable. Time could be wasted. I never watched much of *Gilligan's Island*, but *The Gong Show…* It was easy to find serious people who thought *The Gong Show* (1976–80; 1988–89) was ridiculous and trashy. No one could claim it served any necessary purpose. I loved it.

Charles Barris was born in Philadelphia in 1929 and known as Chuck (or Chuckie Baby). He was a page at NBC before he got a job on *American Bandstand*. That pushed him into the music business and success as a songwriter. Then ABC appointed him to devise and produce new game shows. His first coup was *The Dating Game* (1965–73), in which attractive young men and women asked questions to find out which of three contestants they wanted to date. It was on the risqué side, and the audience carried it from being a daytime show into prime time. Next came *The Newlywed Game* (1966–74), where recently married couples competed for prizes. Again, the questions were provocative and sometimes surreal. Many game shows were, as Minow reckoned, weeds in the wasteland. They passed your time, if you remained awake. But Barris was discovering that the form was ripe for parody.

The Gong Show went over the top. Its format was that of an amateur talent show, in which the acts were painfully bad. Decades before *American Idol*, Barris had anticipated and destroyed its format. There was a gong that could terminate the acts, and three panelists were regular executioners: Jaye P. Morgan, Arte Johnson, and Jamie Farr. Johnson helped remind us that *The Gong Show* had some of the

BARRIS HAD DELICATE TIMING, WARMTH OF HEART, AND A DAFT CHARM.

energy and the manic drive of *Rowan & Martin's Laugh-In*. There were regular eccentrics who wandered in and out: the Unknown Comic and Gene Gene the Dancing Machine. But the show hinged on Barris, serving as a host who himself deserved to be gonged.

He had not appeared before on one of his shows. He really was as shy as he was intelligent. There he was, shuffling, missing his cue marks, and fudging his lines, laughing helplessly as the show deteriorated, like an overgrown and half-drunk kid at his first big party. There was a tough edge in the show: Some acts were embarrassing and were dismissed with cruel abruptness. The whole project seemed to say that talent was a myth. Television was whatever you could get away with. But as this artful shambles went on, it became clear that Barris had delicate timing, warmth of heart, and a daft charm like few others on the box. The show was funny a lot of the time, constitutionally unpredictable, and its other essential purpose was to say, "Look, don't you see that most of TV is junk?" Let's hope Newton Minow liked it. Many people said it was the epitome of disgrace; others saw it as a grandchild of the Marx Brothers.

You can't have a mass medium without a mass. This was always central to the movie business when it took control of the popular imagination (approximately from the onset of the Great War until just after the conclusion of the Second World War). In that age there wasn't really a film-literate audience, or much critical commentary directed at it, though that began to emerge in the forties in the work of Otis Ferguson, Manny Farber, and James Agee. Audiences did not look for searching reviews, just as they were not concerned with newspaper reports of box-office action. They were fixed narrowly, and confidently, on having a good time. That habit fed itself and bypassed choice. That is a characteristic of any mass medium, as witness the popularity of electric light and air to breathe.

In the "golden age" of cinema, there were far more films made that any critical consensus would have called bad—or worse. But a proportion were brilliant—or better. Nor was this simply measured in money. It was plain that pictures were a business, and one that had helped carry the nation through the Depression. Yet no one automatically assumed an equation between big budgets, revenue, and diminished quality. Some of the great successes were outstanding or ambitious projects in their time (and that's what matters): *The Birth of a Nation* (1915), *The Big Parade* (1925), *The Jazz Singer* (1927), *It Happened One Night* (1934), *Snow White and the Seven Dwarfs* (1937), *The Wizard of Oz* (1939), *Gone with the Wind* (1939), *The Best Years of Our Lives* (1946). It was taken for granted that a smash hit could be a very good film, and that tradition lasted until at least *The Godfather*, which was the biggest box-office film ever made when it opened in 1972.

YOU CAN'T HAVE A MASS MEDIUM WITHOUT A MASS.

Television followed a similar course. It began as a marvel that easily forgave so many imperfections, not just in picture and sound quality but in terms of ambition. The medium quickly reached its power position, keeping people at home and out of movie theaters. But that was an era of moribund programming stability, with shows that had millions of loyal adherents but are close to unwatchable now.

A poignant example of that is *Father Knows Best* (1954–60), a title worn proudly once, and without irony. It featured the Anderson family in a Midwest town named Springfield. Jim was in insurance. Margaret was his wife, and mother to their three kids, a stay-at-home voice of reason. The problems the five of them faced were typical and low-key, but the parents did their level best to talk them through. That this mundane caring stayed on TV for years—with ex-movie names Robert Young and Jane Wyatt as the parents—was a measure of entertainment lapping over into advertising's belief in the American way. Millions liked the show and took it to number 6 in the ratings; Young won Emmys for "best continuing performance" in a series. It seems quietly monstrous now, and something in it ground on Young. He quit as Jim Anderson because he felt his own unhappiness was dwarfed by the character's stability. He would have another hit series playing a wise older doctor, *Marcus Welby, M.D.* (1969–76). This became a number 1 show. Young was beloved and copied, but his endlessly positive scenarios were enough of a wasteland for him to become depressed and attempt suicide.

The same solid ground included hundreds of hit shows, from the celebrations of family to the ritual endorsements of guns and order in the West. A remarkable thing about the era of the TV Western is not just that it may have endorsed America's stance and confidence in the Cold War, but its total indifference to what was happening then in the American West. After 1945, no part of the country moved forward as rapidly as the West. Yet no show took note of that, or thought to cover the excitement and transformation of Las Vegas, a new city that overturned so many ideas and ideals in the country. Bugsy Siegel and the raffish glamour of southern Nevada became current, decades later, in shows like *Vega$* (1978–81), not to mention several poker series. But the reality of casino life, with the nuclear test site as its near neighbor, never intruded on the dynasties called *Gunsmoke*, *Rawhide*, and *Wagon Train*. The medium was more alert to the viability of old story formulas than it was attentive to the state of the nation.

But there were remarkable things in that dull, absentminded age.

Out of the mass of domestic sitcoms arose *I Love Lucy*, a prodigious success in money terms, and a revelation of incipient madness and repressed feminism in the American household that has stood the

A REVELATION OF INCIPIENT MADNESS AND REPRESSED FEMINISM IN THE AMERICAN HOUSEHOLD.

test of time, perhaps because few of the people making the show were aware of those subtexts, and because the shows freed a reckless genius in Lucille Ball. Live dramas like *Marty* touched on an authentic working-class life and taught us that good acting (as opposed to routine presence) was possible on television. On *Your Show of Shows* (1950–54), Sid Caesar and Imogene Coca offered a sophisticated, satirical vein of comedy that got high ratings. *The Ernie Kovacs Show* (1952–56) was an unapologetic display of eccentric comedy, with a central figure who broke many rules of the era: He was not there to be lovable, and he was definitely not someone it would be so nice to come home to. The ingratiating piety of fifties lead players on TV seems a kiss of death now. And even the best shows of that era have dated in many ways. But television is not made for posterity, and so for all its play on nostalgia it corrodes our feeling for history.

I am working toward several chapters on the best of television, and I won't give too much away here. I'll just mention *Breaking Bad*, which may be close to "masterpiece" status in the minds of those reading a book about television, and which undermines most notions of Dad's omniscience. But when that show began in 2008, it had an audience of just over 1 million. Decades earlier, that would have been a harbinger of cancelation. Even at its close, in 2013, it was getting an audience only around 4 million. But that last season grew strikingly—as if the public sensed an event—and it concluded with 10 million viewers. *Breaking Bad* made money, it won many awards, and it is established now as a modern classic. It was also a welcome glimpse of the real modern West, consistently well written, and superbly acted (Bryan Cranston, Anna Gunn, and just about everybody else). It had many writers and directors, but it was utterly consistent. You may put that down to the inspired creator of the show, Vince Gilligan, but our appreciation of the creator or showrunner is a modern phenomenon. It has to do with the establishment of cable television, the technology and business system that has made for so many bright wildflowers in the wasteland.

Plus, *Breaking Bad* was beautiful. What do I mean by that? Well, start with the unscathed blue sky of New Mexico and so much screen time being devoted to that. You may respond, "Well, there has to be a sky," while losing sight of the decision to see it and glory in it. I came to television from movies, and there the idea of beauty was commonplace. In *The Passion of Joan of Arc*, director Carl Dreyer and his actress Maria Falconetti made us see that the face could be beautiful (as well as hideous), and it understood that the constant close-ups of the film were a measure of spirituality. On *Citizen Kane*, one revelation was the way in which lighting, décor, and the deep-focus view

Walter and Skyler White in **Breaking Bad**

that held them together were a path to psychological insight. In John Ford's *The Searchers*, the backdrop of Monument Valley (Ford's favorite location) was a source of epic adventure and tragic potential, no matter that in ordinary life there has never been a white ranching life in the valley.

I doubt Ford ever told his director of photography, Winton Hoch, "Make it beautiful!" That word was as uncommon in Hollywood circles as "art." But the hard-headed and gruff Ford was an aesthete, too, and sometimes that swayed his judgment. There are moments in *The Grapes of Wrath* (photographed by Gregg Toland, just before he did *Kane*) where the pictorial values get in the way of the harsh existence that is the subject of the film. "Beauty" always runs that risk of becoming self-conscious. Still, the cinema, with its big screens, was a medium where some movies and directors were famous for doing "good-looking work" or having an exceptional eye.

For decades, such a thought was absent from television. You can explain that in terms of picture size, the rough image, and the general attitude that if the TV came on and stayed on, that was nice and comforting enough. In time, household TVs got larger and they acquired high-definition imagery. That helped, but I don't think it mattered as much as the institution called cable. Cable expanded on the notion that some people cared enough to pay more, that it was possible to work in long shot and to assume that the picture could be beautiful without being too fancy or arty. *Breaking Bad* looks and feels like a good, extended movie not just because of its skies but because of the inventiveness of the interiors and its trust in Skyler and Walter. Beauty needs to be unstressed to work in narrative form; it has to be natural—and television has reached that state, because it is comfortable with a far more modest audience than watched *Father Knows Best*, *The Fugitive*, or *Gilligan's Island*.

So one person's wasteland may be another's garden, but the orthodoxy of the wasteland settled in. The blast from Newton Minow led to very little, just as the FCC has had no effective grasp on the medium. (It did get upset over Janet Jackson's brief breast, but it ignores all the others.) It is up to us whether we see desolation or wildflowers in the sunlight. Without the flowers, we might never have noticed the light. I loathe *The Jerry Springer Show*, but it is one of the few modern television shows that attempt an unsentimental view of working-class life—though some of the people seem more interested in being on TV than in working, or life.

IT IS UP TO US WHETHER WE SEE DESOLATION OR WILDFLOWERS.

A split began in movies in the sixties and seventies, and as the gap widened, we could see that it was separating mass-audience pictures from something rarer, more difficult, and more elitist. That was inevitable, but it leads to the curiosity of Oscar ceremonies where the most popular films of the year hardly get a significant nomination, while art-house pictures gather the awards. The Academy knows the dangers in that, because it needs a huge audience on Oscars night to sustain the TV show that pays for most of its year-round activities. A similar thing has occurred in television as cable has opened a gap between essential viewing (often as habit-forming as *Friends* or as tense as a fine Super Bowl) and something more specialized, where characters can curse, take off their clothes, and face what was anathema to early television—American Unhappiness (a title still awaiting use).

The change is unstoppable, and you can regard it as an advance in maturity, but it means that television is not exactly a mass medium any longer. That range of choice we have with the remote is proof of aimless pluralism, bland variety, and discerning choice (as opposed to just turning the set on and letting your remote wander). It may even occur to you that the magical tool makes *you* remote. But the vacuum in mass media is not incidental. Our society is increasingly crowded, and as lonely as it has ever been, and subject to the abrasions of race, poverty, and gender in new ways. Such a packed and insecure world needs a mass medium and the chance of being one entity, a people and an audience. If a large enough crisis overtakes us (imagine it as you see fit), we will need something we can all attend to.

Or are we *not* a society or a commonality? In 1987, Margaret Thatcher voiced her bold hope that "there is no such thing as society." Still, in crisis we need somewhere to go, and that need is now often filled by the screens of the Internet. The average Internet user checks his screen thirty times in an hour, fevered yet bored. That seems like a sign of neurotic insecurity, but it alludes to a medium made to foster that unease. So be afraid of a breakdown in that godsend service, especially if God is elsewhere, watching some other show.

||||||||||||||||||||||||||||

"WASTELAND" HAS ANOTHER MEANING. We most of us feel secure or smug watching something "good" on television—that is what *we* do, while millions of others watch something "bad" on all the other numbered outlets. So we have an oasis and the desert as a model of our cultural landscape. Moreover, it seems to match American aspirations that as people came to the empty land, the wilderness, and built it up, they did well. In that spirit, you can point to the radical, vertical building styles pioneered in Manhattan and Chicago, the Victorian residences of San Francisco, and even the Anasazi cliff cities at sites like Mesa Verde in Colorado.

Such innovations seem to defy the threat of "wasteland," but the monumental achievement of those old cities is in decline—from greed, development, laziness, and the loss of aesthetic and social conviction. San Francisco is being undermined by its own heedless prosperity. Skyscrapers that once inspired awe and ambition can now seem intimidating and brutal, not least because they are kept empty. In that shift, the building attitude of Los Angeles and Las Vegas becomes more telling, for in those cities architecture has been affected by the culture's craving for change. So buildings surrender the monumental and become set-like, atmospheres that can be altered every few years. Structures also understand another threat, less pressing in the East, that of weather and the old empire of desert. The boom years of Las Vegas

Technology leaves its dead behind, unburied.

may never come again. It is a swell toy city waiting to be reclaimed by desert or a wasteland more lasting than the fatalistic mindset that prevails in its casinos.

Eastern strongholds—Miami and New Orleans—have been put on alert as most vulnerable to rising sea levels. The thought may yet strike home that wasteland, desert, or desolation have always been natural American landscapes as well as the source of its deepest beauty.

I hope this is not too roundabout, or sinister. But it prompts another thought. Naturally, you and I are very much in favor of good, built-up, architected television. That fits in with every dream of progress. But is it possible that the wasteland is the inescapable canvas on which those brave daubs appear?

IS THAT AN OASIS?

AN AGING, DISCRIMINATING CULTURAL CLASS STILL EXISTS IN AMERICA. Such people buy and read books, and they keep personal

libraries. They tend to have had a "good" education—they went to college—and, better still, they decided that their development and happiness depended on their own *increasing* curiosity after school, and on their duty to educate themselves. They take newspapers, and prefer them as paper. They go to the theater and to live music, even if they have to budget the ticket prices. These are not the wealthy few who fund or own orchestras, ballet companies, art museums, foundations, and retreats. They favor foreign and independent movies, and they are proud to see how those genres have won Oscars as well as audiences. They are devout over Turner Classic Movies and Netflix. The majority of people reading this book are of that class. And their overall view of television is to say, "Thank God for PBS." That idea seems like a saving oasis, to be measured with Social Security and

Medicare. These people are growing older, in a society that does more for seniority than any in history.

The oasis has been glorious and nourishing, but it has struggled with its coming to the desert too late. So it fights against the encroachment of terminal dryness and does not always credit its power to alter desert. The BBC has been so large, so whimsical, and so English it can easily be made fun of. But it was and is like one of those hallowed movie studios in that it creates shows as well as distributing them. In comparison, PBS has been a handler of other people's shows—a kind of United Artists. It has always lacked the advantage of the BBC, which seemed not just to carry television to the people but to *be* the medium. It was always there, holding to an economic contract that seemed as fair as it was productive. Generations grew up in Britain believing this was the way for television to operate.

PBS HAS ALWAYS LACKED THE ADVANTAGE OF THE BBC.

I have mentioned the demoralizing and maddening impact of advertisements. Allowing commercialism to infiltrate common discourse may be the greatest of our cultural tragedies. But that peril has had one bulwark, the inherent benefit of a contract whereby universal public funding can pay for programming and free it from interference (just as we want a picture quality without flicker, break-up, or white noise). But contracts slip. By 2015, the case for the British license fee was under threat. It had obvious demerits: Rival broadcasters said it was not fair; the BBC was prey to comic budgetary disasters like any entity the size of a small nation; and access to television in Britain as everywhere had been so compromised and complicated by digital media. We do not all watch television on our television. So maybe the license is archaic. Still, its contract is as vital as the notion that the state should try to care for its citizens—that there is or ought to be a thing called society. I realize there are ideological elements that long to be rid of that sentiment. And media technology is on their side. At the same time, the technology has excited some of the most creative minds we have had.

PBS as an entity did not arrive until 1969, but there had been honorable gestures toward it for years. In 1952, wishing to be identified with cultural enlightenment while promoting its brand name, the Ford Foundation initiated a television program called *Omnibus*. It was conceived by James Webb Young, who hired Robert Saudek to produce the show. *Omnibus* was a magazine on the arts, new enough to appreciate the chance of interviewing artists and of having live events in a studio dressed up like a Bauhaus cabaret. Saudek asked Alistair Cooke to be its host. He was forty-four, born in Manchester, England, but a naturalized American (as of 1941), a journalist from the *Manchester Guardian* and a radio man for the BBC, someone whose capacity regularly lived up to his emerging ambitions.

Omnibus found a safe Sunday-afternoon slot, playing usually for an hour. It was funded by Ford (at a steady loss), and it was taken on by CBS (1952–57) before relative failure sent it to NBC, to ABC, and then to darkness. Did not enough people watch? At its best it had an audience of between four and five million. That is more than now watch the best shows on our cable television—and the population has doubled.

A lot of *Omnibus* can be tracked down. Much has dated but it's clear that Cooke was an urbane yet mercurial host—open-minded, quick-witted, acerbic, transatlantic already, knowledgeable, knowing, and as good as a smart teacher. He could take the innovative and make it feel

OMNIBUS RAN THROUGH OVER $1 MILLION OF FORD MONEY.

unthreatening. The show interviewed Frank Lloyd Wright and Agnes de Mille; it led Leonard Bernstein into talking about music in an educational spirit; it did a life of Lincoln, written by James Agee and directed by Norman Lloyd, with Royal Dano as Abe. That's where Peter Ustinov won his Emmy as Dr. Johnson. And it could launch out in the daring of a *King Lear* in seventy minutes, directed by Peter Brook, with Beatrice Straight as Goneril, Natasha Parry as Cordelia, Micheál MacLiammóir as Poor Tom, Alan Badel as the Fool, and Orson Welles as Lear. That was broadcast on October 18, 1953, four months after the coronation of Elizabeth II: It was cheerfully chaotic and under-funded compared with the state occasion, but it was a more penetrating vision of the plight of kings and queens—and it was an astonishing, ramshackle portent of what television for its own sake might be.

Omnibus ran through over $1 million of Ford money (they had more)—and did its wonders on a commercial network. Moreover, Cooke and Saudek did not conclude their television careers. Cooke is a lasting figure in this book, and Bob Saudek would carry on as a producer (*Profiles in Courage*), as a key member of the Carnegie Commission that led to PBS, and as a founder of the Museum of Broadcasting. When Saudek died in 1997, Cooke spoke at the memorial:

> You'd never have guessed it from this modest, earnest,
> rather scholarly man. The great thing was his inventiveness.
> It wasn't enough to say, "Let's have a ballet." He'd say, "I'll
> tell you what we do. We bring in Sam Snead and have him
> show the most beautiful golf swing, we get a tennis player
> to demonstrate an elegant backhand..."

The end result of that was a small ballet for athletes, choreographed by Gene Kelly, with Cooke as the Everyman spectator. Genius has to be trusted and not asked to convince committees. Alas, you don't see much of that wit and invention on PBS now.

At the same time as founding *Omnibus*, the Ford Foundation began the process that led to PBS. In 1952, Ford established National Educational Television to serve as an exchange for local stations seeking educational programs. It had no production function, but its service led to it being called "the university of the air." In time it took on documentary films that had national scope and urgency. But by the mid-sixties, Ford was reluctant to continue. That led to the Public Broadcasting Act of 1967 (in the Johnson administration) and the establishment of the Corporation for Public Broadcasting (CPB) and PBS.

The CPB was funded by the federal government, with a nine-member board of directors, chosen by the president but approved by Congress. That board was politically balanced, but the balance indicated how far PBS was at play in terms of partisan struggle. Coming later in the day than the BBC, and as a measure passed by a liberal administration, PBS would never gain the sense of neutrality that the BBC had and which protected it from many interventions. PBS had a production function, but only after twenty years of busy commercial broadcasting, so it was never like the pathfinder that extended cultural horizons in Britain.

The CPB's budget was $445 million by 2014. This money, augmented by corporate funding and the donations of audience members, funded both PBS and National Public Radio (NPR), but there has been a constant tension between PBS and right-wing interests who feel it shows a liberal bias and have threatened to reduce or stop funding. (A left-wing dismay at its crippling caution has seldom found voice.)

This has led to serious disputes within PBS. In 2005, Kenneth Tomlinson, appointed to chair the CPB board by George W. Bush in 2003, resigned over charges that he had been active in trying to muzzle PBS, not least by campaigning against one of its leading voices, Bill Moyers. In 2010, KCET in Los Angeles, the largest station in the network, withdrew from PBS over funding disagreements and fears that proper radical expression was being curbed within PBS itself.

There are many sides to these disputes, but there is no doubting the historical detachment or isolation of PBS. As a large organ of independent broadcasting in the most open media society in the world, with powers to commission and make programming, its record is abject. At its best, it has elected to be tame. The *NewsHour* is an invaluable institution, and if it sometimes seems cautious and institutional, remember

SOMETIMES *THE NEWSHOUR* FEELS AS NOSTALGIC AS TURNER CLASSIC MOVIES.

that it has resisted many charges of unfairness (from many sides) to become the most reliable television news program in America. It was ahead of everyone else in assuming that the News deserved an hour (or more). That is marvelous, if you think an hour is adequate in a world that goes on all the time—just like TV.

It started as *The Robert MacNeil Report*, soon renamed *The MacNeil/Lehrer Report* (1975–83), not just hosted by but also created by Robert MacNeil and Jim Lehrer. MacNeil, Canadian by birth and experienced in British television, was dry, austere, and less ingratiating than his colleague. Lehrer, raised in Texas, was warmer, funnier, and closer to the image of a professional journalist. But they admired each other and they made a good team. Their show became the *NewsHour* from 1983 to 1995, and then, after MacNeil retired, *The NewsHour with Jim Lehrer* (1995–2005). After that, it was hosted by a group led by Judy Woodruff, Gwen Ifill, and Hari Sreenivasan (the stress on women and nonwhites is welcome, but more honorable still is the faith in ability over glamour or charisma). The *NewsHour* goes on (life is unthinkable without it) and its audience is more than 2.5 million a night, with eight million people seeing it at least once a week.

If you want a measure of the *NewsHour*'s archaic charm and idealism in the age of social media, look at the regular Friday conversations between David Brooks and Mark Shields (in the same room, using talk, and crediting politeness). Those two are hired in to stand for the right and the left, but they are amused by the distinction, they are friends when they disagree, and that suggests their trust in compromise. They are arguably better as TV chums than as writers. But they are a model in an era when so many news shows have encouraged or directed discussion into shouting matches auditioning for Jerry Springer. The state of Congressional deadlock and futile but mounting anger cannot be separated from the way television itself has promoted this crossfire (a term that does imply weaponry). Indeed, as the *NewsHour* holds firm with a view that is calm, verifiable, and unsensational, the possibility looms that it is reporting on an imaginary country. Sometimes the *NewsHour* feels as nostalgic as Turner Classic Movies, even when it's discussing today.

There are other major achievements at PBS—the work of Ken Burns and *Frontline*, for instance—and I will come to those. There is also *Sesame Street*, an astonishing hit, created in 1969 by Joan Ganz Cooney and Lloyd Morrisett, one of the first formats for Jim Henson, and so good that Renata Adler once said it might be the best thing on TV. Think of *Sesame Street* as counter to the infernal madness of Disney and the violence of so many cartoons. Think, even, of the days when television catered to children, as opposed to those children who claim the pay-grade status of adults. Indeed, one lesson of *Sesame Street* was that there might have been a show as fruitfully dedicated to fact, story, and fantasy for adults. But in many ways *Sesame Street* was led to mimic the styles of commercial television. Still, it recognized fantasy as a legitimate strain of experience—and that is something rather hushed up for grown-up au-

MASTERPIECE THEATRE HAS BEEN A MEEK, EAGER CUSTOMER OF BRITISH TELEVISION.

diences. So surreal in its own nature, TV has resisted that voice or tone in most programming. It is an enormous failure of the medium that in its fearful and depressing stress on "realism" it has buried dreaming as a human enterprise. Why should that be left to the commercials and their gross ulterior motives?

I am not forgetting *Nova*, *Antiques Roadshow*, or *Charlie Rose* (though I do not remember much of them), but in over forty years there is not much that seems challenging, beautiful, or transcendent. For decades, *American Masters* has been plowing its furrows, created and presided over by Susan Lacy. That product is respectful and accumulative (it feels for culture in the mood of a banker), and surely it has sent fresh audiences to the work of all these artists—are they all masters (more than two hundred so far)? Does that status permit retirement? The shelves of that show stand like one of those Time-Life series, like their multivolume history of the American West, richly illustrated, blandly written, and finally a burden on the shelf more than fireworks or mind-altering spasms. *American Masters* has an institutional tread that says art, too—even the best—can be made orderly and tranquil. It need not ruffle the aspic assurance of our lives. They have not done Chuck Barris yet.

You know what comes next: It is *Masterpiece*, or what was *Masterpiece Theatre* before that. That brand name is enough to make one wonder whether excessive use of mastery in titles doesn't reveal an itch for servitude. The other word, "Theatre," is revealing: It harks back to a certain snobbery, and it does gently extricate itself from any thought of "masterpiece television." I think it may be a given at the public broadcasting oasis (beneath the shady palms) that television is not quite worthy of that word.

For many, *Masterpiece Theatre* is the heart and soul of PBS, yet this independent American broadcasting operation has been a meek, eager customer of British television. Most of its material has come from the BBC, though *Upstairs, Downstairs*—very important at the beginning—was a show made by London Weekend (1971 in Britain, starting in the United States in 1974). It was the creation of two young actresses, Eileen Atkins and Jean Marsh (who also played one of the maids), and it showed the "progress" of a Belgravia family in the first three decades of the twentieth century. It was genteel soap opera, and it traded on an excessive American respect for the British class system. The same could be said for the TV *Brideshead Revisited* (1981), made by Granada but shown on PBS, which endorsed clothes, décor, and the enchantment of stately homes. Both shows were cleverly written and prettily played—just think of Gordon Jackson and David Langton at 165 Eaton Place, or Jeremy Irons, Anthony Andrews, Diana Quick, and the ranks of English theater in *Brideshead*. Like many *Masterpiece Theatre* offerings, these shows exploited a fondness for valuable old possessions, just like *Antiques Roadshow*, which was itself a BBC show originally, derived from the earlier *Going for a Song* (1965–77), which had made a household god out of Arthur Negus, an elderly, owlish antiques appraiser, and the chuckling wizard uncle who could price things found in your attic.

There's not too much difference between *Upstairs, Downstairs* and *The Forsyte Saga* (1967) and *Downton Abbey*. You can imagine the same chaise longues and copper warming pans being used in all three. The pained masters and the cheeky maids are the stereotypes, and they say the same things over a span of forty years. And for twenty-one years Alistair Cooke presided over their presentation, speaking from a set that was supposed to be a gentleman's study. I saw Cooke's own study once, on the Upper East Side of New York, and there was no resemblance. The set was an ad for trading in an embalmed lifestyle with benefit of literary attitude. There were better shows than *Upstairs, Downstairs* or *Downton Abbey*, but Cooke had begun to seem like the captain of a cruise ship touring through outposts of culture's empire.

There is engrossing work on *Masterpiece Theatre*: Think of *I, Claudius* or *The Jewel in the Crown* (two baleful portraits of empire). Recollect *A Question of Attribution* (1991), written by Alan Bennett and directed by John Schlesinger, with James Fox majestic and hollow as Sir Anthony Blunt and Prunella Scales as dainty, fussy, and sturdy as the corgis as Elizabeth II. (That witty, touching show actually provoked Alistair Cooke's waspish unease because of its kindness to traitors.)

Still, I cannot escape feeling that "Masterpiece" is a velvet cloak to suffocate its own enterprise—and which asks the American public not to notice that home-grown material has seldom been used. So Masterpiecery falls in line with so much of PBS in promoting a refined world that is English-speaking, well-mannered but waspish and witty, white and determined to pass as upper-class.

It is sometimes hard to credit. I was in conversation with a friend and we were arguing over *John Adams* (2008), the television miniseries that tracked the life and times of the second president. We agreed we admired the meticulous recreation of period and place, and appreciated the severity of life then compared with the comfort in much of *Masterpiece*—the Adamses were not rich people; their lives were harsh. (But the 500-minute show had cost $100 million.) We recalled that it came from David McCullough's well-researched book. We were deeply impressed with the acting—Paul Giamatti as Adams, Laura Linney as his wife, Stephen Dillane as Jefferson, and Tom Wilkinson as Franklin. (How do English actors horn in on so many American heroes?) "You can count on PBS," sighed my friend.

I told him I thought not.

How could that be? he wondered. Didn't this cultivated drama have the feeling of a project Ken Burns might have authorized? Surely such material drawn from American history was the natural province of PBS? It turned out to be HBO (which may explain the $100 million). That is not to denigrate the show or the work of its English director, Tom Hooper. *John Adams* was an astute American copying of what had become a British idiom. It was a tribute to independence that still expected to be seen and felt in a masterpiece tradition. But would a British audience sit quietly by if American television dared make dramatic serials from the works of Dickens? So the question arises: Why has PBS not dug into the classics of Dreiser, Dos Passos, Faulkner...the line goes on? Yet American television seemed very pleased when the BBC had the subversive élan and the resources to offer Alistair Cooke's *America*.

The oasis can be appealing as a getaway resort, but I fear its water supply is artificial and endangered. This is so like Las Vegas it can be worrying.

PART TWO
THE MESSAGES

A PLAY, FOR TODAY?

THE NEW OWNERS AND MANAGERS OF TELEVISION quickly realized the charm and convenience of series that might run forever. A man in

charge of a new network affiliate in New Hampshire told me (in the late seventies) that his nightmare was waking up and wondering how he was going to fill his airtime. All of that passive temporal space—the first wasteland? No one of us at home can endure the threat that TV will stop or go blank. That's an absence that produces sofa rage or panic in ten seconds. It's also a peril that suggests any "on" will do, and there have been stations everywhere that would play anything they could find. In that witty and wicked film about local TV, *To Die For* (1995), that's how Suzanne Stone (Nicole Kidman) gets to be a weather girl at WWEN in Little Hope, New Hampshire.

So the infant medium cherished sitcoms and Westerns and police stories that had years of life in them, doing more or less the same thing week after year, from pilot to syndication. *Today* and *Tonight* soaked up hours of time at either end of the day. Baseball would become a season of over 150 games. Yes, winning a Series was dandy, but the TV stations wanted the season to last as long as possible—to go to series. Cute ads played and played as punctuation in our watching.

Thus, it's all the more impressive that television, early on, also acquired a taste for shows that were one-off. They had to be thought of, written, and played out of nothing, without hope of longevity. If you think about it, these adventures were insane, which leads to the thought that maybe television allows itself too little insanity.

These things were called plays.

Was that "home theater"? Or just an opportunity for beginners, the cheapest raw material—young actors? Take Grace Kelly. You probably think of her as a successful movie star who married a prince, thereby fulfilling the old belief that there was something royal in stardom. She was in some famous Hitchcock films—*Dial M for Murder*, *Rear Window*, and *To Catch a Thief*—and she won an

IT'S A WONDER NOT TO BE FORGOTTEN THAT THE NEW MEDIUM VOLUNTEERED THIS.

Oscar in a film that is seldom seen now, *The Country Girl*. That is for the best, because it's not very good. Her Oscar was a tribute to how adored she was in 1955: Her mix of class and sexiness was something to make a Don Draper fold. In fact, Kelly made only eleven movies. But by my estimate, she had accumulated thirty-seven credits in television, essentially between 1950 and 1954, and most of them were in "drama."

Her movies are preserved, but a lot of her television is lost. In February 1950, when Kelly was twenty, on the *Philco Television Playhouse* on NBC, she played the title character in "Ann Rutledge." This was regarded as a play, about the love between Ann (who died aged twenty-two) and Abraham Lincoln (Stephen Courtleigh). It ran sixty minutes (or 47.5 in the commercialized format), the script was by Norman Corwin and Joseph Liss, and Gordon Duff directed. It's lost now. Two years later, on *CBS Television Workshop*, Kelly was Dulcinea in a thirty-minute version of *Don Quixote*. The director was a young man named Sidney Lumet, and Quixote was played by Boris Karloff. Don't you want to see it?—Lost. Later in 1952, Kelly and Dick Foran played a married couple who go back to his country home and find trouble. This was for Westinghouse's *Studio One*, from a script by Reginald Rose and directed by Franklin Schaffner. You can find this odd harbinger of *Straw Dogs* on YouTube. It's not very good, but that's hardly the point, and Kelly has a desperate close-up at the close of Part I (before the soothing demonstration of Westinghouse's latest refrigerator) that Hitchcock may have noticed as beauty under stress.

On that close-up, you can feel Kelly moving up to her mark with the eager camera tracking in on her frightened eyes: It's all been planned, of course, yet it was live. We are in the golden age of television drama, a heroic enterprise made in defiance of mishap and accident. A series of adjoining sets were constructed; a line of action was set up that involved the minimum of costume changes; there were a few days of rehearsal, more for the camera crew than the actors; and then at an appointed hour, a story unfolded, in sequence: filmed, cut, and transmitted live. When there were mistakes, they were golden, too. In working out the shots and the angles, with several cameras, the playmakers were repeating the invention of film language that had first occurred in the silent era—and in nearly exactly the same manner. But they were doing it live.

The process of live drama was fiendishly, comically difficult in an age when television still worried over a clear picture and audible sound. Why was it done—at peak viewing hours on the networks? The only answer is that enough people (at home and in the studio) felt an affinity between this new medium and drama that might match the best work being done on stage. There was a creative urge!

It was a form that developed new writers and directors after the war, and a training ground for up-and-coming players like Grace Kelly. Nowadays, that moment seems the more fabulous in that much of the work done then did not survive. But in the long historical view, it was the postwar itch to do drama that would lead to the second golden age of dramatic long-form series. Even if it needed an ad for a Westinghouse refrigerator, this was something of value. (And during the ad, a new set could be readied, and actors changed costume!)

It's a wonder not to be forgotten that the new medium volunteered this gesture, and carried a large audience. There were so many competing theaters of the airwaves: the *Kraft Television Theatre* (1947–58); the *Lux Video Theatre* (1950–57), a development of Lux's tradition of redoing hit movie scripts on radio, often with new actors; *Studio One* (1948–58); the *Goodyear Television Playhouse* (1951–60); and *Philco Television Playhouse* (1948–55). Perhaps the most remarkable thing was that the genre was driven by writers, normally the most exploited and derided form of life in Hollywood. The anthology series put out the word that they needed new stories—ideally set indoors (exterior sets were difficult in live work), with not too many characters, essentially realistic (given that the audience was not to be troubled), and by tacit agreement kind or accommodating to the major corporations that were sponsoring the series. Most of the plays were broadcast on Sunday nights, so as not to conflict with stage schedules. They might have as much as a week of rehearsals. The budgets were very low—an original script seldom received more than $2,000, and the actors were treated like kids desperate for the opportunity. Perhaps the actors didn't quite notice, but these anthologies became major hits: By 1950–52, there were three or four in the annual top twenty-five shows.

The field was the more open in that the movie studios (clinging to existence) often forbade their contract employees from doing television. Here's how it felt to one young actor:

> It was all new, and very exciting. We were making up a new medium. I remember a little suspense story I did in which I had all the lines. Not long afterward I did another piece on the same program: I was in every scene and never spoke a word. These were little thirty-minute stories where you could try anything. CBS's Studio One was the classy show where we did serious drahh-ma. For them, in a few months I went from the Brontë sisters to Turgenev to TV's first spectacle, a story about the sinking of the battleship Bismarck. As the credits rolled, the studio was thick with smoke and ankle deep in water, with two cameras shorted out and cast and crew wet as water rats. I loved it!

That's Charlton Heston. He did a 50-minute *Wuthering Heights* in 1950, with Mary Sinclair as Cathy to his Heathcliff. Hal Wallis, a chief executive at Paramount, saw the broadcast, called the actor, and so his movie career was launched. From James Dean to Grace Kelly, the kids were looking for that break. The wind still blew toward the West coast. In 1955, Philco put on *The Death of Billy the Kid*, written by Gore Vidal and directed by Robert Mulligan, with Paul Newman as Billy. This was far from a standard Western. An alert viewer could get the hint that Billy might have been gay. Three years later, Newman was replaying the role at Warner Bros. in *The Left Handed*

THE LIMITATIONS TO THE TV PICTURE OFTEN ADDED TO THE HOPE FOR REALISM.

Gun, a regular movie directed by Arthur Penn, who had himself done a number of TV plays, including *The Miracle Worker* (written by William Gibson) for *Playhouse 90* in 1957, with Teresa Wright and Patty McCormack. That Helen Keller story reached Broadway in 1959, and the big screen in 1962. In valuable ways, television was pumping life into the ailing picture business.

One of the most influential emerging writers was Rod Serling. Born in Syracuse, New York, in 1924, he had served in the Pacific in a parachute regiment. From that, he drifted into radio at a Cincinnati station, and wrote more scripts than he could remember. It was his memory of military command that inspired *Patterns*, a critical study of American business methods. Fielder Cook directed it for Kraft; Ed Begley and Everett Sloane were lead actors. And the *New York Times* said it was so good it ought to be played *again*. From that, Serling went on to *Requiem for a Heavyweight* (1956), with Jack Palance as a used-up fighter. Both shows won the teleplay Emmy, and Palance won as best actor. *Requiem* is hokey and sentimental, but it had a raw look: The limitations to the TV picture often added to the hope for realism, which could be at odds with the increasing use of color in movies. The following year, for *Playhouse 90*, Serling wrote his best single work, *The Comedian*, which featured an alarmingly vicious performance from Mickey Rooney as a comedian who behaved like a tyrant. No movie of that time would have depicted a show business

*Mel Tormé,
Mickey
Rooney,
and Kim
Hunter in*
The Comedian

personality as such a monster (though Elia Kazan's *A Face in the Crowd*, about radio as well as television, came close). *The Comedian* had fine supporting work from Kim Hunter, Edmond O'Brien, and Mel Tormé, and it was directed by the up-and-coming John Frankenheimer. *The Comedian* took the Emmy for best single program of the year, and it may be as good as anthology drama ever reached. That Rooney missed an Emmy (it went to Peter Ustinov playing Dr. Johnson) may have been because too many people couldn't believe this cruel monster was really their Mickey.

Serling did not like people too much: The bad guys are usually his most interesting characters. On the other hand, Reginald Rose was liberal and humane and optimistic. All those traits can be seen in *Twelve Angry Men* (1954), done for *Studio One* and drawn from Rose's own experience of serving on a jury. It was ideal live TV, and idealistic, too: a single set, continuous action, and a chance for intense sweaty close-ups. Of course, it suggests that one rational doubter, Juror #8 (Robert Cummings), can calm and persuade a room of bigots and indifferent onlookers who just want to go home. Barack Obama would turn out to be a sad follower in the juror #8 tradition. When Henry Fonda played the role in the movie, wearing a white suit, he was an emblem of civic virtue. Alas, real juries are not as reliable or manageable—or as quick. The TV version won Emmys for Rose, Cummings, and director Franklin Schaffner, and it's still a great comfort—if you do comfortable.

Rose's career never regained that eminence. Serling would go on to lead *The Twilight Zone* (1959–64), the lasting source of his reputation. But the most notable writing career in live TV drama is that of Paddy—or Sidney Aaron—Chayefsky, born in the Bronx in 1923. Wounded in the war, he is said to have started writing in hospital. He

Twelve
Angry Men
(1954)

tried plays, movie scripts, and radio before gaining a foothold in television with an adaptation of Budd Schulberg's novel *What Makes
Sammy Run?* for Philco, starring José Ferrer. He turned increasingly
to intimate, realistic studies of ordinary life, and in 1953, for Philco
again, he wrote the play most associated with live drama—*Marty*—
which is by now the epitome of a sentimental but respectful treatment
of working-class experience. Indeed, it may be a role model for that
attitude in many people who are comfortably middle-class.

It's a love story between two people who feel they've missed out
on love and romance and who are oppressed by family expectations,
especially about marriage and "settling down" to
the code of television commercials. "I'm a fat little
guy and girls don't go for me, that's all," says Marty.
The "that's all" is a measure of Chayefsky's lifelike
talk and the play's lack of self-pity. Marty may have been the last
person to make such an admission on TV.

IT MADE THE COMMERCIAL SEEM FRAUDULENT.

The couple were played by Rod Steiger and Nancy Marchand in
the meticulous minimal naturalism that was being promoted by the
Actors Studio. But Steiger especially is very good—a lot better than
Ernest Borgnine, who won an Oscar in the film. So it's a fond, studious
television play about the kind of people who didn't get on television—

and still don't—and their heartache. Marty ends up in love; but if he hadn't, you trust that Chayefsky would not have had him turn into a mad-dog killer or join the Mafia.

Sixty years later, *Marty* feels dated, slow, and it can seem patronizing, but that's less important than the impact it had in 1953 in suggesting there was a life elsewhere, much of it in the dark, watching television. At one point, Marty and his pal say they'll stay home and watch Sid Caesar because they can't think what else to do. Delbert Mann directed, and he and Chayefsky went on to do the overdrawn, plaintive movie (with Borgnine and Betsy Blair), which won the Oscar for Best Picture. Granted that so many of these TV plays were swiftly turned into movies, it's a wonder the film studios didn't realize their terrible error in shunning TV. But would Hollywood have ever made *Marty*, or *Patterns*, or *Twelve Angry Men* first?

Nancy Marchand and Rod Steiger in Marty

What happened to drama on American television? By 1960, it hardly existed in the great mass of formulaic dramatic series where writers were hired to feed the machine with projects that ran for years and thus had no closure. The arrival of videotape wiped away the urgent uniqueness of live drama and made an irresistible commercial case for re-runnable, episodic eternities in which "drama" might be pacified. Most of the talents mentioned so far had taken their chance to make movies instead. In 1959, John Frankenheimer directed a two-part TV adaptation of Hemingway's *For Whom the Bell Tolls*, with Jason Robards and Maria Schell. Two years later he was off on a run of movies that led to *The Manchurian Candidate*, jittery with alarm at what television was doing to the country. Ten years after he played a cut-price Heathcliff, Charlton Heston was Ben-Hur. The movies were a different way of life, bringing much more money, and apparently more significant and valuable than television.

Still, it's strange that television drama subsided just as the difficulty of doing it was being overcome. Videotape was invented in 1956, so there was no longer a need to record dramas on kinescopes (usually of poor quality). Kinescopes were photographed copies of the TV image. Magnetic videotape was a workable resource in the easy dissemination of material. By 1960, most television was created and shot like cheap movies, and that permitted a loss of visual daring. In the TV *Marty* there are prolonged and unbroken shots of Rod Steiger inhabiting the role, with a moving camera, because that was the easiest way to film live. Without that need, television shooting became as formulaic as most movies. It almost made itself, and in terms of mise-en-scène, most television ground to factory-like stasis. Too much television, to this day, has little sense of the unique medium and different ways of filming waiting to be tried. The best experiments in TV style—and often the most beautiful—have come in the coverage of live events, especially sports. There's that word again—"live"—and the possibility of the loss of vitality once it is forgotten.

Nancy Marchand and James Gandolfini in The Sopranos

There was another factor. When *Marty* played, there would have been commercial breaks. They might have been for that Westinghouse refrigerator, the latest Chevrolet, cigarettes, beer, or just the longing to be part of some rich, glamorous world. There's no commercial I can think of that would not disturb the humdrum life Marty is leading, even if he finds a woman to marry. The look of the show, its patient commitment to duration, and the uneasy, undecided element in Steiger's acting, are all contrary to the romance of advertising.

Erik Barnouw noticed this tension in his fine book *Tube of Plenty* (1975), where he identified the discomfort advertisers felt in the face of realistic dramas:

> Most advertisers were selling magic. Their commercials posed the same problems that Chayefsky drama dealt with: people who feared failure in love and in business. But in the commercials there was always a solution as clear-cut as the snap of a finger: the problem could be solved by a new pill, deodorant, toothpaste, shampoo, shaving lotion, hair tonic, car, girdle, coffee, muffin recipe, or floor wax. The solution always had finality.

Chayefsky and other anthology writers took these same problems and made them complicated. They were forever suggesting that a problem might stem from childhood and be involved with feelings toward a mother or father. All this was often convincing—that was the trouble. It made the commercial seem fraudulent.

And too many people noticed that gap in the 1950s. As we shall see, the power of drama would return—Walter White on *Breaking Bad* lives in such hardship or conventional failure that he finds a way to break out of it. And when he breaks, he becomes not just extraordinary but someone who would defy Marty Piletti's comprehension. That made a great show, yet ironically it played not commercial-free on HBO or Showtime, but on AMC, broken up by ads. The same was true of *Mad Men* that recreation of the atmosphere and attitudes of advertising. Both those shows were appreciated, though by a smaller portion of the audience than would have watched *Marty*. But in sixty years, another sort of gap had appeared: Marty's life was filled with pain and disquiet—but imagine him as a series and a sit, and you can feel the pain being drained away by repetition and familiarity.

THE BBC DRAMA DEPARTMENT BELIEVED BRITAIN NEEDED A GRIM WARNING.

Equally, *Mad Men* said it was fixed on the disaster or the chaos of being "Don Draper," but those perils were softened because the show was a success and a ditto device. Something in our own inner systems, in the potential for social criticism, had been turned off. And even Walter White had "solved" his predicament by becoming an unwitting or inept example of the master criminal that violent melodrama dotes on. He had transformed his existence. If you're dying, *Breaking Bad* is a wild, enticing commercial for cutting loose.

If you think back to *The Fugitive*, so popular in the sixties, isn't it clear that what Richard Kimble is really fleeing is not the policeman who has vowed to get him, but the dread of ordinary, insoluble, un-magicked life? How does he have no money worries and such a good haircut? Compared with Steiger's Marty, David Janssen's Kimble feels and behaves like a man in a commercial who has that secret hunch that a golden Angie Dickinson is waiting for him in the next town he comes to. And the next.

||||||||||||||||||||||||||

THINGS DID NOT HAVE TO WORK THAT WAY. Rudolph Kacser was born in Vienna in 1904. He trained with Max Reinhardt, and he was making films for Ufa when the Nazis came to power. So in 1933, en-couraged by a friend, Billy Wilder, he went to Hollywood, but he couldn't make that career work. In 1935, he moved to England, and not much is known about his next fifteen years: What could an intel-ligent German-speaker do in Britain during the war? He had worked as a writer and producer, and in 1952 he was offered a job by Michael Barry, the new head of drama at BBC Television—not just a new head, but a new position. By then, Kacser called himself Rudolph Cartier, and Barry told him things at the BBC needed shaking up. They were surely inspired by reports of live drama in America, but it's not clear how much of it they had seen. Shows didn't travel yet.

Cartier admired screenwriter Nigel Kneale, and they planned a science-fiction serial, to be shot and transmitted live. It was called *The Quatermass Experiment*, and it involved a British spacecraft crash-landing in Wimbledon, with only one of its three man crew left. But there were spores on board, too, alien forms that might destroy much more than Wimbledon. Most people who watched found it very frightening; they were irked by the occasional technical delays but never gave up on the serial. It was done in six episodes in the summer of 1953, with Cartier directing as well as producing. The audience started at three million but it was over five million by the close. Only two of the six episodes survive, in rough quality, but it was not long before a movie was made, and not a good one.

Quatermass wasn't a play, unless you regarded it as a three-hour drama fit to scare you, and it inclined to say science is all very well—but watch out. Encouraged by the success of *Quatermass*, Cartier and Kneale proceeded to do a two-hour adaptation of Orwell's *Nineteen Eighty-Four*. It starred Peter Cushing and Yvonne Mitchell; it was faithful to the novel; and it gripped and distressed the audience (seven million this time). There were no commercials to provide relief, and every sign that the BBC drama department believed Britain needed a grim warning about where the world might be going (and what television could do to post warnings). The still bombed-out desolation of parts of London served to convey the desolation of Orwell's Oceania.

You can find this *Nineteen Eighty-Four* on YouTube. The picture and the sound are poor; you see the occasional microphone boom; the focus is wrong sometimes. But the story has a conviction and a terror that still hold. As I looked at it again, seeing the lead characters, I wondered if there had ever been as heartbreakingly beautiful a character on TV as its vibrant rebel Julia (Mitchell) before she is reduced by torture, brainwashing, and the actress abandoning conventional makeup and prettiness. The dread was not cliché. Thirty years ahead of Orwell's threatened date, a real movie had been made.

There was talk in the House of Commons that the BBC had gone too far (especially with those rats in Room 101), but defenders proposed a very un-American response: "Well, if you don't like it, you can always turn it off." That simple wisdom lasted at the BBC for three decades or more, and it still breaks out occasionally, though the BBC has acquiesced lately in the drab habit that viewers shouldn't turn it off. But in making stuff for "everyone," the risk of dull work increases. In the controversy over *Nineteen Eighty-Four*, the new queen and her consort, Prince Philip, said they had seen the show and found it terrific.

Elizabeth II played a part in television history. She had become queen in 1952 at the age of twenty-five, a weird fairy-story figure even if the young woman at its heart was rather grim. A lavish coronation was planned for the spring of 1953, and the idea arose that perhaps the event might be televised from inside Westminster Abbey. Prime Minister Churchill (born twenty years before movies began) was against the idea, but the young queen insisted—let's do it. In 1969, the same queen consented to *Royal Family*, a documentary made in a mood of rather awkward spontaneity, but a key step in turning the royals into an ongoing spectacle and unwitting celebrities, something they would live to regret. It wasn't out of cunning or media insight, but the royal family was on its way to becoming a TV institution, a soap opera version of prison, a kind of *Downtonia* written by Harold Pinter or Samuel Beckett.

The televised coronation happened, with RAF bombers flying the footage directly to Canada for that audience. It is believed that 20 million people watched the coronation in Westminster Abbey. I was one of them, because of the set my grandma had bought for the occasion.

WATKINS WENT TO THE HEART OF MODERN DANGER WITH *THE WAR GAME*.

It was the first thing I ever saw on television, and it's a good thing I saw it, because there hasn't been another coronation since.

When the Canadian Sydney Newman took over as head of BBC television drama in the early sixties, he initiated a series called *The Wednesday Play* (it lasted from 1964 to 1970). That label demonstrated a wish to make the writers all-important, even if this was the era in which film directors began to receive a new adulation and respect. It was also Newman's intention to add impetus and ideas to a shake-up underway (at last) in British society, and to match the cheek and irreverence of shows like *That Was the Week That Was*. The time slot for *The Wednesday Play* was after the *Nine O'Clock News*, and Newman always hoped for a kind of television drama that felt like an overflow from the news. For a time at least, it was possible to wonder whether the overall programming of the BBC was a unified force with an educational purpose. The sixties in Britain are often taken to mean pop music, shorter skirts, and the Pill. But television was there, too.

Alas, few in American television thought that the upheavals that we now call the sixties were a fit subject for ongoing drama. Richard Kimble has his problems, but they have little to do with what America was experiencing as he roamed the nation.

An early sign of what Newman sought was *Culloden* (1964), written and directed by Peter Watkins, but intended as a brutal recreation of a battle fought in Scotland in 1746, the last act in the suppression of the Bonnie Prince Charlie uprising. Watkins viewed the event as a battle being fought today, and he deliberately made it look like a documentary (though everything was invented, costumed, and designed). It was a startling work, for no theatrical movies to that time had shown battle in such shocking detail. Still, *Culloden* was watched with fascination because it seemed to be working under the safe cloak of "history." Wasn't it just a fresh way of doing documentary?

The next year, Watkins (and Newman) went to the heart of modern danger with *The War Game*. This was not history, but the future—if only days away. The show proposed that China had invaded South Vietnam, whereupon the United States had threatened strategic nuclear attacks on China. So Russia came to the support of China. The action switched to Berlin, where American forces suffered defeat in a land battle. Now nuclear war was "on," and missiles began to strike at air bases in England. Once "on," that bomb threat is so hard to turn "off," a matter addressed comically in Stanley Kubrick's 1964 movie, *Dr. Strangelove or: How I Learned to Stop Worrying and Love the Bomb*. *The War Game* was just fifty minutes, and it was scheduled to be broadcast in *The Wednesday Play* on October 7, 1965. (Two weeks earlier, over Vietnam, an American fighter and its pilot were shot down by a Chinese plane.)

The BBC were anxious. *The War Game* was a play, or a movie, but whenever possible it used the abrupt, broken style of raw news footage to show radiation sickness, food riots, martial law, and devastation in the settled countryside. Watkins was attempting to shatter British complacency and ignorance about what nuclear war would mean, and he was eager to dismantle the complacent distinction between news and fiction. Here was a film that had the nature of television as its ultimate target. As Watkins said:

> In this film I was interested in breaking the illusion of media-produced "reality." My question was—"Where is 'reality'?…in the madness of statements by these artificially-lit establishment figures quoting the official doctrine of the day, or in the madness of the staged and fictional scenes from the rest of my film, which presented the consequences of their utterances?"

The Cuban Missile Crisis was only three years back, while enough people in Britain as well as the United States were already alarmed at the potential for world war in Southeast Asia. But the film's mention of a game suggested an attitude that was sardonic, salutary, and even a little nihilistic. Plus, the film was very scary. In the crisis, the BBC opted to withhold the film because it was "too horrifying for the medium of broadcasting." Yet, wasn't it clear that if a real nuclear war broke out, television would be the only means of showing it to the public—instantaneous and harrowing—until the cameras melted? Instead, *The War Game* was released as a movie (for a much smaller audience). The final irony was that this carefully created work then won the 1966 Oscar for best documentary.

THERE WAS A SIMILAR NATURALISM IN *UP THE JUNCTION*.

There was a similar naturalism in *Up the Junction*, and it upset a large part of conservative Britain. This play came from a loose collection of stories by Nell Dunn, published in 1963. The project was taken up by the team of Tony Garnett and Ken Loach and turned into a cinema verité movie (though done with great skill) about life in working-class south London—the junction is Clapham Junction, the site of an important railway station. Dunn's TV version kept the idiomatic chat (it wasn't really dialogue), authentic settings, and the preoccupations of young people—clothes, music, sex, money, and sometimes abortion. It was Loach's first job of direction and the start of an authentically socialist artistic career. But what was more impressive still was that *Up the Junction* focused on three young women (played by Carol White, Geraldine Sherman, and Vickery Turner)—not educated, not quite moral beings (in Henry James's lofty sense), and with no clearer destination in life than Marty had had. True, they were above average in looks, but many in the audience for this barely shaped narrative felt the slice of life like a wet fish hitting their face. There were protests, which was what Newman, Garnett, and Loach had wanted. Time and again *The Wednesday Play* was based on this principle: Turn it off if you can't take it—or shut up and watch. It was part of one of the healthiest relationships between the public and the media that has ever existed.

A year later, 1966, Garnett and Loach applied the same method to *Cathy Come Home*. As written by Jeremy Sandford, this was the story of a young couple (Carol White and Ray Brooks). They come together, they have a baby, and they get a house. But then the man loses his job and the family is evicted. As homeless people, they squat in empty buildings until social services take away their child. Twelve million people watched (from a population of about 52 million), and many had previously been unaware of what homelessness meant. Again, the language and the camera style were rough, but this time the

The family from
Cathy
Come Home

social problem was felt. Shortly after the first broadcast, the charity Shelter, dedicated to trying to eliminate homelessness, was formed. I don't know if there were fewer homeless people because of *Cathy Come Home*—it's simpleminded to think that art can dress our wounds in a tidy, healing way. But the scheme for television as a medium that would not let the public look away and claim ignorance was made clear. Fifty years later, *Cathy Come Home* is as much a cultural landmark as the De Sica movie *Bicycle Thieves* (1948).

What do I mean by saying we could not look away? Homelessness is a wide-reaching issue: The people in prison are homeless; millions more who are "free" live in insecurity over their residence. As you watch television or read tonight, there may be people sleeping on the sidewalk on your block. You know them, more or less; they are neighborhood people. And if you walk past them tomorrow before they are up and "on" like the rest of us, you may sneak a glance and then look away if it is returned. You may give them a dollar and a kind word. You may assume that charity only buys liquor or drugs. You say to yourself that the authorities should clean this whole damn thing up. You are part of the silent, unwatching majority who believe action is futile. You hope you will never be in that predicament. But television is our great chance to look, to understand and act.

Imagine an hour a day of simple surveillance of the barely sustained existence of a derelict. "Oh, people don't want to watch that!" you hear. So let them revel in the astounding special effects of a film like *San Andreas* (2015), with the Golden Gate Bridge buckling under the playful onslaught of a tidal wave.

Nell Dunn and Jeremy Sandford did not write much more for television (and their marriage ended in 1968). But *The Wednesday Play* discovered other excellent writers. Dennis Potter was born in the remote Forest of Dean area in 1935, the son of a coal miner. He never went to university; he usually had some kind of illness and was emotionally burdened,

POTTER IS A MORE ENDURING SEARCHER AND DRAMATIST THAN PADDY CHAYEFSKY.

in part by his having been sexually abused as a child. After doing his National Service, he went into journalism, and stood as a Labour candidate in a general election. He wrote novels, and he was one of the writers on *That Was the Week That Was*. He was endlessly productive, but in hindsight it's clear that television made him, partly because of the opportunity it offered for plays and scripts, but also because it could be like a scalpel opening up the nation's sensibilities. His first significant offerings were two Wednesday plays in 1965, *Stand Up, Nigel Barton* and *Vote, Vote, Vote for Nigel Barton*, which told the story of an ambitious socialist on the make, without piety or undue respect.

The Wednesday Play then gave way to *Play for Today*, and at the turnover Potter wrote *Son of Man*, a play about Christ in which the naturalism was calculated (if not determined) to upset many churchgoers. By then, Potter was a free agent, and he worked as often for commercial television as he did for the BBC. But he surpassed mere naturalism and found his way to increasing fantasy in dramas for television. In an age and on a medium obsessed with naturalism, Potter is a poet of disturbed inner lives. I'll mention only a few of these works: *Brimstone and Treacle* (1976), in which a Satanic figure (played by Michael Kitchen—it was Sting in the later movie) rapes a handicapped girl, and always knows he's in a TV play—this was banned for years; *Pennies from Heaven* (1978), where Bob Hoskins plays a 1930s sheet-music salesman driven to adultery and murder, and in which the character mimes to several popular songs of the 1930s—Potter was always alert to ways in which pop culture had affected attitudes to love and sexuality; *Blue Remembered Hills* (1979), in which adults play the roles of children in an exquisite but pained evocation of childhood (Helen Mirren was one of them).

IT WAS BEAUTIFUL IN A WAY THE SMALL SCREEN HAD SELDOM ATTEMPTED.

These are major works (all produced by Kenith Trodd) that leave one wondering how to describe *The Singing Detective* (1986), one of the few occasions in which genius emerges from the steady workaday mass of television. It was a six-part miniseries in which a man named Philip Marlow (Michael Gambon) is in hospital suffering from debilitating psoriasis (one of Potter's own complaints), with his mind wandering between the detective fictions he writes, his childhood in the Forest of Dean, and London during the war. Once again, pop songs and musical routines ran through the whole show. Jon Amiel directed a cast that included Joanne Whalley, Patrick Malahide, Janet Suzman, Alison Steadman, and Bill Paterson. Many found the show offensive or disturbing; its sex was uncommonly explicit. So *The Singing Detective* was too inventive or rare for a large audience. But it played on the BBC in the spirit that no one needed the largest audience all the time, and it is that unusual thing in this history, a TV show that seems better now than when it first played. It was modern noir, fusing so many strands in British culture.

One episode starts with London and the Thames in 1945. The river "glistens and blobs in the moonlight." Marlow speaks:

> The thing about the moon is, it gives you the creeps with a capital K. Am I not right? It makes dirty water look like silver, turns flotsam into the crown jewels, and causes poor slobs in the cuckoo-house to think they are Jesus Christ or F. W. Woolworth. Am I right?

It was movielike, asking difficult questions, and beautiful in a way the small screen had seldom attempted, as well as a forerunner of long-form television, but Potter had reached this point as an artist because of the excitement of television drama in Britain.

Today, that era seems as precious and remote as that of live TV drama in America. Only a few years before *The Singing Detective* opened, the playwright David Hare wrote and directed his first significant play for television, *Licking Hitler* (1978). It was a companion piece to his stage play *Plenty*—both starred Kate Nelligan, and both treated the subsequent dismay of young, emotional idealists who felt they had won the war. Decades later, Hare described the moment with reverence:

> In the 1970s, television was regarded as a uniquely important medium. No playwright would dream of condescending to it, or of not giving it their very best work. *Armchair Theatre* and *The Wednesday Play* had initiated the practice of good dramatists and actors setting out to tell truths about the lives of all the people watching at home.

ABOVE:
*Michael
Gambon in*
The Singing
Detective;
BELOW:
*Melvyn Bragg
and Dennis
Potter*

Times changed. The originality of one-off plays and their respect for closure meant that the works might be "lost" in the mounting collection of boxed sets for multi-season dramas. Writing in 1999, Mark Lawson lamented how hard it was by then to see *Licking Hitler*. The same difficulty arose with *Saigon: Year of the Cat* (1983), a play or a movie Hare had written for Thames Television, and which Stephen Frears directed. Set in 1974 in Saigon, it has a love affair between a British bank manager (Judi Dench) and a CIA operative (Frederic Forrest). It's very good, and it ought to be remembered. But now you have to go to Amazon to search for a tired DVD. That *Saigon* is relatively unknown because it never went to series.

Dennis Potter did much more than I have mentioned—novels, TV serials, film scripts, public appearances in which he relished offending important people and stale ideas. He had the vitality of someone never quite well. In 1994, he succumbed to pancreatic cancer, but at the very end he was loyal to television. So he did an interview with Melvyn Bragg in which he was funny, truculent, resigned, and simply Potter. He referred to his cancer as "Rupert" in a lethal homage to Rupert Murdoch, who was becoming an ever more powerful mogul in the medium Potter loved.

Potter is a more enduring and searching dramatist than Paddy Chayefsky, just as the potential of difficult and even purposeful drama shown without commercials still seems vital to our expectations of television (and something to be guarded). All too often, commercials have masked from Americans their understanding of how deserving of criticism their country is. Do we yet realize how far "the greatest nation on earth" is itself an ad slogan that blurs insight and misleads progress?

But I want to close this chapter with something that suggests how sometimes even commercials can be handled if set in a sardonic or creative framework. In March 1963, Associated-Rediffusion (one of the commercial production companies in Britain) broadcast an original 60-minute play by Harold Pinter. It was called *The Lover*, and it had a married couple (Alan Badel and Vivien Merchant) whose happiness together is sweetly nourished by an intrigue in which they sometimes act as each other's adulterous lover. The wit and mischief of the two players are still like fresh flowers. *The Lover* was directed by Joan Kemp-Welch (a luminary of commercial television), and in its interplay of actuality and fantasy it is like one of Luis Buñuel's last films—though before Buñuel got to make them (*Belle de Jour* was four years away).

Take one moment—and you can see it on YouTube. We see the wife getting dressed. Sitting in a black slip with a lace edge, she puts on stockings and secures them with garters. Then she adds a cocktail dress and high-heeled shoes. This is close to the voyeurism of an ad. She is getting ready for her lover's visit. Nothing is said. The image is black-and-white still, and you can feel the crew holding their breath so that the sensual rustle of the clothing may be heard. Pinter was early in his career, but this is an exquisite fable, and that one scene has things no one had thought to put on television before: eroticism existing in pieces of clothing as much as in the larger scheme of games we play with reality; and fantasy as the engine in furtive pleasure. So much of TV has been stolid with realism, blind and deaf to the inward dream (that treasure of the movies). But here it was, as early as 1963, a startling advertisement for human nature.

11
TALKING HEADS

AT FIRST, THERE WAS THIS CRUDE, diminutive screen abuzz with interference. What could any scheme do with it except stick a head in the rectangle, as if it was a hatbox or the basket at the foot of the guillotine? And if you were going to put faces on television, in the hallowed cause of human interest, shouldn't they talk? Everyone in news admitted that radio was more sophisticated, swift, and informative than the assembly of film might be on television. Still, when network news started in 1947–48, the only evident way to organize the show, or hold an audience, was to have a commanding face and a big voice in the studio reassuring the audience that the show would work. It was Douglas Edwards at CBS and John Cameron Swayze at NBC (on the *Camel News Caravan*). Swayze tried to explain the clips, his own role, and the audience's uncertain participation, before saying, "That's the story, folks. Glad we could get together." The medium had to tell us it was real, and that it was OK to watch. A new kind of "togetherness" was being attempted.

But there were doubts, too. In 1950, John Gielgud brought the Christopher Fry play *The Lady's Not for Burning* to Broadway. He went on television to be interviewed with his actress, Pamela Brown, and was asked to perform. The two of them did a scene from *The Importance of Being Earnest*, and then Gielgud offered a Hamlet soliloquy. But he was not impressed: "[A] long and tedious business—4 hours for a short session of ten minutes… I cannot help feeling it is abominably undignified to act to interruptions of advertising Pepsi-Cola!" Whatever Gore Vidal might say, the fuss of appearing on TV is still onerous and futile compared with the ease of going on radio.

On early TV, the right talking head could seem to be telling amazing truths. Edward R. Murrow had been born in Polecat Creek, North Carolina, in 1908. He was handsome, grave, and dark, and he had a voice made for radio. As such, he had become known for his newscasts from Europe at war, especially London during the Blitz. But he never doubted his place in television. Murrow had a romantic sense of himself; he might have been an actor. He would have been more obvious casting for *Dragnet* than Jack Webb, and he often smoked on air (it still looked stylish) even if doing reports on tobacco and lung cancer—which killed him at fifty-seven.

At CBS, he became host for a documentary magazine program, *See It Now* (1951–58), the forerunner of *60 Minutes*. He and his producer Fred Friendly were increasingly irritated by and scared of the influence of Senator Joseph McCarthy, who was spearheading campaigns against an alleged Red menace in every walk of American life. By 1953, McCarthy was urging the resignation from the Air Force reserve of Milo Radulovich, a young lieutenant whose father and sister had been accused of Communist

A NEW KIND OF "TOGETHERNESS" WAS BEING ATTEMPTED.

sympathies. Murrow and Friendly determined to put this case on *See It Now*. The network permitted this (its boss William Paley, and Paley's wife, Dorothy, were Murrow fans), but when it came to modest promos for the show, CBS went quiet. So Murrow and Friendly paid for them themselves.

In the Radulovich item, a circumspect account of what was a minor case in McCarthy's agenda, Murrow concluded by speaking to

the camera. His words were carefully weighed, but Murrow's touch of Bogart was good enough to seem impromptu and heartfelt. He was asking us to recognize his reliability:

> Whatever happens in this whole area of the relationship between the individual and the state, we will do ourselves; it cannot be blamed upon Malenkov, Mao Tse-tung, or even our allies. It seems to us—that is, to Fred Friendly and myself—that it is a subject that should be argued about endlessly.

Murrow was a natural self-dramatist and he realized he was taking on McCarthyism in a new public arena. He looked into the camera directly and said, you can trust me. *See It Now* pushed against the reckless senator and his chronic, casual lies, a campaign several newspapers had already been embarked on without dislodging him. In 1954 that led to the Army-McCarthy hearings, in which both sides accused the other of acting in bad faith.

The dispute built around the Army's claim that McCarthy's associate Roy Cohn had attempted to get special treatment for another colleague, David Schine, who had had to join the Army in 1953. Eventually, hearings were announced for the Senate's Permanent Subcommittee on Investigations. In truth, this was an argument that had swollen out of proportion. A smarter McCarthy might have seen he was being set up for exposure and retreated.

In a move to build its audience, ABC, the weakest of the three networks, announced it would televise the hearings. It was during those proceedings that a lawyer, Joseph N. Welch, clashed with McCarthy. When the Senator tried to blacken the name of Fred Fisher, his young assistant, Welch delivered what are still lines in America's history:

> Until this moment, Senator, I think I never really gauged your cruelty or your recklessness. Fred Fisher is a young man who went to the Harvard Law School and came into my firm and is starting what looks to be a brilliant career with us…Little did I dream you could be so reckless and so cruel as to do an injury to that lad.

Welch was speaking in anger and sadness, without a script. But he was a canny performer, and his eloquence was markedly at odds with McCarthy's clumsy bluster: The senator couldn't read a line as plain sincere. So Welch nailed him with what came into his talking head on the spot:

> Senator, may we not drop this? We know he belonged to the Lawyers Guild…Let us not assassinate this lad further, Senator. You've done enough. Have you no sense of decency, sir? At long last, have you left no sense of decency?

That was June 9, 1954, and it was an important day in America. The sale of television sets had increased: 26 million households had a television by then—for the first time, more than half the nation. It was tempting to think that "decency" had won the day, and certainly McCarthy's power was ending. Though he was acquitted in the hearings, his popularity fell off fast. He had played badly on the air, and came to be canceled. But the lasting victory was for great lines (sound bites) and how to handle melodrama. A few years later, Otto Preminger cast Welch as the judge in *Anatomy of a Murder*.

Though little noticed at the time, the material of news was gathering a performing glow, and anyone aspiring to power or attention needed to be capable of being one of those talking heads. (It could be more useful than using the same head for thinking.) For the 1952 election, the Republican nominee, General Dwight D. Eisenhower, had selected Senator Richard Nixon of California as his vice presidential candidate. Whereupon a rumor built that Nixon had been the beneficiary of an illegal fund from supporters that had enabled him to live above his means. These charges were unjust, but Nixon's status was threatened. Spurred by advisers, notably Murray Chotiner, and left to dangle by Eisenhower, Nixon resolved to speak on television in his own defense. This occurred on September 23, 1952, at the El Capitan Theatre in Los Angeles. He actually spoke on the empty stage, though a small set of furniture and curtains was arranged for him. The Republican National Committee paid $75,000 for the event, and it was carried by NBC on sixty stations. It played at 9:30 P.M. in the East, right after Milton Berle and the *Texaco Star Theater*.

Nixon wrote the speech himself, though Chotiner and a few others advised on it. He wrote and rewrote and still he managed to be conversational with it. His first big television appearance was a success. He had his wife, Pat, on camera as a support and a prop, and she duly smiled at some of his points. Nixon told the world that Pat did not have a mink coat (as some rumors had suggested), "but she does have a respectable Republican cloth coat." (See how far the tropes of advertising were taking over discourse.) Then he took charge of the night:

> One other thing I probably should tell you because if I don't they'll probably be saying this about me too: We did get something—a gift—after the election. A man down in Texas heard Pat on the radio mention the fact that our two youngsters would like to have a dog. And believe it or not, the day before we left on this campaign trip, we got a message from the Union Station in Baltimore saying they had a package

for us. We went down to get it. You know what it was? It
was a little cocker spaniel dog in a crate that he'd sent all
the way from Texas. Black-and-white, spotted. And our little girl Tricia, the six-year-old, named it Checkers. And you
know, the kids, like all kids, love the dog, and I just want to
say this right now, that regardless of what they say about it,
we're gonna keep it.

Adorable pets had been turned loose on American television.

||||||||||||||||||||||||||||

THE PRINCIPLE OF THE FACE, and what it might yield to sustained
scrutiny, did not have to be stressed. It had been a condition of the
movies for at least four decades. Drama and comedy drew upon it all
the time: It was the antic reactions of Lucille Ball that made her hilarious and alarming. Newscasters were chosen because they seemed mature, reliable, and calm. But another lesson sank in on a medium that
was often desperate to fill its own time. People will talk. They'll ago-
nize, trying to get the right answer. Agony is interesting. And people
will do interviews if they believe it will sell a movie, launch a book,
further a cause, or generate a political
campaign. The interview is absurdly
cheap as an air-filler: Most of the people turn up for free, because they think
television is doing them a favor. The
mechanics of the show are simple, especially on a standing set, or with
a table like Charlie Rose's. All you need is a questioner who can listen,
heed the time, comb his hair, and seem respectable to the audience.

> ANYONE ASPIRING TO POWER OR ATTENTION NEEDED TO BE CAPABLE OF BEING ONE OF THOSE TALKING HEADS.

No one filled more time with small talk than the NBC executive
Sylvester "Pat" Weaver (also the father of Sigourney Weaver). In the
early fifties, he established the format for both *The Today Show* and
The Tonight Show, thereby accounting for four or five hours every
weekday for decades. If that seems ungrateful, just remember the minutes and years of quick newscasts, weather predictions, and showbiz
interviews in the morning magazine show that knew very well that its

chief duty was to tell the time, get the kids to school, and stave off morning despair. Many able hosts passed through the shows over the years, and many foolish things were taken seriously. It's still quite hard to remember anything that actually happened on *The Today Show* (or *Good Morning America*). The network says *Today* is a moneymaker, a franchise cornerstone, and an alert to so many other things NBC is playing. Yet maybe it still leaves the question as to whether anyone ever needed morning television. A shower, orange juice, clothes, and a little hope—yes. But a fresh today is marvel enough—we have woken up again, or turned ourselves on—so *Today* can seem like overkill.

The honorable professionals from *Today* can say, "Well, of course it's lightweight and trivial—that's what it was meant to be." But sixty years of the trivial can impinge on our sense of climate and leave life seeming flimsy. It makes all the todays alike and indifferent—there is philosophy in that—and it can leave the human beings persuaded that their duty to time is to waste it, or stay "on" with it. With *The Today Show* and all its equivalents (at any time of day) a warning option is raised—what if you turned me off? And it's only gradually that we realize what courage that takes, or what proof of the suspect notion of US exists in the mere title of *Good Morning America*.

The Tonight Show is a different matter, because our status then is so different: At the end of the day, we are coming to rest but lively enough for something else. *Tonight* was never a magazine show. Even before Johnny Carson, with Steve Allen and Jack Paar (two inquisitive men with conversational talent), it offered the prospect of getting to know someone. The interviews were longer and a little edgier than in the morning shows. The guests were more compelling, even if they were mostly show business. But Carson was somewhere between a ghost and an angel, a distinctly uneasy man who understood his task to make the nighttime easy. For thirty years, he was both reassuring and unpredictable, likeable but lost, always there yet distant. We never rumbled him. Johnny Carson came and went as an unknown figure, maybe the most intriguing model of American maleness since Cary Grant—which is a way of saying he was problematic, elusive, and as anxious as anyone holding down a big salary. But he liked talk, comics, pretty women, nifty suits, timing, and being unknown but in charge. Ed McMahon was his pal, his Fool, but sometimes his potential betrayer.

For his farewell, Carson did his best to be moved. But when he stopped, he was entirely off. Marinaded in audience for so long, he went cold turkey. None of the replacements on *The Tonight Show*, and not even David Letterman, have taken away his myth and its mystery. Carson is perhaps the best TV example we have of how unknowable we are. To adapt Robert Musil a little, he is the charmer without qualities. Anyone who watched him for long has his voice, his timing, and his parched double takes in their heads.

No one going on *Today* or *Tonight* or on the legion of shows that took interview as their essential ingredient expected to be attacked or "exposed." If someone famous enough went on the shows, there was a tacit contract: I look good, I talk and laugh, and in return the show makes nice and I am promoted along with my latest venture. For all the halfhearted air of news, these shows were usually extensions of the commercialism on which television was constructed.

But occasionally something could go wrong. In Britain, for the BBC, a show called *Face to Face* (1959–62) drew attention because it seemed more searching. The host was John Freeman, a war hero and a former Member of Parliament. He was handsome, intelligent, and cool in his manner—though the show seldom employed more than his voice or the back of his questioning head. His show was not intended as an interrogation or even a confrontation, but it had a more austere structure than was common in America. The black-and-white show began with inventive cartoons by Feliks Topolski and classical music. But it ran only thirty minutes, which rather belied its gravity and let most interviewees stay clenched in their responses—though Evelyn Waugh admitted cheekily he was doing it for the money.

Freeman was off camera, not "with" the subject, and never offered friendship or chat. (He ignored Waugh's admission.) His preparation and his questions were thorough and his style was that of judicious scrutiny. He was asked once about the secret to his interviews and he said approximately this: He asked a question, listened to the answer, then paused, because it was in the nature of such sittings that the subject grew nervous at silence and started to say something that was not calculated in advance. Some truth might spill out. But most of his subjects handled him comfortably and avoided revelation.

THAT POSSIBILITY OF TOUGHER TALKING EXISTED BUT FEW SEEMED READY TO GRASP IT.

Quite often, Freeman went for very respectable subjects, not just show business celebrities. So he interviewed Carl Jung, Adlai Stevenson, Martin Luther King Jr., Bertrand Russell, as well as race car driver Stirling Moss, and assumed that enough of the audience knew what these faces were talking about. This was a touchstone at the BBC and on British television generally. It is not that the British public was more intelligent or better educated than the American. But there was an attitude in programming that did not submit to a lowest common denominator. Britain has enjoyed television quiz shows—like *Mastermind* and *University Challenge*—where many of the questions are too difficult for the public. Isn't that what education is about?

For one show in 1960, the subject on *Face to Face* was Gilbert Harding. He was not in the league of Jung or Russell. He was only famous for being on television, as an acerbic panelist on *What's My Line*, where he had been known to be rude to ordinary contestants. He was neither well nor happy; he was a closeted gay at a time when homosexuality was illegal; he was a man from an earlier, repressed culture. But in the course of the interview he wept over the death of his mother and all that involved. The audience was surprised and alert for more: A kind of voyeurist glee had been released. Nobody thought Freeman had meant to embarrass Harding, though it's possible that he doubted whether this subject was quite worthy of the show. The program caused a great stir, which was added to when Harding dropped dead of an asthma attack only a few months later. The possibility arose that heads on TV might be targets.

That possibility of tougher talking existed, but few seemed ready to grasp it. At CBS, from 1953 to 1961, there was a show called *Person to Person*, with a very strained format. Edward R. Murrow would sit in the studio while a camera filmed the subject, talking from his or her own home. The subjects were famous, of course, covering a range from Marilyn Monroe to Fidel Castro and from John Steinbeck to Margaret Mead. No one ever broke down or gave much away. The show never transcended celebrity chat. Senator John Kennedy was on the show but he was clearly in a campaign mode, acting on assumptions about the camera he had known most of his life.

Which brings us to the careers of Dick Cavett and Charlie Rose, providential figures for those in the literate class looking for an intelligent retreat, and hosts who have accumulated a treasury of interview material with valuable people of their time. Cavett was born in a small town in Nebraska in 1936. As a teenager, he met Johnny Carson (another Nebraska resident), who was doing a magic act in a church in Lincoln. Cavett went to Yale, where he majored in drama, and he became a fanatic on showbiz knowledge, as well as a wit and a devotee of wordplay. There was never going to be a chance of Cavett being Carson, though arguably no one appreciated Johnny better. He was hired as a writer and talent coordinator on *The Tonight Show* in the era of Jack Paar—one of his Paar lines was "Here they are, Jayne Mansfield," as an intro for that star.

Cavett was cheeky yet learned, physically small but brave, merry though depressed beneath that. Television needed him as an alternative possibility. Above all, it needed his urge to work in the mainstream and make it smarter. Cavett liked talkers and liked to talk—he would have appealed to Kasper Gutman in *The Maltese Falcon*. He liked music and acting, and he often employed those areas to leaven his interviews. He understood that he needed stars and felt no pain in that. He loved them, he knew their work as well as they did, and his training and skills helped him ask questions that opened them up. *The Dick Cavett Show* started at ABC in 1968. He would do classic conversations with Groucho Marx, Bette Davis, Katharine Hepburn, and many others that helped reintroduce these looming figures to a new America. He

A CAGED PHENOMENON, A MONSTER.

seldom did people he didn't admire. He had writers, like Norman Mailer, Truman Capote, and Gore Vidal, and he would sometimes referee their battles. It was on a Cavett show that Mary McCarthy questioned the veracity of Lillian Hellman—"I said once…that every word she writes is a lie, including 'and' and 'the'"—and got herself into legal trouble. He managed to be both a stargazing kid and a hip Boswell. He revealed people without ever thinking to attack them.

His archive is a godsend to history, but his show never worked. ABC tried their best. They gave him a band and some musical routines. They switched his day and his time slots. He had in the region of three million loyal followers, but it was a hard lesson of network television that three million was not enough. Above all, he had the integrity that would not—could not—lower his own standards. Never mind: In hindsight he is as important as Carson and not so different. The two Nebraska boys were shy, funny, and hidden.

Cavett ended up at PBS (1977–82), which had always seemed his natural venue, though one suspects Cavett sometimes sighed at the mention of public broadcasting as a respectable dead end. He wanted the big show, as if he had been Chaplin or Bob Hope. And if talk failed with him, it was America's sad loss. If you want an example of Cavett, try this. In 1979, his office received a call from Jed Harris. Cavett was startled: He had assumed Harris was dead—but he was the only TV interviewer fit to be surprised and to understand. Harris, born in

1900, had been missing for a long time. But he had been a master of American theater in the twenties and thirties, on the cover of *Time* in 1928. He had directed and produced *The Front Page*, *The Green Bay Tree* (with a young Olivier), *Our Town*, *A Doll's House* (with his lover, Ruth Gordon), *The Heiress*, and many others. He was famous for his meticulous stagecraft, for psychological suspense, cruel intimidation of actors, and just for being hateful. Olivier said that he had modeled his Richard III on Harris.

By 1979, Harris was broke and sick, but he had not mellowed. He had written a memoir, and he was shrewd enough to guess that Cavett on PBS was its best promoter. The two men met. A studio was found in Los Angeles and a crew hired. How could Harris not know that this was his swan song? Against medical advice, he smoked during the shooting. He was hideous and alluring, and he knew it. Time and again, he let his large hands roam across his face, holding a cigarette as if he knew it was his nightshade. He was arrogant, yet he remembered enough and he was piercing in his sense of detail and in the hint of how he had commanded moments onstage. Cavett knew the story well already, and he never thought to intervene. He realized he had a caged phenomenon, a monster, an odious genius of sorts. The cameras rolled, and Harris died just months later. PBS guessed that "no one" had heard of Jed Harris, but now we have the record of a special serpent. The Harris interview was allowed to play for five nights, the longest time Cavett had ever given anyone. But surely fewer people now know who Harris was than was the case in 1980. A treasure trove is laid down for a culture that often ignores its own wealth. Without Cavett, our posterity would not know that a beguiling Satan had passed by.

Charlie Rose was born in Henderson, North Carolina, in 1942, and he went to Duke. It is possible that that school and its basketball tradition mean more to him than almost anything. He probably would sooner interview Mike Krzyzewski (Duke's basketball coach) than Vladimir Putin. He worked for Bill Moyers at PBS for a while and proved himself in a 1987 interview with Charles Manson. Rose is not as quick-witted as Cavett, or as depressive. He is earnest, well prepared, and interested in a wider range of people. Rose does a lot of interviews with businessmen and political figures, and he likes to move in power-broking circles.

Soon after he started his PBS show in 1991, he shifted his studio base to Bloomberg Television (to ensure a better high-tech image and satellite links). That also brought him closer to wealthy company, adding to his long relationship with Amanda Burden, a stepdaughter to William Paley, the founder of CBS. It matters to him that he knows the right people, and sometimes he is too gentle with them.

He is curious about many things—his series on the brain, assisted by Dr. Eric Kandel, was an education for the layman without cheating on the science. He is less astute on show business people than Cavett, but smarter on medicine, money, and media news. In person, he has become involved with CBS and *60 Minutes* and even their morning show. But he has always understood that his kind of talk requires PBS. He lacks Cavett's mercurial flair, and some people will watch Rose for a few years steadily and then take years off without a sense of loss. When you come back, he is as courteous as ever, as one-paced, and deeper in his own earnest mannerisms, but he is focused on big issues and the belief that talk can help our problems. It's not his fault if the world seems to be getting worse—though that is a pointer to the nature of television.

||||||||||||||||||||||||||||

WHEN ROSE TOOK ON THE BRAIN, there were diagrams and educational tools, but whenever possible, the show preferred talking heads and the chance to have experts chat. Television has always had mixed feelings about overt "education." That approach can seem boring, high-minded, and out of place on a fun box. But that partiality for unalloyed entertainment can lose sight of how formative the entirety of television is.

Consider this example of barefaced education. In the mid-1950s, BBC in Britain had a show called *In the News*, where for thirty minutes a group of interesting people discussed current events. A producer on the show, John Irwin, decided to visit one of his people, A. J. P. Taylor, a professor of history at Oxford. He attended a Taylor lecture and was impressed by the professor's fluent directness and intellect. He wondered if these lectures would work on television. Taylor was intrigued. He was a well-known academic and writer, but he enjoyed writing for the popular press, especially the Beaverbrook papers. He said he would like to give it a try.

The result had to be seen to be believed. Irwin put Taylor on the otherwise empty stage of the Wood Green Empire theater. The professor would speak for thirty minutes. His first topic was the Russian revolution, covered in

THE OPEN UNIVERSITY WOULD BROADCAST A SERIES OF LECTURES OR LESSONS.

three lectures that played on Monday evenings at 6:00 P.M. He had no script, no autocues, no Telestrator. He gave the engineers his opening remark and a closing line so that they could cue the show. Otherwise, this small, intensely alive man strode forward, looked at the camera, and delivered his lecture, without pomp, coyness, or concession. He didn't need a script because he had been lecturing extempore for years. And he was so expert that he always came in on time.

This started in 1957, and by the mid-sixties he had done forty lectures. And they were lectures: Television was so young, it had no shame or discretion. Taylor's audience had started out at 750,000 but it grew to four million (a million more than Cavett got in a country with about four times the population of the UK). Taylor was riveting, and many people woke up to the idea that television might galvanize education in a country where in 1960 only a small portion of young people went to university. Taylor was enough of a socialist to be excited by this prospect: "I expect we shall have a tremendous university of the air in no time," he said. It was in 1965 that Harold Wilson's Labour government proposed an Open University, and put it in the hands of the Minister for the Arts, Jennie Lee.

The plan was simple but extraordinary. Using television, the Open University would broadcast a series of lectures or lessons on various subjects. There would be set books. The students at home would have to do papers and assignments, and there would be meetings (at the Milton Keynes campus) where students would convene for seminars and tutorials. The TV content was seldom at Taylor's level. But when the Open University started to teach in 1971, it had 25,000 students, many of them past regular college age. This was in a country where the total university enrollment was still only 130,000. The OU is still there, with a campus for research. It has graduated over 1.5 million students so far, and it helped alter British attitudes to higher education and the prospects for people who have had a poor start.

A. J. P. Taylor

Taylor did not bother to be sophisticated with the camera. He was content to talk in a full shot, his body animating what he said. Sometimes his producer cut to close-ups, but Taylor was unaware of the refinement. He was a moviegoer, fond of silent comedy, oblivious of what we might call mise-en-scène. But we cannot afford to be so casual. In the culture of talking heads we have been deeply affected by the look of people talking, listening, and agreeing to understand, or not. What I'm talking about is akin to the three-camera technology Karl Freund and Desi Arnaz developed for filming sitcoms. It is as old as the movies and so familiar we may think we hardly notice it. But television often hinges on processes we do not "see."

In life, if two people talk while sharing the same space, they are a shifting spatial continuity. Sometimes they gaze at each other intently; sometimes they can hardly bear to look. But there is a way in which a conversation deserves to be filmed in what I'll call a two-shot, a shot that keeps the two people in the same frame. You can observe that method in many films by Jean Renoir, Robert Altman, and Kenji Mizoguchi, to name just a few directors. It is an approach that sees harmony in physical context and talking rapport. Of course, you can break this up if you wish, with a cut to a close-up to indicate surprise, deep feeling, or insult.

Television does not often do that. If you watch the *Charlie Rose* show, there may be an initial establishing shot of Rose and his guest at the same table. But once they start to talk, the style of the show enters into a pattern of crosscut close-ups. This editing, done live during the filming, may be managed with skill and tact; its format is built into the convenient shooting method. But it is also a shaping intrusion that says, "This is how the conversation is going; Charlie is getting the point." That notion of "understanding" helps us feel we have understood, too. A Rose conversation doesn't work if Charlie isn't getting the point and feeling reassured. If Charlie didn't get it, I suspect we'd change the channel out of uneasiness.

Think of a telephone conversation. The technology of the phone has imposed a crosscut close-up routine upon us. Do you see and feel how sixty years or so of television interviews have imposed an irresistible pattern in discourse? To such an extent that it is common for our private consciousness to fall into an interview back-and-forth. We are talking to someone in our life, but we are being interviewed by some kind of notional Rose. That presents us as a character, as a figure a little outside ourselves. I am not sure whether this process is positive or negative—or whether it has to be either. But I believe our monumental, albeit casual and forgetful commitment to television has set this up as a wiring structure in our minds. And it lets us feel apart from others, and even from ourselves. A subtle detachment or solitude comes from it. That removal is vital to television. (It's worth a program in the Rose-Kandel examination of the brain.)

So here's a cut, to something the very smart and excited A. J. P. Taylor said about his middle-aged discovery of himself as a performer, or a ghost. Had any TV performer intuited the split in performing identity with such humor or appreciation?

I have nothing in common with the screen figure whom I think of vaguely as Him. He has mannerisms which had never occurred to me. He says things that astonish me— sometimes penetrating remarks that I should never have hit on, sometimes rash generalizations that seem to me a trifle unscholarly—but he always seems to pull through somehow. Occasionally I think of something he ought to say and is going to miss. Just when I have despaired of Him, he says it after all. I rather like Him, though I am glad I am not Him or anything like it in real life.

The Open University has been very influential. One can watch series of lectures now by good (and bad) academics on the Web. But its influence may not be complete yet. In Britain, the education system has begun to charge for the university experience. In the United States, fees up to $60,000 a year just for tuition have become a systemic problem. The debt on college loans is well over $1 trillion, a drag on the economy as well as a shadow on the lives of young graduates who find getting a job in their major harder and harder. So questions arise over whether university education is still the valuable or unique experience we want it to be. Once upon a time, going to college was a significant adventure. But these days, kids travel on the Net from an early age, and have the chance to direct their own education, and do it in less than three or four years.

Traditionalists dislike this trend. But in Britain, education has recently been busy applying new value tests to its own work, so why should parents and students not test career plans against investment? Television technology can act with disarming speed. So it's neither absurd nor futuristic to wonder if higher education might one day be a process done at "home," screen to screen. In so many ways, it has been happening for decades. But it's a matter of ironic quandary as to whether that prospect excites or alarms you.

||||||||||||||||||||||||||

THE HEAD AND THE FACE ARE CHANGING. When A. J. P. Taylor looked into his first television camera, I doubt he thought about it, or worried. He believed he was being straightforward—it was only later that he appreciated the doubling of himself. Ed Murrow wanted to be trusted (perhaps he longed to trust himself), but he never lost that sultry actor's hesitation, for he had thought about what he was doing. He saw the gap opening in himself. And in seventy years or so—it is a key to modern times—we have become wary of the face. Look at the Checkers speech now and it may be hard to grasp that Richard Nixon believed what he was saying and was committed to his stance before the cameras. It's hard because we learned how two-faced the same man would become once he knew the challenge of being on television.

This is not just the plight of politicians, though it is a catastrophe of politics that we do not trust these people. We have seen too many faces striving for sincerity. Return to the look of *The Fugitive* for a moment, and one of the haunting charms in the series was that David Janssen was never quite "right." The narrative rested on the wronged innocence of Richard Kimble, but in the inescapable Janssen there was the placid face of an actor worn away by the task of looking sincere for hundreds of hours and having to mask an innate uneasiness. (Harrison Ford actually got outrage as Kimble in the 1993 movie.)

We have been sapped by our uncertainty: It comes from a lifetime of having to look at actors and abide by the dream that they are telling their truth, that they are authentic or sincere. Yet we know that actors make it up every time, and we have realized how like actors we are in our own everyday masquerade.

So many thousand hours of talking heads have taken their toll— think of the stamina it must require in a talk-show host or a president to keep going on and telling us a kind of truth about the weather in Burbank or how we got bin Laden at Abbotabad. In that light, it's easier to be impressed by the immense, taunting unknown in Johnny Carson, the man whose candor lay in wondering, "Well, maybe I'm a fake." It's like the mainstream of commercials that know the folly in asking us to believe anything. You can't hope to sell stuff now, unless you're tongue in cheek—the talking head is always crossing its fingers.

As I was pondering over this, an example came along that I honestly want to share with you. Harland David Sanders was born (probably) in 1890 in Indiana. He is an instructive American pioneer and a small fountainhead for television. He fought with the US Army in Cuba in 1906, having lied about his age. He worked on the railroads and took a law degree. But that career ended when he fought, physically, with a client. Then he sold insurance, ran a ferryboat, and went into the tire business. That got him a job running a service station in North Corbin, Kentucky. As people on the road stopped for gas, Sanders thought to serve them fried chicken and gravy. He had a local rival in that trade, but somehow or other that rival got convicted of murder, which gave Sanders a freer run.

The chicken business thrived. In 1935, the governor of Kentucky made Sanders an honorary colonel. He found new ways of cooking the chicken fast and let it be known that he had a "secret recipe." In time, he started franchising his operation and he traveled as its spokesman. He wore a white suit with a black string tie, white hair, and a white goatee, and he talked a little Kentuckian. By the early sixties there were 600 KFC outlets—you learned this at your parents' gravied plates—and there are 18,000 now. In fact, in 1964 Sanders sold the whole operation for $2 million, but he insisted on staying on as its spokesman and its godhead in commercials. He liked his image more than the chicken. Sometimes he criticized the very restaurants he was promoting—he was sued once for saying that his secret recipe gravy had turned to "wallpaper paste" in some places.

Sanders died in 1980, aged ninety. But you wouldn't know it. The white-suited fraud went on and on in advertising. Then in 2015, the company reckoned on a new trick for their stale ads. They determined that everyone by then knew the colonel was bogus—and beloved just because of that—so they hired actors to play the role and make fun of it—Darrell Hammond first and then Norm Macdonald. These ads won a lot of new attention, and some people took offense at the kidding. Like many great American issues, this is not resolved yet. But it is part of the talking head business, and I'll leave you with this chatroom entry, 5:57 P.M., October 18, 2015, from Kevin [all *sic*]:

I have to admit I didn't really appreciate the first round of commercials. But Norm has put on a little different spin. With the wink he gives us, he knows he's not the real deal and it is humerious and entertaining. Kind of takes you back when things we a little simpler. You have to put the right spin on it. I guess the advertising worked on me. We went out and picked up some chicken at KFC! Just sayin.

||||||||||||||||||||||||||||||

WHEN I CAME TO this chapter, I took it for granted that "talking heads" was a building block of television, or axiomatic. Moreover, it is still the case that whenever you turn on your machine you are likely to see heads that are speaking, or announcing, or lying, or acting…so many things that are not quite talking. That medium shot is in our understanding of nature and ourselves, like the full figure in a crucifix, or the full shot of Fred Astaire moving to music.

But seven decades of talking heads has changed us, or made us sour. The benign principle doesn't always apply. A newscaster tells us what has happened and I only know the account is inadequate. After several years of doing without Charlie Rose I came back and he was plodding along in the hope that being sensible made useful sense and masked the frequency with which he was promoting something…a show, a celebrity, or the idea of sense.

I watch a lot of television, but I can't recall the last time someone on the screen working at the general level of information (or talk) interested me, surprised me, or woke me up. Then Trump.

Do not run away with the hope that Donald Trump is absurd, insane, reckless, or not nice. Those verdicts are accurate enough, but they are so incidental to the context of what he has absorbed from television about talking to us. He may be ridiculous and irresponsible, but he is not a fool, and he is an inspired, mercurial handler of TV. He is a natural.

12

POLICEMAN, SAVE MY LIFE

"COPS AND ROBBERS," WE USED TO CHANT, hurrying to the movies. The mood was excited, for adventure was promised, with the serene safety net of knowing the cops were on our side. Wasn't there something almost ethnically unclean about robbers? The game left you knowing that cops were *our* guys, and so we thought until *The Godfather* (1972), which had only a single cop, corrupt, brutal, and stupid, and dead in his own pasta.

His name is McCluskey (Sterling Hayden), and he's a disgrace, even with that noble actor. So remember the better names from TV, the "guys": Sipowicz, Furillo, Benson (female, 100 percent proof, but a guy), and Stabler—we trust those cops, even if we seldom speak to real policemen. As a breed of hero, they have taken over from that lone rider cherished by Westerns. But they are ghosts such as real cops must envy. We were brave, out on the streets after dark, going to a movie; but in our own home we clung to law and order and a need for

As Z Cars *began, over 60 percent of UK households had no car.*

safety. So TV—out of respect for domestic reassurance?—seldom got into systemic police corruption, a subject familiar in movies for decades. In real life, it's not always cops or robbers; sometimes the same people are both. So cops may seem urban, modern, and gritty (they're written rough and modern), but strip those moods away and what's left is like a Western, filled with modest nobility and the blind probity of a Gary Cooper.

Take *Law & Order*. In that immense, dynastic enterprise, the detectives are always on. They seem to have left personal life far behind. They clear away the corpses and the outrages, and hand the evidence to the lawyers in plastic bags. They are weary, long-suffering, and without illusions—or with the few that their pay grade permits. They bear no grudge at good and evil leading to plea bargains, and cynical arrangements among the lawyers. They are in a city of fantastic pecuniary scale and malfeasance, where TV crime serves to stop us asking dangerous questions about larger crooked deals. So billions are appropriated in official redirection and ordinary privilege, yet these cops do their work, in danger, filth, and deceit, for maybe $90,000 a year, before tax. The contract in cop shows is very strange, and it resembles the couch philosophy that says: "I think the world may be very bad and scary, but I am on my couch, paid up for the month. So I will pretend that 'crime' (the *c* next to cancer) is entertaining, instead of something people may do to me. I know, it's weird having an elephant in the room, but he is kind of like a pet. He looks after me—doesn't he?"

A PROGRAM FULL OF SIGHS, SHRUGS, AND WHAT-THE-HELL ATTITUDES.

Creator Dick Wolf's extensive franchise carries an air of dogged, weary thoroughness—it's a program full of sighs, shrugs, and what-the-hell attitudes. It *was* hard work, over decades, getting Wolf's net worth up to $350 million. One can imagine detectives Benson (Mariska Hargitay—$400,000 per episode) and Stabler (Christopher Meloni) dealing with cases as if moving heavy furniture. But once a corpse or a wrong is found, the routine solemn answering service can start—"In the criminal justice system, the people are represented by two separate yet equally important groups: the police who investigate crime and the district attorneys who prosecute the offenders. These are their stories." Mike Post's music dawns (it's an optimistic, cleansing theme) and we're off on another episode of the franchise that might still make "law enforcement" an attractive career and a security blanket for uneasy citizens. I put "law enforcement" in quotes just to give a nudge: We like to assume our law is enforced, as opposed to handled.

For some of us, the show has been there most of our lives, so we regard it with a mix of fondness and disbelief. It seemed so real once, so fabricated now. The grungy disorder of the city is so swiftly wrapped up in plot; and the wildness in human nature and the savage economic and racial dysfunction of our

"MY NAME'S FRIDAY. I'M A COP."
—JACK WEBB ON *DRAGNET*

society are neatly repackaged as *Law & Order*. Isn't it pretty to think that's how justice works? Unsolved crimes rarely get on the show. Failed cops seldom work as entertainment.

From the vantage of today, you might think that the police have always been a staple of television. That's not quite so, and it's why *Dragnet* (1951–59) was so decisive, as well as an early indicator that NBC would be associated with police procedurals. Like many TV shows of the fifties, *Dragnet* came from radio, but Jack Webb (producer, director, and lead actor) saw Los Angeles as a wide-open setting for a tribute to the police. (Sixty years later, its views of that lost LA are the most intriguing part of the show.) The show talked about presenting "your police force" in an educational spirit. Most people then had little idea how real police functioned, so hope filled the gap. In fact, *Dragnet* was so locked in a hard-boiled idiom that it soon prompted parody. Sergeant Joe Friday (played by Webb) was "just a cop," without a surrounding life or actorly attitude. He was novel but hardly interesting. He was dedicated to "the facts" of a case and never doubted their existence. The terse authority and no-nonsense cult were devoured. The show was steadily in the top 5 and sometimes it played to 48 percent of the audience. It won one of the first Emmys (best mystery, action, or adventure program), and in its emphatic music, its interrogatory format, and in the drained hawkish affect of Webb himself it is still instantly recognizable as "early TV." It's like James Ellroy under heavy sedation.

Naked City started in 1958, and young people today have never heard of it. But it was among the most successful twenty-five shows of the day, which included ten Westerns, from *Gunsmoke*, *Wagon Train*, and *Have Gun—Will Travel* (the three most watched shows in the country, with 35 ratings and above) to *Zane Grey Theater*, *The Texan*, and *Cheyenne* (all over 25). It's not that cops and crime were missing from the American scene. But television was averse to real-life violence and afraid of glorifying criminal behavior. Gangster films had been vetoed during the war, to boost civic morale. Jack Webb had been wary of handling guns on screen. Many of the Westerns were versions of a law-and-order show, and their gunplay—from history, encoded in myth, and steadfastly conservative—seemed safe or inoffensive. The gun came with the horse and was as loyal. To suggest that the actual Americana of the fifties was threatened with crime was more than the medium or its advertisers wanted to hear. *Dragnet* rarely examined criminal personality or the socioeconomic pressure within crime; it favored routine, systematic rectitude.

In Britain, there was a pioneering police show that was deeply respectable and a genteel promotional tool for the police. In 1950, there had been a successful British movie, *The Blue Lamp* (that lamp was the symbol and logo of policing), in which a decent, amiable, and unarmed copper, PC George Dixon, played by national favorite Jack Warner, had been shot and killed by a young thug—played by the very polished Dirk Bogarde.

In 1955, through the agency of the writer Ted Willis, the BBC resurrected Dixon for a series, *Dixon of Dock Green*, that would be built around PC Dixon and his work at a suburban London police station. Dixon was a cozy figure, almost a parish priest. He introduced every story with a little chat—"Evening all," he'd say—and he was surely intended to make young viewers feel good about policemen. This was underlined by the 6:30 time slot on Saturday evenings: It was family fare. The show was never more than folksy fluff, yet people remarked on its realism. It defies belief now that it lasted until 1976, by which time Jack Warner was eighty and hardly mobile. By then, many British policemen

THE SHOOTING WAS MORE REALISTIC THAN ANYTHING SEEN BEFORE.

were armed (because of the Irish troubles), and the public was aware of police corruption and brutality, things unimaginable in 1955.

Long before 1976, British attitudes to their police had been revolutionized by *Z Cars* and its successor, *Softly, Softly*. *Z Cars* began on the BBC in 1962. It understood that a lot of crime could be linked to poverty or disadvantage. The British show was created by Troy Kennedy Martin and Allan Prior, and it gave up Dixon's pedestrian beat for pairs of policemen who used cars to patrol the Merseyside area. That was fresh, and in 1962 four young men were forcing Liverpool into world consciousness. The shooting was more realistic than anything seen before, and for the sake of urgency, the studio scenes—at the station, for instance—were shot live. The series was acclaimed, and it had an audience of 16 million an episode from a population of only 52 million. It made a household figure of the actor Stratford Johns, who played Inspector Barlow, an abrasive, less than fully honest, and far from Dixonian boss. The show explored the life of real and often minor criminals—much of the material was domestic—and it pioneered an understanding of the stresses felt by the police themselves, surrounded by dishonesty, violence, and the pressure to be above criticism. The writer John Hopkins was key to the show—he

Jeremy Kemp in Z Cars

wrote well over fifty episodes—and he was fascinated by the cop who turns nasty and rogue. The seeds of a good film called *The Offence* (1973, directed by Sidney Lumet and written by Hopkins), in which Sean Connery's copper kills a suspected rapist (Ian Bannen), were in the TV show.

Z Cars never played in the United States, though *Naked City* was seen in Britain. As someone who lived with both shows, I think *Z Cars* felt better and truer to life in the early 1960s. Not that *Naked City* should be forgotten. It was created by Bert Leonard and Stirling Silliphant (one of the most energetic and inventive writers in American television). In fact, the model for the show was the 1948 movie *The Naked City*, directed by Jules Dassin and produced by Mark Hellinger, much of it shot on location according to the studious neorealistic aspirations of the postwar years. The movie had spoken of there being five million stories in the naked city, but by the time Silliphant got to work, that had to be upped to eight. A lot of the TV series was shot on the streets, and in actors like John McIntire, Horace McMahon, and Harry Bellaver an attempt was made to keep the cops working-class and unglamorous. The word "gritty" was heard. On the other hand, the model-like Paul Burke was also one of the cops, and he had Nancy Malone as a girlfriend (an appealing actress who would go on to be a producer and the first female vice president at Twentieth Century Fox Television).

Naked City was discontinued in September 1963, just over two months before that day when the police and the nation were suddenly naked and stricken. That was only part of a wider cultural change.

Jack Webb as Joe Friday

Movie censorship was breaking down to concede sex and violence such as the screen had barred for decades. Television was more cautious than the movies, but as the sixties advanced, it could not ignore a new dimension of violence— like Jack Ruby shooting Lee Harvey Oswald live in a police station in Dallas. There were assassinations of public figures; the Manson gang raided a secluded property on Cielo Drive in the Los Angeles hills and murdered pregnant actress Sharon Tate in February 1969; there was violence in the South and on city streets in the North; above all, there was Vietnam, sometimes thought of as a police action. Not all of this was criminal, but most of it required police and a troubled definition of their role that put their behavior and American power in critical focus. There was the new possibility that cops and crooks might not be white.

Among the other police shows crowding in, there were two set in San Francisco: *The Lineup* (1954–60) and *The Streets of San Francisco* (1972–77). Only the latter is remembered, and that because of the Bay Area being known as a hotbed of liberation, and because of the flamboyant presence of a young Michael Douglas, teamed with a veteran cop played by Karl Malden. So where did *Hill Street Blues* come from, and who knew it could be as good as it was when its two creators, Jeffrey Bochco and Michael Kozoll, were reluctant to do the show?

BY THE LATE SEVENTIES, RESPECTABLE MIDDLE CLASS AMERICA WAS INCREASINGLY AFRAID OF CRIME ON THE STREETS.

Brandon Tartikoff was only thirty-one when he was appointed head of entertainment at NBC, but he was an old-fashioned showman in the vein of Irving Thalberg, Darryl Zanuck, David O. Selznick—and Fred Silverman. He was hired to have ideas for programming, and NBC was then third among the three networks—television was still a board game for ABC, NBC, and CBS. His astonishing success was an example for his type of executive in an era when such bosses flourished.

Tartikoff wanted a police series—no one knows why, except that the cops had worked before, and by the late seventies respectable, middle-class America was increasingly afraid of crime on the streets and hopeful about the prowess and integrity of the police. To be alive and alert in the United States was to feel the political implications in "crime." It was also easy to believe that the "reality" of cop life had scarcely been touched on in earlier shows. Tartikoff joined NBC in 1971 and would take over leadership there from Fred Silverman in 1980. He would make a good partnership with the next head of NBC,

Grant Tinker, the cofounder of MTM, the production company that had delivered *The Mary Tyler Moore Show* (1970–77) to CBS, consistent in the ratings and as an award winner.

Tinker asked Bochco and Kozoll to furnish a cop show, to create it, and they started to write *Hill Street Blues* (1981–87). The assignment went against their grain at first, but they stuck at it. They envisioned an ensemble show, with the station as its heart and a family of actors all working at about the same weight. They wanted several stories going on at the same time. They may have been affected by the ensemble movies of Robert Altman (*Nashville* especially). They may have seen or heard a little of *Z Cars*—*Hill Street* resembles it in many ways.

They chose to set it in a generic American city, not a particular locale. They wanted a mobile handheld camera and overlapping talk, and they wanted drama and humor mixed in so fast you never quite knew what was happening. They saw the station house as the locker room for a team, with oddballs, eccentrics, aberrants even, but a team we might want to belong to. It was the assumption that you can't do a successful TV show about the police without being on their side. Will there ever be a cop show that sees past the imperative of the "side," or recognizes that we ask for the impossible with our police? There's always a lurking question in cop shows, beyond reach or the attempt at reaching: Is crime natural in humans, or is it the result of our socioeconomic flaws? If it's the latter, the cops are into politics.

Hill Street had two black actors (Michael Warren and Taurean Blacque) and one Latino (René Enriquez). There were even women. Betty Thomas was a blonde in a blue uniform. Barbara Bosson (Mrs. Bochco at the time) played the ex-wife of Captain Frank Furillo (Daniel J. Travanti); Barbara Babcock was the florid love interest for Sergeant Phil Esterhaus (Michael Conrad); and Veronica Hamel played the one lawyer in the show, Furillo's new romance—sometimes it seemed possible they were having sex, if only to ease the pressures of the job. *Hill Street Blues* played at 10:00 P.M., and there were innocent notions that that was a safe time—whatever "safe" is. Television was still secure in the dream that kids watched at certain hours, and when they were allowed to. The inner threat—that domesticity had been

invaded and occupied by a barbarian force (or an amiable elephant)—
is still being struggled with.

Until Conrad died, Sergeant Esterhaus was the rock to the show
and its voice. As desk sergeant he would do an outline of the day's
events, ending in a soft-spoken but heartfelt "Let's be careful out
there." We felt that advice was intended for the cops, the city, the law,
and us, the citizenry. As a gentle urging that our American systems
could work decently, despite compromise, confusion, and human
nature, it was on a par with a later hit show, *The West Wing*
(1999–2006).

The audience enjoyed the comradeship, the characters, and the
actors: Television seldom strays far from likeable people, and that
curse has smothered intelligence and candor in many politicians. The
show was well reviewed, but it did not thrive. By intent, the narrative
was fragmented and difficult, and thirty years of television fiction had
trained us in story lines that were comically tidy and predictable. *Hill
Street Blues* was pushing against resistance and simplicity, and when
it was renewed after its first season it had the lowest ratings of any
renewed series. But it was gambling on its vision and on the rigor of
the writing. Not for the first or last time, audiences felt this precinct
might be "real." Bochco and Kozoll themselves wrote 144 episodes:
They have never done better work. Other names with writing credits
would loom large one day in television history. Jeffrey Lewis wrote 84
episodes; David Milch did 63; Mark Frost did 35; and Walon Green
(a movie writer) did 11. It became an envied job: David Mamet and
Bob Woodward squeezed their way into an episode each. A novice
named Dick Wolf wrote 8.

In only one season did *Hill Street Blues* make it into the top twenty-
five shows: 1982–83. But four years in a row, from 1981 to 1984, it
won the Emmy for outstanding drama series, and eventually acting
Emmys went to Daniel J. Travanti (twice), Barbara Babcock, Michael
Conrad, Bruce Weitz, and Betty Thomas. Those prizes encouraged the
word of mouth on a spectacularly different show in a medium beset by
staleness and the attempt to pass off the archaic as fresh (fabrications
like *The Love Boat*, *The A-Team*, and *Magnum, P.I.* were all very popular then). In those years, *Hill Street* was whipped in the ratings by

such shows as *Dallas*, *Dynasty*, *The Cosby Show*, and *Cagney & Lacey*. But something significant was happening. The top shows of the seventies—like *All in the Family, Happy Days*, and *Laverne & Shirley*—had had ratings in the thirties. But in the eighties, most top shows had slipped to 28, 26, 25. Only *The Cosby Show* consistently kept its head above the 30 line; by 1989–90, that was still the top show, but at 23.1. The following year it was *Cheers*, at 21.3. Was the audience bored, or was the television set beginning to offer so many alternatives that being top meant living at a lower altitude? In its "difficulty" and its appetite for human variety, naturalism, and a greater sense of thematic danger, *Hill Street Blues* was a harbinger of cable. HBO had been formed in 1972. It was still only a toddler ten years later, but it would be an answer to questions very few had yet thought to formulate.

NO SYMBOL OF TELEVISION IS MORE DATED THAN *TV GUIDE*.

I am trying to outline the history of a crowded medium while picking on a few shows and exploring what they and their genres meant. This has to be the way, for one of the most pervasive things about television is its mix of order and untidiness. Nothing illustrates that more than the way a choice among three or five or even ten channels was getting out of hand. No symbol of television in the late seventies and eighties is more dated than *TV Guide*, the weekly publication that made a fortune by letting a viewer know all that was playing. In the sixties and seventies, it was the most widely used magazine in the country. But the prospect was becoming plain: The viewing choice was expanding so fast, your show might be over before you'd found it.

Hill Street Blues was outstanding television, perhaps great in its day—the first half of the 1980s. I watched it with pleasure; I regretted missing an episode. But do we want to see it again? The seven-season show came out on boxed-set DVDs in April 2014. It had gone into syndication once, but after that it was hard to see. I'm not sure how the boxed set fared; how easy would it be to persuade someone not born when the show played to sit down for…140 hours? The actors, so familiar then, are not current. The language and action could seem tame. And who has time for *Hill Street Blues* in an age that is supposed (with reason) to be golden for long-form television drama? Can one hold Frank Furillo and Walter White in the palm of the same hand, or in the cockpit of shared fiction? Will *Breaking Bad* seem as compelling in 2042?

Still, the idea of looking at some of *Hill Street* is tempting, whereas revisiting *Cagney & Lacey* (1981–88) is harder to credit. But that was an important series, well made and regularly more successful than *Hill Street*. Barbara Corday, a writer, had read Molly Haskell's landmark film-studies book *From Reverence to Rape*, first published in 1974. She had talked to Haskell, who told her there had never been a female buddy movie. Couldn't there be one in the emerging era of feminism? Corday had set out to write a movie (it had the working title *Newman & Redford*) but it got nowhere. She told her boyfriend, television producer Barney Rosenzweig. One thing led to another and, with Barbara Avedon as her partner, Corday turned the idea into what would be *Cagney & Lacey* for CBS. It had two women cops, one a careerist, the other a working mom—they ended up as Sharon Gless and Tyne Daly, and both won Emmys. Yet all this came after CBS had softened what seemed at first like an aggressive feminist edge.

A LONDON WHERE RACE, SEXISM, AND POVERTY ARE OVERCAST LIKE THE WEATHER.

How could that concept be denied when television was greedy for any social trend it could turn into likeable people? How could anyone fail to see that *Cagney & Lacey* was light years ahead of *Police Woman* (1974–78), a modest hit and one of the first shows with camp undertones, in which Angie Dickinson was an undercover cop with a jazzy wardrobe—she was always having to pose as molls, dames, and hookers.

The gap between that show's Pepper Anderson and Jane Tennison seems greater than thirteen years and more than the shift from a sleek, desolate Los Angeles to a London where race, sexism, and poverty are an overcast like the weather. *Prime Suspect*, originated and written at first by Lynda La Plante, would run seven seasons over a span of fifteen years (1991–2006)—there was a hiatus when Helen Mirren feared she was risking being typecast. Made for Granada and shown on ITV in Britain, *Prime Suspect*'s seasons never went over five hours, and it had a distinct dramatic closure. That was a challenge on any well-written series: If it was drama and a story, didn't it need to come to a climax? But if it was a television series, shouldn't it go on forever? La Plante liked the idea of a drama stretched out over several nights, a possibility the television business had always resisted.

So *Prime Suspect* felt like an extended but contained movie, though not because of tedium. It was tightly written, well shot, and it turned a fine actress into an international institution. Mirren was sexy without effort or camera worship; that was less the point than her sour intelligence and smothered resentment. She didn't care to be glamorous, and that let her become the sharpest woman cop we have ever had, or simply one of the most believable. Tennison had her own life, worn ragged and compromised by the duties of her job. She harked back to the realism of *Z Cars* and was one more sign that British television had a daring harder to find in America. With money from WGBH in Boston, the show played on PBS's *Masterpiece Theatre* format.

Yes, I am indeed headed back to *Law & Order*, but if you are a television fanatic you will know already how many police shows I am overlooking—and which I can hardly remember. But there are three more that have to be assessed, and they make clear how much of a family-tree structure has operated in this area. Brandon Tartikoff was still head of programming at NBC and he was as impressed as most people by the success of MTV, the cable channel launched in 1981 to play music videos—you have to accept that for more than twenty years rock and roll had got along without accompanying videos. Tartikoff saw that kids had made a habit out of MTV, and its slick, hectic style had affected much of television, not least its commercials. Why not a cop show that felt like MTV? he suggested.

The memo was taken up by Anthony Yerkovich, who had written thirty-four episodes of *Hill Street Blues*. He became the creator of *Miami Vice* (1984–90) and the most regular writer on the show, though he soon yielded creative control to the executive producer, Michael Mann. Mann was already a proven movie director and now, for the first time, a television show would be famous for a directorial look and its stress on visual and aural style, or varnish. Mann was not once credited as director, but all the named directors attested to the control he had exercised over color, the skidding sheen of lights after dark, the clothes, the cars, and the pounding music (run by composer Jan Hammer). There were pink flamingos and a turquoise ocean. Every woman was a knockout, every guy a dude. The show also marked a departure in violence, with the clear suggestion that Latinos were well dressed but cruel—this was a trope introduced in Brian De Palma's influential *Scarface (*1983), also set in Miami.

Miami was of special interest in America then, because of the influx of Cubans and their music and also because of its assertive modern architecture and the fashion shoots being done in Miami Beach's boutique Deco hotels. Tartikoff's wish had been realized. Few remember the stories in the show, but its look had influenced the culture as a whole, and the techno decadence inspired the various *CSI* series yet to come, where voluptuous women gaze into vivid wounds. Dick Wolf was there again as one of the writers and a producer on *Miami Vice*. The two lead cops on the show had been talked about as Jeff Bridges and Nick Nolte, but this was the tag end of an attitude in which movie stars disdained television. So Don Johnson was resurrected (his has been a career of comebacks) and paired with Philip Michael Thomas, with Edward James Olmos as their iconically cool or impassive superior. A lot of rock singers (like Sheena Easton), boxers (Roberto Duran), and spurious celebrities (G. Gordon Liddy) passed by in the slipstream of TV gravure. It seems comical now, but so what? That's all too late; the show was lethally suave in its few years—the era of crack cocaine and Reagan's forgetful work in Latin America. I'm not saying anyone on the show was on drugs, but they acted as if they were, and this impression was assisted by the premature feeling of film stock turning into something digital. *Miami Vice* won Emmys for sound editing, cinematography, and art direction, and for Edward James Olmos, and in its second season it rose in popularity. It soon slumped, but it made a fortune for Miami and a host of designers and dealers. If you wanted to be fatalistic, you could say there had never been a television show so co-opted by the slippery ethos and the

WHY NOT A COP SHOW THAT FELT LIKE MTV?

moneyed glow of commercials. The title of the show might refer to a police department, but it also imagined a tourist attraction—like "Miami Nights."

The focus of police life moved back to New York in 1993 with the start of *NYPD Blue*—and I'm coming to that. But in the general way of things and with a basic understanding of network scheduling, it's still hard to believe that when *NYPD Blue* began at ABC, on Sep-

Sipowicz

tember 21, 1993, it came only eight months after *Homicide: Life on the Street* had started at NBC. I'm sure *Homicide* was a reaction against *Miami Vice*: It opted for Baltimore as if to warn us how many dull, impossible cities there are in the United States. And as so often before, it told us and itself that no one had done cops for real before. Actual cops must have sleepless nights as their elusive reality is hunted down by television. That's a joke, but consider how television has altered the way police people present themselves in daily life.

Homicide was inspired by a first-class documentary book, *Homicide: A Year on the Killing Streets* (1991), by David Simon, who had been a *Baltimore Sun* reporter. Its precepts were that being a cop was a job, as dull as any other, and nothing to get excited about; that Baltimore was an unalterably African-American city; and that cops were losing ground in a struggle for social improvement that politicians were abandoning. *Miami Vice* surely spurred people to try a weekend getaway in southern Florida. *Homicide* did nothing for tourism in Baltimore. So NBC steadfastly applied itself to making something pedestrian and uneventful? Not exactly. Brandon Tartikoff had left NBC in 1991, but the network had not given up his notion that cops were exciting.

Simon created the show, along with Paul Attanasio: They were credited as writers on all 122 episodes. But other people had a large say, and a claim to creatorship: the writer Tom Fontana; executive producer Barry Levinson; and producers Gail Mutrux and James Yoshimura. Of course, "creator" is a heady title in most fields (the movies have not encouraged it), but by the early nineties it was clear that it brought fortunes if the created television show was a hit. *Homicide* was shot in Baltimore, and a lot of the time it was done on handheld 16mm. It had lead roles for black actors—Andre Braugher, Clark Johnson, Toni Lewis, and Yaphet Kotto. In Richard Belzer, Jon Polito, and Melissa Leo it favored excellent actors who seldom looked starry. And because these cops failed often enough and reflected on a city of underprivilege and institutional hard luck, *Homicide* was the most left-wing cop show the country had ever had. It soon had Peabody Awards to mark that effort.

But the show was not a popular success: We have shown no inclination to stay with stories in which the cops fail our hopes for them. From the outset, *Homicide* heard talk of cancelation. It won Emmys early for writing and directing (Fontana and Levinson), and it got exceptional reviews. But it never went higher than number 24 in the ratings and was usu-

THIRTY YEARS EARLIER HE MIGHT HAVE STAYED A STRUGGLING NOVELIST/POET.

ally in the sixties, with an audience of about 8 million, or up to 50 percent of what *NYPD Blue* would get.

The initial thrust for that other 1993 debut came from Jeffrey Bochco, and in obvious respects it was a sequel to *Hill Street Blues* and its celebration of community in a police station. But Bochco had a co-creator, David Milch, and the longer it went on, the more that intriguingly flawed writer was responsible for the show. Milch was forty-eight in 1993. He had been to Yale and the Iowa Writers' Workshop; he was a published poet. Twenty or thirty years earlier he might have stayed a struggling novelist/poet, but now he was becoming a success in television. He had been a writer on *Hill Street Blues*, and he was drawn to cops whose own lives were in ruins as they tried to maintain law and order. Milch was impulsive, with addictive tendencies, a gambler, and a producer likely to throw out a script (his own even) and go with an improvisation. And so the psyche of a writer would take over a hit show.

It was intended that there would be two lead cops as the show began: John Kelly was of Irish descent, the son of a cop, a straight arrow, and as handsome and alluring as David Caruso could make him—at that time, Caruso was set on making a career as a movie star. But Kelly would become involved with a cop with crime links (well played by Amy Brenneman). When she killed her Mafia lover, Kelly went against the law to protect her. This was good drama, but it was also in response to Caruso's ambition, and pressure to write him out of the show. That meant the attention shifted to his partner, Andy Sipowicz (Dennis Franz), a figure cherished by Milch. Sipowicz was not handsome, or house-trained. He was alcoholic, racist, homophobic, sleazy; he was Archie Bunker with a gun. As Kelly departed, Sipowicz picked up a new partner, Bobby Simone, played by Jimmy Smits—Puerto Rican, very good-looking, a subtler actor than Caruso, and a crowd favorite after *L.A. Law* (1986–92).

NYPD Blue was a deserved success, in the top 20 in its first few seasons and reaching as high as number 7 in 1994–95. As such, it played steadily to an audience in the 10–15 million range. It won the best drama Emmy for 1995, and Dennis Franz would collect the best actor award four times (still a record). There were many other Emmys for actors and writers, but the ensemble virtues depended on Sipowicz, who is one of the most complex characters in American television and a scumbag who over the years made grudging but plausible progress

HE WAS ARCHIE BUNKER WITH A GUN.

toward commitment and decency. He got into a romantic relationship; he became a father; he subdued many of his demons; he was promoted. Franz won the affection of his audience and he proved himself a fine actor, so it is curious that he has done very little since.

In the history of police shows for sure, and even American television as a whole, he was a rounded figure, tragic, or flawed yet noble in his persistence. He deserves to be seen in the company of Willy Loman, Michael Corleone, Saul Bellow's Herzog, Walter White…I am searching for female equivalents but having a hard time. Sipowicz was dramatically large yet horribly ordinary, unforgivable and unforgettable. Yes, he came through in the end, and that vindication might be looked on as fanciful. Not many men as self-destructive as he was avoid a bad end. But he was credible and enduring. In some ways, I'm content that Dennis Franz has not come back. It lets Sipowicz breathe in the imagination; it allows one to think that the actor had given his all and was exhausted. There are so few television characters who managed to stay with us as more than their clichés and catchphrases. Sipowicz lives, and I think he was as much a confession for David Milch as Walter White would be one day for Vince Gilligan.

At the millennium, "blue" had another usage that could be as muddled as Sipowicz. L. Brent Bozell III had formed an organization called the Parents Television Council (PTC). Bozell was conservative and Catholic, but liberal, agnostic parents understood what he was worried about. Television might have seemed once like a technological endorsement of family life, a means of education, frank discussion, and civic progress. But soon enough, kids had got their own TV sets and discussion had turned into horrid sniping, and the "content" was close enough to indecent, even if sometimes the language and the positions had to be explained to parents. That was not unlike the devices themselves, so if parents invested in a blocking device that could eclipse pornography after 10:00 P.M., they often required the kids' insolent skills to make the censoring work. All too often, the essential situation comedy of television, and the most rueful, was what the children were seeing and hearing.

In 2003, the PTC published a report, "The Blue Tube: Foul Language on Prime Time Network TV." There were First Amendment devotees who mocked the alarm, but no one could contradict the numbers in the report: "Foul language increased overall during every timeslot between 1998 and 2002. Foul language during the Family Hour [8:00–9:00 P.M.] increased by 94.8 percent…and by 109.1 percent during the 9:00 P.M. ET/PT time slot."

It wasn't only language that troubled the PTC, and in fact, in most of the pornography that the council had not quite caught up with, the participants were diligently silent, except for moans and sighs and slapping. "Blue" in the title of the report was mindful of *NYPD Blue*, where many "bullshits" were counted. Worse still, the show seemed to think that cops and crooks had sex, quite a lot of it, for which nudity was often a prerequisite. There were episodes of *NYPD Blue* that incurred FCC fines, though some of those were overruled on appeal. The show had a reputation for being "dirty" as well as blue (and that may have persuaded twelve-year-olds to stay up into the 10:00 P.M. slot when they had finished their four hours of homework and reading Emily Dickinson with their parents). But how could one have Andy Sipowicz as a character without the possibility of dirt?

It's not a frivolous segue to say that *Law & Order* is seldom dirty or blue. That's a sign of how circumspect, businesslike, and conservative it has been. Dick Wolf was forty-one in 1988, a graduate of the University of Pennsylvania who had worked in advertising and in Hollywood screenwriting before he got attached to *Hill Street Blues*. He was ready to move, and he had the idea of a show in which every episode began with cops and ended with lawyers. In forty-eight minutes, and with "gritty" realism and legal expertise, a case was settled. He found support for the idea at Universal Television, but the scheme was turned down by Fox (Barry Diller's mistake) and CBS before Brandon Tartikoff and Warren Littlefield allowed that it might work at NBC.

With recurring characters and actors, it might seem like an ensemble show, but its true subject was the process indicated in the title, along with the tacit assumption that law and order worked (if not quite as thoroughly as the show). *Law & Order* has always been a formidable study in efficiency, with so much plot to be conveyed in so short a time, with everything clear, tidy, and credible. It works, and if I sound disappointed or let down, it's only because that functioning is not enough. That famous *ker-chunk* music that separates scenes is not moody or atmospheric, but it's like a smooth gear change. The show is wild about the streets of New York, but never diverted by spontaneity or the inessential. Everything we see and hear is strictly necessary, and so character suffers. Long before the end (and we are talking twenty-five years for the larger franchise of sequels) we conclude that cops are functionaries in a positive process. The trial proceedings do not always get or believe in a "just" result, but there is a result, and it admits the invisible plea bargaining less often than it now occurs in life. So there is nostalgia in the show, for cops who get the job done and lawyers who, while being far from Perry Mason, can say "Case closed." The conservatism of the show implies that we have the best system possible and that it is worth enjoying. It's no surprise that Rudy Giuliani and Michael Bloomberg appeared on the show and gave it mayoral endorsement.

The show made its debut in September 1990, and the original *Law & Order* ran for twenty years, putting it second only to *Gunsmoke* (1955–75) in live-action longevity. *Gunsmoke* feels like an antique now, but it's close to *Law & Order* in its adherence to formula and its support of the status quo. Yes, the franchise has opened up problems in the law and in police work in a perfunctory way, and it has often taken off from real cases. But its effectiveness in shooting, editing, and acting should not conceal its indifference to character and explored experience. This is only instinct, but I suspect the show plays especially well to the elderly, to those living alone, and to those who hope that the law and order of America itself can go without question or undue criticism. If you have serious doubts about the structure of our society, our economy, or our way of life—in short, if you are thinking of change—I'm not sure this is the show for you. And as it plays in marathons in syndication, with one show overlapping the end of another, its wall-to-wall feeling can be stifling. The system works, but there is not time for life. The sprawl of *NYPD Blue* seems revelatory in comparison.

I WATCH IT WHEN I'M TIRED AND ANXIOUS.

Yet I watch it when I'm tired and anxious—this aspect of television has been manifest in many shows, but not often in one that touches on ugly crimes. The virtues are obvious. The speed and tightness feel exemplary in an age when movies have forgotten those habits. The acting is as good and brisk as you can expect, granted the superficiality of the writing. When it began, George Dzundza and Chris Noth were the cops; Dann Florek was their chief; Michael Moriarty and Richard Brooks were the district attorneys; and Steven Hill was their unsmiling boss.

Ker-chung—there was turnover. Some actors fretted at the formula. Research said the show needed more women. Jerry Orbach arrived as the archetypal sour cop (pre-written and phoned in), until he died. S. Epatha Merkerson took over from Florek. Sam Waterston became the district attorney, Jack McCoy, the liberal but pragmatic heart of the show, buoyed by a line of pretty young assistants—Jill Hennessy, Carey Lowell, and Angie Harmon—with whom he had no time or inclination to flirt, even if they were dressed (very tastefully) at a wardrobe level beyond what real assistant attorneys could afford. The cops and the lawyers had little private life, and that meant they hardly seemed to need it. A subtle suggestion was in the air: that if you had no private or inner life, you might be more law-abiding.

Dick Wolf might say that the largest spin-off, *Law & Order: Special Victims Unit*, was a response to any suggestion that the original show was unduly clean. He said he had been inspired by the Jennifer Levin/Central Park case of 1986 to get into cases that involved sexual crimes. It was in keeping with that aim that the two detectives—played by Mariska Hargitay and Christopher Meloni—were

the couple in the entire franchise with the least resolved chemical feeling. You felt that they might get at each other, if an episode gave them time, and Detective Stabler was sometimes unhinged by the nature of the crimes he was pursuing. In 2016, Hargitay is still with the show, which stands at 389 episodes. She is also the only one of its regular actors to win an Emmy (in 2006), though that does scant justice to the legion of players who had their moment on the show. *Law & Order* has been in the hallowed tradition of having guest stars (often very famous) to do their showy bit for twenty minutes or so. Several of them have won guest Emmys on *SVU*—Amanda Plummer, Leslie Caron, Cynthia Nixon, Ellen Burstyn, Ann-Margret (the show took that Emmy five times in six years).

Dick Wolf has said that he and everyone else try to keep the standard as high as possible. Why not? That's a mantra for McDonald's, Sony Entertainment, Walmart, and Congress, too. So long as you recognize the possibility of quality, you have to keep it high. But suppose that much TV actually functions in terms of presence, rather than quality: We don't think to say, "Oh, that's good electric light today." In all *Law & Order* series as of December 10, 2014, there had been

1,062 episodes. That includes *SVU, Criminal Intent* (which pairs Vincent D'Onofrio and Kathryn Erbe, and where frequently something startling seems about to happen between them—but not yet), *Trial by Jury*, and *LA*. There have been what are called "iterations" in Britain, France, and Russia. There are video games derived from the franchise. It goes on and on, and I sometimes dream of waking in the night with Ice-T in my head delivering some one-liner of plot information, like "Warn the Archduke!"

Meanwhile, in 2014–15, America the nation faced increasing problems of racial hostility, profiling, and excessive violence in its own police forces, as well as our irrational expectations where cops are concerned, expectations boosted by TV. Successively over the years, we have congratulated a new "realism" in police shows. But by now we have to admit our fond and unrealistic regard for these shows, which have been advertisements for policing and an encouragement to believe that we do have "law and order." Police shows (for all their quality in acting and writing) overlook the structures of disorder, in which the poor are punished for stealing from the rich while the opposite transaction goes undiscussed. Most police shows smother the chance of political discourse. We have talked about reforming the police so long, we may be weary of the hope—hope can wear you down as much as futility. There is a terrible peace in giving up hope.

Clearly, the police have to continue, whatever drastic or surreal reforms we entertain. (Make the police the official bad guys, licensed for crime, trained and equipped, unionized, and very tough on freelancers who try to intrude, but taxed at 22.5 percent so long as they keep the whole thing organized on a "we only kill our own" basis. Face it: Organized crime is an appealing concept, and an eternal dream of crime on screen. That was vital to the novelty of *The Godfather*.)

I'M NOT SURE WHETHER ANY POLICE SHOW HAS EQUALED THE LOCAL REALITY OR THE POETIC HORROR WITHIN *RED RIDING*.

It's the raw spontaneity of violence that we flinch from. So the longer a cop show persists, the more comfortable and beyond reproach it becomes, and the more artificial the crimes seem. Thus, so many police shows begin to reveal themselves as glorified commercials for order. Which leaves a lot to be said for short form and its insistence on damage and closure. I'm not sure whether any police show has equaled the local reality or the poetic horror within *Red Riding*.

This was three related films, played on Britain's Channel 4 in 2009. It was created for television by Tony Grisoni and David Peace and drawn from four novels by Peace that refer to real criminal events in Yorkshire, but which are written in a frenzy of disturbing psychological insight. It's the story of police efforts to track down or ignore a serial killer, stretched over several years, but it becomes a portrait of what motivates such a killer, what sentiments and self-interest guide the police (who want to "own the North"), and how all of this fits a part of England comprised of old and failed industrial centers on the edge of wild country. *Red Riding* never doubts the role of police corruption—or their abandoning of their own codes. The three films were directed by Julian Jarrold, James Marsh, and Anand Tucker. They are terrifying, and we feel in advance how far the characters are exposed to dramatic closure. They will not stay on forever.

That was one of the first television shows to find beauty in decay, desolation, and fraying cities surrounded by moorland—its influence on the first season of *True Detective* is clear. It was done in Yorkshire dialect, yet it played in America as a movie, and won high praise. It had exceptional performances from a cast that included Paddy Considine, Andrew Garfield, Sean Bean, David Morrissey, Rebecca Hall, Maxine Peake, and the uncannily frightening Peter Mullan. *Red Riding* was fiction and proud of it; it was also a fevered take on real crimes in Yorkshire that were known to many British viewers. It was the News as if told by Louis-Ferdinand Céline, and a scathing portrait of the police or of those elements in society that liked to be reassured by police presence.

Red Riding was a television event, as terrifying in its portrait of bureaucratic burial procedures as in its glimpse of murderous pathology. But it was antique in its assumption that "crime" overtook vivid human characters and worked itself out in narrative strategies Dickens would have understood. Remaining that old-fashioned was good television, and ruinously sentimental. It depicted a Yorkshire in which too much went unseen and unacknowledged. That worked, just as

Dickens always grasped the potency of incidents half lost in the past and then retrieved. But in that first decade of the twenty-first century, a technological portent was being ignored: Britain was becoming the society most subject to video and electronic surveillance, even in places as remote and seemingly wild as that part of Yorkshire.

The precinct station and the gang of cops, honored from *87th Precinct* (1961–62) to *Law & Order*, may not last. Cops see only so much. We now have camera and computer technology that can move the data as swiftly as it can track through the blood vessels in corpses. I am no enthusiast for the hi-tech CGI effects of *CSI: Crime Scene Investigation* (that's William Petersen and Jorja Fox) or *CSI: Miami* (that's David Caruso and several amazing pinup lab girls). But those shows testify to technology on the job. They are old hat already, because now we see that the computer is the best bloodhound, as well as the advised in-strument for the most sophisticated crime. Such things as mugging, actual physical robbery, and murder may come to seem as archaic as words like "footpad" and "highwayman." So much criminal fiction registers through the meek acceptance of attitudes to disorder or misdeeds that are as archaic as Joe Friday or George Dixon. For some time now, we have been in an age of "organized crime," whereby old criminal actions are reassessed as "business as usual." This is especially true in very large matters of financial conduct. As a whole, we are drawn to "organized crime" because it segregates it from the kind of nasty, violent things done—generally—by poor and deprived or insignificant citizens. So, if law itself becomes an embodiment of institutional unfairness, then criminal statistics can be categorized as "security lapses," "password errors," or "street altercations." Murder, that old favorite, is a weird, personal sport, so much more emotional or self-indulgent than the conscientious pursuit of fraud and social engineering.

THE NEWS, OR ISN'T THERE ANYONE?

WE STILL CALL IT "the News," not "a News" or plain "news," so we are left wondering what ideals that title and the capital "N" are clinging to; and how does that allegiance leave us ill-informed and vulnerable? There was an age of television—it was dominant from the sixties through the eighties—when many conscientious Americans were in the habit of watching the News at 6:00 P.M. (In Britain the News played at 9:00 P.M., in prime time.) Viewers were usually loyal to one network or newscaster: CBS and Walter Cronkite had an edge on esteem in an era when the News itself seemed to be gathering pace and becoming the institution of record that radio had been during the war.

The News on television was not as obvious as it seemed. If tonight's headlines are a coup in an African nation, an emerging but inscrutable scandal on Wall Street, and the death of X (she was beheaded very untidily by a fan or a terrorist), what does TV do? It has no camera crew in the African country, so it hustles together some stock footage to play behind a phone call from a journalist in the African capital who says it's unclear what is happening. Since financial scandals tend to be invisible, a few Wall Street scenes must suffice, with a talking head trying to explain the inexplicable—in *The Big Short*, Margot Robbie is enthroned in a bubble bath to explain one process. That done, she tells us briskly, "Now, fuck off." Which is not so far from the way expert opinion acquits itself on the News. And since you don't have—and don't want to show—X expiring, you throw together a 15-second obit and you have one of X's ex-husbands or managers saying what a princess she was.

It's not compelling, or as cogent or useful as radio or newspapers will manage. A lot of TV News is radio with vague illustration, or print under the handicap that we have given up reading. So TV develops an unspoken longing for televisual news—like the kind of camera-friendly disaster that speaks for itself.

In the sixties, there was *the* assassination and then the other killings; there was the space program, unfundable without its TV show; there was Civil Rights and an unruly younger generation; there would be rock and roll, drugs, an explosion in fashion and sexual liberty; there was Vietnam, the first TV war. Most 30-minute newscasts had more than enough material, and there were audiences—mature or middle aged—who needed reassurance or explanation as the mayhem was delivered. In time, "Watergate" would be called a crisis in constitutional government, but it was compelling entertainment, too. There must

HOW DOES THAT ALLEGIANCE LEAVE US ILL-INFORMED AND VULNERABLE?

have been TV executives who thanked God for the crisis and its startling viewing figures, even if they were Republicans. Calling the story "Watergate" won near universal recognition and simplified the need to understand it. We have lived with "gated" community scandals ever since.

But was it *the* News? Did it have time to keep up with "quiet" developing events and ideas in Iran or Afghanistan, say? Was it tracking the steady abuse of children in the Roman Catholic Church, since tidied away in *Spotlight*? Were we prepared for the final debacle in Vietnam? Did Cronkite know about global warming? Was there news of the computer age about to break? How often did the News admit that it was offering a convenient sampling, restricted by the posting of correspondents and camera crews? Wasn't the ideal behind the News that we, the people, were getting the whole story in a selection process that was judicious, fair-minded, and still not too far from omniscience? There might be blood, death, and riot on the News. There might be horror, where the footage was tempered to suit popular taste. But the News was handling it, and keeping it under control. There was no program called "The Chaos." There still isn't, but by now the Net's helpless coverage of *stuff* hardly needs it.

||||||||||||||||||||||||||||

IN BRITAIN, BY 1963, I had lived with television for several years, even though it only entered my family home in the late 1950s. I realize now what an archaic creature I was without TV, but I had the movies, radio, a lot of homework, sports, and girls. Television hadn't made itself essential.

On the evening of November 22 (I didn't know that date for sure then, but the knowledge now is fixed for life), the woman I was going to marry—her name was Anne—and I were walking through Chichester in West Sussex to have dinner with a friend. It was dark and cold and we held hands. We were so much in love. I think we got to the friend's house sometime around seven.

I HAD NEVER SEEN ANYONE KILLED ON LIVE TELEVISION BEFORE.

Does that fit? Dallas was on Central Time, six hours behind Greenwich Mean Time. The shooting in Dealey Plaza occurred at 12:30 P.M. local time. The motorcade was going to a big lunch, and we were looking forward to dinner.

When we got to the friend's house she was huddled at the radio (she didn't have a TV) and she told us what she knew about the shooting. Moments later we learned that President Kennedy was dead. Walter Cronkite had declared that on CBS in America—with a tear that some of us know as well as we recall Kennedy's flirty smile.

I was going to say this was a shock such as we had never known. But seeing ourselves on-screen has pushed us into dramatizing our experience—that is a big part of TV's imprint. Still, that November 22 was astonishing, terrible, and very frightening. In the next few days, I was what is called "glued to" the television. A shock on the set is like an earthquake: You don't sleep, waiting for the after-tremors. I can't remember where I was when I saw what I remember next. But it was one of the most unsettling things I have ever seen.

It was just after 11:00 A.M. Central Time at Dallas police headquarters on the twenty-fourth, Sunday morning. There was live coverage, with NBC serving as the network pool, and Lee Harvey Oswald was about to be transferred to the county jail. This was the first significant chance to see Oswald and wonder what he looked like. So Britain was watching, along with most of the world. Oswald wore a black sweater and he was urged forward by plainclothes policemen on either side. Then a man in a dark suit and a gray fedora hat came out of the crowd—there was an untidy mob of people in the basement as well as a television camera—and stuck his gun against Oswald's body. It was 11:21 A.M. and you could hear the shot on television. Oswald was pronounced dead in less than two hours. I had never seen anyone killed on live television before.

We had been stricken by the death of the president, yet many of us resisted early fears that it might have been part of a conspiracy, rather than the lone action of a troubled person. We wanted to feel sane about it, and to keep it no worse than a savage affront to security or reason. I preferred to see the assassination as an aberrational incident, and not part of a design. But when Jack Ruby shot Oswald I could not help but believe there was a script being worked out. This

was *News, the Movie*—I don't think I'd seen anything as immediate or decisive (outside sport)—but it was a conjuring of paranoid dread, too. I was excited and I felt urgently alive.

In England, it would have been just after five in the afternoon when Oswald was shot, and I believe I saw the shooting on a live feed, but it might have been a moment or so later. It felt live, and though Dallas was "far away," that distance of 4,750 miles seemed erased. More than I had ever done, I felt American, while seeing that that country was fermenting in melodrama.

The News is the attempt by the media to tell us "Keep in touch—the world's *hope* is for us all to know what's happening." And agree on it? Clearly and by necessity, the News is an edited and editorialized account of things that happen, things that are new. It tries to tell the story. But suppose the events resist story; suppose they are random or inexplicable. Then there is a risk that hope withers.

On September 11, 2001, something happened—and compared with the action of November 22, 1963, there's less doubt about what it was. The deeper burden of that news was how we would react to it, and that is still unfolding—and too untidy for any 30-minute *Nightly News*. Yet so many things happen that cannot make the News. On August 4, 1961, for instance, at the Kapi'olani Maternity & Gynecological Hospital in Honolulu (can we all sign on to this?), a baby was born: Barack Hussein Obama. It may not have been the most straightforward or promising human event, but it would prove to be news one day of a kind that no American should disparage. That is not taking sides in politics; it is just recognition that this was preparation for a momentous change if someone as humble, ill-starred, and underprivileged as Lee Harvey Oswald might become president. But the networks didn't notice, just as they didn't report ball games played that day, picnics, or lovers walking across town in the cold and the dark.

But ordinary ball games sometimes make the News. On July 11, 1962, before Obama's first birthday, moments from a day game at Wrigley Field, the Cubs against the Phillies, were beamed across the ocean, live, thanks to the Telstar satellite. We had this new reach, and fans at Wrigley, told of the coverage, stood up and waved at the camera in the lazy good nature of a seventh-inning stretch. I waved back, from London. This was new! And if it was mundane, it could help change your life. The possibility dawned that everyone could see everything at the same time.

Of course, a lot of news is unknowable, or out of sight. CBS didn't run daily footage from Auschwitz in the early 1940s. People who believed as devoutly in enhanced interrogation as Vice President Cheney were at pains to keep coverage of it off the News—though surely that footage would have shown how diligent and thorough our nation was in guarding liberty while preserving fear.

Whatever happened in Dallas, we have not made up our minds about it. Oliver Stone would provide a nightmare film, *JFK*, on what we might have seen, or the wonderings we could not get out of our heads. It was a movie less about journalism than paranoia. And that's a pressure on TV, which likes to provide an answer after thirty minutes. Aware of public unease, and a large society's longing for certainty, the US government investigated the

OF COURSE, A LOT OF NEWS IS UNKNOWABLE, OR OUT OF SIGHT.

shooting in the plaza. The Warren Report said Oswald had done it, on his senseless own. That did not hold. There were spreading doubts and anxieties, and some urgings to disprove the verdict and expose cant and cover-up in our law and order. That bitter confusion was a part of what we call the sixties and the seventies, and in 1978 a second committee of inquiry (the Stokes committee) decided there *had* been a conspiracy. By the end of the century, as many as 70 percent of Americans doubted the Warren Report's completeness. That number has declined somewhat since then, though over 50 percent are still unwilling to accept the official explanation. The doubts they feel—that *we* feel—are inseparable from the disquiet in the country, and it is part of this mood that the News has failed in its declared function. But no one ever guaranteed that a great mass medium would be reliable, reassuring, or free from a loneliness in which we have to struggle with conflicting truths and live for another day. More or less, a little over 50 percent of us now trust very little of what we are told. That is hardly a tribute to television News or the blur of breaking stories on the Web.

‖‖‖‖‖‖‖‖‖‖‖‖‖‖‖‖‖‖‖‖‖‖

IN 1964 IN VIETNAM, a fresh group of American advisers were arriving—a crew of seventy-five, including special strike forces named Jill St. John, Janis Paige, and Anita Bryant under the command of Bob Hope. This was one of fifty-seven USO tours Hope would lead in his lifetime, paid for by the Army with a large assist from NBC, who would film the tour for one more *Bob Hope Christmas Show*. A mission like Vietnam and the nation's confidence were still bound up with the reign of network television. Bob's being there with NBC suggested the war was under control. And it was during this tour that the Brinks Hotel in Saigon was blown up, killing two and wounding sixty-three. Hope and his party missed that explosion by just a few minutes. Years later it was revealed that they had been the intended target of the bomb. The Vietcong had felt the need to get on American television.

At the Bien Hoa Air Base, wearing a baseball cap and carrying a golf club, Hope strolled onto the open-air stage to an outpouring of applause and affection—this was years before GIs in Vietnam would boo Hope. He went into his stand-up routine, always the fruit of several writers and Hope's cutthroat timing. He had a string of jokes before he came to this: "I asked Secretary McNamara if we could come here." Then came the Hope pause—for several generations, that wicked delay and his shifting gaze were in our DNA. "He said, 'Why not? We've tried everything else.'"

Five thousand troops burst out laughing—it's still a funny line, and there's no rapture like that when everyone gets a joke. Within a month, this wisecrack was part of Bob's TV special, a show that reached 24.5 million homes. It was the biggest audience yet for a Hope special, and it is a number that network television today rarely approaches. The focusing power of television was unquestioned then: It was of acknowledged importance that Hope and NBC were going to Vietnam in an age of *Bonanza*, *Bewitched*, and *Gomer Pyle*. That may suggest that American society now has nearly despaired of focus.

Nobody believed Defense Secretary McNamara had really said that to Bob, and no one who knew Hope thought he was anything but a supporter of the war and the forces fighting it. But jokes have a life of their own, and humor can discern awkward truths. So Hope's fancy at official helplessness was not out of the blue, or absurd. Most Americans got the point, and within the charade of Bob being Hope there was this germ that already, in 1964, the Pentagon didn't know what to do. This was three years before Walter Cronkite would admit on CBS that, "It is increasingly clear to this reporter that the only rational way out then will be to negotiate, not as victors, but as an honorable people who lived up to their pledge

"VIETNAM WAS LOST IN THE LIVING ROOMS OF AMERICA." —MARSHALL MCLUHAN

to defend democracy, and did the best they could." That was "stalemate" as perceived by "the most trusted man in America." His judicious estimate was instantly famous, and it is still cited as a landmark in television commentary, from a newsreader supposed to be neutral. But Hope had been there first, more penetrating and yet more carefree. He had addressed the nation.

There's another conclusion: We know Cronkite pondered what to say, or whether to say it, with superiors at CBS. He believed it was an important step, and history reckons it had an impact on public faith in the war. Cronkite's remarks concluded a "Report from Vietnam" on February 27, 1968. On March 31, Lyndon Johnson—on television—told America, "I shall not seek, and I will not accept" nomination for re-election, but would give all his time to running the war. For veterans of network news on television, that sequence is a touchstone, and it goes along with the sentiment that it was regular televised coverage of Vietnam that persuaded Americans out of trust in or sympathy for the war. One can imagine Will McAvoy on Aaron Sorkin's *The Newsroom* (2012–14) knowing what Cronkite said by heart (though McAvoy would have been only thirteen at the time). Bob Hope believed he was tossing off a wisecrack and was not to be taken seriously.

Today, no one on television would expect to be heeded in that way. There are network newscasters still, though you may have a hard time naming them. In December 2014, it was announced that one of the most recognizable of them, Brian Williams, had signed on for another long-term contract as NBC news anchor. He would get $10 million a year, and he had about 9.5 million viewers a night, which made him a narrow ratings leader among the three traditional networks. Deborah Turness, the president of NBC News, said that, from Hurricane Katrina to the case of Edward Snowden, Williams had "taken viewers to the heart of the stories that matter most in a way that's uniquely his."

Williams was able enough on television; he was handsome and well spoken; he seemed smart, considerate, and alert. I could believe that some viewers tuned in for him, but I doubted that many of them felt the need to trust him. How could that be in an era when, apparently, Fox News is the most trusted source of news on television, and when it is also the most nakedly biased and least reliable of the cable news stations? "Most trusted" in that context means the most appreciated, or agreed with. But Fox News on a good night gets about 3 million viewers. Take the three networks—ABC, NBC, and CBS—and the three cable networks that provide regular newscasts—Fox, CNN, and MSNBC—and I doubt whether 10 percent of the nation (call it 30 million viewers) have the News "on." Whereas, in the sixties and seventies, in the era of Vietnam, the space shots, and then Watergate, Walter Cronkite alone had an audience of 20 million a night, while running behind Chet Huntley and David Brinkley on NBC for much of the sixties. (About 60 million are thought to have watched network news some nights then.)

THE MOST IDIOSYNCRATIC ANCHOR OF THAT ERA WAS DAVID BRINKLEY.

So it may not be exactly that so many Americans ever trusted Cronkite, or needed to. Was it more that in his era they trusted television and the principle of reporting? Was the persistent esteem for Kennedy's presidency equally a measure of the cultural attitudes to his office and his uncommon appetite for the medium? FDR was clearly a radio president who relied on not being seen. Truman was blankly averse to media attention, and even Eisenhower (who had much more public attention) seemed to take the attitude, "Well, sure, since I'm the president, you're going to want to televise me—so let's get it over with." Whereas Kennedy seemed to look at the presidency and say, "Gee—I can be on TV!"

I don't mean to say people didn't like Walter Cronkite. He seemed like a good guy. A Mr. Television. Bill Moyers observed that Cronkite had a bond of candor with the public, but those things are easy to talk about. Cronkite lasted: He did the *CBS Evening News* from 1962 to 1981, and he was more personally attached to the space program than other anchors—and that was a rarity, a major news opportunity that was upbeat and successful. Still, the most idiosyncratic anchor of that era was David Brinkley.

Born in Wilmington, North Carolina, Brinkley seldom disguised his Southernness. He drawled a lot of the time and gave every sign of pondering and relishing what he said, and wrote: More than any other news people on camera, Brinkley preferred to write his own urbane material. He had served in the Army during the war. Cronkite had seen action, too: As a reporter, he had flown on bombing raids. But whereas Cronkite was well behaved, formal, and respectful of or obedient to the news, Brinkley made it clear that he had a wry, acerbic attitude to the scams and liars who got on the show. He was mannered, funny, and rather Mencken-like. Today he would be judged eccentric and elitist. Just before his retirement, on the eve of Bill Clinton's presidency, Brinkley was heard to say, "The next four years will be filled with pretty words, and pretty music, and a lot of goddamn nonsense." He might have been fired if he wasn't going already.

The networks have feared such rogue and unpredictable figures—you can think of their fictional model, Howard Beale (Peter Finch), in the uncannily prescient *Network* (1976), written by the author of *Marty*, Paddy Chayefsky, and directed by Sidney Lumet. Beale is the veteran being fired from the UBS network who is seized by visionary frenzy and the mantra, "I'm as mad as hell and I'm not going to take this anymore." He is a far-fetched creation of agonized genius, a man who goes crazy while he's on. Most real anchors congeal in stability, saying "That's the way it is" (Cronkite's tagline). Since 1948, the United States has had twelve presidents but only seven CBS news anchors: Douglas Edwards, Cronkite, Dan Rather, Connie Chung, Bob Schieffer, Katie Couric, and Scott Pelley. (You are expected to know the presidents yourself.)

But Beales have come and gone in other guises. In November 1962, on Saturday nights but running open and live, with a studio audience and cameras in view, the BBC introduced *That Was the Week That Was*, created by Ned Sherrin and presented on camera by David Frost at the start of his curious ubiquity. It was a program of songs, sketches, talking heads, and anything they could think of, and much of the "satire" (that was the new word) was directed at current politics and public figures. The writers included John Cleese, Richard Ingrams, Kenneth Tynan, Dennis Potter, Peter Cook, and Bill Oddie, and the show identified an educated and cynical audience better than any previous show had done. It teased the format of newscasts and the precious solemnity of people in the news. *TW3* ran for a year and was canceled because 1964 was an election year in Britain and the BBC were nervous that their impartiality would be challenged. It found an audience as large as 12 million (*The Daily Show* with Jon Stewart, on Comedy Central from 1996 onward, got under 2 million). *TW3* shifted to America, still with Frost as its presenter, but again it was terminated when the Johnson-Goldwater election required decorum to avert disbelief.

In Britain, there had been a surprise with *That Was the Week That Was*; you could feel it in the performers and in the audience, too. We were all amazed that the great parental edifice of the BBC had let us get away with this show and have such a good time. And 1963, its year, was a time of convulsion. The entire world was either in recovery after the Cuban Missile Crisis of October 1962 or deranged because of it. For Britain, it was a year in which the ancient class folly of society was coming to a head of sex and scandal. The stupefied aplomb of Prime Minister Harold Macmillan was deflating. It was under his suave administration that Britain had emerged finally from the war and its hardship. "You never had it so good," he told us, and he was right, if the good was prosperity, greed for more, and a gradual evolution into raw behavior with an assist from technology—television was doing that, pouring advertisements into our ears, a drug that made you feel free but desirous when you woke up. Another technology, the birth control pill, was working in a similar way.

In '63 (with the Beatles building in the background—"Please, Please Me" was released in January) the complacency and the corruption of tired rule and class, not to mention the clash between the naivety of the old guard leaders and the new reach of media, made for a scandal. John Profumo, a cabinet minister, had an affair with a whore and lied to the House of Commons. Pictures of a Miss Christine Keeler, twenty years old, ran in the Sunday papers (the cutting edge then) and aroused the country. Some wanted to think of fucking her, while throwing out the toffs who had got there first. The whole thing was absurd, a sex farce, but it was changing Britain before our eyes and ears, and *That Was the Week* was where you could feel the damage and the glee. It seemed OK to

THE SHOW WHISPERED, "COME SEE THE WRECK HAPPENING."

do it and see it because the BBC was permitting it. The smothering authority of that institution remained even if the Edwardian gent, Macmillan—Supermac in Vicky's newspaper cartoons—was coming apart like the cat in *Tom and Jerry*, brick by brick, mustache by mustache, cocksure grin by shattered teeth. The show whispered, "Come see the wreck happening." And TV is a knockout with wrecks.

In October 1962, for days, people had clung to the television set while being afraid to turn it on. Literally, you wondered if you would see the enormous explosion, the big bang, starting on the sweet horizon (still in black-and-white, of course) and coming up to claim the cameras, the intervening space, our sets, and our houses themselves. The fire this time?

There was nothing like *That Was the Week* in America yet, where television was a serene institution, the technological comfort that the BBC hoped to keep possession of. In 1963, the airwaves in the United States were calm or somnolent with *Wagon Train*, *The Beverly Hillbillies*, *Dr. Kildare*, *Perry Mason*, *The Fugitive*, and even *The Dick Van Dyke Show*. In all these programs, and in all the others, a show appeared on time, the way it had been last week; and in the stories wrongs were righted, dysfunctional lives were put straight, production codes were adhered to, and happiness and purchase prevailed. You rode the story arc and you got the message, from Chesterfield, Lux, or Chevrolet, in just the way the surge of patriotic wartime movies had ended with "Buy War Bonds as You Leave This Theater." You had to search hard for any hint of insurrection in TV, but it was there in a frivolous, playful marvel called *Candid Camera* (1948 onward), the one show in which the medium winked and said, "You're not trusting us, are you?" Its host, Allen Funt, was a likeable fellow, a benign real-life Joker, captivated by people and amazement. But provocative questions came from his fun.

TIME HAD NEVER PASSED LIKE THIS BEFORE ON TELEVISION.

Just over a year after the ordeal of the Cuban Missile Crisis, there came the sequel. That started in Dallas with the motorcade. In the assault on the Republic and its assurance, television had its greatest boost and vindication. In fact, the *CBS Evening News* had gone from fifteen minutes to thirty only two months before Dallas, but now the News went on and on, unbroken and unstoppable. Cronkite and a few others were there all the time, visibly shaken and unshaved, older and so much sadder. Time had never passed like this before on television, and it was the prolonged crisis that had put a camera in the basement of the police station, waiting for Oswald to show. The shootings turned into the funeral, and Cronkite came out of all this in horrible and helpless eminence, because he had been the most constant and reassuring presence. Brinkley was grave and eloquent, but he couldn't be wry anymore. Cronkite was faithful and stoic, and that was closer to the technological presence of the medium. He was on, and there is a way in which the television has never gone off since then.

So when I said that Brian Williams of "our" NBC seemed to be an able newscaster, I didn't mean to sound patronizing. I liked him, as far as I could, watching him three or four times a year. I could hear what he said, and feel he'd thought about what he was saying. He covered Katrina admirably, and he did have an interview with Edward Snowden. But Brian Williams never had the opportunity to become iconic or to become the news—until his admission that he had sometimes exaggerated his own presence in news events, like a kid wanting to be in an adventure movie.

So he was suspended, and not long thereafter it was claimed by jackals that Deborah Turness had very little experience running the News (inaccurate; she had edited the News at Independent Television in London). Worse, she was English (true; she was born in Hertfordshire).

For here is the conundrum of the News. We expect it to go on every day at a fixed time in a sober way. We want Brian looking trim and alert. We don't want him in a ruined studio where you can see the barbarians or the rising tide in the gash in the wall. If we smile fondly at the tradition of Cronkite saying, "And that's the way it is," we respond to the confidence he believed in conveying. And if that way stays fine and firm, like picnic days in summer, that's all well and good. We have all said from time to time how much we yearn for "good news," and sometimes news shows make a concession in that direction. The Internet is full of amusing but touching pet videos and wardrobe malfunctions. But television knows we will not watch good news for very long without becoming restless and changing the channel. That tranquillity we aspire to has no fascination or compelling power. With the best will in the world, there must have

been a part of Brian Williams that waited to be woken in the middle of the night and dragged in front of the camera, with no tie and un-combed hair. He wanted the big one. He put it more tactfully when he met his new contract. "I admit that I'm a one-trick pony. I am, I think, designed and put on this earth to do what I'm doing now—and that is to eat, sleep, and breathe nonfiction and the news going on in the world."

Williams knew that the audience for network news had been in decline for at least twenty years, and the one thing to arrest that pro-cess was something as drastic as aircraft crashing into the World Trade Center one sunny morning. I could believe Williams was decent enough that he might have said, "No, I really don't want to have to see that and talk about it." But I wonder how he would handle this follow-up: "Very well, Brian, you're off that day. We'll give it to Peter Alexander or Ann Curry. Or maybe Tom Brokaw can come in and sub for you."

The thing we call 9/11 was evil and terrifying, but it was con-tained, and it was what we have to regard as a show. Please don't misunderstand me, but it took place in a major urban center at a time of day that would grab ratings. As an event and an outrage, it was precisely focused, with iconic imagery worthy of a big movie. My family saw the images in San Francisco. Early in the morning, I had seen on my computer that something unusual was occurring. I hurried upstairs and joined the children, who were getting ready for school; I turned on our television in time to see the second aircraft entering the tower. That was 9:03 A.M. in Manhattan—6:03 in San Francisco. Our younger son, who was a few weeks short of six, asked, "What movie is this from, Dad?"

If you think of the disaster movies of that era—or from the his-tory of the movies—it was easier for a child to believe that this scene had been arranged as a spectacle than that it was actual damage. It could be watched, and surely the people who arranged these scenes had calculated the facilities for coverage available in New York City. The attack was not launched on Mount Rushmore, a cornfield in the prairies, or Hoover Dam, because coverage would have been less likely in those locations, just as delivering the planes there would have been more problematic. The criminals who made the plan intended to get on television.

On July 17, 2014, a Malaysia Airlines aircraft was shot down by an antiaircraft missile in eastern Ukraine. Two hundred and ninety-eight people were killed. We do not know exactly what happened, but we believe it was a reckless action taken by Russian forces or pro-Russian elements in Ukraine who meant to register the justice of the Russian cause in that area. It was a crime and an act of terror. As far as we know, there is no film of the crash or of the plane being struck. How could there be when it was so unexpected and in so desolate a place? All of which stresses the concentrated mise-en-scène of 9/11 and the cunning that anticipated that outrage live on network television, fit to shock and amaze everyone in the world. It was something done by people who understood television, and it was inconceivable before this medium.

9/11 WAS SOMETHING DONE BY PEOPLE WHO UNDERSTOOD TELEVISION.

It follows that if you were to poll Americans on "What is the greatest disaster of modern times?" I believe the events of 9/11 would win—moreover, "9/11" is itself an emphatic, modern title such as no one forgets. Now, let me ask you what happened on December 26, 2004. That's over a decade ago, and attention spans are not always reliable.

I'll assume that after a few moments, some of you will guess, "The tsunami?" Others may respond, "Which tsunami was that?" The event I'm thinking about has several different names—the Boxing Day tsunami; the Christmas tsunami; the Sumatra-Andaman earthquake; or the Indian disaster.

Those names are not as emphatic as "Katrina"—I think you all know about that, even if you're not sure when it happened. Was it August 30, 2006; July 31, 2004; August 29, 2005? Does it matter? Put it another way: Is the known total of fatalities from Katrina 1,245; 1,833; or 2,205? And if the answer to that second question matters, what does it say about your uncertainty?

We have vivid, poignant still photographs of the aftermath to the Malaysia Airlines disaster (which has to be distinguished from the other Malaysia Airlines loss, Flight 370, over the Indian Ocean, from which fragments of wreckage have gradually been discovered). There was a lot of aerial coverage of Katrina hitting New Orleans, and more on the devastation that resulted. But the Indian Ocean tsunami was so widespread and scattered, and so sudden and hard to film in remote places, that most of the imagery was of the ruin left behind. The death toll was extraordinary by the standards we are discussing here, and it was spread throughout Indonesia, Thailand, Sri Lanka, and India. "We know that," I hear you saying. But was the death toll 60,000; 160,000; 230,000; or 310,000? If so much range seems playful or tasteless, recognize your hesitation in answering and the way the difference in those numbers amounts to maybe eighty times the number lost on 9/11.

There's something else to be faced. The dead on 9/11 were nameable lives and tragedies that could be presented as recognized narratives. So to speak, those lives were insured on our scale of values. But the news changes in urgency or drama when it happens far away. So many of the dead in the Sumatra-Andaman earthquake and what followed it were Asian, and those lives do not count in the same way on our News. In 2012, a theatrical movie was made of that tsunami, *The Impossible*. To convey the tidal wave of destruction, it used digital effects as well as five weeks' shooting in a real tank and simulated effects done in slow motion. Much of the damage seen is startling and fearsome. It's not a bad film. But it is a movie about a white family who were on vacation in Thailand when the tsunami hit. There were such people, and some of them were killed. But in *The Impossible* the parents and the three children all survive. In other words, the entertainment was so constructed that a white audience in Europe, America, and Australasia could feel better about it all at the end. The essential experience of the tsunami—death and life-altering damage for native peoples—was a secondary concern. And so the peoples who did suffer such casualties had to feel an indifference or assumed superiority in the culture that made the film.

This aspect of the news is of enormous cultural consequence in determining how the crises of the world will work out. For example, without being a scholar of the Vietnam War, I have it in my mind that 57,000 American deaths occurred during that war. That number is like an ATM password or the orthodoxy that six million died in the concentration camps in the event known as the Holocaust. But if you look Vietnam up now, the official figure is actually 58,000. Then ask how many Vietnamese were killed, granted that the potent newsreel coverage and several disturbing movies about that war have concentrated on American characters? Were the Vietnamese losses 250,000; 750,000; two million; or three? The answer is in there somewhere, but the range is so large it illustrates our lack of precise concern and the feeling that it might as well be story. [Answers to these questions will be supplied in a footnote at the end of this chapter.]

So here is the ultimate riddle in TV News. I said earlier that watching the shooting of Oswald, I had felt excited. I'm sure that was a feeling of having been witness to something momentous, and seeing it as a living document. There had been the surprise—and who is not exhilarated by surprise, whether it is the shock of death or ecstasy? But there was something else not to be missed: I was rewarded for watching. The world of chance or random cinematic life had given me a spectacle. In that context, you have to recognize the implicit contract in watching—it is the fundamental deal in movies: You have to show me something, like a wow. And so I am watching to be amazed, moved, terrified. At that point, you are close to seeing how far the News has to be drastic, disastrous, or worse. Tranquil and contented days will not cut it. The News in which nothing happened today is not news.

NEWS RELENTLESSLY SEARCHES FOR MOMENTS AND THE MOMENTOUS.

So News relentlessly searches for moments and the momentous, and if they aren't there the pursuit may be encouraged to create them or design them. The intelligence in the terrorist design of 9/11 is not too far from a newsroom's shaping of the vast untidiness of what has happened.

The News is thrilled with danger and its own precarious safety net. Few things illustrate that better than the CNN coverage on the first night of the bombardment of Baghdad (January 17, 1991) when the network had Peter Arnett, Bernard Shaw, and John Holliman in a hotel in the city with electronic equipment sufficient to get television out to the world—if the regime in Iraq would allow it, and they did.

Some hunch or ineptness told the Iraqis to be prepared to dramatize themselves, even if that entailed their defeat and humiliation. The urge to be on television is often irrational and unquenchable.

Equally, the instinct in authorities to limit that urge is natural and sensible from their point of view. There are still governments in this world, neighborhoods in what is sometimes called the global village of television and social media, that determine to expunge or ignore certain embarrassing events and situations. They will not allow them to be seen or referred to on their television systems. Russia couldn't see the point of talking about Malaysia Airlines Flight 17.

THE NEWS IS ENFEEBLED, DEMORALIZED, AND . . . INSECURE.

And even those as enthusiastic as Vice President Cheney about enhanced interrogation, its vigor and effectiveness, its point as freedom in action, were reluctant to have unambiguous film coverage of their proud achievement get on the *Nightly News* and were likely to invoke the interests of national security to prevent it.

In free or unfree states, claims on behalf of "national security" often reflect an unease in rulers, and their consequent, and often unconscious need to spread "insecurity" to give them more of a free hand. It's not that such governments are always determined to be dishonest, or manipulative. Most strive to think well of themselves. But they know how far the public estimate of security and its opposite can hinge on media descriptions—and official PR. Their instinct is to have the latter crowd the former. So it's necessary to say that after seven decades of television, the News is enfeebled, demoralized, and…insecure. The news may become almost anything anyone cares to post; in which case, it begins to be ignored. But be wary of the thought that "open" coverage in the media will simply lead to more benign liberty. There was a naive assertion in the "Arab Spring" that cell-phone communication in Tahrir Square, Cairo, in 2011 had "brought down" the unpleasant Mubarak regime by organizing gatherings and signaling the appearance of freedom at work. It is a hope in young activists that tyranny can be overthrown in a night or a weekend: We have been thrilled by that scene in so many movies. But some of these concepts—"Arab Spring," "social media," and "bringing down"—need to be kept in quotes. Four years after "Tahrir Square," Egypt again has repressive military rule, and Hosni Mubarak has been first tried and convicted, then exonerated and freed, then retried and convicted, fined, and made subject to imprisonment.

No one is sure what to do with the old man, or how to separate the national hero from the scoundrel. Several American administrations had dealt with Mubarak for thirty years. He was received with respect in the White House and the Vatican. He contributed men to the mission to free Kuwait. We looked on with equanimity and ignorance and regarded Mubarak as a force for stability in "a chaotic Middle East" (or one the West had despaired of understanding or solving). The News seldom did Egypt. So Mubarak strove to be unobtrusive and relied on the technology of our onlooker culture.

That onlooker culture has been a creation of film and television, though it is added to now by the multitude of smaller screens where "breaking news" reports may be sensationalized and invented, in a rising ferment of news din that makes us ready not to bother. You can regard the culture as a new, radicalizing means of bringing the things seen (the world) into our homes for our appreciation and experience—like a gift. But that formula is not enough. It loses awareness of the conditioning elements in the process of screening, and thereby seeming to control, the experience of chaos—in that sense, the gift can be a misleading trick. If you want a simple, startling illustration of that, consider how far in watching the News we enjoy the terrible things seen.

Am I saying that we take pleasure in 9/11, Katrina, the death of JFK, and so on, on television? Let that upsetting question linger. "Pleasure" is not the best word. Try confirmation, security. Still not enough? There is a part of us that has been trained in watching screened reality for all of our life. If you watch Marion Crane being murdered in *Psycho*, it is appalling, emotionally damaging—in 1960, for sure, it drove some viewers out of the theater. And yet, most of us watched and recognized that we could not intervene, no matter how real it seemed—and did not have the responsibility of trying to save her. If you happened to be in a strange motel and saw the start of that murder through an open door, you would do something—wouldn't you? You could call the police, you could sound a fire alarm, turn on every electrical appliance in sight, or you could attempt to overpower that forbidding tall woman with the knife. But when you watch the movie, you know that you can sit there and observe without being noticed. The thing seen may be very powerful and deeply distressing. But you are not responsible. And that allows you to see the excitement, the beauty, and the amazing spontaneity in the event. It is a movie—as Hitchcock himself said, "*only* a movie."

That has gone on all our life now, and it's no exaggeration to say that at times of our life—impressionable times—we have spent four or five hours a day in this observance. That training is something we have hardly bothered to examine: Our systems of schooling still labor over the word and verbal constructs and hardly acknowledge cinematic literacy, let alone its pressure toward illiteracy.

But suppose being a helpless observer or even a connoisseur of film has gradually cultivated a kind of detachment or irresponsibility that comes close to dismayed futility. Does that help explain your own weary realization that the political conduct of this country is in a state of stalemate, yet so torn by fury and hatred that it is too sad to contemplate? Or does it bring credence to the violent contradiction in our practical intelligence: that our climate is being pushed into a disturbance or a loss of balance that can destroy us, but we are doing too little about it? Do observers take less and less responsibility because they feel an institutional separation from the thing seen? Because solitude seems to be a part of the technology? From all of that, contemplate the possibility that great disasters are spectacles for us in which the chaotic sense of tragedy begins to be organized. Then consider the furtive gratification that this time it's not us there on the shores of Indonesia, in Vietnam, or in the ruins of Fukushima. It's someone else. Not this time—though we have a foreboding that one day we may go to television to see the beginning of the end, and it will be coming for us.

These are things this medium has done with the mass of us, and they are beyond politics, reason, or science. They say that technology is less our tool than something that makes tools of us.

Imagine the television coverage of some future disaster. Think of Brian Williams handling it all, without a crack in his voice or any attempt to run for cover—I'm sure he would perform admirably because he wants to be there and on. But then imagine that we lose Brian (a failed connection), and think of an eroding HDTV image that falters and fragments, reverts to black-and-white and begins to look like old, mottled film. Still, visibility persists and there's no mistaking the advance or its threat to our existence (call it "civilization"). It might be the extending fireball of a great explosion. It might be the horde of those who have had nothing or so little that rage took them over—they want food, energy, water; they want our TVs. Or it might be a tide rising.

We have been here before, in the name of science fiction or wicked entertainment. Once upon a time (call it Halloween 1938, *The War of the Worlds*—good old radio), a commentator on top of Broadcasting Building in New York City described an alien advance intent on destroying the city. Then his voice cut out, and after a pause we heard just the call of a lone operator, from somewhere and nowhere, trying to make contact:

"2X2L calling CQ New York…
"Isn't there anyone on the air?
"Isn't there anyone on the air?
"Isn't there anyone…"

*Professor R. J. Rummel, a political scientist at the University of Hawaii, places the total of Vietnamese deaths (military and civilian, North and South) in a range from 1.15 million to 3.20 million. The US Geological Survey estimates that 227,898 died because of the tsunami. The death toll from Katrina stands at 1,245.

WOMEN, WIVES, AND WONDERERS

14

WOMEN WERE ALWAYS ASSUMED TO BE ESSENTIAL TO THE TELE-VISION CONTRACT. That was the estimate of the men "in charge."

Just because women were at home, waiting, they would watch. Didn't that keep them off the streets? Weren't women then as problematic as kids? This was a domestic medium, so it was natural that women with as little to do as Donna Stone would watch during the day until their gang came home. Daytime soap operas sprang up (not educational programs on the female orgasm, doing your taxes in case "he" abandoned you, or handling male rage). There were handsome male cyphers on the soaps (often gay ideals), but the fantasy agenda the shows pursued was female—and not respectable. You seldom heard of men who were devoted to those shows (imagine if Archie Bunker watched them secretly). But most American soaps were genteel, with nice clothes and décor, and social aspirations. In Britain, *Coronation Street* (1960 and still going) for Granada was happily working-class, with an audience of 20 million. Among its characters, Ena Sharples, Elsie Tanner, and Annie Walker were as widely known as the queen (but more believable).

The numbers on most soaps are absurd but verified: *Search for Tomorrow* (1951–86, 9,130 episodes); *The Guiding Light* (1952–2009, 15,762 episodes); *As the World Turns* (1952–2010, 13,858 episodes); *General Hospital* (1963–, 13,318 episodes); *All My Children* (1970–2011, 10,755 episodes); *The Young and the Restless* (1973–, 10,677 episodes). You begin to see how episodic modern life has become.

Here was the real telethon, more surreal or dreamy in narrative structure than anything else on TV; much more open to sexual adventure and variety than prime-time shows; deeply suggestive of a thriving and justified madness in American society; the only thing in the world for some people; locked into ads for products women might want (chainsaws, poison, double indemnity life insurance?); and with a pattern of termination around 2010. Was that because the economy plunged? Because far fewer women were at home? Because Internet pornography had arrived to match dream energy? Or was the ecstasy of disbelief unsustainable, and even overshadowed by the farces running on news reportage? Had lack of respect for soaps really broken through? Did those shows imprison women; did they make for prisoners who thought they were free; or were they part of an unruly awakening? Academics study daytime television, but tenure often expires before they've had time to see it all. You had to have seen these shows when they played, just as there was a time when Donna Stone seemed an ideal figure, a role model, and not yet a breakdown getting ready to occur. But don't sneer: *General Hospital* sometimes reached 17 million households. In human history, there had never been such a mass medium, or such a profuse pressure from the social-sexual underground. Soaps were like B movies in the forties: Because few took them seriously, they were free to go wild.

Moreover, you can't appreciate *I Love Lucy* without seeing that she was like someone who watched those shows, her reality touchstone blown to the wind. Imagine another version of that show, where Lucy watches soaps and then tries to act them out. Imagine a *Lucy* where she knows that Desi is a liar, a scoundrel, and a womanizer. That was more or less the reality show of the Arnaz marriage—and it wouldn't have got a sponsor.

Lucy was a marvel, entirely unpredictable if you place it in the mores of the early 1950s, yet mysterious even now. The set-up was domestic, and offered in a spirit of light-hearted optimism—but the antics involved were so desperate as to suggest not just that this marriage was "rocky" or "surreal," but that all marriages might be against nature. (Fifty years later, that conflict has moved close to the heart of so much television—at a time when advances in same-sex marriage cannot mask an unease over marriage as a whole.)

WHAT DID WOMEN WANT THEN, AND WHAT DID TELEVISION EXPECT OF THEM?

As I have observed before, the title changes in the show did confer a kind of ownership on Desi, even if it drove him mad. That simple, barbed fact can set you thinking in an effort to place Lucy Ricardo in her context. What did women want then, and what did television expect of them?

In the movie *The Best Years of Our Lives* (1946), there is an exquisite moment; it's still touching, decades later, and it must have been overwhelming when the picture swept the country (it won Best Picture with eight other Oscars). A soldier is home from the war (Fredric March). He comes to the door of his old apartment. His children let him in. He hushes them because he wants to surprise his wife (Myrna Loy). She is in a room at the end of a long corridor, but she hears the odd silence. She appears in a doorway, and husband and wife come together in that precious corridor. If you haven't seen it, go and find it now, for it is a seed moment for television domesticity and a lasting tribute to corridors.

The wife doesn't do much else in that film, because wives in 1946 didn't have too much opportunity. She doesn't rediscover sex with her man, or wonder if he met other women at war. She doesn't say, "Look,

I took a job while you were gone and I liked it and I want to keep doing it." She never wonders if she likes him anymore. The beautiful scene I described, and the closing space between them, is what the man had been dreaming of while he was away (and what he assumes she is dreaming of). More or less, postwar movies gave us that kind of re-union, while steadily pushing forward in the old cause that wanted to keep women gorgeous, sexy, and uncritical. A voyeurist urging begins after the war (it's profound in film noir) for women to slip out of their habit and into a sexual mood (like Donna Reed playing Lorene in *From Here to Eternity*).

The movies were reaching out for greater sensuality, and that only made television more cautious. It was not really until *Charlie's Angels* (1976–81) that the system took the plunge of making women sexy on the box. That was called "Jiggle TV." Because the stuff was going directly into the home, the small screen believed it should be restrained and family-friendly. It wanted generations of women to keep watching; it wanted them to be as content as the corporations sponsoring the medium; so it ignored the possibilities that were invading the big screen. More than that, no one reckoned at first that television was suitable for conveying beauty or glamour—the image didn't look good enough compared with the lush black-and-white texture of movies or their explosions in color. Look at the gaudy display of Russell and Monroe in *Gentlemen Prefer Blondes* (1953) and it's easy to understand that television believed it couldn't compete technically, let alone in any narrative sense.

That's a pointed comparison, for *Gentlemen Prefer Blondes* is eye candy but it's also Howard Hawks and a version of Anita Loos doing a film that celebrates female pursuit of jewels, money, and men as handsome but stupid consorts. It actually harks back to the glory of talk and competition between the sexes on the big screen that had existed in the thirties and forties in *Nothing Sacred*, *Bringing Up Baby*, *Midnight*, *The Lady Eve*, *His Girl Friday*—the heady era of screwball, and still the best women have looked and sounded in the history of American movies. Those women talked back.

Attractive, smart, independent women like Katharine Hepburn, Carole Lombard, Barbara Stanwyck, or even Bette Davis in those films never showed up on television. Women didn't talk or think (those habits are linked) on television for nearly two decades. There are so many hit shows of that first age of television where the girl was for emotional hat-checking, like *Dragnet* or *Perry Mason* (where Barbara Hale's Della Street was attractive, helpful, and eager, but never given a day in court). Miss Kitty was there in *Gunsmoke*, and she was a hint

at naughtiness, but Matt Dillon never really noticed her. In the majority of Westerns, the heroic men soldiered on, with a horse as their best companion. They might rescue a pretty woman in one episode, or feel briefly aroused in another. But their lives were like their series: dedicated to male self-sufficiency. That's the imprisoned spirit of *Wagon Train*, *Cheyenne*, *Rawhide*, and even the innovative *Maverick*. By the time you get to *Bonanza* (1959–73, and top show from 1964 to '67, years of amazing turmoil and social/sexual change in America), that Ponderosa household of guys is so exclusive and self-satisfied, so ponderous, you might wonder if gay thoughts ever arose. It wasn't that these guys never had sex; they were a species that did not think of it. Plainly, the show's appeal was in defiance of the alterations in American life. The sexual suggestion on television was confined to the commercials.

So, what the hell was Lucy up to—and why did it take the medium so long to learn about her appeal? I have talked about how the show grew out of a radio show, *My Favorite Husband*. There is a fascinating memo on what the TV show might become, written by Jess Oppenheimer, the lead writer on *I Love Lucy*. It's simple, candid, and as startling as plans for war:

> He is a Latin-American bandleader and singer. She is his wife. They are happily married and very much in love. The only bone of contention between them is her desire to get into show business, and his equally strong desire to keep her out of it. To Lucy, who was brought up in the humdrum sphere of a moderate, well-to-do, middle western, mercantile family, show business is the most glamourous field in the world. But Ricky, who was raised in show business, sees none of its glamour, only its deficiencies, and yearns to be an ordinary citizen, keeping regular hours and living a normal life. As show business is the only way he knows to make a living, and he makes a very good one, the closest he can get to this dream is having a wife who's out of show business and devotes herself to keeping as nearly a normal life as possible for him.

It didn't exactly work out that way, of course: A normal life at the Ricardo household is hard to find. But that's the fun and the comic desperation that animates Desi, which can only be explained by love. Isn't it actually the case that these two are classically at odds? In turn, doesn't that get at the show's understanding of marriage—that it is best between people who are ill-matched? If we recall that hallowed corridor in *The Best Years of Our Lives*, the Ricardo household seems mined with booby traps, not just as a prompt to slapstick but as a way for Ricky to keep discovering Lucy's nightmarish schemes. The fun came from Ball's considerable skill at physical comedy—call it slapstick—and Arnaz's adequate bewilderment as a long-suffering stooge husband.

The role of show business is there, and it's what allowed the stream of illustrious guest stars on the show, but it gives way to the view of home as a kind of prison Lucy may destroy if she can't escape. Yes, she is a stargazer with show business, but really she just needs something to do. That frenzy was employed, if never quite satisfied, in her having children.

But the sense of show business and normalcy indicates the hope in Oppenheimer and the ruling class on television for how the medium could relate to its audience. In that light, television was taking over from the movies but sustaining the old equation of dream or desire with ordinariness. Dreaming had always been more problematic than Hollywood wanted to admit, and the problem grew more intense when TV desire focused on the purchase of advertised products as well as the mythology in a show. The sit was the Ricardo home, but the situation was the expansion of the American economy—in fact, the golden age of television coincided with a surge in prosperity and economic opportunity, so it was not hard for TV to think that it was responsible. But the erotics in early TV were in the shiny products.

The audience was tickled because it felt it was watching a version of reality that depended on Hollywood. Lucy and Desi were a well-known couple; even if neither had become unequivocal stars, their eminence hung over the show. It was written; the apartment was a set;

and Lucy and Ricky were "characters." But it was more tangled than that. When Lucy got pregnant, Lucille Ball was herself expecting. And the marital mayhem survived on a choppy sea of stories about the real marriage being unsteady. So *I Love Lucy* was what we now call a sitcom (and the proving ground for so many others), but it was a reality show, too, long before that term became current, and one that turned on the tormented position of a wife. America loved Lucy, and laughed at her comedy. But it's hard now to look at the show without seeing a bizarre screwball version of *A Doll's House*.

One writer noticed the double act:

> The show was built on an entrancing pseudo-effect of the real: that the very ordinary couple portrayed was played by a real couple, one of whom was extremely famous, successful, and rich. Lucille Ball, a real star, became a goofy housewife named Lucy Ricardo, but nobody was fooled. Didn't we smile when we saw the heart-shaped logo at the end...?
>
> That was the fun of it—the confusion and mixture of televised fantasy and voyeuristically apprehended reality. A dose of fantasy. And the insinuation that we might be watching something real. Which has turned out, fifty years later, to be television's perennial, still winning formula.

That was Susan Sontag.

||||||||||||||||||||||||||||

BY 1961, IF YOU WERE GOING TO THE MOVIES, the parade of women was changing. There were fabulous beauties still, from Elizabeth Taylor to Sophia Loren. But they were verging on the archaic, and when Taylor played Cleopatra, the film was a helpless dish for the paparazzi feast over its making. We were only a few years away from nudity and overt sex. The lineup of screen women also included Natalie Wood craving release in *Splendor in the Grass*, the several "girls" in *Some Like It Hot*, and even Mrs. Bates in *Psycho*. In that

Mary Tyler Moore statue in Minneapolis

troubling context, Laura Petrie was a throwback to clean, single-minded cuteness, loving obedience, with great legs.

Mary Tyler Moore had been born in Brooklyn in 1936. She was a teenage dancer in some Hotpoint commercials and she was making a tough way in television until creator Carl Reiner cast her as the young wife in *The Dick Van Dyke Show*. Dick's character, Rob Petrie, was part of a scriptwriting team on *The Alan Brady Show*, which was loosely based on Reiner's experience writing for Sid Caesar. (Whenever Brady appeared, Reiner played the part.) The part of Rob had once been talked about for Johnny Carson. The other writers were played by Rose Marie and Morey Amsterdam, and Richard Deacon was their foolish owl producer. The antics of the writers were as comic as the dialogue, and Laura was often on the edges of the fun. But really she was Rob's wife, Ritchie's mother, and a meticulous housekeeper who looked like a Midwest model. In other words, she was mainstream, and trained for it—Laura had married Rob at the age of seventeen, when he was twenty-eight.

The Dick Van Dyke Show played on CBS from 1961 to 1966, and it was steadily popular. Rob and Laura may be the most appealing, untroubled marriage just short of fakery or coma on television. They had a timing together that showed not just skill but warmth, yet it was a rapport like that of players in an ad. Not that they did more than kiss. And not that Laura did anything really, except look spiffy, smile forever, say the right thing, and persist. She was like the nurse Lucy needed. The show won three Emmys as outstanding comedy and Moore twice won the Emmy for lead actress in a series.

It was a mark of Moore's popularity that her next show was called not *WJM in Minneapolis* but *The Mary Tyler Moore Show*. During the *Van Dyke* show Moore's first marriage had ended, and she married Grant Tinker, who became the producer of her next show. Indeed, the couple formed a very successful production enterprise,

MTM. *The Mary Tyler Moore Show* was built around a television newsroom at a local station, where Mary Richards had arrived to work as a producer after a failed love affair. Thus, in 1971, she was recognized as an independent career woman, open to marriage but not dependent on it or desperate about it. She had affairs during the show; sex could be assumed but not shown, and there was neither passion nor heartbreak.

Mary was the center of the newsroom and the sounding board of the show, which was created and largely written by James L. Brooks and Allan Burns. Compared with the *Van Dyke* show and most other sitcoms, it was grown-up and plausible in its relationships and its talk. And Mary talked, so people had to listen. The show was good on friendships between women, office politics, and the evolving attitude to homosexuality, infidelity, and that old chestnut, happiness. Mary had neighbors where she lived, Phyllis (Cloris Leachman) and Rhoda (Valerie Harper), who were wilder than she was. There was Lou Grant (Ed Asner), the grumpy and unhappy boss; Ted Baxter (Ted Knight), the self-admiring newsreader; and later on there was Sue Ann Nivens (Betty White), ravenous for men and mischief.

Lena Dunham

The show was adored, and it stands up well as a confident comic entertainment. It was during the years of *The Mary Tyler Moore Show* that one might realize that the movie screen no longer seemed to know how to do this type of comedy. From 1975 to '77, *The Mary Tyler Moore Show* won three Emmys as best comedy series. Moore herself won four Emmys as actress in a comedy series, and supporting awards went to Cloris Leachman, Ted Knight, Valerie Harper, Betty White, and Ed Asner. In time, all those surrounding players would get their own series, often playing their character from *MTM*: *Rhoda* (1974–78); *Phyllis* (1975–77); *Lou Grant* (1977–82); *The Betty White Show* (1977–78)—and *Too Close for Comfort* or *The Ted Knight Show* (1980–87), the only one not at MTM and CBS.

The abiding figure in this plenty was Grant Tinker, born in Stamford, Connecticut, in 1925 and educated at Dartmouth. He was the leader of MTM Enterprises, but in 1981, just as he and Moore divorced, he moved on to become chairman of NBC, where he would launch *The Cosby Show*, *Family Ties*, *The Golden Girls*, *Cheers*, and *Hill Street Blues*. This is one of the outstanding executive careers in television, sufficient to place Tinker in the tradition of classic Hollywood moguls, not that they match the maturity and consistent effectiveness of Tinker's work.

> IN ONE EPISODE OF *TILL DEATH*, ALF IS READING MARY WHITEHOUSE'S BOOK, *CLEANING UP TV.*

But if you want to gauge the achievement of entertainment television in the seventies, and the range of female life to be seen on the small screen, you should recall that at the Emmys *The Mary Tyler Moore Show* was regularly in competition with *All in the Family* (which was at its peak from 1971 until 1979/80). Why do I pick the latter date? That's when the show yielded to the actress's pleas and said that Edith Bunker had died of a stroke. She may be the most endearing woman television has ever had.

In Britain, in 1965, the BBC had launched what proved to be a controversial sitcom, *Till Death Us Do Part*, created and written by Johnny Speight. It was a broad-brush portrait of a working-class bigot, Alf Garnett (Warren Mitchell). He was ignorant, opinionated, racist, intolerant of social change, and a relic by the standards of the time. He used the word "bloody" freely, and language was breaking open. In the same year, 1965, live on a late-night talk show, *BBC-3*, Kenneth Tynan had given "fuck" a debut, almost certainly with intent. There were motions in the House of Commons saying he should be prosecuted. Mary Whitehouse, a self-appointed moral guardian, thought his bottom should be spanked, little knowing how much that might have appealed to Tynan. In one episode of *Till Death*, Alf is reading Mary Whitehouse's book, *Cleaning Up TV*, with approval.

Alf Garnett had a wife, Else (Dandy Nichols), whom he called "a silly moo." She was cut from his cloth but she seemed to despise Alf as much as he loathed immigrants or liberals. Their daughter lived with them in their small house in Wapping (in the East End of London) with her lazy, left-wing husband. The show was very funny, if you were disposed to see it as a satire on bigotry; but equally compelling if you were pleased to hear the rough candor of Garnett's view of life. The BBC rode along with protests over a hit show, as well as the first serious view of working-class life on British television. Johnny Speight was upset: He had wanted universal horror and outrage at Alf Garnett—but that took too little account of the charm in acting and the charismatic odiousness that Warren Mitchell managed.

The Americanization of the Garnetts did not happen quickly, though there was competition over the show and a thrill of anticipation that someone might make a series exposing American working-class vulgarity. In the event, Norman Lear won the rights and took the project to CBS. The British title was softened: Death was out and instead it became *All in the Family*, set in Queens, at a rather higher income level than the Garnetts had enjoyed. Carroll O'Connor would be Archie Bunker, and Jean Stapleton was Edith. The kids were played by Sally Struthers and a young Rob Reiner.

All in the Family was controversial, too, but there was little evidence that viewers were offended enough to turn it off. It was often funnier and gentler than the British show, which has never played in America because of the deal but also because a lot of its local references would not travel. *All in the Family* went to number 1, with a rating over 30, and it stayed there for five seasons. It won the outstanding-comedy Emmy from 1971 to '73, and

THE BRITISH TITLE WAS SOFTENED: DEATH WAS OUT AND INSTEAD IT BECAME *ALL IN THE FAMILY*.

again in '78. Jean Stapleton won Emmys for 1971 and '72, and again in '78, and O'Connor got it for 1972 and '77 through '79. Other awards would go to Struthers and Reiner. This happened over forty years ago, but the first years of the show feel as present as ever, even if the seasons after Edith's death were a letdown.

It's still spoken of as "the Archie Bunker show," which is fair enough: He was the loudmouth of the household and the engine of most of the jokes. But Edith seems more essential. She was a plain woman, without a trace of glamour—and there have not been many of whom that was true on television. She dressed shabbily, or without interest. She never seemed to think anyone might be looking at her, though Jean Stapleton was only forty-eight when the series began (the age Nicole Kidman reached in 2015).

AN UNRESTRAINED AND UNCONSCIOUS DECENCY EMERGED IN EDITH.

But she had grace, kindness, and patience. She was not nearly as aggressive or dismissive of her husband as Else in the British show. Edith really was there until death, even if she had worn out love or romance for Archie. She came through slowly as someone dismayed by much of what he said. Not that she was what is called smart or educated—if she had been, she couldn't have stayed there. An unstrained and unconscious decency emerged in her, as touching as the revelation that in the heart of such women there might be endurance and a passive nobility. She was a character Faulkner might have written, though as a black woman. It may be that real Bunkerism watched Archie and gave him a cheer, but that was harder to do when the show cut to the face of Edith. She was a role model for women who wouldn't know what that term meant.

We may take pride in what women do on television now. Not that it's easy to find women at the executive level of Grant Tinker. In the wealth of long-form shows in recent years, *The Affair* (2014–) was co-created by Sarah Treem and Hagai Levi (and before that, they collaborated on *In Treatment* [2008–], a show Levi had originated for Israeli television). We have dominating female performances from Claire Danes (in *Homeland*, 2011–), Julia Louis-Dreyfus (*Veep*, 2012–), Julianna Margulies (*The Good Wife*, 2009–16) and Maggie Gyllenhaal (*The Honorable Woman*, 2014). These are series about central female characters—some of them very tough, smart, and independent—on which the actresses are often producers, too.

We have a confident Ellen DeGeneres with a talk show; we have people like Katie Couric and Diane Sawyer who have run the News; Judy Woodruff and Gwen Ifill are vital to the *NewsHour* on PBS;

on MSNBC, Rachel Maddow is one of the better talking heads around. Barbara Walters has only just retired (whatever that means) after one of the most varied and distinguished careers in television. Oprah Winfrey has had her show and her network, and she is a cultural enabler of the first order. We have only just lost Joan Rivers, who could be wickedly funny or plain wicked. In addition, Rivers struggled between

thinking she was not quite a beauty, in the movie star sense (she *was* pretty), and then mocking that lofty condition. Judge Judy, after more than 5,000 shows, is making $47 million a year. On *Girls*, the leading quartet includes a few faces and bodies that would not have made it on television ten years ago, to say nothing of the steadfast intellectual integrity of Lena Dunham's own rowdy nakedness.

On the other hand, I don't think we're ever going to see Erin Andrews naked on television, even if that remote prospect explains her presence. She does the unnecessary on-field interviews and reports during football and baseball for Fox. A few years ago, *Playboy* voted her "America's sexiest sportscaster," but she may have disappeared before this book reaches you. Until then, she asks a Madison Bumgarner what it felt like, and the poor pitcher struggles to be polite and coherent and to deserve these meretricious TV moments after owning the show a few minutes earlier. Andrews does a breathless, subcompetent job, but she is attractive in the way of twenty or thirty years ago (she looks like an untidy Charlie's Angel).

Television has many women commentators on male sports events now, some as good as any reporters. It happens that they are nearly all of them conventionally "attractive"—like the newscasters on Fox, or like the women in commercials for beer, cars, shampoo, and aids to erectile dysfunction. Apologists for the TV business will say that these figures are there to build the female viewership for what were once male preserves. But that fails to deal with the way TV accommodates "unattractive" or plain men, while putting

JOHN MADDEN "KNEW" FOOTBALL; A WOMAN BUILT ON THE SAME SCALE HAS NOT YET BEEN TESTED.

women to a stricter and sexist test. John Madden "knew" football; a woman built on the same scale has not yet been tested. The legend of pretty women and magic is not gone yet.

Andrews's flashy presence at big games, like that of other women field commentators, is at odds with the desperate wish of the NFL to eradicate reports of sexual violence among its players. If you pursue Andrews (she has done *Dancing with the Stars*), you can find views of her as relaxed as the slender young women recruited for the beach-scene ads extolling this beer or that. A similar class of "babe" can be found on many modern sitcoms and in the generality of advertising, where the women are anonymous but delectable assistants to the dream called purchase. That tradition endures, despite PhD candidates' theses on sexual objectification. On *Masters of Sex* (2013–), a bold Showtime series with actual sexual behavior as its subject, Virginia Johnson (Lizzy Caplan) was far more naked than Dr. Masters (Michael Sheen), and a good deal more conventionally glamorous and movielike than the real Virginia E. Johnson.

"We can always get a girl," Hollywood told itself for decades. A few of those "girls" became treasures in our memory. But the system proved itself correct over and over again. There were young women who went into hard training and dietary hell to look "cute" for a few years, dressed and undressed. They were hired and passed over in the business's confidence that the line of novices started outside its door and would work for lunch money. So the women were called "girls," and it was very few who could dispel that word and its assurance with one glance or Bette Davis eyes. Women who look ordinary (which can be terrific or enough) are still treated like Communists by TV. They seldom make it to ads, to series, to Fox newscasting, or sideline color. They are not often sufficiently the center of a series or a show that it will pause for them to think and talk—unless they are Marge Simpson.

Women are more widely employed as writers and directors on TV than they are in the movies—but that still leaves it very hard for them to succeed. When a Jon Stewart or a David Letterman retires, the system has difficulty in thinking of a female replacement. Anna Gunn, as Skyler, was very good in *Breaking Bad* (and attractive), but some viewers took against her because she was a spoilsport to Walter White. Why? Because Walter was living out a fantasy while Skyler asked, "Can we stay real?"

Edith Bunker's nakedness was of the spirit, in language and response, and true to her predicament in life. That does not show up often enough on television, or in the other arts. But the treatment of our women is a good test to bear in mind, just because the institutional and commercial bias of the medium is so ready to exploit women, and men's attitude toward them. To go back to the start of the chapter, that is why *I Love Lucy* is so astonishing. I don't think it was deliberate, or even conscious, but the show presents us with a conniving, manipulative, desperate woman under the influence of trying to live up to expectations of her. She seems a mile away from Edith, or from Shelley Long's Diane in *Cheers*, but they are models for the medium, and women doing their best under intense pressure.

THE LONELINESS OF THE ROLE MODEL

"IT'S MORNING AGAIN IN AMERICA," said a Ronald Reagan commercial in the 1984 election. The nation seemed tempted: The president won forty-nine of fifty states, with 525 votes in the electoral college, the highest figure any candidate has ever attained.

The Cosby Show was the top-ranked television program for the next five seasons, from 1985 to 1990, and one of the more beguiling and uplifting comedies ever put on television. It won the Emmy for outstanding comedy series in 1985. Prior to that, Bill Cosby had won three Emmys as lead actor in a drama series for *I Spy* (1965–68), where he was the first black actor to fill a lead role in a regular series. In 1998, he was a Kennedy Center honoree in a list that also included Shirley Temple. In 2003, at the Emmys, he was given the Bob Hope Humanitarian Award (chosen by the Academy of Television Arts and Sciences). Many viewers felt that Cosby possessed comic timing and gruff charm that

amounted to genius. He was spoken of with awe and judged to be a benign teacher; he liked to spell out his degree in education in the credits to *The Cosby Show*. It was observed that the Cosbys were a role model writ large, not just for black families but for white people watching them, too.

Sometimes the audience for *The Cosby Show* was as high as seventy million. Today, a Cosby interview—live and unpredictable—might win more viewers, but he would have to confess his broken life to Oprah or some other trusted listener. It would be a grisly public occasion, respect turning to ashes. But don't rule out the medium's readiness to take it on—with an "O. J.: The Truth" to follow. The obverse of thoughtless trust is vengeful shaming.

The audience in the late eighties loved Cosby and found the man enchanting and his family situation idealized, sweet, but a construct that passed most belief tests. Why not? For years, there had been happy-family shows on television that won large audiences without ever approaching the exact comedy that Bill Cosby created or his show's lifelike relationships of parents and children. And for decades there had not been such black characters on television, as appealing and admirably decent as Mary Tyler Moore, Fred MacMurray on *My Three Sons* (1960–72), or Mr. Rogers.

Cosby was a natural performer; everyone had said that from his start, without necessarily asking what that term meant. He had a performing quality that let you think the camera could really see into people. And if shows such as *Father Knows Best* (1954–63), *Happy Days* (1974–84), and *Family Ties* (1982–89) had been pleasing, respectable, positive entertainment with good values that might encourage young Americans to behave, be happy, and do no harm, why should a show not attempt the same thing for families of color? Especially when it was a better show.

In the era of his great success, it was easy to write an encouraging biographical note on Bill Cosby. He had been born in Philadelphia in 1937, the child of a maid and a Navy cook. His father was away in the war and afterward. Cosby was a good athlete at school, though he failed to graduate high school. He took on all manner of small jobs to help the family, and then he served four years in the Navy. It was 1961 before he completed high school and entered Temple University. He had always been a class clown, an amateur comedian, and before he could graduate he was off and away doing stand-up comedy in that lively, subversive rush of the sixties.

For a couple of decades he did anything he could think of, which included comedy acts, records, *I Spy*, movies, hosting the cartoon show *Fat Albert and the Cosby Kids*, and, in 1969, a sitcom, *The Bill Cosby Show*, which ran two seasons but never took off. America was struggling to absorb its black history. The nation had been shaken by Civil Rights demonstrations. Old attitudes altered, but regular America still disliked anger in black citizens. It had felt disturbed, or offended, by the demonstration by athletes John Carlos and Tommie Smith at the Mexico City Olympics in 1968. It admired Dr. King and Muhammad Ali, but it was fearful of Malcolm X and even Richard Pryor. Still, the society was laboring to get young

REGULAR AMERICA STILL DISLIKED ANGER IN BLACK CITIZENS.

blacks into colleges and schools, even if that meant busing and quotas, which upset some people. In other, odious ways, the country was more open to black citizens: It sent far more than their mathematical proportion in the population to Vietnam; it kept a disproportionate number of them in prison.

On television in the early seventies, the Jeffersons were derided neighbors of Archie Bunker, and they would get their own show, *The Jeffersons* (1975–85). Norman Lear took another British show, *Steptoe and Son*, and converted it into a black American setup, *Sanford and Son* (1972–77), where Redd Foxx (birth name John Elroy Sanford) became a favorite rascal. That show was steadily in the top 10, as was *The Flip Wilson Show*, a pioneering triumph for a brilliant comedian. You could look at those shows and feel encouraged by American race relations, and if you turned your attention to sport, that scene could not have functioned without new legions of black stars. It was the time of Reggie Jackson, Arthur Ashe, Kareem Abdul-Jabbar, and O. J. Simpson. But ownership, management, and coaching in those sports did not extend to minority groups, and there were few black television commentators on sport.

There were a few black actors on white TV shows (John Amos on *The Mary Tyler Moore Show*), but many shows stayed white as far as the eye could see. The black shows were tight gatherings, with the tacit assumption that most white people did not know black people, did not have black friends to dinner, and did not have their kids play with black children. If you look back at the generality of seventies television, the reasons for hope and encouragement existed, but were set in a context of cultural segregation. Thirty years from now, we may look back on 2015 with similar regret. There have still been so few sitcoms (with comic timing and charm) about a mixed-race marriage. In the great age of rock and roll, white musicians had appropriated a range of black music, the energy of black performers, and sometimes their voice of pain (the blues), without much public commentary, adequate residual payment, or shame.

Still, there was an extensive and earnest wish for the country to do better; it came to fruition at ABC, where *Roots* became one of the major events in television history. It played one year after the bicentennial, and it was principally the work of three men.

Alex Haley was born in Ithaca, New York, in 1921, and he would serve twenty years in the Coast Guard. Retired from that, he set himself to writing. He became the lead interviewer for *Playboy* and did groundbreaking pieces with Miles Davis, Martin Luther King Jr., Muhammad Ali, and Jim Brown. In 1965, he coauthored *The Autobiography of Malcolm X* to great success. Eleven years later, he delivered a book of epic, breathtaking simplicity—*Roots: The Saga of an American Family*—a novelization of a family like his own, starting with the birth of Kunta Kinte in Africa in 1750. The book was a sensation in 1976 and the number 1 seller for over five months.

David L. Wolper produced *Roots* for television because he had done so many documentary surveys on American history. He was a key figure in seeing the opportunity presented by television and the mass of newsreel to celebrate national history. His work was not profound or critical, but his energy and clarity led

ABC PERSUADED ALEX HALEY TO ADD A WHITE CHARACTER NOT IN HIS BOOK— A TROUBLED SLAVEMASTER.

his field and helped sustain the notion that energy and clarity would get at the truth. His work includes *The Rise and Fall of the Third Reich*, *The Race for Space*, *Four Days in November*, and *Hollywood: The Golden Years*.

Wolper and Haley could envisage *Roots* on television, but they needed a mogul who would insist on it. Fred Silverman, born in New York in 1937, was one of the leading network executives at a time when networks were the game. At CBS, he had OK'd and presided over *All in the Family*, *M*A*S*H*, and *The Mary Tyler Moore Show*. But in 1975 he became president of ABC, which was running behind the other two networks. His record there would reach from game shows to *Charlie's Angels* and *The Love Boat*. Silverman was cheerful about his own common touch and his alertness to passing fantasies. But he had a taste for a new form of television, something that would be called a miniseries.

The medium had known series and serials, though it was wary of tightly linked serials because it was never sure that an audience would follow along with every episode. For the American bicentennial, Silverman reckoned to make a miniseries out of an Irwin Shaw novel,

Rich Man, Poor Man (published in 1970), in which we follow two brothers, one a businessman, the other a boxer (they were played by Peter Strauss and Nick Nolte). It was twelve hours, stretched over seven weeks in February and March of 1976. Dean Riesner wrote all the scripts and Bill Bixby, Boris Sagal, and David Greene shared direction. It's no more than routine melodrama with a starry cast, conventional if not laborious narrative structure, and unusual production values. But it worked, and it came in second in the ratings. A large audience stayed to see it through.

Still, Silverman was not confident. You couldn't do *Roots* as other than a black story, but ABC worked hard: They persuaded Haley to add a white character not in his book—a troubled slave-master (played by Ed Asner, who had won an Emmy in *Rich Man, Poor Man*); and when they promoted the show, the white faces got more than their due quota of screen time. Commercial spots in the show were not selling. Some early reviews were dubious. Silverman elected to be brave and cautious at the same time. He gambled by playing the show eight nights in a row in January 1977. If it succeeded, the effect would be sensational, with word of mouth building all over the country. If it failed, it could be swept away quickly and ABC would get back to the Osmonds, *Monday Night Football*, and *Happy Days*.

It worked, less because of its quality as a movie than because of daring presentation, the novelty of the material, and a range of appealing performances from a cast that included LeVar Burton, Cicely Tyson, O. J. Simpson, Louis Gossett Jr., Leslie Uggams, and Ben Vereen. And surely because the national conscience—so slow in history's terms—was ready. The *Roots* audience built from about 28 million households to 36 million. It was estimated that 100 million people watched the last episode. The show took the Emmy for outstanding limited series, and individual awards went to Asner (again), Olivia Cole (she was black), Louis Gossett Jr., and director David Greene. There was controversy: Some said the show was unfair to white characters; others felt the barbaric cruelty revealed was just a matter of "period" accuracy. Of course, *Roots* moved the country forward and served as a history lesson. But then, in 2013, Americans were once more moved and shaken by *12 Years a Slave* (actually done by British filmmakers), as if the wound remained open. Looking back, one has to say that the television careers of LeVar Burton, Leslie Uggams, Olivia Cole, and Ben Vereen did not move forward as effectively as that of Ed Asner.

ROOTS BUILT FROM ABOUT 28 MILLION HOUSEHOLDS TO 36 MILLION.

There was a sequel, *Roots: The Next Generations*, in 1979, shown every night for a week. This brought the story up to date and ended with James Earl Jones as the adult Haley. Henry Fonda and Olivia de Havilland played a nineteenth-century couple who abandon their son when he marries a black woman. The sequel was popular, though its audience dropped off significantly from the original. Again it won the limited-series Emmy, and an individual award went to Marlon Brando, who played the neo-Nazi George Lincoln Rockwell (in one episode).

A book like this has to note the "event" of *Roots* and respect its impact and its context. In the same year as *Roots*, O. J. Simpson's NFL season at Buffalo was cut short by injury—he was close to retirement, yet only thirty. He also met Nicole Brown that year. Jimmy Carter had just been sworn in as president. He straightaway pardoned all those who had evaded the Vietnam draft. He seemed to carry a wish for candor and reconciliation. The audience presented itself for *Roots* in huge, earnest numbers. Was there some hope for change in the air, a wish that Watergate and Vietnam might be put to rest?

So *Roots* unfolded—predictable, powerful, but heavy-footed. I went back to reexamine this television monument, and I couldn't sit through it. The show had helped ordain the term "African-American," when I was not American myself yet. But I guessed in 1977 that black Americans—for their own sake and for the sake of all Americans— were going to have to be plain Americans, and as plain as the rest of the country. (Although being plain in the United States goes against the steady urge towards exceptionalism in the struggle between reality and dream.)

One burden *Roots* bore was being perceived as a lesson and a role model. There was an awkwardness in its concept—between Wolper's educational thrust and Haley's fictional urge—that is close to the ruinous condition we have now with so many movies that tell us they are "based on a true story" while garbling and spoiling the history but compromising the soaring flight of fiction. Figures from life and history must be created anew for art to have the best chance of explaining history.

Think of the movie *Steve Jobs* (2015), directed by Danny Boyle and written by Aaron Sorkin. That apparent biopic does not always resemble or deliver history's verifiable Jobs: Michael Fassbender does not look like the man, as Ashton Kutcher strove to in *Jobs* (2013). Many people involved in Jobs's life (like his associate Steve Wozniak) admit that much in *Steve Jobs* is inaccurate or invented—its details did not happen. But then they say that its essence, *its story*, is true. Anna Karenina, Charles Foster Kane, and Jay Gatsby did not exist, but their fictional lives are now emblematic of their society. Sorkin, I think, set out to make a film about a character trembling on the edge of genius and authority. So the greatest value of *Steve Jobs* is to let us feel the passion and danger in being close to an inspiring American fascist (someone who imposes his will and vision on those around him), a genius of new enterprise and the kind of leader we keep saying we need.

This Jobs is not the object of a biopic; he is a fictional character in a movie that is actually not too concerned with Apple and its fruit. But *Roots*, I fear, was fatally a commercial for progress—which doesn't mean it was less than well intentioned, or that we the public didn't need to put on some speed and make progress. Which brings me back to Bill Cosby.

||||||||||||||||||||||||||||

THE BIG SHOW WAS NOT COSBY'S IDEA IN THE FIRST PLACE. It was the vision of Marcy Carsey and Tom Werner, TV programmers who had met at ABC and developed such shows as *Mork & Mindy* and *Soap*. They left the network and struck out on their own as Carsey-Werner, and they dreamed of a hit sitcom, for its own sake and for the business revenue. They both enjoyed the humor of Bill Cosby and felt that he had never been adequately focused for television. So they talked to him about something new.

Cosby wanted a family show, educational in the broadest sense, and featuring a working-class family. It seems that it was Cosby's own wife, Camille (they have been married since 1964 and had five children), who wondered if the parental couple could be professional people, middle-class and gently rising, as if to say that such a staircase was possible for black families. Above all, the scheme involved a range of children in the family, not only because Cosby wanted to provide models for parenting, but because his own comic impulse was stimulated by kids. He could be true to them, fond and supportive, while throwing us a raised eyebrow or a slow burn that said, "Kids!" *The*

Cosby Show was driven by other people at first, but gradually it became his atmosphere. Anyone could see what a charmer he was, and the benign father figure he wanted to be, but you could feel, too, that he was the writer and the director, urging it all along. He was a wizard in his cave, and very soon it became clear that the cave—10 Stigwood Avenue in Brooklyn Heights—was a kingdom.

Cosby knew that any real dad could look like a chump with every other word he said. But in giving us that frailty, he underlined his eminence. He was a big man, bulky but soft in his famous sweaters, and you could tell he had been a fair athlete. He had moves, steps, head feints, and wraparound vision. The kids liked to cuddle him. And Cliff Huxtable had a pretty wife, Clair (Phylicia Rashad), who was actually eleven years his junior. The longer you watched, the easier it was to credit that as the show went on so Cosby dominated more and more of it, and breathed its championship deeply. A day would come when he even wondered aloud if he might buy NBC, the network that his show had rescued.

From the outset, some critics said the show was too sweet and overcalculating. They complained that the Huxtables did not seem to know white people, or even other people, and that there was a kind of hush law operating in the house to smother anything controversial. Some felt Cosby was just dunking us all in Jell-O pudding (made with wholesome milk), the confection that he advertised for years with enormous success (again, playing with children and giving the impression of improvisation). But even critics admitted that Cosby was brilliant in the way most of us admire comics and their mechanics. Perhaps we are manipulated, but there's no ill will in sight, and the comic's charm rests in his relaxed performance. It's like being in the hands of a great magician. In trying to describe his persona on the show, I have endeavored to stay faithful to what I felt at the time. And surely Cosby deserves that, as much as O. J. Simpson cannot lose his achievement as a running back.

As of January 2016, nothing has yet been proved in court against Bill Cosby, though there was an undisclosed settlement in 2006 in the

IT'S LIKE BEING IN THE HANDS OF A GREAT MAGICIAN.

action brought by Andrea Constand, where a dozen women threatened to make similar claims. That is now the cause of felony charges of sexual assault in the state of Pennsylvania. The case will be hard to win—and it may be distended by television coverage. But is more proof needed? It appears Bill Cosby behaved atrociously to a number of women, beyond molestation to the point of rape. I believe that as much as I have always felt that Simpson murdered his ex-wife, Nicole Brown Simpson, and Ronald Goldman in 1994.

Cosby is seventy-eight as I write (2016), and his career is finished, for his reputation and role model have been destroyed (or replaced). He did maintain a tour of stand-up comedy nights as the charges built against him, and there were reports of audiences giving him ovations, but any talk of new television shows came to an abrupt close, and it is hard now to find *The Cosby Show* in reruns. If he gets back on TV it will be in his trial. The accusations have been dreadful, and Cosby turned to silence. Nothing in this history was more arresting than his studio presence on the NPR radio show *Weekend Edition Saturday* on November 15, 2014, when a concerned and respectful Scott Simon asked if Cosby wanted to comment on the allegations, and silence filled the air.

Cosby has been helpless in the Internet nightmare. The authority he once had on-screen, and the way he controlled and projected his attitude, have gone mad with ravaged celebrity. He is now open to a frenzied court worthy of Prometheus, in which he is gnawed at every day on the Net, whose judgments are probably more final than court proceedings. But this is what the screen does now—using that word to cover the total electronic broadcast of imagery through space. The implicit crosscuts, from *The Cosby Show* to Jell-O pudding

ads to this Internet chaos, make a more compelling portrait of television than *Roots* (in hindsight), and far more immediate in the light it casts on where race is now.

The O. J. Simpson affair came at a cusp: The Internet was only just getting up to speed, and filmed news was still a mainstay of journalism. The trial was one of the most tedious and inescapable events in our television history (it ran nine months). Years after the Simpson case, I was doing a documentary beneath the HOLLYWOOD sign (isn't that what it's for?), and in a lull as we waited for the wind to drop, the cameraman told me how the Simpson case had been the heyday of his business: hiring out his equipment and himself to visiting TV news crews. For more than a year, he was making money as fast as he could—there would be estimates later that the United States had lost productivity to the tune of $40 billion just because so many people stopped work to watch the case and the trial.

ROOTS, I FEAR, WAS STRICTLY A COMMERCIAL FOR PROGRESS.

For so long, television had worshipped at the feet of Justice in ways that were blind to injustice. How could a medium honestly promote the American Dream without specious claims of fairness? *Perry Mason* (1957–66) was a ludicrous show when it first played, with haphazard rewritings of legal procedures, the invincible record of one attorney, and a district attorney who never won a case, but it was steadily in the top 20, and Raymond Burr won two Emmys as lead actor in a drama series. There were other legal series—from *The Defenders* (1961–65) to *L.A. Law* (1986–94)—that took on increasing reality and cultural doubt over court results. But the Simpson case was a breakout event and blatant disclosure that Justice was replaced by a TV show close to nightmare but, in this case, more alive with American racism than anything else on television.

The Simpson trial had so much: a sports idol whose heroic beauty and camera cheerfulness were suspiciously brittle; a white wife who was the epitome of blonde centerfold cool; momentous bloody violence, a feast for the new science of DNA testing; black attorneys just as eager to win and cash in as their white counterparts; incompetence of shocking proportions in police and lawyers; one fully identified racist cop; and a jury of Angelenos who were mostly women and black, because of the shifting of the action from Santa Monica to downtown Los Angeles. Even so, would the travesty have been moderated if it had not been on television? With that decision, the event became a series, not a show (134 days in court), and national productivity was sabotaged (100 million watched the verdict—the same number as saw the last episode of *Roots*. We always have 100 million for a big wow.)

There was idealism contained in that decision. For we are eager to think that showing events and actions is informative, open and even democratic, no matter that we know so many of our most important decisions are taken privately, secretly, or "in camera." There was also a certain shy vanity in Judge Ito. (Judge Judy would have settled the case in three hours—that's one reason why we love the harsh lady.) In an open democracy, should our procedures not be open to the scrutiny of the camera, albeit a camera that behaves as plain, detached, and "objective" as surveillance? Do we have cameras in the Oval Office recording every compromise and sigh? Do we record the deliberations of the Supreme Court? Have we got steady coverage of the financial boardrooms, the bankers' offices where the design of the economy is manipulated and its rhetoric scripted? Do we have full video coverage of Abu Ghraib, Gitmo, and any other location required for necessary enhanced interrogation? Don't we have the screen rights on Kim Kardashian's bathroom—or does it just feel like that?

If *Roots* had been a drama about the travails and vindication of a black family, and a black presence in America, its simplicity was exposed by the ongoing OJ and Cosby series, in which the psychic and cultural tensions of being a black American exploded. Once civil rights had been defined and enacted, the races in America were plunged into the turmoil of psychic hope and dread in which role-modeling was as spurious as the mythology about what made a pretty woman or a decent man. Why was Simpson called "OJ" except in a kind of branding or headlinese that said, "Look, this guy is sweet, wholesome, and nourishing (and 'Orenthal' is just too fancy)? You can have him for breakfast." (And "Sweetness" and

WHY WAS SIMPSON CALLED "OJ" EXCEPT IN A KIND OF BRANDING?

"Sweet" are nicknames often given to black men.) Is "OJ" that far from Jell-O? Wasn't that extended advertising campaign a way of saying you can trust our pudding because Bill Cosby likes it—sweet, wholesome, and pretty?

Why should an actor not take advantage of the money to be earned by doing a commercial? Don't they all do it now? But the pressure of branding is corrupting and destructive, because it takes away from any sense of an actor's integrity. Imagine a network newscast telling us that this story was brought to us by…that's hideous, but it's what some radio sportscasters have to do all the time. And if we don't quite believe in these stars and celebrities, surely life becomes a little harder for them. To be identified as a role model is not to lose a lot of human variety; but it's stress that can deform a person. And if we believe the very worst about Simpson and Cosby, then we are looking at a disaster born in success. Both those men had risen far beyond the circumstances of their birth, and in the US there is latent resentment,

an instinct for vengeance, that waits on success—for this is a nation of so many failures if measured against the ideology of its advertising, and the pounding impetus of its required "greatness." The huddled mass worships the shining light, but it loathes it, too. That urge comes down especially hard on minorities cast as newcomers, aspirants and searchers wishing to inhabit the American dream. That is how an Eldrick becomes a "Tiger."

OJ had lost his playing career (and any great athlete faces a crisis in that); he may have been close to the end of his broadcasting and acting careers because of drug dependency; and he had lost a trophy wife who was now going out with other men. Suppose a life of sweetness masks a capacity for anger. As for Cosby, he had been adored to such a point that he could have felt he was adorable, and thus a gift to women. He met many women who saw him as a star and someone who might help their careers. So perhaps he took advantage of that and let loose a monstrousness that he had restrained for so long, in the way of black people who were once told to be polite to whites. As if politeness, or even nonviolence could dispel coarseness, racism, and hostility in much of white society. William Cosby the citizen may have made grave and criminal errors; and he may have to take the consequences for them. But William Cosby's own privacy was obliterated by his fame and by his essential presence as a performer.

I am not raising these points to exonerate either man, though in American show business Cosby has never been alone in taking advantage of women. Movie moguls, many of them, used the auditioning process to impose sexual rights. Don't marvel at that, or succumb to naive horror, for all of us at the movies or watching television have employed these beautiful strangers in our own fantasy romance. The one transaction is more brutal than the other, but don't lose sight of how the two are related. It can be a torment for stars to be told by crowds of strangers that they love you and are yours. Equally, the astonishing light of celebrity can persuade some of its beneficiaries that they are immaculate, uncatchable, beyond law, reason, and the constant observation that imprisons them. We have had presidents yield to that temptation, leaving us to decide they must be human after all. But do we allow role models to be human? An actor doing Jell-O pudding commercials is not to be seen spitting out a mouthful of yellow glop and saying, "How I hate this stuff!"

Loathing white stuff is hardly illegitimate. In *The Fire Next Time* (1963), James Baldwin asked why blacks should be expected to aspire to white American society. Was it really so admirable or supreme? Over the years, some of the most remarkable black lives have been beset by that tension—think of Louis Armstrong, Miles Davis, Martin Luther King Jr., Richard Pryor, Muhammad Ali, Tiger Woods, and even Barack Obama. King is frequently designated as a saint and then attacked by enemies because he was not flawless in private. As for Obama, though he has not complained, one wonders how far a lifetime of racial insecurity and traditional obedience determined his being trapped in rationality sometimes when blunt politics was called for. He has worked hard to be calm, lucid, moderate, modest, clear-thinking, so many qualities that his opponents feel are far-fetched in black life. In the same way, a part of Cosby may have hated himself for the very charm that white people cherished.

He was a safe black man on television (a thing that makes Richard Pryor seem braver still in admitting the danger and disorder in his life). The charm could work in baffling ways. In January 2015, Cindra Ladd joined the long line of women who said they had been exploited by Bill Cosby. She gave a harrowing account of being drugged and then raped, and explained why she had never reported the event. But then she added this remarkable statement: "I watched *The Cosby Show* at its zenith and was a fan [this was long after her rape]. But as I watched Dr. Cliff Huxtable, so compassionate and kind, so honorable and wise, I could never reconcile that image with the Bill Cosby I encountered so many years ago." She kept watching the show?

You might look at black experience in America fifty years after the Voting Rights Act and feel encouraged. There are distinguished black citizens in every walk of life, (though too much of the black population is still at the levels of brutal poverty and disadvantage). Job opportunities, educational access, real estate liberty have all been opened up to black participation. We have had a black president, and Oprah Winfrey may be the richest woman in the world. Denzel Washington and Morgan Freeman have a case for being among the best and best-respected movie actors in America. So much is for the better.

And yet, in 2014–15 there were clashes between mostly young black men and children and mostly white police that disturbed or dismayed the nation because they spoke to abiding prejudices and systemic unfairness. And the Supreme Court is steadily reversing a series of measures that once sought to be more welcoming to black Americans.

||||||||||||||||||||||||||||

THE FORCES THAT COMBINED TO PRODUCE *THE COSBY SHOW* wanted a hit and the spoils that came from it. It would be fatuous to expect that prime-time television did not have that in mind. I don't exclude Cosby himself from that feeling, yet no one had more hopes for "inspiration" or example than Cosby. But like so much mere entertainment, *The Cosby Show* seeped into deeper levels of understanding. The show fit very well with the vacant optimism of "morning in America" in proposing a black life that was settled, secure, happy even, and part of the glow of economic progress. It was a view of life that sustained the spirit of advertising and which let a large white audience believe there was nothing to fear or feel threatened by in black experience.

But the more you think about it, the more spurious that mood seems. Why do white Americans need to be given confidence, or tranquillity, about a black presence? It's as if after centuries of brutal exploitation of blacks, white America requires psychic forgiveness enough to overwhelm any black suggestion that there might be reparations—and most of liberal white America feels that would be fanciful and foolish. And useless—don't poor people mishandle their money? By every measure, a majority of blacks continue to be underprivileged in America, especially vulnerable to police suspicion—and condemned to be judged as "role models" if they do as well as Cliff and Clair Huxtable.

Another remarkable black figure on television was Clarence Thomas, on his uncertain way to becoming a Justice of the Supreme Court in 1991. He was a rage for a moment, not just the new show but a means for American society to plunge into profound topics, from the importance of blacks being promoted in our life to the ugliness of sexual harassment. Then, in an astonishing way, Thomas receded. Twenty-five years later, we hardly know him, but for the few moments of melodrama. But it is hard to forget his grievance or anger when he charged the Senate Judiciary Committee for setting up "a high-tech lynching for uppity blacks." That is a line in history and it could have come from *Roots*, or from some canny coaching scriptwriter in the Republican administration that had nominated Thomas.

The televised hearings of the Judiciary Committee were hideous yet riveting, and we were all incriminated. In fact, the legal vetting of Thomas was nearly done with when the Committee believed he might have been lying and given grave offense to Anita Hill. They brought Hill forward as a witness. That story within the process was not resolved, in part because the Committee proved timid about letting supporting witnesses have a say. The process was ugly in every way, and demeaning. The Committee were torn between being judges themselves or showmen with a scandal.

It was hard not to wonder—Why is this on television? But Joe Biden (chairman of the Committee) surely shared every vague thought that the processes of democracy should be seen and heard by us. Equally, one felt that Biden was caught in our horribly confused feeling: Must you show me this? but don't stop, please.

It's hard to think the Thomas-Hill confrontation served much purpose. It did not settle any truth; it did not clarify the reputation of either party; it did not do honor to the Senate; and it had little to do with "transparency." Hill said later that it was "a disservice to everyone." And after Thomas was approved, he ultimately fell silent in questioning sessions for ten years, because, as he has stated, he felt others would ask his questions. No matter whom one believed, the thought lingered: Would a white nominee and a white clerk have received the same level of intense television exposure?

The ordeal of being a black character in the living theater of television is immense, because the atmosphere of theater is so hard to escape. We need the forthright voice of black experience: It was there in Billie Holiday, Charlie Parker, James Baldwin, Richard Pryor and in the bold handsomeness of the Black Panthers. It is there in the boyish pleasure with which Steph Curry sinks an outrageous three-pointer— that is speech; it was there in the seething fusion of beauty and the sinister in some Michael Jackson routines; it was remarkable in Chris Rock's brave, witty, and exact opening monologue at the 2016 Oscars. I think it was there when Barack Obama wept in the attempt to speak about gun damage in America. But there are also despairing silences, like that of Justice Thomas; of "Tiger" Woods struggling to comprehend the loss of his magic; of Bill Cosby on the radio; and of the shuffling, demoralized O. J. Simpson at the Lovelock Correctional Center, incapable of making a direct testimony about what he did, and why he did it. After all, he is beyond incrimination or reward now, but he has something to offer in the drama of how an O.J. becomes the Other. It is only such revelations that can lead all of us to abide by the unremarkable, ordinary, and natural presence of black people as Americans.

So the larger problem in our use of screens derived from television is that the condition of role-modeling, branding, or profiling has become so pervasive. So Clarence Thomas is *the* black man on the Supreme Court (and he did replace the first black justice, Thurgood Marshall) and not his complex self. In a similar way, Tavis Smiley and Trevor Noah are less-than-white talk-show hosts who haven't quite made it at the top level. *Empire* and *How to Get Away with Murder* are "exceptions," hit shows about black characters, even if they rely on a criminal backdrop. And so on. This drab categorizing can be applied across the board of television offerings, and it's only when we come to sport that it becomes redundant, because that is the truest multicultural enterprise in the nation—even if it is the one aspect of our activity where nonwhites predominate.

This impedes the chance for whites of seeing black people as if they were not of any one race or type, but as odd, eccentric, unpredictable, unaccountable as any of us. Many will sigh and say, "Well… haven't we made progress? Isn't there reason for hope?" Perhaps, but do we have the time to wait? Barack Obama came to the White House with the burden of being profiled or role-modeled as the black president. A similar load awaits a woman—because white males are accustomed to their own originalism. One interpretation of Obama's office has been his steady wish to be a president instead of a black president, in a culture that is rife with unspoken (or barely spoken) feelings of disapproval and hatred of such a public figure. I am not being partisan; I am not saying he was a great president or one who might have been great. (I don't know what a great president is supposed to be, as opposed to a president.) I am simply suggesting that he was unlucky enough to take up a role-model position that could eclipse his chance to find himself.

The greater threat to our culture and our discourse is that this kind of branding is descending on everyone, and nearly everything we do, because of the technologies that television and domestic screens have furnished. We are all of us being profiled all the time as part of the techno-commercial system by which our corporate structures (private and governmental) attempt to keep charge of us and keep us in order as predictable elements in the market. Elsewhere, I propose a contrast between Mary Tyler Moore and Edith Bunker. Mary was a clean role model (the single working woman), she was Miss Perfect, chipper, bright, everyone's friend, attractive, smart, able—it was a killing and entertaining package and it may have hurt the real Mary Tyler Moore as much as it did American women who tried to be like her. But Edith Bunker was not a role model: American television does not offer middle-aged women of modest education and common looks as role models. Mary was credibly someone who might watch the commercials and follow their lead—she was famous for her snappy dress sense. But Edith was the kind of person advertisers pass over. You couldn't think of her buying much except the same old groceries. You couldn't persuade yourself, or her, that she was in a position to "reinvent herself" along with the surge of "morning in America." Yet Edith was human, humane, all without stress, and she was believable as a real woman. Has she had any successors?

The individuality left in this mass society is our demographic profile, and where we fall on the statistical curves that track our social security, our educational history, our résumé, our "vital" statistics, our credit record, our passwords, our purchasing record…our dot-com. But once we're part of the curve, our particle identity may vanish: This is close to what Werner Heisenberg recognized in his uncertainty principle (1927). In an age of increasing fears over identity theft, it is easy to lose sight of how identity has been ebbing away through the net of our discourse. That may seem alarming, but we go along with the system happily enough. We work to remember all our passwords, and worry that forgetfulness means Alzheimer's. We understand that our information and our whims on the Internet are being used to place us and serve us with "what we want." And shouldn't we be content if we have what we want—even if those desires are increasingly codified? We welcome systems of discourse that embrace voluntary limitations on language and communication: The restricted alphabet of Twitter is a step toward schemes in which we may have to answer "like" or "not like," yes or no, on or off.

And in language itself—the most hopeful of our technologies?—we now have a scheme of calls, responses, or hit-button phrases that do not quite mean what they seem to say: "happy hour," "have a good one," "delete," "homeland security," "the red carpet," "lol," "btw," "breaking news," "A minus," "the sexiest man/woman/pet alive," "outside the envelope," "social media," and "the greatest nation on earth." These are signals that undermine the complexity of particular messages and begin to bypass language. It's as if the curtailment of intricate or debatable meaning from ads has infected our general discourse.

This linguistic code accompanies a typology of images that has been present a hundred years in movies and intensified in ads: the strong man, the beautiful woman, the villain, the hunted look, the sexy gaze, the honest face, the happy smile, the confrontation, the car chase, the shoot-out…The list is immense, and it's not that such situations, or sits, don't have roots in life or their place in story. But there has always been the danger that their accumulation depletes our appreciation of the real thing, life. So the black man can be a badge on television such as blacks go mad trying to bypass. And that frustration may be coming to all of us now. The technology is a system of understanding, but is it also a way of abbreviating sense?

This system is all the more natural in that no one ever made the decision to adopt it. Our participation and our vote were bypassed. We need to reassess the cultural threats we face. The tragic ending of *Nineteen Eighty-Four*, in 1954, was delivered in the crushed figures of Winston and Julia, whose rebellious intimacy had not been permitted by the state. The sight of Yvonne Mitchell's radiant Julia demolished may have been the first great emotional moment in TV history. In 1954, this was close to memories of resistance movements from the war. That is how Winston and Julia had tried to fight Big Brother. But time moves on, and now the corporate state might respond to resistance with more calm:

> Very well, you may keep your privacy, your intimacy and "independence." That's what you like, and it comes as fantasy, personal opinion, drugs, pornography, passwords, the Net, or loneliness. The state does not care or need to care about that. Because privacy has been cut off from action. You do not count amid such vast numbers. The mass prevails and we are skilled at guiding it past the whims of privacy. So let privacy settle for isolation.

16

MR. PRESIDENT

THIS ACTOR HAD BEEN AROUND IN MOVIES FOR FIFTEEN YEARS by 1954, but he was amazed at how his life had recently altered. "I am seen by more people in one week than I am in a full year in movie theaters." He reflected on that experience; it changed his life— and ours.

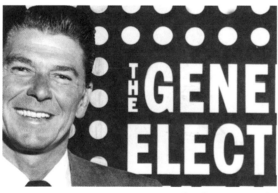

In December 1954, he did a 30-minute melodrama for *General Electric Theater*. He had a cozy arrangement on that show. His agency, MCA, had proposed him as host and actor for *GE Theater*. He might even do public events on the road, speaking at General Electric establishments. There was a little more to it: The actor (who was also president of the Screen Actors Guild) leaned on his guild to allow MCA to produce the GE shows through its subsidiary, Revue, a liberty that went against SAG rules and which made a fortune for the agency. It was Lew Wasserman who constructed that deal for MCA and advised Ronald Reagan that television was the big new thing— so many people saw you; perhaps it was everything.

In that December 1954 episode, *The Dark, Dark Hours*, directed by Don Medford, Reagan plays a doctor. At 3:45 one morning, he and his wife are sound asleep in their twin beds in their nice home. But then there's an insistent buzzing at the front door. The doctor gets up, grumbling, and puts on an expensive dressing gown. He goes to the door and finds two kids, one of them shot, the other looking after him. As a doctor, he is prepared to treat the kid wounded by gunfire. But he is bound to call the police because he's an upright citizen. Then the kid who's not shot pulls a gun: "No cops, man," he orders. This kid is acting his head off, but it's to little avail because the story keeps shooting him from behind in order to concentrate on Reagan's Doc. Yet the kid is James Dean, just before he made *East of Eden*. Dean was another new thing, fidgety, moody, Methody, muttering, trying to be a riveting, jittery hoodlum. Reagan is deeply old-fashioned, stoically dull and settled. But he was the future more than Dean, and television was working.

Reagan's contract was $125,000 a year—the best he'd ever had—and for that he did the shows, traveled promoting GE for fourteen weeks a year, and found he was meeting and greeting 100,000 workers a year. It was his first campaign, and it felt sweet because the people he met knew him from television and because he did a terrific greeting. To this day, commentators remark on how a movie star became president, but that's not the secret to Ronald Reagan. More accurately, he was the man on television, cooler, calmer, and less charismatic than movie stars. On the big screen, Reagan had been a pal, a support, an amiable sidekick. But after Reagan it was fanciful for any movie star—from Warren Beatty to George Clooney—to have a stray thought of running for the big job. Instead, it needed a TV veteran who understood the humdrum job and the virtue in being genial or easygoing, and being on.

I have already touched on the first notable presidential use of television (see chapter 11), though Richard Nixon was merely struggling to stay a vice presidential candidate when he delivered his "Checkers" speech in 1952. It's important to recall that that coup established an insecure figure. Yet the beseeching effort did characterize Nixon. As Mark Feeney says in his searching book, *Nixon at the Movies*:

It created a template for both how he viewed himself (as honest and embattled) and for public doubts about him (as shifty and shameless)… Forever after, he managed to seem simultaneously sanctimonious and unsavory.

The Checkers speech had Nixon alone—his wife was off to the side, but as a piece of theatrical furniture (that may have been oddly revealing). The speech was that of a man, locked in courage and apprehension, who felt isolated. In television terms, that would become prescient. In the crucial electoral debates with John Kennedy in 1960, it seems to have been Nixon's exposure to company that undermined him.

There had never been such televised debates before, and there were worries over their legitimacy. Section 315 of the Communications Act insisted that television was obliged to give equal time to all candidates—and there were a dozen or so running for the presidency. The networks hated that much balance; they wanted stars without distractions. In inviting Kennedy and Nixon to debate as soon as they were nominated, they were putting pressure on a government waiver of Section 315. Eisenhower signed off on that in August, though he was not always Nixon's best ally. Asked by *Time* magazine's Charles Mohr to

JOHN KENNEDY'S FATHER HAD BEEN IN THE PICTURE BUSINESS.

name a big Nixon initiative during his administration, the president had said, "If you give me a week, I might think of one."

Kennedy jumped at the debate, so Nixon had to join him. But as a semi-incumbent and the better known person across the country, he saw the natural advantage Kennedy would have—and the risk he was exposing himself to. If you review that first debate (September 26, in Chicago, for CBS), it's easy to feel that Kennedy is excited to be on television, while Nixon would rather not be there. John Kennedy's father had been in the picture business; the youth had met movie stars; and he had an appetite for being photographed and having the camera like him. What does that mean? It's hard to define, but it is a modern secret in politics and the pulse of television. Do you want to be on TV? Do you think you deserve it? Do you believe you will be "good" on camera? Answer "No" to those questions and you might as well get out of politics. But if you have that manner (naturally or from training) you may go far: Few were horrified when Ben Carson said Obamacare was the worst thing since slavery, because he said it in his relaxed, affable way.

Kennedy respected the 1960 debate and anticipated how it might work. He had been campaigning in California and let his tan build. Then he rested for a few days before the show. Earlier in the year, in the Wisconsin primary contest with Hubert Humphrey, Kennedy had been filmed on the stump by Robert Drew, Richard Leacock, and Albert Maysles for a film called *Primary*. This was an early example of what would be known as cinema verité, done with light-weight cameras and tape recorders, with the filmmakers catching the candidates impromptu, without warning, just "being themselves." Kennedy's sense of the moment and his appetite for risk responded to that method. If you were interested in being "on," you might as well be on all the time. It might not count as verité, but it seemed "real." The medium's tortured pact with "reality shows" was beginning. A candidate might deliver an elegant plan for civil rights, Middle East peace, and "Is the earth getting warmer?" (it was already), but if he farted out loud in a press conference, he was finished.

IT MIGHT NOT COUNT AS VERITÉ, BUT IT SEEMED "REAL."

By contrast, Nixon had no rest, no tan, and he had only just recovered from illness. He chose to wear a light-colored suit. His hair was freshly cut short. His collar looked just a little loose—was it the wrong size? His neck seemed scrawny. As the debate gathered, the candidates were asked whether they wanted to use makeup. Kennedy said he had no need and Nixon went along with that implicit dare, though events would show he had needed it badly. He looked a little haggard and unshaven. That was bad enough. But then the debate began and something best known as mise-en-scène took over.

The director for television was Don Hewitt of CBS News (later a major figure at the network and the creator of *60 Minutes*). It was Hewitt who made the editing calls on which image to show at any given moment. You might anticipate that in a debate, the camera would concentrate on the candidate speaking. That happened most of the time. But Hewitt knew enough about how TV worked to realize that reaction shots, or listening moments, could be just as interesting as talking heads and maybe more revealing. The result was remarkable—and it passed instantly into the playbook of political campaigning on television.

Kennedy listened, like an appreciative actor in a two-shot; he attended to Nixon; he even smiled occasionally at some of the things Nixon said—not in mockery (he was too smart for that) but to show the process of analysis or judgment at work. It wasn't quite as good as watching Cary Grant listen, but it was akin to our ability to see an intelligence working in Grant (and many other actors). On the other hand, Nixon was inclined to freeze while Kennedy was speaking, waiting for his next turn and radiating that essential nervousness and the idea that he felt alone up there while he was on.

IT WASN'T QUITE AS GOOD AS WATCHING CARY GRANT LISTEN, BUT IT WAS AKIN TO OUR ABILITY TO SEE AN INTELLIGENCE WORKING.

If that makes the first debate seem like a landslide, that's a mistake. Somewhere between 70 and 75 million watched it, nearly half the country, and polls suggested that reactions were very close. Kennedy had just shaded the result, but that was less significant than the way he had introduced himself and settled the doubts that he was too young, too glib, too irresponsible, too pleased with himself, too Catholic, whatever. None of those possibilities was really disproved. You could say that he was pleased with himself, or that he was easy in his skin. He liked being on TV. There was a clear poll response that JFK had proved himself a serious candidate and an intelligent or well-spoken guy. He brought the election to a state of equality and uncertainty, and Nixon hated uncertainty. Edmund Morris, one day the biographer of Ronald Reagan, defined the 1960 election as "Apollo v. Cyclops," because Nixon's eyes seemed to come closer together under the gaze of the good-looking guy. Within a couple of days, no one could remember what either man had said or promised.

Kennedy had writers, but he trusted instinct, too. In one of the later debates (there were four altogether), Nixon accused him of a "barefaced lie," and JFK shot back to say he couldn't return that

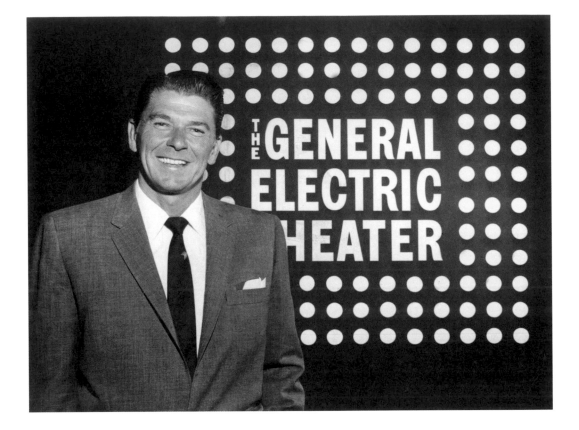

charge, because "I've seen him in a television studio, with his makeup on." We don't have to rank that as the first sound bite in electoral history, but Nixon was bitten just as much as the jab lodged in public memory. There were wide-eyed declarations at the time that the television debates were bringing in a brave new world of active democracy and public participation. But there was a chance, then and there, before election day, that the debates would begin to be boring, unless there was a camera angle or a bite to hold on to. There had been a solid fifty years of movies by 1960, enough to teach us how deadening small talk and speechifying could be on-screen. People needed to talk in lines and act as if they had just precious seconds to live.

That grasp on *now* was essential Kennedy, and the proof of what movies and movie people meant to him. The political show was highly entertaining in the early sixties, and yet it was superficiality written on our wall, or our screen, too. I don't mean that as an accusation of intellectual shortcoming—it was Kennedy's unmediated insight that the presidency was going to have to be superficial to play on television. So he got off great lines, from "Ask not..." in his cold-morning inaugural to "I'm the man who accompanied Jacqueline Kennedy to Paris" at a state banquet hosted by President de Gaulle. It was JFK's personality that often brought this immediacy close to melodrama or horrid brinks. He played the Cuban Missile Crisis of October 1962 like a suspense movie. Nothing happened in that desperate tension that we could see, day after day, but we were attached to the television set to see if it would.

And so that witty, tousled "now" head was blown to pieces in November 1963. No, I'm not suggesting in any causal sense that Kennedy was assassinated like an event in a movie, but do not overlook the possibility that in the muddled mind of Lee Harvey Oswald, Kennedy was the celebrity head of the moment that he needed to hunt. Ask what was accomplished in the administration of John Kennedy and it's hard to give a list of serious political decisions. But the movie of those thousand days is vivid and jittery with our attention and, finally, our crushed feelings.

As the new means of observation and reportage, television was seeping into politics and staining it. If you look at John Frankenheimer's eerie movie *The Manchurian Candidate*

(released October 24, 1962, at the height of the missile crisis), you see a young director (raised in live TV drama) obsessed with television screens and rising to the idea of assassinating a candidate on TV as the latter makes a key speech. It's not the fanciful intrigue of Communist conspiracy that is frightening, it's the feeling that television is an eye impatient for terrible action.

The rise of a television president doesn't happen overnight. All his political life, Lyndon Johnson had been a physical operator: He got other people in person in a small space; he grasped them, grappled, hugged, and scolded them. He is a figure from an ongoing play, not a television person. So when he took to the screen he was lamer, slower, plaintive, and so intimidated by the medium that he abandoned his natural way of speaking. He was not as good or present as Nixon. And when Johnson made his most significant broadcast, it was to announce his retirement from the contest. By many tests, Johnson was a more complete and effective politician than Kennedy, but he knew he had been eclipsed by the glow of his departed master.

Eisenhower was the first president to speak to the people through television, though his press conferences were filmed first and edited if necessary before being shown. He was seldom comfortable on television, but in hindsight his limitations feel honest. On January 17, 1961, days before the inauguration of his successor, he decided to make a 15-minute farewell speech on television. It has a moment that is one of the things he is best known for. This famous general told America, "In the councils of government, we must guard against the acquisition of unwarranted influence, whether sought or unsought, by the military-industrial complex."

He did not describe that complex, and most people then were uncertain what it was. But wasn't there something uncanny in a nearly finished leader coming to the people and warning of some large yet vague conspiracy? Wasn't that why he was asking for "an alert and knowledgeable citizenry" to protect the nation? Moreover, there was an extraordinary phrase embedded in the speech—"whether sought or unsought." It wasn't simply that this large complex of self-interest *intended* to undermine liberty. It could even be that it had no such plan. But the inexorable processes of technology were bringing it about. And he was tossing out his message in a bottle for us on a medium he seemed to count on, even if he didn't quite like it—a medium which could be seen to be a part of that "unsought" pressure, all the harder to resist because it was not designed.

The oddity of this farewell made it remembered, and that was a sign of how television might alter the balance of political procedure in America. After all, how else was a president to reach the people? There had been the long age of public speaking and written addresses. Roosevelt had proved the power of radio. But a president has few opportunities. He delivers the State of the Union speech, and he can call press conferences or special addresses. But he is not a fixed part of the ongoing

WHEN JOHNSON TOOK TO THE SCREEN HE WAS LAMER, SLOWER, PLAINTIVE.

governing process, in the way a British prime minister sits and speaks in the House of Commons and is obliged to take questions there regularly. He has no forum. But TV is his. As Newton Minow would write: "His ability to choose when and how to appear without cost before millions of viewers is completely unmatched by his political or Congressional opponents."

We sometimes think of Richard Nixon on the rack of television. But sometimes he used it well. Nobody worked harder at trying to master the medium. No president grasped that task better than the man who had helped lose the election of 1960 because he seemed wretched on television. It was on November 3, 1969, with Vietnam unsolved and after revelations on the secret bombing of Cambodia, that Nixon called for a prime-time spot and said, "And so tonight—to you, the great silent majority of my fellow Americans—I ask for your support."

Just as Eisenhower had implied, in the broad gray light of TV, that there was a special trust between him and the people, so Nixon was identifying the anonymity of the mass, whether they liked it or not, and claiming them as his. This was no different from the way people on television assumed the existence of a public by talking to them. It was Alfred Hitchcock introducing a grim tale with "Ladies and gentlemen…"; it was Carson promising "We'll be right back"; or it's some cute movie star in a commercial looking at us and asking, "What's in your wallet?" as if we were being robbed?

The "silent majority" has passed into folklore as a classic sound bite, and as a helpless warning on where political discourse in a land of the free might be headed. For it implies a mass of people who could not be heard—so was it more legitimate and sensible for them not to speak, or

WATERGATE BEGAN AS A LIVE TELEVISED EVENT. IT WAS DAYTIME TV.

think? That majority was being placed as helpless—and it is us as well as them. The concept was also a signal that the role of Congress was being marginalized as a TV event—how many memorable bites have been uttered in Congress during your lifetime? So television, decades in advance, was outlining a futility that hangs over our politics.

Nixon was not in the least reassured by his own mastery. His insecurity was such that he permitted the extensive campaign of dirty tricks when all he faced was a landslide victory. The thing we call "Watergate" (like a sea that can hold all streams, outlets, and flushing devices) was so unnecessary. Yet it would briefly reinvigorate Congress and supply one sound bite that you do recall. On May 17, 1973, the Senate committee established to investigate Watergate began as a live televised event. It was daytime TV carried on all networks at first, and then by one of them in a rotation process. Committee chairman Sam Ervin—truly like someone from a John Ford film—became a household figure, a rural Joseph Welch. Eighty-five percent of households were said to have watched some of the hearings, live or in evening highlights. But it was the minority leader on the committee, Howard Baker, who had the line that captured the summer and which has infiltrated all of modern noir, fact and fiction: "What did the president know, and when did he know it?"

It is an irony that Nixon told himself the Ervin hearings would bore the public—how little he understood his silent majority and their appetite for nearly anything on television, especially if they sniffed the melodrama of scandal. He was bewildered that three networks kept playing

White House counsel John Dean for five days, because he regarded Dean as an unimpressive minor official. So the man who had created the concept of the silent majority failed to appreciate the appeal of imminent humiliation. He hadn't watched enough daytime soap opera.

The summer of '73 was as crowded as a soap opera synopsis. Ehrlichman and Haldeman resigned. Dean was fired. The hearings went forward, with the drab-voiced admission from Alexander Butterfield that there were sound tapes! Archibald Cox was fired. Spiro Agnew was convicted, on unrelated charges. Gerald Ford was appointed vice president. On October 21, in Game 7, with a two-run homer from Reggie Jackson, the Oakland A's took the World Series from the New York Mets.

On November 17, at Disney World, President Nixon held a press conference on live television. He was brilliant, even if most of the silent majority knew he was a goner. Maybe he knew that, too; maybe he wanted the humiliation. It's hard to understand Nixon without some sense of psychic self-destruction. He was very good on television by then. His voice was deep and steady. He moved with purpose and intelligence. For once, he knew what being on television meant, and at last he seemed fulfilled by it.

The immediate purpose of the conference was minor: It had been charged that he had been making money out of the office and his career. He knew this was untrue and that no American would cavil over minor money. So there he is at the podium in a packed room, his arms holding the lectern like a captain steering a ship. He is loaded with the facts. He counts off the monies he has earned over the years. And the ABC coverage is extraordinary, for we have not just the frontal shot of him speaking. There is a cutaway to a close-up of his hands as he enumerates his sources of income. He had fabulous hands, with eloquent long fingers. If he'd used those hands more on camera, who knows what would have happened?

He's faring very well, even in a lost cause. But then he does it. He comes to his climax and there's genuine, controlled anger—for God's sake, he knew the money thing was a bum rap, a softball he could do a Reggie Jackson on. And he put us all on alert by saying that his message was not just for that roomful of journalists, but beyond that to the television audience:

> In all of my years of public life, I have never profited, never profited from public service…And I think, too, that I could say that in my years of public life, that I have welcomed this kind of examination, because people have got to know whether or not their president is a crook. Well, I'm not a crook. I've earned everything I've got.

"Crook"—why did he let his thick voice use that old-fashioned word? "Crook" is from the forties, and it suddenly reminded everyone what this man was about. He put the unkind word in the public mind, and it was a rod on which so many other crystals gathered. Remember "Republican cloth coat"? He needed something like that, something plain, humble, and clean. Yet he said "crook." It would be months yet before mercy arrived. But in August 1974, in what he told us was his thirty-seventh address to America, he said, "I have never been a quitter," and he quit, suggesting that it was an honorable sacrifice so that the other processes of government could move along without being slowed. He was doing it for the nation and for fluency, and for the sake of keeping the national show "on."

He was not finished; indeed, post-1974 may have been the best time of his life. Early in 1977, the idea arose for a series of television interviews. Was it David Frost's scheme, for the British TV personality was without a show? Or was it Nixon's? As if to prove his honesty over finances, he admitted to being in need of money. The two men made a deal, agented by "Swifty" Lazar: For $600,000 and 20 percent of any profits, Nixon would sit down for a series of interviews with Frost. The American networks said they would not carry the shows because money had changed hands. So Frost took the chance and financed the venture himself.

The interviews were shot in a house in Monarch Bay, California, in March and April, and the four main interviews were broadcast in May. Frost had worked hard on preparation, and it is still the general reckoning that he caught Nixon at one point in an admission that gave away nearly everything. But by then, we all of us knew enough about everything. There was no chance of legal proceedings. And perhaps Nixon was willing to be caught. He was still on television, with a large audience, and he was more relaxed than he had ever been. He did make the startling claim that "When the president does it, that means that it is not illegal." Only a few years earlier, in *The Godfather Part II*, Michael Corleone had said in a matter-of-fact way that "they" could kill anyone if they wanted to. As Mark Feeney put it, in *Nixon at the Movies*, speaking of the privilege available in breaking bad in movies and on television:

> Any crime can be committed, any action carried out when there's only a two-hour statute of limitations. The appeal of the movies at their most visceral is not about size or simulation or even the effect of light dispelling darkness. No, it is about the abolition of consequences.

The thing about the silent majority is that they don't protest such things. They can't get on the screen.

Between Nixon's resignation and his resurrection, there was a movie that caught both the current state of television and its future possibility with unnerving prescience. It was a fantasy and a satire, yet it was written by a man who twenty years earlier had been regarded as a pioneer of unaffected naturalism. This was Paddy Chayefsky and the film was *Network* (1976). It contains an early expression of what a television president might be.

Howard Beale (Peter Finch) is a newscaster who has gone insane. His network, UBS, and his old friend Max Schumacher (William Holden), are about to take him off the air when Beale's madness turns into ranting about the whole world being mad. This reckless act greatly improves his numbers. At one point he is called before Arthur Jensen (Ned Beatty), chairman of UBS, and put on the receiving end of a fulsome, unwinding sermon (there is very little conversation in *Network*— nearly the whole thing is done in Statements):

> Am I getting through to you, Mr. Beale? You get up on your little 21-inch screen and howl about America and democracy. There is no America. There is no democracy. There is only IBM and ITT and AT&T and DuPont, Dow, Union Carbide, and Exxon…We no longer live in a world of nations and ideologies, Mr. Beale. The world is a college of corporations, inexorably determined by the immutable bylaws of business. The world is a business, Mr. Beale. It has been since man crawled out of the slime. And our children will live, Mr. Beale, to see that perfect world in which there's no war or famine, oppression or brutality. One vast and ecumenical holding company, for whom all men will work to serve a common profit, in which all men will hold a share of stock, all necessities provided, all anxieties tranquilized, all boredom amused. And I have chosen you, Mr. Beale, to preach this evangel.

"Why me?" asks the amazed Beale. And here comes the bite that eats us up: "Because you're on television, dummy."

"Dummy" is a touch unkind or aggressive as an address. I prefer "buddy," close in sound and embrace. For what Jensen is suggesting is that once you're on television, there's no need to sermonize, to rant, go crazy, or take things seriously. Just be there, be cool and calm, for the authority rests in that mere, empty presence, being "on." The thing that handicaps Howard Beale and Richard Nixon is

NETWORK CONTAINS AN EARLY EXPRESSION OF WHAT A TELEVISION PRESIDENT MIGHT BE.

their strenuous urge to save the world, or set it straight. If only they could see that since their urgings point in opposite directions, the urge is immaterial. Once you're there, striving and extensive thinking fall aside, just as the butterfly lifts off from the husk of the pupa. If you want a nutshell demonstration of this negative capability, think of Chance, the gardener in Jerzy Kosinski's novel *Being There* (1970). He is amiable but alien, and he regards television as horizon-like, as beyond explanation or qualification, as a garden where things grow and pass. Chance would no more criticize TV than **"WHY ME?" ASKS THE AMAZED BEALE.** he would challenge nature. He likes to watch because he has no meter for boredom or excitement. He is cool with being there, so null, chill, and glassy he is as much like a screen as possible.

I know this seems unfair or ungrateful to candidates after they have labored so long, and with such loss of dignity, to become president. Above all, I do not mean to be harsh about Reagan, or to claim that he was a nonentity (or even that these days presidents do little except sustain television). Reagan did plenty: He intensified the Cold War by increasing US military expenditures, and then moved in on Mikhail Gorbachev to negotiate a lot of weapon systems away. And so the Berlin Wall came down in due course, and the "evil empire" he had identified in the Soviet Union passed away—didn't it? He reduced taxes and then raised them. He cut inflation and raised employment. He saw it as "morning in America," and he established the superiority of the wealthy class that we still confront. He saw the threat in Grenada and invaded. He launched a war on drugs—"just say no." He involved us in the tangle known as Iran-Contra, though it is likely that he never fully understood it personally. He tripled the national debt, and he was upset about that, though again it is not clear that he could explain the process. But these were all things he did, or things that happened: Presidents can hardly help but do things in four or eight years. They're like kids.

What protected Reagan from sensible political criticism was that he was an actor, and even a poor or dull actor, who carried on bravely nonetheless. There was a foolish or lightweight side to him, to be sure: He got carried away with the Strategic Defense Initiative, just like a kid in love with *Star Wars*, and he never saw that it was daft. And as to Iran-Contra, well, it is quite possible that he was told about it at some meeting or other. But as the wry political commentator Jack

Germond guessed, "They told him, but he forgot." And no, I'm not using that as a mean way of suggesting that his Alzheimer's condition had begun some time before the end of his administration. I'm just saying he might have forgotten. We all forget things all the time. Mark Feeney has a lovely story about that and how judgments about him didn't quite matter. Nixon was talking about Iran-Contra when there was thought of criminal wrongdoing. "Reagan will survive," said Nixon, "because when all is said and done, he can get up and say, 'I am an idiot and therefore can't be blamed,' and everyone will agree. I never had that option."

"Idiot" there is too much; it shows Nixon's mean streak, just as Arthur Jensen could have called Howard Beale "buddy" instead of "dummy." Reagan was nowhere near an idiot, but he knew not to make an issue of intelligence. It offends too many viewers, and easily smacks of villainy. Reagan had been a lifeguard once, proud of the lives he had saved, and he always had a look that said, "Hey, buddy, I'm here, I could save you"—so long as the threat was just drowning and not a Laffer curve. He wanted to be helpful, to be needed and liked. That's how he and the presidency were so good for each other.

REAGAN PLAYED THE ROLE OF A POSSIBLE FRIEND.

You may think I am saying this tongue in cheek, as a way of mocking Reagan. Not so, but in the not so, I am touching on something that may be more disconcerting than any chance that he was an idiot, or unqualified. Reagan was an acting buddy: He played the role of a possible friend. To that end, he was impressive and endearing at very commonplace things—like crossing a lawn from a helicopter to the White House; giving a cheery wave; chuckling at a joke (whether or not there had been one); standing up at a microphone and saying, "Well…"; or smiling when someone said something—it didn't matter what. You're going to argue that those are petty assets, absurd to note in a president, but they are the stuff of television, and Reagan was the first man in that office entirely comfortable with the empire of such things—a very amiable empire, warm but cool. He did those little things to silly perfection, the things that are usually cut out of a movie to concentrate on the "important" or "meaningful" things.

But movies aren't television, and movies can often look antique, arthritic, pompous, and moribund in comparison, puffed up with their own dramatic self-importance. That's what betrayed Nixon—he was no good at being casual or dull, perhaps because he didn't want to think himself capable of such things, but also because he was so bad at relaxing with television—or with anything else? We were learning that ease was vital to a TV president or to candidates for the office, and might cover for ignorance, carelessness, and a recklessness that was still startling when a Donald Trump exhibited it.

Presidents are still capable of doing BIG things—like Abu Ghraib, Health Care, and Monica Lewinsky. Perhaps they are just **big,** or *big.* A president could yet terminate existence or help it last a while longer. My point is rather that television has introduced the possibility of presidents who do very little except walk across the lawn, get up to speak, say "Well…," and give you a good-buddy shake of the hand without quite knowing or caring who you are. They are the one on television; they are there. That feeling comes from having watched Reagan closely for eight years, from thinking about television most of my life, and from reading Edmund Morris's reckless, yet inspired book *Dutch*, in which we see the emptiness of the actor fading into the deserted shell of dementia, and feel as touched as in reading any book about any president.

On January 5, 2016, Barack Obama appeared at the White House to offer proposals on the regulation of gun usage in the United States. There were television cameras to record the occasion, as well as relatives of victims of our various gun tragedies. The president's proposals were modest. They did not address the willful misreading of the Second Amendment. They only touched on the regularity of shooting incidents in schools, or the quantity of firearms in the nation. There was every fear that any moderate executive actions would be opposed, and mocked.

TELEVISION HAS INTRODUCED THE POSSIBILITY OF PRESIDENTS WHO DO VERY LITTLE EXCEPT WALK ACROSS THE LAWN.

The president wept. He was immediately attacked for that show of feeling. Some said he was acting for the camera. Who knows what happens in the mind of a weary, dismayed president? Who knows how much secret knowledge of our perils he lives with? Who knows how far a humanist is on edge and exhausted after several years in a maddened society, and in the midst of an election campaign that horrified so many would-be voters and reminded us of grotesque TV shows?

||||||||||||||||||||||||||||

SO THE MAN WHO GOES ON TELEVISION FOR US wept and was decried as an actor. Is there time left for us to grow up?

I concluded a revision of this chapter on the morning of Super Tuesday, March 1, 2016, wondering if the events of that day would ensure that Trump had the Republican nomination for president. At that point, his own theoretical party was plainly and belatedly devastated by his performance, and by the way he had unleashed storms of "reality TV" on what might have been a considered process for rational voters. This onslaught had been grisly, and there was every reason to blame Trump personally—and to note that we have been unable to subdue him with the reasoned criticism, humor, and judgment that we think are expected of us. We had been powerless, as in so many other respects, while abetting the possible delivery of power to a monstrous "Other."

Some called this politics as usual. In the *New York Times,* Ross Douthat proposed that the Obama administration had itself paved a way for Trump. I think that was unfair and inaccurate: Obama had striven to seem an old-fashioned gentleman on television—Trump played as a deliberate lout. But the nature of television as a technology was more potent, and less resistible, than any individual style or decision. We were having a presidential campaign that grew out of television itself. Trump's acuity was in feeling that slide towards chaos and riding it like a skier in a slalom.

It was my estimate that Trump had never anticipated being Mr. President: He knew how tedious and impotent that job was. His aim was to be Mr. TV on a new show, every night perhaps, in which he

attacked the next president and any other politician in sight—and regularly "fired" them. Douglas McGrath wrote a *New Yorker* fiction in which he imagined Trump conjuring up ever more outlaw remarks or stunts in the hope that they would ruin his prospects. But at every fresh outrage, his numbers only improved. Could he be trapped on his own mud slide?

So, *is* there time left for us to grow up?

17 LIVE?

WHAT DO WE EXPECT FROM LIVE TELEVISION, and how quickly does that get into ruminations over what is lively, lifelike, or life itself?

For myself, the chief reason for having a television set has always been to see certain events as they happened. These ranged from the coronation of 1953 to the tense funeral of Princess Diana on September 6, 1997, when there was a feeling that the British monarchy might be at the brink of its own extinction, or nonrenewal. (That funeral had an estimated world TV audience of 2.5 billion.)

I can think of others: the World Cup final of 1966 when England beat West Germany 4–2; the moment when the Queen Mother's horse Devon Loch collapsed while leading the Grand National steeplechase of 1956—five lengths clear and forty yards to go; and the dread instant when the ball went through the bow legs of Bill Buckner at first base and the Mets won Game 6 and tied the World Series of 1986. Of course, the Mets then won Game 7.

I watched Buckner's misfield in a bizarre and ill-mannered way. While attending a dinner party, I was sitting with a small television hidden on my lap. It may have been the first time I watched life on TV while apparently politely attending to it in reality. My reaction at Buckner's lapse led other guests to think I was having an attack of some kind. I was. Years after, I also saw the older and sadder Buckner return to Fenway Park after twenty years of dismay, to throw out a first pitch. He got a four-minute standing ovation, and I was moved to tears.

But now I recall that I did not see that ovation live; it came to me as a highlight later in the day, and I'm sure the ovation was shortened for the sake of all the other highlights. "Highlights" is another of those code words, and livelike is not live. I'm not sure that I would have wept at Fenway if I had been there that day. It's different watching on a screen, because the frame chooses, pauses, and romanticizes a moment, if only because it says, "There was *this*!" It is so reminiscent of movie moments where our tears have been calculated and timed by the moviemakers. Do those different grades of tears have a different atomic structure, or is it just context, watching or being there?

WHILE ATTENDING A DINNER PARTY, I WAS SITTING WITH A SMALL TELEVISION ON MY LAP.

I treasure live television for its sports coverage, and for the most part the medium keeps faith with true world time. You only have to think of NBC's shameful delayed coverage of many Olympic events to appreciate that. But NBC would argue that, having paid a fortune for Olympic rights, it is their option to show the stuff when it suits them best. (NBC have signed a $7.75 billion contract for Olympic rights through 2032.)

There are memorable Olympic moments, of course: Bob Beamon's jump at Mexico City, where it was nearly impossible to believe what you'd seen; Nadia Comaneci's several perfect tens at gymnastics in Montreal in 1976; Joan Benoit's marathon victory at Los Angeles in 1984 when, for the first time, a camera tracked a runner all through the race, allowing for commercial breaks (where she had to keep running). In fact that was the first Olympic marathon for women, and the live action lasted two hours, twenty-four minutes, and fifty-two seconds.

But a study of the Olympics on TV quickly discovers other things to see and be moved by: In 1972 in Munich, in addition to Olga Korbut's disputed 9.8 on the uneven bars (the audience felt she deserved higher), coverage shifted over to the terrorist invasion of the Israeli team's quarters in the Olympic Village and the tragedy that ensued—it was "lucky" that so many cameras were there, though the live coverage was fragmentary, incoherent, and impossible to understand; at the 1989 World Series in San Francisco, blimp cameras were looking down on Candlestick Park on one of the most beautiful days the city has known, but then the earth shook and the cameras hurried north to the city to report disaster. These side benefits don't have to be disastrous. When the marathon was run at the Beijing Olympics in 2008, the total coverage was a first, incidental opportunity for millions of us to see and feel what Beijing might be like.

Beijing put on one of the finest opening ceremonies the Olympics have ever had—it was a four-hour pageant of music, dance, fireworks, color, advertising, exuberance, and cool calculation, said to have cost $300 million. The Chinese film director Zhang Yimou was overall director; Ang Lee was a part of his team; but Steven Spielberg withdrew to protest Chinese support of outrages in Darfur. The TV show was a crucial demonstration for the proposition that China was a modern nation, driven by a new prosperity as well as old cultural traditions. It was a major international television event with a worldwide audience estimated as somewhere in the 1–4 billion range. NBC delayed it twelve hours to get its best share of the numbers.

THE GAME HAS BEEN ALTERED AND EMPHASIZED BY THE COVERAGE.

Like many in the world, I find great pleasure in watching sport, especially soccer—the thing I call football. But I have not seen a live game for years, in part because I haven't been in London at the right time, but also because I could hardly sustain the cost of tickets for me, a son, and grandchildren—that would require close to £200 (about $300). On the other hand, through my cable package I can see nearly every game Chelsea play, in real time, if I get up early enough. That ability has transformed soccer and helped turn Chelsea manager José Mourinho into a Howard Beale cut with James Cagney. As such, he has upstaged his own players and seems certain to be somewhere else by the time you read this.

When I watched a game live at Chelsea's Stamford Bridge stadium in the fifties and sixties, I believe I got in for sixpence (less than ten cents) in an economic system where player wages were held at a maximum of £20 a week. There might be crowds of 60,000 to 70,000 people, most of them standing packed together on the terraces and subject to alarming surges in that mass. I saw Jimmy Greaves live, like a sparrow floating over the mud, slipping ball after ball into the net. It was grand.

In February 2015, England's Premier League, the top level of club soccer, made a new deal for television rights. They sold them to Sky (a part of the Fox empire controlled by Rupert Murdoch) and to BT for three years for just over £5 billion. That was a 70 percent increase on the previous three-year contract, and part of the shift that has allowed many foreign-born players to join English clubs for enormous transfer fees and weekly salaries. Chelsea paid Atlético Madrid £32 million for Diego Costa and agreed to pay him £150,000 a week for five years. He was decisive and lethal for about two months before he became a surly problem on television.

The games seem the same as they were in Greaves's day; the results are vital and the skill levels are better than ever. But soccer is now a television event. It relies on many close-ups, where viewers can read the logos and advertising names on a player's shirt. The players work fast, but they know they are part of a system of close-ups and slow motion. They are more fastidious about their appearance; they have acquired an insolent capacity for flopping at possible fouls; and they indulge in post-goal celebrations that would have been regarded as tasteless fifty years ago. They are stars who endorse other products and dreams. They model clothes in fashion magazines; they appear on "reality" shows; they know they are being photographed and so their skills have turned into performances. Their named uniforms are sold around the world at $60 a shirt. The mud of the late fifties has become money. And kids who once paid sixpence to watch can't get in because the seats have gone to businessmen, stars in other fields, and people who can afford the tickets. So the kids stay home and think of football as a TV event.

That shift is everywhere. When the New England Patriots beat the Seattle Seahawks in the 2015 Super Bowl, the show loomed larger than ever. It was a good game, with a fourth quarter in the balance until the very end, with calls and plays that were being diagnosed long after the game. Two plays in particular on the Seahawks' last drive were replayed many times in exquisite slow motion, and slo-mo has been current in American football for years to give the officials a clearer view of what actually happened. That adjustment derives from the way viewers at home have had that privilege for a far longer time. Slo-mo multi-camera replays are not allowed to slow the fluidity—the liveness—of a soccer match, though they are used to determine post-game penalties for "unsportsmanlike conduct."

Slow motion slows the course of a game and adds a weird distortion and a dreamy beauty to its liveness. The 2015 Super Bowl had over 114 million viewers, which made it the most viewed sporting event ever on American television. Consequently, commercial airtime during the show was being charged at $4–4.5 million for thirty seconds. There was a prolonged, flashy, yet dull halftime event, featuring Katy Perry, that ran close to twenty-five minutes. There was the pre-game show and postgame interviews. There were lots of exceptional plays, and the NBC commentary from Al Michaels and Cris Collinsworth was as good as it gets. More than that, nearly all the ads were playing for the first time and they were showcases in their novelty, humor, and daring. Next day, the media rated the ads as well as the players.

The whole show ran four hours, in which just one hour of football was required. But then absorb the latest research reporting that with meditative huddles and precise measurements, the ball is in play, or live, in that hour of stop-go contest for about seventeen minutes. The equation between four hours and seventeen minutes says a great deal about American culture, and about television's urge to control liveness.

It seems obvious, but it's worth stressing: Most live television occurs where the cameras are and is shaped by their placement. At every major sporting event, there are fixed camera installations and a mise-en-scène schematic that can predict the shot selection in advance of the game. Cameras and sound recording strive to convey the physical impact of the game. Sometimes players and coaches are miked and equipped with miniature cameras. That is not part of a campaign to warn the country of links between repeated collisions, concussion, and subsequent brain damage. It is done to heighten the thrill for the armchair audience; in other words, it dramatizes and celebrates the violence just as football cultivates enormous young men who often fail to graduate from college and sometimes carry the cult of violence off the field and into their private lives—until an elevator has enough surveillance coverage to catch Ray Rice and his fiancée and push the NFL into deciding what it felt or ought to feel about that case.

It's not just that football is thoroughly covered by the medium. The game has been altered and emphasized by the coverage. It was George Will (a keen sports fan) who observed: "Football combines the two worst things about America: it is violence punctuated by committee meetings." But that is not quite the impression you get at a live game, especially if you're sitting as far away as your budget demands. In seeing the whole field, you recognize patterns and high skills. You

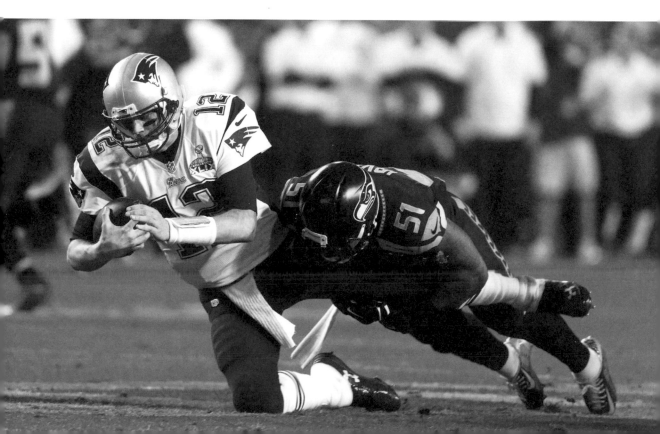

feel the pitch, the weather, and the crowd's involvement. Some of that comes through on television, but the cinematic sophistication emphasizes the things Will is talking about: the combat and the huddles. On television the coaches become vital figures, and sometimes self-dramatists. But at a real game you hardly notice them. You feel the crowd and your part in it.

It's fascinating to trace the evolution of the NFL on television. Our football heritage owes so much to Ed Sabol, the founder of NFL Films. In 1962, Sabol made a movie of a championship game, which led to a long-term deal with the NFL. These were movies, shot on film long after videotape was available, and constructed as dramas. Sabol created camera angles and close-ups on a game that are axiomatic now. He freely overlaid dramatic music and he found John Facenda, who became one of the most treasured and effective voice-overs on television while working in newsreel cadences established in the 1930s. In Sabol's obituary it was said that Sam Peckinpah opted for slow-motion slaughter on *The Wild Bunch* (1969) after being stirred by NFL films.

Those football highlight movies never felt live. They were meticulous and very slanted re-creations. Today, HD television lets you see the beard and the sweat on players, the spiral of the ball and the blades of shining green of the grass. Anyone can see the technical advances, but the ethos of the sport and our idea of an attitude toward it come from Sabol (1916–2015).

||||||||||||||||||||||||||||

TELEVISION HAS COMPROMISED THE SPORTS IT LOVES MOST DEARLY. Sometimes the event is prolonged beyond tolerable limits just to stay on the air and earn the maximum revenue from commercials. Sometimes the opposite happens. So tennis introduced the tie-break system to terminate prolonged sets. That was said to rescue weary players (and nervous TV schedulers), yet fatigue is an inherent part of sport. Tie-breaks made a match more manageable on television, and so we lost the rare delight of a game like Pancho Gonzales v Charlie Pasarell at the 1969 Wimbledon Championships, when Gonzales outlasted his younger opponent, 22–24, 1–6, 16–14, 6–3, 11–9, in a game that stretched over two days.

Penalty shoot-outs are good television, but they distress most fans nearly as much as the introduction of television time-outs would if they stopped the proper flow of soccer. Yet some would argue that soccer's dislike of those time-outs has been an impediment to the reluctant advance of the game in the United States, compared with its rule in Europe and South America. The thing that spectators cherish, the uninterrupted live sequence of the game, is antithetical to commercial television.

Sport may be the best ongoing version of live television, but that phenomenon includes the terrible afternoon at Hillsborough, Sheffield, in 1989 when an FA Cup semifinal was interrupted by disaster on the packed terraces. Cameras set up to film the match panned sideways a little to see the crush in which ninety-six people died and hundreds more were injured. The intensity of the live action rose several levels to observe death. At a

SAM PECKINPAH OPTED FOR SLOW-MOTION SLAUGHTER ON *THE WILD BUNCH* AFTER BEING STIRRED BY NFL FILMS.

more trivial level, but absorbing still, in 1956, live on air, talking about the recent Jewish wedding of Arthur Miller and Marilyn Monroe, the brilliant but wayward Oscar Levant blurted out, "Now that Marilyn Monroe is kosher, Arthur Miller can eat her." The studio audience for *Words About Music* gasped and Levant was dismissed. Later on he said he hadn't meant it the way it sounded, but people that are depressed are often prey to their own inappropriate remarks. Later still, Levant admitted, "I suspect that my subconscious had led me into saying something outrageous enough to get thrown off the air."

The risk of live TV is always alluring. There are fabulous newscasts where the studio setup and the groomed newscaster are sent into panic by an earthquake. In the era of live drama, there could be moments when the audience saw a camera, or when the play stopped and went dark for a few minutes. At the Super Bowl halftime show in 2004, Janet Jackson had a wardrobe malfunction when Justin Timberlake pulled at her costume, and for a second we saw her breast (or a picture of her breast). We survived, though her career suffered, in part because there was some suspicion that the mishap had been managed. Ten years later, the wardrobe malfunction, or the "nip-slip," is a standard genre in the Internet's coverage of "life." More significantly, that Super Bowl flash was what prompted Jawed Karim to launch YouTube (where you can still see the MTV-produced halftime show).

Liveness is carefully guarded now. On many live shows there is a ten-second delay intended to give the staff time to cut out an "indecent" image or remark. All along, "Live from New York...it's *Saturday Night!*" has played three hours later on the West Coast. But there are precious live moments that play whenever they occur—the verdict at the O. J. Simpson trial, Neil Armstrong stepping onto the surface of the moon, Jack Ruby shooting Oswald, Niki Lauda's Ferrari erupting in a fireball at the Nürburgring in 1976. Or Howard Beale going off script?

Am I kidding? Well, no more than Janet Jackson and Justin Timberlake. You may recall the moment early on in *Network* when the UBS anchor Howard Beale tells his audience that he has been fired and begins to improvise:

> I don't have to tell you things are bad. Everybody knows things are bad. It's a depression. Everybody's out of work or scared of losing their job [this was 1976]... We know the air is unfit to breathe and our food is unfit to eat, and we sit watching our TVs while some local newscaster tells us that today we had fifteen homicides and sixty-three violent crimes...So I want you to get up now. I want all of you to get up out of your chairs. I want you to get up right now and go to the window. Open it, and stick your head out and yell—*"I'm as mad as hell and I'm not going to take this anymore!"*

UBS are poised to take him off the air, but the veteran producer says let him run. And people do go to the window and shout out. All of a sudden, Beale has shed the reasons why he might be fired. He has captured live television and made it riveting. Quick as a thought, the ambitious program producer Diana Christensen (Faye Dunaway) sees

the chance of making Beale a figurehead in a new approach to the
news. He'll be "the mad prophet of
the airwaves," with re-creations of
terrorist robberies and a dramatization of the news that has been
left prosaic by old-fashioned journalism. The UBS ratings soar.

As written by Paddy Chayefsky in 1976, that was satire and
surreal. Diana Christensen would
be seventy-five now—sitting at
home with her TV, or owning some
network. But she was the real

prophet in *Network*, for her reckless zeal had guessed at a future
where the News was a show, with anchors at Fox as glorious as Dunaway, with pitched-battle arguments, a little bit of footage, and yards
of spin. At NBC, for instance, the executives were despondent over the
revelations of Brian Williams's overactive imagination. But Diana
might have seen Brian as a new way ahead, even if Williams himself
had an archaic handsomeness that reminded one of the fragile,
pumped-up look of Tyrone Power or Rock Hudson. Surely she would
see that Brian had broken through and found that fantasy or twilight
zone where we wanted to be in this imaginary world of news, behaving like Robert Redford in *All the President's Men*—which is to say
acting. So could Brian get a new show in which he speculates on the
news, makes jokes about it, and wonders what is true or not—or
whether anything could be true now? The audience could then vote on
the plausible height of his tall stories. If that seems far-fetched, is it
really so unlike Jon Stewart's *Daily Show* on Comedy Central, where
in so many ways the ideal and theory of news was mocked? He and
Williams were friends, and Stewart announced his retirement the very
week that Williams was suspended without pay for six months.

Williams did return to offer breaking news on MSNBC, but he
will not return to reliable anchoring. Because the phantom of "anchoring" has dissolved in the ocean. NBC and its rivals have to recognize

that that sober mode is gone with the wind. At the time of the Williams revelations, *NBC Nightly News with Brian Williams* had just over nine million watchers a night, which made it the most popular news show on television. The largest segment of that audience was women over the age of fifty-five, whereas Jon Stewart had cornered a part (albeit a very small part) of that more desirable demographic, the 18–34 age range. But suppose Diana Christensen could see the prospect of a format that got both those groups. It would have to be live,

LIVE-NESS IS CAREFULLY GUARDED NOW.

because we would need to feel that Brian was on the edge, Beale-like, inspired like a storyteller but nearly mad as hell and frankly uncertain when he was telling the Cronkite truth and when he was expressing what he wanted to be true. This is the pattern of commercials: the apparently hard facts of sticker price, cash refund, money down, terms of payment, gas mileage, all married to the flawless romance of shaped metal and the dreams of where this streamlined transport could take you. The autos in ads have been the first vehicles impelled by desire.

The ads and the movies may be the least live things on television, along with the factory formula of so many long-running shows. For decades, the truly wild personalities tended to have a short career on the box—think of Ernie Kovacs, the Smothers Brothers, and Oscar Levant, always at risk of being canceled.

But suppose one day that the eloquent depression of Oscar Levant, live, had led to his taking out a gun and shooting himself, all in a couple of seconds, with the blood spurting and falling on Zsa Zsa Gabor or Kitty Carlisle before the engineer could take the show off the air. I suspect the gloom-ridden Levant thought of such a coup, and was smart enough to realize that live television could not help but inch toward death, as if yielding to gravity or destiny.

Once upon a time, in 1971, Jerome Rodale, a promoter of organic food, slumped over dead while taping *The Dick Cavett Show*. That episode was never aired, "for obvious reasons," the story goes. But in February 1968, a still photographer, Eddie Adams, and NBC cameraman Vo Suu were on the streets of Saigon to see the summary execution of an alleged Vietcong terrorist, Nguyen Van Lem, by General Nguyen Ngoc Loan. The policeman shot the man point-blank in the right side of his head. This was not played live, but it was on screens within a day, and it was regarded as one of the most shocking actions ever seen on television. Some say it helped end the war, but people like to believe in such proper consequences, and the conflict in Vietnam had years to go.

No one doubted that this hideous scene was real, though decades of movies had laid the groundwork of suspicion. A gun, a shot, a man falling, some blood on view—these are the ingredients of many of the thousands of killings we have seen on television. These days, I suspect that sort of death is more common on screens than the prolonged kiss, in which we seem to have lost interest. Yes, the scene from Saigon had a rough, verité air, it was as casual as it was terrible, but that tone has been imitated in many feature films. When Charles Van Doren went on the NBC game show *Twenty One* (1956–58), he defeated the resident champion, Herb Stempel. That was the design of a show that had decided Van Doren was more telegenic than Stempel. But the live show took no chances, and it primed Van Doren with the questions in advance and coached him in acting as if he was struggling for an answer. He was found out and brought to a kind of disgrace, though his career as an author carried on.

The objective function of the news has been assaulted by the very measures that terrorists are taking to intimidate us. They define their mission, callous to life but respectful of how television functions. 9/11 was conceived as a live television event, and in a dire way it is exactly what newscasts are waiting for. They would not like to admit this, but they know how swiftly authentic disaster boosts their viewing figures. The zest of Diana Christensen is far from dead, but it is hooked on being live. Whereas the action at the Twin Towers had to be shown live, TV newscasts are still reluctant to play the video of terrorist murders by throat cutting, firing squad, or putting a victim in a cage and setting light to it. These hideous actions may become more ingenious, and they may be arranged as live events.

Live surveillance is a mounting enthusiasm. Surely there was a temptation for the mission that eliminated Osama bin Laden to record itself. In fact, they did have footage from a drone, and that was what the president and his advisers were looking at in the Situation Room.

Could night-vision footage have been played live to the nation? Technically yes, but caution feared giving the game away to Pakistani authorities, to say nothing of exposing an embarrassing failure. But how long will that caution prevail? Why should a military raid, or a drone attack, not have self-coverage? There is increasing pressure to define the public right to know what our masters are doing.

There is talk already of policemen having a small video camera as part of their uniform. That could create a record of incidents on the streets. But the video could be beamed back to headquarters quite easily. Actions could be known and challenged as they happened. Perhaps a policeman's weapon could be disabled by remote control.

This may seem like science fiction, but suppose there was continuing live coverage of polar ice caps shrinking, or of the explosions in Siberia when carbon dioxide and methane break through the ever flimsier permafrost? Why not endless observation of Aleppo, nuclear research facilities in Iran, or the interrogation rooms at Guantanamo. Of course, the authorities will tell us, "You can't see that. It would violate security or human rights." (How does an inmate at Guantanamo know where those rights begin and end?) But we have a diminishing faith in security, while live coverage is reaching deeper into our lives, adding effectiveness and erasing privacy.

Suppose those police cameras work pretty well—wouldn't you welcome one that let you know where your children or your spouse are, and what they're doing? Isn't that a development of GPS, that very handy TV? Why not a personal audiovisual system that tells you where you are and how to get to where you want to go, that forecasts weather and tells you who is coming toward you, that gives your vital signs and has automatic access to your memory? Some of this is sci-fi, but a lot of the technology exists already or is foreseeable.

That electronic oversight of your memory is the crucial step, because it introduces the possibility that your brain can be tracked and schooled. So you might do fewer foolish or perilous things—but you might become a different sort of human. And all of this stuff has to be live, just to keep you alive.

A television news system that has an anchor and a selection process of what items to play (because there was a camera there) is already antiquated and likely to put pressure on the anchor to be a star. We realize vaguely that "news" tends logically towards some infinite surveillance. Isn't that close to how ideal national security operates? Wouldn't it be more useful to have a wall of small screens that run continuous coverage of Aleppo and all the other "hot spots"? There could even be surveillance of your own den, your bedroom, or your bathroom. If you have a stroke in the shower, "they" want to know—isn't that your best chance?

Of course, the best chance of big numbers that a network newscast has is catastrophe. The tension felt in October 1962 over Cuba and the sea surrounding it has not been repeated very often. The old film of nuclear explosions has turned into the iconography of nostalgia instead of disturbing warnings of disaster. But the surreal prospect exists of the back wall of a newscast being suddenly blown out so that ISIS terrorists wearing black can rush in—or will it be the rising tide, not to mention the chaotic army of our own dispossessed?

||||||||||||||||||||||||||||

THERE IS A DERELICT SOMETIMES ON OUR STREET. He is there today. He slept on the sidewalk in a ragged sleeping bag with his shopping cart of possessions, many of them taken from the colored garbage holders of the city, the ones in blue, black, and green that are emptied into a Recology truck once a week, with warnings from the workers if you put the wrong refuse in the wrong colored bin. So we are clerically correct in ridding ourselves of waste, and this derelict and others outfit themselves from the same bins.

I don't know how old this man is. He has ragged hair and an untended beard. His face is burnished by hardship, living in the open, and a kind of madness that seems to grip him. He cries out sometimes; he sings unknown songs; and he goes into foulmouthed tirades. But I don't know his age because I don't want to go close enough to look at him properly. I am not alone in this feeling. You see people who cross the street to avoid him, or who look away in the hope that he is not there.

But he is there, even if it would be no surprise to find his corpse one morning in that filthy sleeping bag. Then Recology, or someone, would have to come to take him away. Before people are up. He may not register in our systems. I doubt he has a social security number or a bank account; he seems to have no address (think of him as a Richard Kimble). I have watched him enough to know he has no iPhone, no portable battery television, no computer. To that extent he is not quite one of us; he has not been counted. So he seems like a throwback to a Dickensian world where outcasts, vagrants, and the homeless had to live on the street or in ditches sheltered by hedgerows. You may tell yourself that in an optimistic world, these outcasts will disappear in time thanks to welfare, health care, charitable repair schemes for the crazy…and medication.

But I also wonder whether he is a harbinger of a time when poverty will intensify and make for a degree of homelessness and danger that has to be policed and controlled for the security of the very few who are safe. There are countries all over the world already where that condition prevails and rules out the chance of democracy, law, education, and a good cable package.

I also wonder if the savage look and life of these people is not a glimpse of what Earth could be like if a few of our imminent catastrophes make an alliance. That could be like the wasteland in Cormac McCarthy's novel *The Road*, where survivors are on their own and when the televisions no longer turn on. We are so close to a decision point—on or off.

DOCUMENTARY?

WHEN MOVING PICTURES WERE FIRST SHOWN TO THE PUBLIC, in Paris in 1895, the subject matter was more incidental than significant.

What counted was the living imprint of actuality and a sense of time passing. So Auguste and Louis Lumière shot whatever they could think of that was available, simply to prove that their *Cinématographe* functioned—a train coming into a station, a family picnic, workers leaving a factory. There was no attitude or design in these choices, but the first spectators supplied the meaning. When the steam engine came toward the camera, some people screamed and ran out of the salon. They thought the locomotive would break through the screen. Or if they didn't really believe that, they were taken with the pretending. This still works, and has confused us.

Exactly the same thing happened with television, with the extra proviso that the medium performed domestically. So there was an inherent but rarely explained affinity with the medium and an attempt to bring reality into our living rooms. For many people, that seemed to be the primary purpose of television. But there were ambiguities that slowly became apparent. Visual appearance and narrative interpretation are all very well, and they are the material of documentary, but they are not as reliable as they seem.

Consider Abraham Lincoln, a president whose grasp on posterity owes so much to the arrival of photography. There are a few portraits in film emulsion of previous presidents, but we don't bring them to mind easily. Whereas the bleak but humane gaze of Lincoln the leader is as strong and uncertain as any good photograph. There are a number of photos of the later Lincoln, and they make us think of the burden on a president. He was only fifty-one in 1860, but he looks older and sadder. Is he ill, or depressed? Is it that his resolute calm at being depicted, and his declining to smile, convey a certain resignation?

THE EFFECT WAS MILDLY SHOCKING: SHE DIDN'T QUITE SEEM LIKE "OUR" VIRGINIA WOOLF.

We have had great actors play Lincoln in movies—Walter Huston, Raymond Massey, Henry Fonda, and Daniel Day-Lewis. These are fine performances, and sometimes those actors have worked hard to resemble the real Lincoln. But do they match that handful of still photographs and their gravity, fatigue, and sense of abiding? These photographs have an atmosphere that we cherish whenever film or television have given us even a few seconds of someone we wanted to *see* alive. In 2014, at the National Portrait Gallery in London, I saw something of Virginia Woolf that surprised me. In our collective imagination Woolf is a grave, serious author, a woman on her way to suicide and immortality. When Nicole Kidman played her in *The Hours* (2002), she made herself look unlike Kidman but not that close to Woolf. I don't remember Kidman smiling once in that film—and she won the Oscar, in part because Woolf's grim and melancholy eminence had rubbed off on her. But in the Woolf show at the National Portrait Gallery there was a strip of stills taken in rapid succession at a party in a garden where Woolf was gay, a little flirty, skittish, and having a very good time. The effect was mildly shocking: She didn't quite seem like "our" Virginia Woolf. But perhaps for a moment or two she was herself? There are pictures of Hitler chatting with children and playing with animals. But in most documentaries on television that need to show Hitler, the makers of the program pick a harsher, crueler image, more tyrannical or crazed. That's our Hitler—thc profile, the brand, the anti-role model.

People learn to act, to pose and present a side of themselves. Animals are easier because their identity is fixed in outward appearance. So early television loved wildlife, guessing we would feel the same. They were right. There is still a compulsive draw in telephoto film of leopards hunting a young buffalo until the outraged mother appears to chase the predators away with her horns. We know that story—we revel in it, just as it's hard to resist www glimpses of pets doing strange things (even if close viewing suggests those bits of cuteness may have been rigged).

David Attenborough was born in Isleworth in west London in 1926, the younger brother of Richard. He got a degree in natural sciences at Cambridge, and in 1950 he applied for a job at BBC radio. They didn't want him, but the application reached the desk of the head of "factual broadcasting" at BBC Television, and they did hire him. He then began to develop a tradition of wildlife films, which he produced and presented: *The Pattern of Animals* and *Zoo Quest*. These programs were academic and as detached as possible: Attenborough despised the Disneyfication of wild animals in films like *The*

A SERIES OF-THREE DOCUMENTARY PROGRAMS THAT DEFINED THE POSSIBILITY IN TELEVISION.

Living Desert (1953), which won the documentary Oscar despite some musicalized insect scenes. He preferred patience, respect for the animals, and a voice-over commentary that was expert and enthusiastic at the same time, without going too far in either direction. He was becoming one of the heroic figures in television history.

In 1957, the BBC set up a Natural History Unit at Bristol (it's still there). Attenborough could have led it, but he opted to stay in London. He actually dropped out of broadcasting for a while to get a postgraduate degree in social anthropology. But that never came to fruition, because he was offered the chance to be controller of a new channel, BBC2, which began in 1964. Attenborough never gave up his own wildlife films, but he was the leader who galvanized BBC2, which was always meant to reach a more discerning audience. Among many

*Kenneth Clark
does Degas*

other things he did there, he initiated these shows: *The Old Grey Whistle Test* (an exceptional pop music show, based on expert knowledge, striking opinions, and recital-like appearances from musicians); *Call My Bluff* (a very successful game show); *The Money Programme* (the first British television reporting on finance); and an oddity called *Monty Python's Flying Circus*. The impresario's range of interests was amazing. No one was doing more to inform the British imagination. He was quite simply a great leader in the tradition of John Reith, but he was so much more amiable and contemporary than Reith.

He was only just beginning. In the next few years he gave the go-ahead to a series of three documentary programs that defined a possibility in television. He asked Sir Kenneth Clark (formerly director of the National Gallery) to write, produce, and present on camera a series to be called nothing less than *Civilisation* (1969). It felt sweepingly thorough (which means it had the confidence to leave out a great deal); it was fixed on Western culture; Clark was immaculate, fully upper-class but droll and with a paternalistic common touch that guided the public through an urbane tour of the history of art. Every art gallery and museum in Britain, any publisher of art books, and the entire business of art owe their existence in part to Clark. To watch the series now is to marvel at the languid assurance of a revered don lecturing to obedient masses, and the notion of a benign nobleman distributing civilization to us all, like a lord of the manor handing out tips to his tenants at Christmas. You couldn't get away with it now, but it was vital and transforming then. Plus, it was among the first glories of color TV.

Chuck Barris does the Gong

Less serene in its tone, but deeply provocative, was BBC2's next large venture: *The Ascent of Man*. This was a 13-part series on nothing less than human evolution, not just as a species but as a social and intellectual animal. The series was supported by Time-Life and produced by Adrian Malone. But its author and on-camera presenter was Dr. Jacob Bronowski. He was a remarkable man, born in Poland in 1908 and with a PhD in mathematics from Cambridge, where he also played chess for the university. But at the end of the war, when he had been sent to observe Hiroshima and Nagasaki after the bomb, he switched his studies to biology and the sources of human violence. He was known on television in the fifties as a panelist on *The Brains Trust*, but he was a bold and inspired choice for *The Ascent of Man*.

He had passion—not a striking quality in Clark—for the theme and for the precarious condition of mankind. And he chose not to follow Clark's smooth narration. His show had a script, but as he visited the crucial locations, Bronowski was inclined to fall into improvised monologues. That made life itself seem more perilous, and it found its climax in the episode on genocide, when Bronowski was at Auschwitz and he reached down for handfuls of the muddy soil there with the DNA of corpses. It was one of the most arresting things I have ever seen on television, and just as Attenborough hoped, it was personal but universal.

These shows were enormous popular successes, and they seem now like an assertion from the BBC that a simple but vivid form of education was possible on documentary television, good enough to satisfy experts and engage the masses. The third show was in many ways the most obvious.

IT WAS ONE OF THE MOST ARRESTING THINGS I HAVE EVER SEEN ON TELEVISION.

Alistair Cooke was a beloved voice on BBC radio because of his weekly *Letter from America*. He wrote regularly for the *Manchester Guardian*. He had also done pioneering work as host on the American television show on the arts, the very daring *Omnibus* (1952–57), where Cooke sometimes entered a maze of different items—an early version of the crazed house of television. So he seemed the natural writer and presenter for what became *Alistair Cooke's America* (or *America: A Personal History*) an easygoing declaration of opinion that became an epic, and which pleased everyone except those requiring more structured political commentary. Oliver Stone's *The Untold History of the United States*, done in 2012, was often clumsy but it was refreshingly critical of so many orthodox and optimistic views. It helped reveal the rapture and innocence in Cooke's view of America, where the canyon country of the Four Corners states was as spectacular as in John Ford's movies, yet Cooke was more moved by its natural beauty. He was on camera much of the time, a slim, silver-haired ironist; he spoke his own narration in a conversational mood; and he was encouraged to use personal stories, for he was a man who had found himself in America. Cooke adored jazz, so there he was, playing piano in a New Orleans bar. He had known H. L. Mencken, so the first episode in the show stood up for Mencken as a classic American—

and a man not so far from Cooke himself. Seen again today, the show is as irresistible as the thought that no one would now have the nerve to make anything so sweeping and yet so personal.

1972 was far from America's best year, but the series showed how widely the nation and its idea were still cherished. It was another international success, enough to transform Cooke's own economy (his BBC fee for *Letter from America* had stayed fixed for decades), and then it turned into a handsome illustrated book (from Knopf) that sold two million copies. This esteem helped promote Cooke's appointment as the host on *Masterpiece Theatre* (the PBS format for British literary serials). He reigned there from 1971 to 1992, sitting in the semblance of a gentleman's study, advising us on what was to come (and candidly horrified by the homosexuality in Nigel Nicolson's *Portrait of a Marriage* and by Alan Bennett's defense of the spy Anthony Blunt in *A Question of Attribution*). The American Cooke (he became a naturalized citizen in 1941) was an English mix of populist and reactionary. As an elderly gentleman, he was a loyal watcher of Vanna White on *Wheel of Fortune* (over 6,000 episodes, not all with Vanna, who is now fifty-eight).

The flourish of these BBC shows inspired Thames Television (part of the commercial channel in Britain) to mount its own 26-part series on *The World at War* (1973–74). The show was deeply researched, unearthing many survivors and discovering never-before-seen newsreel footage in international archives. This is the series that, on reaching the concentration camps, elected to exclude

IN THE SEVENTIES, DOCUMENTARY CAME UNDER PROGRESSIVE THEORETICAL REAPPRAISAL.

commercials, a striking gesture of taste or tact. But it could not help but expose a flaw in the compromised nature of commercial television.

The three BBC series were landmarks, no matter that they were sometimes bland, settled in their attitudes, and a kind of virtual tourism. *The Ascent of Man*, I think, is the best, because it was the most far reaching and political, and the most spontaneous. It might have seemed like the start of a wave, and in fact Adrian Malone did go to America to produce *Cosmos* (1980) with Carl Sagan. But soon enough the epic documentary form with a star host began to slip away. In many ways, Ken Burns is the heir to Alistair Cooke; they had the same love of America and a confidence in a television synthesis of enormous subjects. But Burns never considered appearing on camera, despite his charm and good looks and his unstoppable capacity to speak a speech.

In Britain, Jonathan Miller wrote and presented *The Body in Question* (1978) because he was admired as a performer and because he was a doctor and an intellectual. In America, PBS (through its Boston station, WGBH) mounted *Vietnam: A Television History* (1983), derived from the writings of Stanley Karnow. It was a respected series, playing to about 10 million people, and it was praised for its even-handedness—PBS was already careful to honor fairness doctrines, and anxious about threats to reduce its funding on account of its being too "liberal." There was no host to the show, but the voice of Will Lyman—cool, dry, nuanced, and detached—was noted, and soon Lyman would become the narrator on the admirable documentary series *Frontline* for PBS, without ever establishing himself as a personality who might make the documentary "private" or partisan.

In the seventies, documentary came under progressive theoretical reappraisal, often in the Boston area where WGBH led the way in public television and where Richard Leacock was helping to educate a generation of documentaries that eschewed voice-over, interpretation, or a set purpose and preferred unmediated cinema verité coverage. But for

60 MINUTES CAN SEEM LIKE PART OF A SETTLED ESTABLISHMENT.

that to work, you had to believe that a camera could be neutral, and that editing did not shape the material it might be reducing by a factor of a hundred.

Starting in 1968, at CBS, *60 Minutes* became a Sunday-night marker, with on-camera reporters like Mike Wallace, Harry Reasoner, Morley Safer, Dan Rather, and the humorous postscripts of Andy Rooney. Don Hewitt was the energetic executive producer (and he had worked with Edward R. Murrow on *See It Now*). For decades, it was as much gospel as the CBS News, and it did as well as 20-minute items in a network magazine framework could do.

For nearly fifty years it has been automatic viewing for many viewers and a top-10 performer for twenty-three consecutive seasons.

Sometimes it is called the most successful television program ever made, and it has won over a hundred Emmys. In that process it has exposed many wrongs, profiled significant and ambiguous people, and been the epitome of energetic journalism. But in hindsight, *60 Minutes* can seem like part of a settled Establishment in a time when America has become increasingly unsettled. This dilemma is another instance of how television finds it hard not to be reassuring. For decades, the *New York Times* reported crises and troubles in a fashion and a voice that said things would turn out all right. But such newspapers are now clinging on to status, like elderly lions perplexed by an invasion of rowdy, unreliable electronic gnats, the "breaking news" of the Web, where breakage may be the ultimate achievement. There is such a profusion of uncertain and fraudulent "news" now, that we may find it impossible, exhausting, and demeaning to follow. The idealistic theory of the global village is close to chaos.

FRONTLINE HAS BEEN FAR LESS POPULAR BUT OFTEN MORE SEARCHING AND WORRYING.

60 Minutes still plays (it may be as hard to retire as the British royal family), but it has lost a lot of its audience and relevance, because the society that comes to the set loyally at the same time every Sunday is harder to organize now. One measure of that was the way Lowell Bergman, a producer on *60 Minutes* for fourteen years, lost faith when the show compromised on its 1995 handling of whistle-blower Jeffrey Wigand in a scrutiny of deceptions by the tobacco company Brown & Williamson. That's when Bergman moved toward *Frontline* (1983 onward), far less popular than *60 Minutes* but often more searching and worrying in its reports (and winner of over seventy-five Emmys).

The history of documentary, or the real thing, has become very complex. As late as the seventies, networks would occasionally launch big "reports" on important issues of the day, drawing them to the attention of Americans. The journalism was superficial, the educational impact close to nil. So in time the networks readily passed that duty over to PBS or the growing band of independent documentary filmmakers. But a tougher problem was at hand. *All the President's Men* (1976) had been a thrilling and encouraging endorsement of how journalists could be relied on to get at our awkward truths. Surely many young people went into that trade because of it.

For a moment, newspapers shone bright in our culture. But technology took away that luster, and we lowered our gaze. Printing presses and newsrooms shrank as the computer became active. The ideal of newspapers is still appealing—it was at the heart of the movie *Spotlight.* The *New York Times* (February 2016) can still mount an exhaustive two-part essay on Hillary Clinton's handling of Libya. But that may be too dense and tiring for many readers. Newspapers started to falter and media became the World Wide Web, where many news stories were spurious, flagrantly unfair, and indifferent to any test of accuracy. Equally, pure documentarians and diligent journalists realized that films or TV reports were not always suited to explaining intricate, veiled realities. That still needed books, and original documents (or hacked records), and nearly impossible perseverance as governments became increasingly paranoid over what they were doing and their need for enclosing security. The people were losing privacy, but government insisted on it. Vietnam was the last adventure with open coverage. After that, reporters were embedded and compromised, and so the News itself became a magazine with star figures desperate to hold a shrinking audience. The last forlorn romance in the head of Brian Williams was that he was a journalist rather than an "anchor."

NO ONE HAS MADE MORE IMPORTANT DOCUMENTARY ESSAYS FOR TELEVISION THAN ADAM CURTIS

IIIIIIIIIIIIIIIIIIIIIIIIIIII

IN RECENT DECADES, A new theatrical audience for documentaries has sprung up. So Michael Moore has made several very personal films, where he is an engaging mix of Alistair Cooke and Dennis the Menace. His big pictures, like *Bowling for Columbine* (2002) and *Fahrenheit 9/11* (2004), may have ended up on our small screens, but they were made for movie houses, film festivals, and the discerning audience that exists for independent pictures. *Columbine* won the Palme d'Or at Cannes and the Oscar for best documentary. *Fahrenheit* proved to be the highest grossing documentary ever made (with world box office over $220 million). Moreover, the Midwestern man-on-the-street character Moore favors has gone for very big issues with a mixture of outrage and fun that shows great potential for making changes in the world—until time enough passes to reveal that nothing has altered. This is a crisis that documentary faces at all levels: It takes on urgent problems; it makes strong cases; but the impact is simply absorbed in the indifference of our political process. Documentary doesn't quite work, and that is ominous for any kind of relationship between television discourse and the world in which we are struggling. That's one more way in which television can leave us waiting for the end with the bleak assurance that it intends to be there.

Some of the most striking documentaries have turned to small, eccentric subjects that seem containable and have story value. That line stretches from *Grey Gardens* (made by the Maysles brothers in 1975) and *Tyson* (2008), James Toback's revealing portrait of the boxer, to some films by Andrew Jarecki, who has often worked for HBO, which has a distinguished documentary unit. His *Capturing the Friedmans* (2003) was a thoughtful inquiry into one very troubled family, spiced by scandal and murder yet so constructed as to encourage an open mind. But *The Jinx: The Life and Deaths of Robert Durst* (2015), a six-parter for HBO, was only scandal and murder with uneasy reconstruction scenes that drifted into the worst kind of dramatized documentary. When the show built to a private bathroom comment that sounded like confession from Durst, the media pack exulted in what media could do. But any alert viewer worried over how much Durst—brilliant in his perverse way—might be an actor, or a character in his own story. *The Jinx* needed a payoff to match its own smart title and anticipatory air, but payoffs are rare in real, untidy history. It's difficult for filmmakers to get the attention and funding of HBO, PBS, or the BBC without the kind of Durstian hook that promises a large crowd, with our expectations and discrimination degraded by the Web. So many situations cry out for Judge Judy's irritated decisiveness.

Nevertheless, there are some important filmmakers who seem pledged to television documentary. Adam Curtis was born in Dartford, east of London, in 1955. He graduated from Oxford in human sciences and went straight into the BBC, where he has remained. Starting in the eighties, he made a series of documentaries, with an increasingly pungent sense of argument, on power in modern society and its reliance on academic theory and statistical analysis. Curtis wrote his scripts and he was invariably his own narrator, fired by a feeling that he was getting at profound structural truths about our society. No one has made more important documentary essays for television, or taken on such complicated issues. This work includes the six-part *Pandora's Box* (1992) about systems analysis, game theory, and the larger matter of guiding people in how to think (as opposed to thinking for themselves); *830,000,000* (1996), on Nick Leeson and the collapse of Barings Bank; and *The Mayfair Set* (1999), on how a group of very wealthy individuals (all members of the Clermont Club in London) did so much to plan and divert British economic strategies.

His best work, I think, is *The Century of the Self* (2002). In four parts, this runs 240 minutes. Its subject is startling and immense: How the work of Freud and his nephew Edward Bernays (1891–1995) was used to reveal ways of shaping and controlling the public imagination through media and advertising. Television has never been clearer about its own mechanisms. Bernays was a key figure in the history of public relations, psychological impulses, and auto-suggestion. He was not a wicked magician but a social scientist who believed in the need to control (or reassure) people in a mass society. After all, Hitler taught us how dangerous and irrational that energy of the crowd could be; it was not enough to condemn Hitler, say "Never again," and move on. The fantasy life of the masses had to be controlled. It is in *The Century of the Self* that Curtis traces the deliberate notion, originating in advertising, that human need has to be overridden by our desires. In other words, when people cannot get what they need, they must be educated to feel and prefer desires instead—possibly far-fetched, impossible, and demented.

THE FANTASY LIFE OF THE MASSES HAD TO BE CONTROLLED.

The Century of the Self is a demanding film; it talks a lot (Curtis believes that verbal language is the last safeguard against televisual tropes), but you will not find a work that gives you more insight, or leaves you less optimistic. Curtis recognizes how far "the self" is a romantic diversion (not a humanistic guideline) that helps us lose sight of how collectives actually function.

It is a film that made me determined to write this book, and what has happened since that program was made only intensifies my alarm. Curtis's latest works are *The Power of Nightmares* (2004), on government's need to create the myth of great enemies in order to secure their own control, and *Bitter Lake* (2015), which the BBC streamed, an analysis (in many different forms) of how the condition of the Middle East was arranged after 1945. It has a motto, from Curtis himself: "Those in power tell stories to help us make sense of the complexity of reality, but those stories are increasingly unconvincing and hollow."

WHEN PEOPLE CANNOT GET WHAT THEY NEED, THEY MUST BE EDUCATED TO FEEL AND PREFER DESIRES INSTEAD.

Yet "story" is one of the last great humanist causes: It is the source of novels and movies; Joan Didion has said, "We tell ourselves stories in order to live." But Curtis has offered a lucid vision of the end of narrative sense. His work may be one of the last educational outbursts from the BBC, and it's fitting that it seems anguished or wounded.

Ken Burns is better known than Curtis and more cheerful. He was born in Brooklyn in 1953, the son of an academic father. He graduated from Hampshire College in film studies and began to make a series of well-defined and traditional documentaries in a style that owed a lot to British and Canadian television. Burns gathered documentary materials: live footage wherever it could be found, but stills, paintings, and prints, too, filmed with a rostrum camera. He composed these to a sound track of voice-over and carefully chosen music of the period. His early films—like *Brooklyn Bridge* (1981), *The Statue of Liberty* (1985), and *Thomas Hart Benton* (1988)—were well received. Burns himself was engaging, articulate, and a first-class career strategist (there is no law against that).

So it was that he built toward his magnum opus, *The Civil War* (1990), made for PBS in nine episodes and 690 minutes. The show was five years in the making, time enough for Burns to assemble funding from a familiar litany of sources: General Motors, the National

Endowment for the Humanities, the Corporation for Public Broadcasting, the Arthur Vining Davis Foundations, and the John D. and Catherine T. MacArthur Foundation. That funding meant that he and his company, Florentine Films in Walpole, New Hampshire, owned the project and would be well rewarded in the sale of boxed sets of videos and an elegant book, published by Knopf.

The Civil War was a beautiful, soulful work, a television symphony, illumined by hallowed photographs from the Mathew Brady era, a grave narrative read by David McCullough (written by Geoffrey C. Ward and Ken's brother, Ric), period music and skillful modern versions of period music ("Ashokan Farewell," written in 1982), and the resonant, familiar voices of actors like Sam Waterston, Jason Robards, Julie Harris, and Morgan Freeman reading the words of participants from 1861 to 1865. Shelby Foote became a household name because of his wry on-camera insights about the human detail of war. Though challenged by some academics, the film was a thorough history with particular emphasis on the question of race, which would prove to be one of Burns's most pressing concerns.

KEN BURNS IS BETTER KNOWN THAN CURTIS AND MORE CHEERFUL.

About 40 million people watched—the biggest audience PBS has ever had. Humble documentarians (a group that had lately included Burns himself) were dumbfounded by the coup, and envious. Burns had become a national institution in five years, and he has never stopped. In very much the same classical style (a mode well suited to historical themes), he has dealt with Baseball, Jazz, the National Parks, the Roosevelts, and many other subjects. He is over sixty now, but he is booked up for years with projects. His historical focus shifted just once, when he made *The Central Park Five* (2012) with his daughter Sarah and her husband, David McMahon, a searching inquiry into the wrongful conviction of five young blacks after a brutal attack on a jogger in the park.

Ken Burns is an eloquent idealist and a brilliant film chronicler, as devoted to America as were John Ford, Walt Disney, or Steven Spielberg. His manner and his voice have been imitated and parodied, and only one thing keeps him from greatness. In his earnest dedication

"It's a Ken Burns documentary about Ken Burns documentaries."

New Yorker
*cartoon by
Carolita
Johnson*

to America's hope and its future, he does not always admit how badly the country has suffered in the era of his work. So he loves the baseball of his childhood and before, but may not see the corruption that has infected the game. He is a connoisseur of great jazz, without admitting that that art has been diminished and sanitized. A question that awaits Burns is just what happens if black America faces the failure of hope, reform, progress, and beautiful documentaries. I think Ken was once tempted by politics, but he loves his life and work and Walpole, even if he begins to seem a guardian of the past and a protector of a conservatism that wants to stay there. His history of the Vietnam War (set for 2017), with as many Vietnamese witnesses as Americans, may be his greatest test—and ours, too, for Vietnam was our second civil war.

Burns's films are emphatically directed; they come loaded with intent. But the other adherent to working for PBS is shy of direction, or so he has always said. Frederick Wiseman was born in Boston in 1930. He went to Williams and trained to be a lawyer, but by 1967 he was making *Titicut Follies*, about life in the Bridgewater State Hospital for the criminally insane in Massachusetts. It was a provocative and controversial film, because so much of the footage was close to horror, but it was not an accurate sign of where Wiseman was headed. (The very title spoke of attitude in a way Wiseman has seldom repeated.) He soon became a purist of documentary reticence. He liked to spend as long as possible with a subject, shooting until he found things of interest and then compiling those parts in his editing to make a study of the topic or the institution he had selected. He entered the arena without anger or pleasure, uncertain what he would find and not intending to present an opinion or a decision about it so much as its authentic atmosphere. He rejects narrative or voice-over and he works steadily out of Boston for PBS. This is what he says:

> When I'm shooting, I'm merely trying to collect as many—for lack of a better term—"good" or interesting sequences as I can, all the various activities. There's no time to think of themes or points of view. I collect a lot of material and think about all that later. I don't like to start a film with a preconceived notion of what it's going to be about, as it's then that you miss out on things. If I'm only shooting to support a predetermined thesis, I'm going to miss things. I like the final film to be a response to the shooting of the film.

But does that mean he knows what the "things" are, and why they rate as such? To date, he has accumulated forty-two what I will call institutional films, from *Titicut Follies* and *High School* through *The Store* (Neiman Marcus in Dallas) and *Zoo* to *Crazy Horse* (an erotic club in Paris), *At Berkeley* (the University of California), and *National Gallery* (about the London art gallery). *National Gallery* is three hours long, yet it could be longer—the method of working seems ready for the infinite, though I doubt greater length would reach any conclusion. That's because Wiseman prefers the eternal record as opposed to journalistic closure. He is an esteemed figure, at home and abroad, and he is the model or godfather for films that are tasteful and tactful surveillance as opposed to an essay with conclusions. But it's decades since a Wiseman film has offended anyone, and I wonder whether documentary should stay so passive.

It's clear that Wiseman loves what he is doing, and no one doubts his dedication, his subtlety in observing and editing, or his care. But it's hard to feel that all those films make a pointed, critical portrait of America so much as a tribute to contemplation. Indeed, he is a director who steadily confronts the question, What is documentary for? And then prefers not to answer. Is he our Bartleby? When I thought of that, I meant it as something of a put-down. But the more I think about it, the easier it is to wonder if our television doesn't need more Bartlebys. Imagine one as host on *The Jerry Springer Show*, gently deflating the show's bogus wrath. That may just mean that Wiseman is so advanced or dismayed a documentarian that he realizes his genre can change nothing. So he watches us and keeps his temper. He films the external world in the way Bonnard woke up each day to paint a breakfast table.

Wiseman is often impersonal, yet he is fascinated by ordinary life. It's not condescending to say that his films sometimes feel as if we might have made them ourselves, in an age of household cameras and with a sense of the world being there to be filmed. Academic historians are increasingly interested in that treasury of "home movie" as an unmediated record of what has passed. Television documentary does not often delve into such commonplace lives. But one series seems a model for what might be done more often, and an inspiration to us at home with our recording devices.

In 1964, Granada had a notion of looking at the lives of fourteen English children. Paul Almond directed *Seven Up*, which had children talking and playing in a patchwork portrait of British society—and in 1964, the makers felt sure the country was on the brink of significant and necessary change. The show was unstressed, yet sympathetic and it charmed the public imagination in its gentle picture of class differences.

There was a scheme to return to the group every seven years, and so far there have been eight "episodes," all but the first directed by Michael Apted who was a research assistant on the original show and chose the kids to be filmed. These are not famous or especially vivid lives and the kids grew up with some mixed feelings about the show and its exposure—one of them opted out. The whole thing runs 769 minutes now, and it means to push on towards what may be difficult years. The participants are mostly cheery, in a British way—there is more modest optimism than quiet desperation, and the interviews do not probe uncomfortably. But the *Up* series is unrivalled at something a domestic medium ought to pursue—the lives of ordinary and "unknown" people. Being unknown is a strange but precious right in all the din of fame, selfie culture, and the Kardashians (and they are always busy with their own home movie and its loony epic reach).

19

LONG FORM

ON MARCH 5, 2015, I TURNED TO ABC (a network, if you recall) at 10:00 P.M. I had some difficulty finding the correct channel, but I was  urged there because it offered the premiere of ABC's new long-form show *American Crime*, a title that would embrace most of the shows I will look at in this chapter: *The Wire*, *The Sopranos*, *Breaking Bad*, and *True Detective*. *Peaky Blinders* and *The Fall* are British, but much influenced by American shows and equally crime-minded. Long-form television may be a modern pleasure ground, but it insists on people behaving badly in ways we would hope to avoid in life. It does death religiously.

American Crime had encouraging early reviews—in the *San Francisco Chronicle*, David Wiegand had said Felicity Huffman was "monumental" in it. Then there was the presence of John Ridley as the show's creator, writer, and director. He is a published novelist, a TV writer, and the author of scripts for *Three Kings* and *12 Years a Slave*. But I was also drawn by the sentimental appeal of a worthwhile long-form show playing on one of the ancient networks.

Alas, the pilot show left me jittery with interruptus. In the notional hour slot there were five commercial breaks. I am no longer used to that. Worse yet, the passage of the episode was frequently intruded on by superimposed banners or tags for other ABC shows.

I PREFER TV THAT IS HARD TO FOLLOW, OR ELUSIVE.

That created a desperation that fought against the dramatic anxiety of the episode itself. It meant that the strained face of Felicity Huffman's character (thoughtful, clever, ruined, mean-spirited) might inadvertently look down at one of those tags as if it was a fly that had flown into her screen and her mood.

This chronic fragmentation made the show harder to follow, Ridley having already composed and edited it with rapid and brief flashes—backward for sure, but maybe some were forward. The pilot also offered many characters without explaining their links. I don't mind that—I prefer TV that is hard to follow, or elusive. Decades of relentless clarity and dumb linkage have enforced the medium's dullness and made it less lifelike. Still, the scheme of showing *American Crime* did nothing to assist the concentration its stories deserved. Will networks like ABC never understand that? Will they not see that their efforts to compete with cable demand an understanding of "long form"—a story that goes on over weeks and which possesses narrative form, not just commercial organization?

Within the obstacle course of the show, there was plenty to notice. Set in Modesto, California (but shot in Austin, Texas), it understood the listless affect of so many small and out-of-the-way towns and their refusal to relate to landscape. The story had a promising mixture of races. There was a plain hook in view—who had killed this character, Matt Skokie, and why?—that might last a long time. A lot of the acting was impressive, not just Felicity Huffman, who was close to monumental but a nasty, ordinary nag, too. In addition, Timothy Hutton, Benito Martinez, and Caitlin Gerard were unusual suspects about whom I wanted to know more.

So in April 2015 I wrote a note toward this book: "By the time you read this, *American Crime* may be forgotten, or a national favorite. Some of the actors I liked may have vanished from the show.

I gather that it will soon become a court procedural, and that could lead to many lessons about race in America (so it's serendipitous that the pilot played in the week that saw the Justice Department's report on police procedures in Ferguson, Missouri)."

I trust you remember Ferguson, though I know there can be so many local outrages to keep straight. They are as confounding as all the school shootings, or your bank urging you to create fresh passwords.

It's intriguing to look back on one's first impressions of a long-form show, because uncertainty is never far from the creators' feelings: They want to tell a story that interests them, and "story" does presume some closure or resolution; on the other hand, the business of what they're doing, and their own career prospects, make them yearn for renewal, and more renewals yet to come. Why not go on forever and ignore closure? So many things on television aspire to that longevity. In many ways, long form requires this consideration as a genre, for it gets at television's silly urges to be both new and forever.

From the start, ABC seemed eager to promote the show. Still, having opened with over 8 million viewers, it dropped to half that number by the end of its first series (still a good level for cable shows). It wasn't being talked about enough, and while it was renewed for a second series, it was announced that it would then take up another story arc, in which actors like Felicity Huffman played different characters. Was it a true narrative or an anthology?

Television always believed in its own monotony: We needed the News every day; the same commercials were played over and over again; *Gunsmoke* had 635 episodes in twenty years and then, after it had played, it was syndicated. There might be gunfire and fisticuffs in every episode using the same old sound effects. But those things were given, and in the process the crises became habit, or contrived. (Did the same repetition dull the News?) The characters in a show did not always develop dramatically—they did not change; it was only the guest parts that had any chance of organic existence. One principle of *Gunsmoke* was that life in Dodge City was perilous and insecure but

IT'S INTRIGUING TO LOOK BACK ON ONE'S IMPRESSIONS OF A LONG-FORM SHOW.

Matt Dillon grew older and more secure. *I Love Lucy* had 181 episodes in which Lucy was forever on the edge of disaster, but everything got tidied up—until she and Desi actually divorced.

The majority of shows may have wondered about the serial format, but that posed grave dangers: Would an audience come back week after week? Would they countenance a story that might stretch out over weeks and years? And if you let the writers feel they were in a prolonged but linked narrative, wouldn't they think of the climaxes, and even the closure, that most narrative forms tend toward, as if drawn by gravity. There had been ventures in that direction: *The Quatermass Experiment* had cliffhanger endings and then a week of waiting; still, it was only six 30-minute episodes. The serialization of classic novels went much further: *The Forsyte Saga* had been twenty-six 50-minute episodes. No one quite called it a miniseries in 1967. That label waited on the shows ABC launched ten years later, *Rich Man, Poor Man* and *Roots*. But the cherished *Crime Story* (1986–88) was more than NBC could sustain, even though it dropped moonshine in its mix when it let characters survive a test nuclear explosion in Nevada. Later still, *Rubicon* (2010) was shut down by AMC because its tangled but unwinding story had not won a sufficient audience. Devotees were left in clinical shock, but they had that unfinished ending to dream over.

HERE, AT LAST, WAS TELEVISION CATCHING UP WITH THE MOVIES.

Long form is now a label everyone knows, but don't let that persuade you it can last forever. Or that in the years before long form, in the late eighties and nineties, series weren't becoming tougher or that long storylines weren't being pursued—think of *Wiseguy* (1987–90), co-created by Stephen Cannell, which imposed the "story arc" on the old episodic format. Business models were finding profit in smaller audiences before cable gained traction. After that, the streaming services of Amazon and Netflix made for idiosyncratic shows with very small audiences by old TV standards. In 2010–15, long-forms became an orthodoxy, but programmers and audiences alike wondered if there might be too many to keep up with. Amazon is a giant now, but in the media giants do stumble, and both Amazon and Netflix are making large investments that court disaster—if some new way of watching ever dawns.

Still, *Rubicon* was a regrettable withdrawal. What made *American Crime* intriguing was its being on ABC when long form was identified as a cable genre. Not that HBO or Showtime had been quick to see their opportunity. They had been around for years before they found that inspiration. But long form helped characterize cable, just as it won many subscribers. Here, at last, was television catching up with the movies, taking sex and violence, language and tough subject matter in its stride. Cable was not in a mood to pay much heed to complaints over those things. Look, it said, we're minority channels— we believe in a discerning audience (so long as they're content with endless crime and violence—long form has scarcely touched comedy). Audiences were appreciative, or simply small. While it regularly risked cancelation, *The Wire* (2002–08) had a critical reputation that is still unsurpassed. Many writers said, and still say, it was the best they've ever seen. In *Time*, in December 2006, James Poniewozik wrote: "No other TV show has ever loved a city so well, damned it so passionately or sung it so searingly."

Yet that show was pleased if it got a million viewers an episode. The explanations offered were that the structure of the show was as hard to follow as it was difficult to hear or understand the black street talk. Even fans admitted that *The Wire* took getting used to. That homebound middle-class audience delighted with *Friends* (1994–2004) was likely disturbed by the vision of a large, named city being so dysfunctional thanks to poverty, drugs, and the impossible task of police and government. One million was a figure that network television would have ridiculed (*Friends* often had 30 million per episode). But for a novel, 500,000 book sales would be phenomenal and enough to sway a society in its attitude to all those dark subjects. So *The Wire* mattered because it insisted on an audience facing grim urban realities and feeling the distant chance of a solution. Television had reached a point where it could deliver reality—so long as the audience was loyal to murder, mayhem, and ruined lives beyond the point of responding to commercials. In 2015, the real Baltimore exploded over unceasing police hostility to black citizens.

For some of us, long-form series have replaced going to the movies. They even seem like a reversion to the last great era of American movies, the seventies, when pictures were made to challenge the audience, and sometimes managed that while keeping large numbers. That richness began to dwindle in the late seventies, and the decline has never stopped. There are excellent independent movies being made, and they can find a theatrical audience commensurate with their low budgets. But many mainstream movies have found a rut of absurd violence or gross comedy done with special effects and digital photography that convey a separation from reality that disturbs an audience familiar with the seventies, or films made long before that.

There was a time when big box-office movies were regarded as our best pictures and won many Oscars (*Gone with the Wind*,

The Best Years of Our Lives, From Here to Eternity, Ben-Hur, In the Heat of the Night, Patton, The Godfather). Today, the well-being of the Academy's money-raising night on television is threatened by how seldom the winners are pictures enough people have seen. In 2010, *The Hurt Locker* won Best Picture—and for directing and screenplay—but I doubt three million Americans saw it. In 2015, the only film nominated for Best Picture to prosper was *American Sniper*. It won for best sound editing, but it had grossed around $330 million. (The winning film, *Birdman*, took $42 million.) Clint Eastwood had delivered a well-made film, though many discerning people found it politically incorrect. (Which may remind us that no one yet has risked trying a long-form series about military life. Fantasy shooters are easier to handle than the real thing.)

||||||||||||||||||||||||||||

I WON'T GO THROUGH ALL THE LONG-FORM SERIES, but something has to be said about *Oz* (1997–2003), the first long-form that HBO produced, and probably the toughest to watch. *Oz* was created by Tom Fontana, who had been raised as a writer on *St. Elsewhere* (1982–88) and as a writer-producer on *Homicide: Life on the Street* (1993–99). Oz was the nickname of the Oswald State prison, a maximum-security operation (though no one was ever secure there). Fontana wrote many of the episodes and was responsible for the demonic relationship between Schillinger (J. K. Simmons), an Aryan brother, a jailhouse rapist, and a power in the prison, and Beecher (Lee Tergesen), a lawyer once and rather incongruous at Oswald. Schillinger overwhelms him, rapes him repeatedly, and becomes a satanic tyrant. But Beecher learns to fight back and secures the support of prison guard Diane Whittlesey (Edie Falco). Sheer terror mingled with ghastly indignity in an uncompromising portrait of a prison system that amounted to a state-supported version of criminal life.

That was just the beginning. *Oz* had admirers, as well as people stunned by a revelation of prison life not dared before by American media. There were also critics who felt it was overdone and contrived. (There's only one way to test that argument, but it's not one you want to try.) The show never won an Emmy. That should be kept in mind in considering *The Sopranos*, a major prizewinner, often very nasty but with a halfway endearing central character who trod a delicate line with our sympathies. *The Sopranos* was better than *Oz*, but its success with Emmys reflects a narrative balance in the show as well as our own rapid toughening up.

Oz was still playing when *The Sopranos* (1999–2007) started at HBO. It was created by David Chase, born in 1945 to an Italian-American family and raised in Clifton, New Jersey. He had worked previously on *The Rockford Files* and *Northern Exposure*, but no one could have predicted the scale and intensity of *The Sopranos*. Tony (James Gandolfini) was and is (for this series lives on in our minds and in reruns) a Mafia chief, capable of casual cruelty and exploitation, but humdrum, too. He is a nightmare Marty. He worried over his family life, having a wife and mistresses, his intimidating mother, Livia (Nancy Marchand, a veteran from *Marty* and *Lou Grant*). These worries led him at the outset of the show to a psychiatrist, Dr. Jennifer Melfi (Lorraine Bracco). Their sessions together were often a framework for the story. Chase produced the show, along with Brad Grey. He wrote thirty of the eighty-six episodes, with several other significant writers: Terence Winter (he would go on to *Boardwalk Empire* and writing *The Wolf of Wall Street*), Robin Green (she would do *Blue Bloods,* a CBS series that averaged 13 million viewers), and Matthew Weiner (soon to create *Mad Men*). But Chase was the pathfinder, and it was not hard to find episodes and even seasons where he was drifting along, uncertain whether the situation was sufficient, or did we need to know Tony's fate?

TONY WAS NOT FLASHY, WITTY, OR SUPERIOR; HE WAS A LUMBERING . . .

The Sopranos had unbeatable production ingredients. It was sharply written, but the direction was incisive (Tim Van Patten did twenty episodes) and occasionally dreamlike. (The episode "Pine Barrens," written by Winter and directed by Steve Buscemi, shifted from conventional violence to a surreal state, with two gangsters lost in the woods.) Gandolfini had been around for years playing small parts in movies, but suddenly he was reappraised as a substantial actor. Tony was not flashy, witty, or superior; he was a lumbering, shy chump, raised to violence but discovering something more inside him. Edie Falco now had two important series in a row, while Michael Imperioli, Dominic Chianese, Steven Van Zandt, and Tony Sirico became national favorites. And "national" meant something. Despite violence, nudity, language, and steady darkness, the show started out with about 3.5 million viewers and then rose to the 6–10 million range. Every season, it was nominated for the Emmy as Outstanding Drama, and at first it did not win, perhaps because there was a grievance still against cable channels. But then it won twice, in 2004 and

. . . SHY CHUMP, RAISED TO VIOLENCE BUT DISCOVERING SOMETHING MORE INSIDE HIM.

2007, the first cable show to win that prize. Gandolfini and Falco won three Emmys personally, and, ultimately, prestigious awards (like the Peabody) were being thrown around.

Criminal gangs had been on television since *The Untouchables*— but that is a cop show, and lawmen were hard to find in the Sopranos' New Jersey. *The Sopranos* was more subtle and entertaining—it had a mordant wit, as if aware of its own novelty. Still, I'm not sure it would have kept its coherence and its grim panache without Gandolfini. Regular viewers felt the show would have to end by closing out Tony's story—arrest or death, or whatever you could think of. David Chase came to that last episode with just the melancholy wryness Tony deserved. So the show ended on a glance and a sigh, with every possibility lined up like ducks quacking for bread, but nothing settled. It was one of the most unexpected but assured endings in long form, in which the years-long burden of resolution was finessed—or was it cheated? Alas, Gandolfini was dead only a few years later, so no sequel ever had a chance. He was the show as much as James Garner had been Jim Rockford, or Marlon Brando Vito Corleone.

In *Breaking Bad*, a similar trick was managed as we grew to like a villain. But this was more pointed, and poignant, because Walter White started out as a high school chemistry teacher, a harassed husband, and parent to a handicapped teenage son, with a new baby on the way. Then he turned his ability as a chemist into cooking crystal meth on a business scale. Had a good man on television ever gone so far over to the other side? He died at the end (he had to—his change of life had been prompted by the discovery of lung cancer). It was criminal drama again, but it was also a portrait of what an ordinary American guy might do if his every attempt to play the game of success decently turned into travesty. It helped a lot in this process that Walter was played by Bryan Cranston, who had become endearing as the frustrated dad in *Malcolm in the Middle* (2000–06). As with Gandolfini, a small-part player, someone recognized but not easily named, Cranston became a household figure. But Walter's own house was falling apart.

Vince Gilligan, who created the show, was born in Richmond, Virginia, in 1967—he is the first notable figure in this book born after the turmoil of the mid-sixties, at a time when *Bonanza*, *The Andy Griffith Show*, and *Rowan & Martin's Laugh-In* were top shows. But

"MR. CHIPS BECOMING SCARFACE"– THE ARC OF WALTER WHITE.

Gilligan was more interested in old movies and film noir. He attended the Tisch School at New York University and he tried a few film scripts before he was recommended to Chris Carter, the creator of *The X-Files* (1993–2002), broadcast on the Fox channel. That was an odd mix of FBI show and occult projection, but it owed more to *The Twilight Zone* than to shows that believed in the FBI. Soon enough, its FBI became a mirror image of the paranoid's paradise in which a ghosted America might be consumed by spooks, aliens, crazies, and fever dreams. But the writing was endlessly inventive, even as the scheme of serial suspense came and went. The show rested on the undoubted but untested chemistry between its two protagonists: the skeptical Scully (Gillian Anderson) and the credulous Mulder (David Duchovny). The long-suspended possibility of their becoming lovers was an enticement for the show. Carter supervised the writing, but Gilligan wrote thirty episodes and, as he would say, got an education in showrunning a series by watching Carter.

So equipped, Gilligan went to AMC and pitched the idea of "Mr. Chips becoming Scarface"—the arc of Walter White. His first thought was to set the show in suburban Los Angeles, but AMC insisted on Albuquerque, New Mexico (it would be cheaper), and that proved a blessing. It made the interaction of whites and Latinos so much more plausible, and it established a location of flimsy buildings surrounded by desert scrub. Over it all hung the scathing blue sky that became such a part of the show's color scheme.

Breaking Bad was a show where gruesome actions could not get in the way of the thought that it was cinematic. I don't think a show on TV had ever seemed as confident at matching the look and inner life of great movies. That could be attributed to brilliant photography (fifty episodes by Michael Slovis), superb and seamless writing, watched over by Gilligan but shared with many others, the piercing moments of surrealism, the eerie strain of comedy, and the odd but plausible untidiness of Walt's family life. His wife, Skyler, was played with tender nuances and unstressed sensuality by Anna Gunn, so that it was all the more unsettling when factions of the audience turned against Skyler and Gunn. Somehow, a paranoid male chauvinism had been irritated by the marital equality in the show and the toughness Skyler had picked up to survive. She had a mind of her own, and on television that has always been a tough step for regulation wives. Every part was well cast and played, all the way down to the lawyer Saul (Bob Odenkirk) and the macabre Tío Salamanca (Mark Margolis) with his dainty executioner's bell.

IT READS LIKE A NOVEL BY A MASTER STORYTELLER.

My own experience with *Breaking Bad* was to be impressed with it, week after week, on AMC, despite the commercials. But a few years later I watched the whole thing on DVDs over a period of about ten days. All at once it revealed itself as less a show than a very long but perfectly judged movie. Enough people handle their viewing now in this way to justify the boxed sets for purchase and the availability of more TV on Netflix. When I saw the boxed set, it was like water on parched ground. I felt changed and enriched by the experience, but I wondered if I could face the weekly delivery of a series any longer.

I find *Breaking Bad* superior to *The Sopranos* because it acknowledges consequences and destiny, and knows it is moving toward a climax that cannot be interfered with or delayed for another season. It reads like a novel by a master storyteller (which is why I prefer the

134-minute movie of *The Remains of the Day* to years of *Downton Abbey*). In the New Mexico of *Breaking Bad* I could feel a Dickens at work. Gilligan had an overall construct in mind, but the show had to keep getting renewed for him to deliver it.

Breaking Bad was seldom pretentious, though it could get arty; but it had large ambitions, fired by Gilligan's identification with Walter. *True Detective* (2014–) moved in different directions: It was far briefer, but it stood up for art. Nic Pizzolatto had been a literature professor at the University of North Carolina; he had published a collection of short stories and a novel. He had some work as a writer on *The Killing*. Then he started pitching the *True Detective* idea as a series of limited seasons, done to attract genuine movie stars (a concept less and less clear in the public mind) just because the season was short. It was short long-form, a notion that had been growing in British television. It would be eight hour-long episodes with two detectives. Then, in a second season, the locale would shift and there would be two new detectives.

For the first season, Pizzolatto would write everything and Cary Joji Fukunaga (a promising movie director) would handle every episode (though he got the job when Alejandro González Iñárritu proved unavailable). HBO went with the scheme, and Matthew McConaughey and Woody Harrelson signed on as actors (and co-executive producers). Adam Arkapaw would shoot it; he had just done *Top of the Lake* with Jane Campion, which demonstrated his ability and the readiness of HD screens to make landscape a poetic element in a show. First thoughts had been to film in Arkansas, but in the end it became southern Louisiana. Pizzolatto loved the feeling of wilderness being within sight of the gaunt structures of the oil industry, and the idea of occult practices in a modern world. With Fukunaga, he made the show more atmospheric and creepy than had been managed on television before. As an extra, T Bone Burnett was in charge of the music.

TRUE DETECTIVE WAS SHORT LONG-FORM, A NOTION THAT HAD BEEN GROWING IN BRITISH TELEVISION.

That first season was extraordinary, and yes, it was flat-out pretentious. But if that is permitted in all the other arts, why not in television, too? The show covered at least fifteen years of real time, and it presented the two detectives as partners once, split apart when one of them had a brief affair with the other's wife (Michelle Monaghan), but then reunited as the targets of police interrogations about some other case. This was not made clear, and clarity was generally sacrificed to the intense, dreamy, improv-like performances from McConaughey and Harrelson. The actors were friends, and it was McConaughey who had recommended Harrelson as his partner. Their talk was heady, as the prospect loomed that together they had been involved in a large crime. The writing could remind one of Faulkner or Flannery O'Connor, while still seeming fit for the ambitions of two excellent and daring actors. McConaughey was at the point of emerging from his own early career as a romantic lead, while Harrelson had come such a long way from his naive Woody in *Cheers*. We did not understand Rust and Marty, but we liked them, and some of us were content to have them carry on talking for hours. For those who tried but could not get into the show, Pizzolatto's attitude seemed to be, "So, watch something else."

The night McConaughey won the Oscar for *Dallas Buyers Club* also saw the penultimate episode of the first season of *True Detective* (to an audience of over 3 million, about a million more than it was used to getting). Even at that modest level, the show was talked about furiously; on the Net there were eloquent attempts to fathom its deeper meanings—if indeed there was a plan for depth above and beyond the suspended marvel of its talk. It seemed like an event in television history, and there were reviews and rewards to go with that. Then season two lined up, with Colin Farrell, Vince Vaughn, and Rachel McAdams as the leads. Pizzolatto would still write it, but Fukunaga had moved on. The second season turned out an acknowledged failure, with viewing figures dropping as it ended. The third?

PEAKY BLINDERS WAS A BBC TWO SERIES MADE OUT OF SIX-EPISODE ARCS.

There was mounting competition. *Peaky Blinders* (2014–) was a BBC Two series made out of six-episode arcs. The show was created and written by Steven Knight (the director of the movie *Locke*). The Peaky Blinders were a gang of hardened veterans from the Great War—the title referred to their habit of sewing razor blades into the peaks of their caps for use in gang fighting. The setting was Birmingham in 1920, with Cillian Murphy as leader of the gang and Sam Neill as the Northern Irish police inspector pursuing him. It meant to be dazzling: To the eye, the period detail was reliable, but on the sound track there was modern rock, some of it by Nick Cave. There were viewers disturbed by this incongruity; others realized that the show was a melodrama worthy of the 1920s with good guys and bad. But that limited ambition was lit up by the acting and a trio of compelling women (Helen McCrory, Annabelle Wallis, and Charlotte Riley). Winston Churchill and Charlie Chaplin were among the supporting roles, and in the second series Tom Hardy appeared as a cross between Fagin and the Kray brothers.

Peaky Blinders opened on BBC Two and it got an audience of about 2 million (very close to the American viewership for *True Detective*). For America, the Weinstein Company, who had bought the rights, sold it to Netflix for streaming so that you could watch a six-episode season over a weekend.

The Fall (2013–) was just as well done, but it was deeper. This BBC Two show was created and written by Allan Cubitt, who also directed all of the second season. Cubitt had worked as a writer on *Prime Suspect*; he had adapted *Anna Karenina* for television in a version where Helen McCrory played Anna, but he seemed to emerge from nowhere when he began *The Fall*. It is a police show, set in Belfast, in which Detective Superintendent Stella Gibson (Gillian Anderson) comes over from London to lead the search for a serial killer. The show was proud of its Irishness: It found a young Belfast actor, Jamie Dornan, to be the serial killer, Paul Spector; it used many other Irish players; and it actually premiered on Irish television before playing in London.

What's special about *The Fall* is its bipolar structure. It seemed at first to be a story about Stella, who in the form of Gillian Anderson was probably the most glamorous TV cop since Angie Dickinson in *Police Woman*, but Paul became an increasingly important character. We knew who the killer was from the outset, because we had seen the murders through his eyes and process, which was not that different from Stella's method. She is well dressed and sexually authoritative: She orders a young policeman to come to her hotel room for dutiful sex, without any chance of a relationship. But as the show goes on, we begin to learn about her own insecurities when Paul steals her handwritten journal and discovers an uneasy private woman. In turn, Paul becomes more interesting, for he

WHAT'S SPECIAL ABOUT *THE FALL* IS ITS BIPOLAR STRUCTURE.

is investigating her. He is a cruel killer but a fond father, and he is smart enough to win some sympathy. Moreover, Cubitt himself seemed reluctant to have Paul captured and imprisoned.

The rapport between killer and detective in *The Fall* was not new (Colombo had had a droll double act with many of his rogues), but it's hard to think of a television show of such quality that has explored it so well. There's an uncomfortable logic in this just because so many of these long-form shows mine our fascination with murder. Taken one by one, many of them are intriguing and justified. But if you regard them as a whole, and as a grouping in our imagination, then the emphasis becomes disconcerting. It's a welcome advance in the culture that we no longer tolerate lawmen as virtuous and successful as Perry Mason or Matt Dillon. But we are very close now to being monopolized by killers, people we would never let into our homes. There they are, burning quietly in a corner, or on the wall.

||||||||||||||||||||||||||||

THIS SURVEY HAS OMITTED MANY LONG-FORMS—your favorites perhaps: *The Hour* (2011–12), *Mad Men* (2007–15), *The Affair* (2014–), *Downton Abbey* (2010–15). None of those is quite a crime show, yet sooner or later most lead to a suspicion of something very bad. Being at home with a show insinuates a sense of valuable order and security, but show after show offers misdemeanor as a temptation. Then there is *Game of Thrones* (2011–), based on the appeal of medieval costume and warfare, or crime before that word was known. Did I leave out *Homeland* (2011–), which for a while was riveting and in which Claire Danes gave a remarkable and frightening performance as a bipolar person? I haven't even mentioned *Dexter* (2006–13), an eight-season hit for Showtime in which a police blood analyst in Miami (Michael C. Hall) is also a serial killer in private. But for some people all life has become private; that's a function of loneliness.

We tell ourselves we are in a golden age of long-form television, and collectively we have a shared list of the great shows. The trend is powerful and it has changed the thrust of several directors' careers: Steven Knight may have given up movies for television; Lee Daniels took on *Empire*; Cary Fukunaga made his name with *True Detective*, and not on his very good movie, *Jane Eyre*; Jane Campion's fine work has not surpassed *Top of the Lake*; Martin Scorsese was a busily engaged co-executive producer on *Boardwalk Empire*; Woody Allen has signed on to do a half-hour television series for Amazon. Gillian Anderson is one of our best actresses, active on stage and the big screen, but no one could think of her without referring to *The X-Files* and *The Fall*.

Already there are too many long-forms to keep up with. It's also the case that a connoisseur of the genre learns to need the boxed sets more than the weekly appearance at a set time. It's hard to resist a show if the early word is good, and we realize that cable television plays them to expand its subscription base. Yet long-forms cannot help but emphasize the enhanced experience of taking a whole show in just a few gulps. In which case,

I WAS HOPING FOR A LIGHTER-HEARTED ENDING, AND IT ARRIVED IN EARLY 2016.

the collective experience of television takes another blow. It becomes less of an immediate sensation (9:00 P.M. on Sunday) and more evidence of the way the mass we once were has turned into an archipelago of discerning individuals. It's as intense and solitary as reading.

Cable has been one of the best phases in the history of television. But it is threatened or confused now by other forms of delivery, like streaming. Then you have to wonder whether the creative impulse that has united David Chase, Vince Gilligan, Jane Campion, and Allan Cubitt could be sustained in an altered form of broadcasting that lacks the occasion of a big opening and a developing story line. Nothing much has lasted on television, beyond the commercials and being on or off. I began this book by looking at sample shows of the fifties and sixties, riveting in their day but foolish antiques now. Urgency fades fast. *24* (2001–10 on Fox) was a very influential show for a time, full of suspense, but how many of us want to replay it? The more you stress the momentary, the more you are imprisoned by it.

As it is, I feel guilty over series I have not included here—or not seen properly. The helpless frenzy one can feel over the impossible amount of mind-catching fluff on the Net is rivaled by the mounting list of long-forms that have been recommended. So, what about *Secrets and Lies*, *The Americans*, *Broadchurch*, or all the Scandinavian serial-killer procedurals like *The Killing*? Was there even a show called *Ordinary American Life with Nothing Much Happening*? What about the stunning *Mr. Robot*? I have just read Clive James's arousing book *Play All*, in which the great critic (and onetime TV talk-show host) reclines on his sick sofa in a season or two of binge-watching. He sees so much, and sees so much in it, we have to remind ourselves that he is on that sofa because his health is running out. Then we may realize we are in much the same plight, and wonder how far the fever of long-form immersion requires desperation, as well as chimes at midnight.

I was hoping for a lighter-hearted ending, and it arrived in early 2016, as *Love*, which may stand as an innovation in long formlessness. This was a Netflix show, created by Judd Apatow, Lesley Arfin, and Paul Rust (the latter two are married), set in modern-day Los Angeles. There was no heavy load of plot to handle; it was about a kind of nothing as sweet-sour slackers drifted around each other wondering about the difference between love and sex, engagement and tedium. What impressed was its grasp of uneventfulness and insignificance, the very conditions we may experience watching, waiting, and losing attention. Too much TV is determined to give us a jolt and a shock. Too little honors the sweet, sleepy passing of time. *Love* may not last or hold to its rhythms—I am writing this before the close of its first season—but I can see its leading players, Gillian Jacobs and Arfin again, becoming institutions. I'm happy to have them in the house, a doofus and a daft Delilah—or to eavesdrop on theirs.

LAUGH ON/LAUGH OFF

On April 1, 1957, the respected BBC news program *Panorama* (1953

and onward) ran a 3-minute item on that spring's bumper harvest of spaghetti in southern Switzerland. This item had been the idea of a cameraman, Charles de Jaeger, and it showed a group of trees from which spaghetti strands were being picked. The documentariness of it was aired,
with a voice-over by *Panorama*'s regular host, Richard Dimbleby, a revered figure in British broadcasting and a man whose dignity matched his ample girth (note: "ample girth" is a jokey way of saying things we're not really allowed to say anymore—I doubt TV would employ him now).

Dimbleby understood and relished the joke, and he did his piece with a straight voice, just as if he was commentating an event in the life of the royal family.

I saw the spaghetti hoax and wasn't sure what to make of it. Jokes always have a context, and in Britain in 1957 spaghetti was not on many menus. But I laughed because my mother was giggling. You had to be there in April 1957 to feel the different tugs on credibility and farce. But that April Fools' Day joke is enshrined in British folklore. Viewers were tickled to think that the BBC might tease its own impeccable status and kid the audience. I'm sure some BBC officials deplored the piece and worried that "No one will trust us again!" But trust can impede lively television, just as humorlessness gets in the way of everything.

Now, jump forward thirty-three years to May 21, 1990. It is the last episode (number 184) of *Newhart*. This was a 30-minute sitcom on CBS from 1982 to 1990, created by Barry Kemp but dependent on the wry, likeable decency of Bob Newhart (another candidate for Mr. Television in that he served long and well, without offending, and with tender affection for comic timing). *Newhart* had been the series in which Newhart's character and his wife ran a country inn in Vermont. We met the locals and the visitors, and it was steady mild fun. But it had a miracle for its closure.

How would *Newhart* end, as Japanese interests purchased the small town in Vermont? Newhart's real wife, Ginny, had a brain wave. Bob would get a knock on the head, and the picture would dissolve to…a bedroom in Chicago, just before dawn. "No one" had been told about this in advance, but some in the live audience thought they recognized the set. Wasn't it the bedroom from *The Bob Newhart Show* (1972–78, 142 episodes, also for CBS, produced by MTM) in which Newhart had played a psychiatrist, Robert Hartley, living with his wife, Emily, and meeting their friends and patients? The knowing members

THE KNOWING MEMBERS OF THE AUDIENCE BECAME AN ECSTATIC CONGREGATION.

of the audience became an ecstatic congregation as the couple in bed were revealed as Newhart…and Suzanne Pleshette, who had played Emily in the earlier show. Hardly anyone had noticed Pleshette as she was smuggled onto the set. So Bob Hartley told Emily he'd had this weird dream in which he'd been running a country inn in Vermont!

The dream framework made a captivating joke, but that wasn't the whole point. What ensured that moment's fame (so that "everyone" believes they saw it) was the treasured discovery of the very

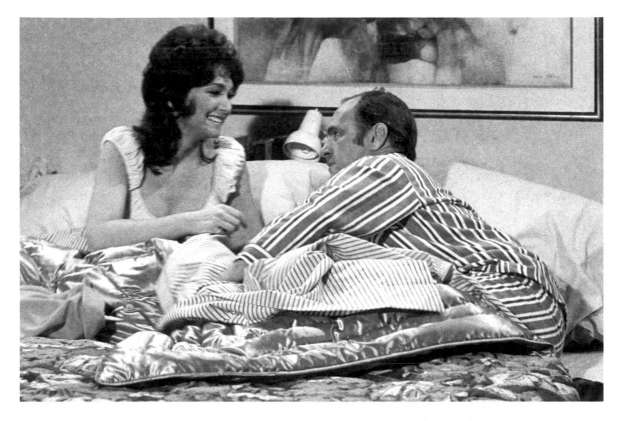

popular Ms. Pleshette. As the actress rolled over, from sleep to drowsy wakefulness, it was as if TV was revealed as one enormous, busy bed in which we were all of us half asleep. Just as the spaghetti episode on *Panorama* signaled a "Don't take us too seriously" caution, so the magical fusion of *The Bob Newhart Show* and *Newhart* indicated that television was a ramshackle empire in which the same rules of story applied across the board and led to delightful coincidences and aberrant insights. It is all one show.

IIIIIIIIIIIIIIIIIIIIIIIIIIII

ASK TELEVISION WHAT ITS DUTY IS, and with lordly measures of earnestness and eye-rolling, the BBC and the FCC and all the other coagulate lumps in alphabet soup will say: to inform, to educate, to sustain the marketplace through advertising, and to give the people "what they want." We pay lip service to this credo and steadily change the channel until we hear an invitation with laughter as its music. If you look back at the origins of television, you can claim that news and commercials were always there—and to one degree or another we have been patient with those worthy and worthless genres. But comedy was there, too, from Milton Berle, *I Love Lucy*, and the shows named after Red Skelton, Jack Benny, Red Buttons, and Jackie Gleason, all the way to Jon Stewart, Ricky Gervais, Larry David, and Neil Patrick Harris. It's not that those comics are all alike (though many old jokes keep getting reprocessed). Their attitude to themselves and their role has altered dramatically. At the same time, their ratings have plummeted. It is harder now than at any time in the history of television to assume that all of America can laugh at the same thing.

IT IS HARDER NOW TO ASSUME THAT ALL OF AMERICA CAN LAUGH AT THE SAME THING.

I doubt that Ricky and Lucy had any design upon America except to be a hit, to be loved, and to make a fortune. The degree of their success is more staggering than ever. *Lucy,* the show, never got less than a 50 share, and sometimes it was up to 70. Intentions didn't matter: *I Love Lucy* was sailing under false and optimistic pretenses. It could have been called *I Go in Terror of Lucy* or *I Can't Stand Her*. Those alternative titles verge on the unkind, but they do place that famous marriage in the company of Strindberg, *Who's Afraid of Virginia Woolf?*…or *Fawlty Towers*, in that the marriage is a disaster kept in place by vows of attachment and residual rights. But if you'd told Desi or Lucy, or CBS, or yourselves, that here was a grotesque portrait of marriage, enough to raise thoughts of murder, you would have been dismissed as tasteless, subversive, and out of your mind. There has never been a marital show so filled with wreckage and misunderstanding yet so pledged to being together as the finale music plays.

Jon Stewart came from a different world. He was born Jonathan Stuart Leibowitz in New York in 1962, the son of two academics. He graduated in psychology from William & Mary and then held an array of jobs fit to spice a résumé before he entered the comedy club circuit. He had a hit appearance on *Late Night with David Letterman* and was personally promoted by Letterman. Thus in 1999 he took over the host job at *The Daily Show* on Comedy Central. That channel had been formed in 1989 as an offshoot of Time Warner and HBO, and when *The Daily Show* started it was hosted by Craig Kilborn with an eye to general matters in the culture. But Stewart took it in the direction of politics, thus putting to the test the channel's claim that it was "a fake news show."

Time and again, Stewart's satirical intelligence led him and us toward the question: Was this a news show tricked up to be funny, or was the news itself so fake, so spun, and so unreliable that the chance of any accurate commentary had passed out of sight?

Stewart himself seemed torn. He talked about entertainment and said he wanted to hear laughter as he ran *The Daily Show* for sixteen years, raising such disciples as Stephen Colbert. One could hear the smart classes talking about Stewart: He had saved their sanity, some said. He was the sharpest voice standing up for liberal or rational awareness; he was a beacon in the wasteland. In doing fake news, he invariably highlighted liberal values. *The Daily Show* played four nights a week in a late time slot; it used street language, lampoon sketches, and it became increasingly antagonistic toward the spirit and personnel of Fox News. But as the years went by, it was observed that Stewart and Fox News sometimes picked up only a little over a million

JON STEWART CAME FROM A DIFFERENT WORLD.

viewers a night each, and were engaged in an enclosed shouting match with each other. No one was being persuaded, opened up, or educated. Antagonism made Stewart and Bill O'Reilly one more odd couple, though seldom on the same screen. The rant of pleasing your own small church held sway. Moreover, Stewart acquired a prestige that was out of proportion with his numbers. His stance was new: that of a scathing, cool intelligence, surveying and mocking the news and all the newsmakers. But was he commenting on an actual world, or on TV's cute globe version of it? Was he beginning to say, this is absurd, what we do and say—when we hardly matter? His audience was young, educated, and liberal, and it surely rose to the enthusiasm for Barack Obama as a new model leader. But, if Stewart grew weary, the raw mess of unreason came back in the form of Donald Trump, a figure who threatened to make satire, objection, or critical thinking seem petty. Did Stewart sense that trending? Was that why he felt he had to step down in 2015, even if it was hard to believe his smart, quick-witted, and attractive persona could be matched by anyone else?

What could Stewart do next? How could *The Daily Show* find rebirth? Stewart was only fifty-two in 2015. He had just directed a film, *Rosewater*, about the imprisoned journalist Maziar Bahari. That picture was unexpectedly conventional and earnest, with Stewart urging the importance of collaboration and having clear goals. (It sounded like Charlie Rose.) The enterprise lacked his dangerous flair or his intimacy with derangement. It even encouraged the hope sometimes expressed by his fans that he might run for president one day. How cruel fans can be once earnestness smothers spontaneity.

I suspect Stewart would be mortified in government, as his rare intelligence was reduced to cliché and safe thoughts. As for the *Show*, it announced that one of its own contributors, the black South African comedian Trevor Noah, would take over from Stewart. This was regarded as a brave, intriguing choice, but within days the Internet was rife with details of earlier Noah jokes that might be judged politically incorrect or hostile to women and Jews. Those remarks were from a while ago, from the more innocent age when Stewart had followed Craig Kilborn into the host's chair. Many educators agree that children's knowledge of the past is drying up like water in California, but we are still thirsty for a cup of damning scandal.

I suspect Stewart needs to do something utterly novel and risky, something that might alter our sense of whatever medium he chooses. Here's the point: As time passes, it's easy to distinguish comedy shows on television that were safe from those that were perilous. I probably like Bob Newhart as much as the next viewer, and I treasure that closing scene from *Newhart*. But we knew we were safe with him from the outset, and he never let us down. We felt we deserved that, and guessed that he deserved us and our caution. An enormous amount of good comedy has functioned like that. *The Mary Tyler Moore Show* was hailed as a pioneering breakthrough for career women, but it ruffled very few conservative feathers and never risked exploring the territory of a woman who breaks up her own family because of her work or her longing—the way men do.

Disruption has seldom been the impetus in long-running comedy shows. That's why *All in the Family* remains so remarkable. The feeling dawned that that show was not really content with the Bunkers. The situation in its comedy was poised to be challenged, not just by the younger people, or even Archie's complacent bigotry, but by the sight and smothered sound of Edith, a simple soul who was ready to disagree.

If early television was ingratiating—please the sponsor, please the audience, give no offense or cause for confusion—Ernie Kovacs was the first insurrectionary. He had been born in New Jersey in 1919, and he had attended the American Academy of Dramatic Arts. Serious illness kept him out of the war, and a salesman's job led him into radio, where he did anything he could find. He was good-looking in a slightly fake way, and he rarely let a twinge of sincerity dispute that air of a confidence trickster who had found a stooge. But he loved television and its opportunities for surreal comedy. He never had a hit show, or even a lasting format. *The Ernie Kovacs Show* played in the early fifties at CBS, and then later at NBC. His best work is a series of specials in the early sixties. He was like an absent-minded surgeon, looking at television humor and tempted by the thought of operating. He seldom allowed that comforting fallacy—that we were looking in on an imagined reality. Instead, he urged us to realize that looking and ways of seeing *were* his show. He talked to the camera, the crew, and the audience; he liked to reveal the apparatus of television being made; and he had a craze for special visual effects.

The world called Kovacs zany or odd. But the critic William Henry III recognized that he was something new, a "video artist." With his director Joe Behar, he took great pains experimenting with the deceptive capacity of the television image at a time when most shows were saying, "Please trust us." In one show, with blackout effects, he contrived to look inside the head of one of his assistants (it was the actress Barbara Loden). He played games with composition and balance; he made a famous *Silent Show* (1957); he did funny voices and foolish characters (like the rest of TV), but he was always devoted to the possibility that the medium was the message: He was Marshall McLuhan as embodied by Groucho Marx. More than anyone broadcasting in America, he guessed that television was so crammed with surreal possibilities and so enormous in its cultural influence that regular shows were very limited compared with the ongoing experiment of how it was done. A brave medium would have given him the News and told him to make a mad news program—but that was thirty years away, and by then that wonderful dream, a mass audience, had lapsed.

Kovacs was killed in a car crash in Los Angeles in 1962. He was forty-two. It was soon said that he was ahead of his time (always the dismissive verdict of a conservative culture), and now I suppose he is dated in so many ways and forgotten by "everyone."

Ernie Kovacs had an endearing affect—he was not as threatening as his work. But Ricky Gervais, it seems to me, is a complacently nasty piece of work, and a gem with sharp edges. He is a great deal more successful than Kovacs ever was, in part because there is a shrewd commercial aim in Gervais's wicked eye. But he still feels like an outsider. One only needs to suggest, "Well, perhaps he'll host the Oscars one day," to appreciate the barbarian force he represents to the besieged mentality of the Academy of Motion Picture Arts and Sciences, the archaic stronghold of what used to be Hollywood.

Gervais has done many things, from being part of a band and doing stand-up comedy to a TV show, *Meet Ricky Gervais*, for Channel 4 in 2000. He was not prepossessing, but he took that challenge in his portly stride. With Stephen Merchant, he wrote and directed the British show *The Office*, in which he played the oily devious boss in a show that enjoyed furtive neurotic behavior in the workplace. The show did poorly at first, but word of mouth savored its tart edge. Gervais and Merchant took *The Office* to America, where it ran nine seasons, most of the time with Steve Carell in the lead part. In 2006, it won the Emmy for outstanding comedy series. Gervais has done much more, as an author of books, in movies, as a stand-up comic, and with his series *Derek* (2012–14). (He is reckoned to be worth $90 million currently.)

ERNIE KOVACS WAS THE FIRST INSURRECTIONARY.

But it is as a stand-up that Gervais has left the deepest imprint. He remains dirty-minded in a very English way that sometimes recalls

Benny Hill (with just a dash of Christopher Hitchens). He comes on in a T-shirt that exults in his potbelly. He is drinking as a rule, and sweating. He is hostile to any idea of sophistication, yet verbally his humor is daring, pointed, aggressive, filthy, and taunting the idea that he might be gay for an audience he believes will be alarmed by that prospect. Benny Hill was always reckoned too local and risqué to succeed in America except on a restricted basis, whereas Gervais resists any prospect of Americanizing himself but feels very comfortable in the United States. Being American on TV is not what it was—as witness the way British actors and other visitors of one color or another are taking "American" roles. Gervais works on an assumption—not uncommon in Europe—that America has ruined the world, but he despises everyone and everything, including himself. The fact that he gets on in America now (when the Smothers Brothers were shut out at CBS in 1968–69) is a sign that official television realizes it is out of control. Playing at any time, on a box that can reach so many channels and streams, how can "standards and practices" mean anything useful?

Gervais can remind us of offense. For three years, 2010–12, he was invited to host the television show that presented the Golden Globes (an invention of the Hollywood Foreign Press Association). Gervais knew well enough the weary derision with which show business regarded the HFPA. It had always been an attempt at self-promotion, a free dinner (with gift bags) and an unnecessary show. It nearly foundered several times in its long history, but by the time Gervais was invited, the Golden Globes were climbing in the TV ratings, in part because they played early in the awards season and had a banqueting format that was friendly to a camera looking for rash moments and smashed celebrities. The show remained superfluous, and only a few steps ahead of the Academy Awards in that respect. Gervais guessed that at home, or in the audience itself, people were making unkind wisecracks about the fake splendor. So he acted on that, like a Kovacs who knew no one would recall or care who got the Globes, while everyone was waiting for scandal, or scandal-like incidents.

GERVAIS RESISTS ANY PROSPECT OF AMERICANIZING HIMSELF.

It was at the 2011 show (the sixty-eighth!) that Gervais let rip. He looked respectful in a black suit and a gray tie, but the filth was unfiltered:

> It's going to be a night of partying and heavy drinking—or, as Charlie Sheen calls it, breakfast. Wow, so let's get this straight: What he [Sheen] did was, he picked up a porn star, paid her to have dinner with him, introduced her to his ex-wife—as you do—went to a hotel, got drunk, got naked, trashed the place while she was locked in a cupboard, and that was a Monday. What did he do New Year's Eve?

The audience in the ballroom at the Beverly Hills Hilton seemed taken aback; their laughter was tentative. Charlie Sheen was an easy target—he had no constituency—but the description was like lurid acid. Then Gervais took on Angelina Jolie and Johnny Depp (with both of them in the room), on account of their wretched film *The Tourist*, which the HFPA had nominated and which had non-dimensional characters. "I feel bad about that joke," said Gervais. "I tell you what, I'm jumping on the bandwagon, because I haven't even seen *The Tourist*. Who has?" There were gasps and some boos—this was not Hollywood nice. There were remarks about Scientologist stars who acted heterosexual. Then later there was reference to the president of the HFPA, with Gervais adding how, to get him onstage, "I just had to help him off the toilet and pop his teeth in."

There was controversy as to whether a thing called "good taste" had been undermined. But wouldn't it have to exist for that to have happened? Evidently many members of the Hollywood Establishment felt that Gervais had gone too far, should have been stopped, and would not be invited again. But the modest world of those interested was abuzz; the show got good ratings and no end of talk. No one sued or challenged Gervais to a duel. He *was* invited back the following year, though he has never quite lost the glow of some infection because of it. But why would he want to lose that toxic halo? For what he had done in a matter of moments was to say that all awards shows were a sham and a shambles, dead meat waiting for vultures. He has never been invited to host the Oscars. In recent years that job has gone to such as Ellen DeGeneres and Neil Patrick Harris, and they have done their brave, team-spirited best before tottering away from the dreadful show saying that it was impossible. In truth, the community that once bound together the Oscars and the people is forever shattered and beyond repair. The Academy Awards show is suffering a long slow death. All Gervais had done was say, "Look. Here is the knife. Do it. Put yourself out of our misery." There was no need to think that Gervais was a pleasant man (not lovable like Billy Crystal), but he had done something that television comedy cries out for—he had performed an autopsy while we still had a technical claim on life.

Even in the United States, where there was a tacit understanding between the positive force of entertainment and the advertising that funded the medium, there had been comics who "trashed" their own show. That could be said of Oscar Levant, Groucho Marx, and the Smothers Brothers. But punishment waited on Levant and the Smotherses; and Groucho had hived himself off in the domain of a grotesque professional eccentric—instead of the intelligent, morose doomsayer that he wanted to be. More or less, those people did stand-up or sit-down routines: They came on in a formalized set and context and they dropped jokes on the public—sometimes harsh, unsettling, and surreal—but the show and the box contained them. They did not have the self-destructive but creatively constructive attitude to control their show and make the medium its subject.

THERE WAS A CONTROVERSY AS TO WHETHER A THING CALLED "GOOD TASTE" HAD BEEN UNDERMINED.

That ability was what made *Laugh-In* so dynamic and inspiring. Yet it's still hard to say how *Rowan & Martin's Laugh-In* came into being. It was created by George Schlatter and Ed Friendly, neither of whom did other work that resembled *Laugh-In*. Friendly would go on to produce *Little House on the Prairie* (1974–83), while Schlatter, raised as a club manager in Los Angeles and Las Vegas, would later do AFI tributes to great stars as well as celebrity showcases for Frank Sinatra, Judy Garland, and several others. Nor was the show characterized by its nominal hosts, Dan Rowan and Dick Martin, who looked like tired, middlebrow comics with no particular edge or ambition. But Martin was a serviceable comedy director—he actually directed that last episode of *Newhart*—and Schlatter's wife, Jolene Brand, had been a regular performer on *The Ernie Kovacs Show*.

So what explained the sustained riot of the show, its host of new personalities, and its instantaneous success with audiences? *Laugh-In* started on January 22, 1968 (a day after the six-month Battle of Khe Sanh began in Vietnam). In time, people would say that the show was the child of the old movie *Hellzapoppin'* (1941), Ernie Kovacs, and even the British show *That Was the Week That Was*. Those are strained arguments for a show that was immediately subversive, sexy, too rapid to keep track of, and profoundly electronic. It had no recognizable social situation other than a bare set invaded by people new to television. *Laugh-In* was energetic and good-natured, up to a point, but it also riffed on disrespect,

LAUGH-IN WAS ALMOST THE FIRST SHOUT OF THE SIXTIES ON NETWORK TELEVISION.

controlled outrage, and the freedom to do whatever anyone might think of. Many skits were very brief, followed by a blackout. As the show extended, so it seemed that the players enjoyed one another's company more and more, and catchphrases grew and became richer. For the audience, there was an illusion of being at a party; they shouted back at the screen to signal plain love for a lot of the performers.

The comedy shows that ruled in the years before *Laugh-In* (*The Andy Griffith Show*, *Bewitched*, and the shows still attached to veteran comics) were staid throwbacks to the fifties, employing routine structures and unthreatening material. But *Laugh-In* was almost the first shout of the sixties on network television: It was abuzz with psychedelia, interruption, smiling insolence, and an ease with irreverence, surrealism, and innuendo that would have been hard to pull off just a few years earlier. It was aimed at a young audience, but it held on to smart, hip older people and it had something for everyone, so much and so fast that if one joke floundered, you had little time to wait for a better one.

The people were living caricatures, without depth, instantly recognizable and endearing: There was Ruth Buzzi as a wizened old lady in a hairnet; Jo Anne Worley as a good-time girl; Alan Sues as an asinine sports announcer (a breed normally treated with solid male reverence); Arte Johnson as a German soldier who found things "very interesting"; the unique comic flair of Lily Tomlin, especially as a kill-joy telephonist, Ernestine, looking to reduce the call load; a torrent of guest stars; and Goldie Hawn.

I don't think you could put that Goldie on television today. She would be pounced on as a sexist stereotype, a remorseless objectification of one more "dumb blonde." In which case, repeat the mantra—you had to be there at the time—and admit that none of us can live anywhere but in our own time. Ms. Hawn (who was twenty-two when *Laugh-In* started) was so slim, and the body painting on her bikini-clad body seemed like growing vines. She did a lot of dancing or shimmying standing still; she messed up her lines, and then dissolved into merry laughter. She flattered the guys and made fun of herself for them. To think of it now is to feel shame as well as changing times. But a lot of people joined me in adoring her and waiting for her next sketch. Not forgetting some of her performances (like *The Sugarland Express* for Steven Spielberg), I think *Laugh-In* was the giddiest and most memorable thing she would ever do.

Immediately, for the 1967–68 season, the show jumped into the top 20. For the next two years it was the number 1 show in America. Some seasons it got 30 million viewers an episode, and it was steadily in the twenties. It ran six seasons and 140 episodes, and was one of the more sensational arrivals in television history. In 1968, in a presidential campaign season, Richard Nixon was a guest, uttering one of the show's regular lines, "Sock it to me." I doubt too many people believed Nixon had become cool, but maybe the man himself felt more hip. His opponent, Hubert Humphrey, declined to go on the show, and later on Nixon would say that he felt his appearance had clinched his victory. All that revealed was that TV presidents would say anything, so long as they didn't have to believe it. But by the time of the next election, *Laugh-In* was dropping like a stone in the ratings. From

A LOT OF FIFTIES-TYPE COMEDY WAS SWEPT ASIDE BY *LAUGH-IN.*

the outset it had been a shock attack. Once familiarity set in, it was over. But so many careers had been launched, and the darker, sardonic mood of the seventies owed something to the nerve and flaunting cynicism of the show. "You bet your bippy!"—another of its lines—became as dated as the Hula-Hoop or bell-bottom pants.

A lot of fifties-type comedy was swept aside by *Laugh-In.* Cynicism was rare, of course, but the ironic voice and a more grown-up level of experience was there in Carol Burnett, Bob Newhart, Bea Arthur (in *Maude*), as well as *All in the Family.* And don't forget *The Sonny and Cher Comedy Hour* (1971–74). I don't want to drag that folly down by suggesting it was a great show, but it had a central image that spoke to a new, sour estimate of married life. Sonny Bono and Cher had been working in music and nightclubs before CBS put them on television. In fact, at the outset, they were a happy couple, but put them side by side, with Cher seeming to tower over Sonny, and a different chemistry emerged. He was busy, eager, and flabbergasted that he had won this beauty, and she was lugubrious, elegant-trashy (she never could make up her mind), with an attitude that said, "How did I get tied to this jerk?" The couple were funnier than their lines, and it was a mixed marriage that was right for the seventies but often as smart as screwball comedies from the late thirties.

They were a treat of an odd couple in an era that liked that formula (*The Odd Couple*, with Tony Randall and Jack Klugman in a state of friction, ran from 1970 to 1975). After they split, Sonny went into what he called politics. Cher started to act: She was impressive in

Silkwood (1983) and won an Oscar in *Moonstruck* (1987), where she is one of the most beautiful women ever on-screen, while largely ignoring the claim that her character is a humble Brooklyn widow instead of a fabulous nightclub performer resting up. But she stopped acting and eventually turned herself over to her true métier—clothes, not that she always seemed "clothed."

I have to skip over many entertaining comedies (though revisiting *Mork & Mindy*, *Happy Days*, or *Laverne & Shirley* is a tougher assignment than you might expect). In passing, in a hurry, I want to note *The Larry Sanders Show*, which ran six seasons on HBO (1992–98). It was created by Garry Shandling and Dennis Klein. In his lethargic way, Shandling played a talk-show host on TV. He talked to the camera and the audience. He liked famous guest stars. And the show took daring steps in saying putting on a show (with all its compromises, deceit, and vanity) was possibly more entertaining than anything within the set situation of a talk show. Shandling made it clear that comedy might be a mind game, elitist and over our heads. But what was that inviting space up there for, if not for us to grow taller in mind and spirit?

A mixture of existential aspiration and contented emptiness was what distinguished *Seinfeld* (1989–98), an immense hit for NBC and a show that received some of the highest critical accolades. It was the creation of Jerry Seinfeld (a stand-up comic) and Larry David, more of a writer but also a club comedian. The two did a lot of the writing, and David would become an executive producer—with all that work, he asked, how could he possibly act, too? I suspect he would have managed, but that might have stopped the show in its tracks.

The rather vague principle of the show was to follow a comedian in his whole life, with emphasis on how things that happened to him worked their way into his material. From the outset, Jerry had an ex-girlfriend, Elaine (Julia Louis-Dreyfus), as well as two unlikely friends in George Costanza (Jason Alexander) and Kramer (Michael Richards). All four were engaging and superficially interesting, but the show was resolutely unconcerned about their happiness or well-being, the dead-end destinies of so many television characters. To match the absence of ingratiating emotionalism, the show had an unusual musical score (by Jonathan Wolff), a synthesized bass line that sounded like a broken spring, kept the proceedings at an intriguing distance, and never attempted to encourage "identification" or likeability. But after four seasons it was the number 1 show, with an audience of just over 30 million. It won the Emmy for outstanding comedy series in 1993.

Famously, it became known as a show about nothing, though Seinfeld and David had never intended that. But it was beyond question that *Seinfeld* liked scenes and conversations that went nowhere, incidents that were so mundane they did not seem like television, and a high level of wit in the often wandering talk. *Seinfeld* had an unsettling core attitude: that nothing really happened in life—that it might be like watching television. As the audience came to it, so did prizes and tributes. *TV Guide* (itself waning fast) would call it the greatest TV show ever.

Behind the scenes it was another odd-couple show in that Jerry was nice-looking, engaging, friendly, and nonthreatening, while Larry David was none of those things. But they had a lot in common: They were both Jewish, from Brooklyn, though Seinfeld was raised on the south shore of Long Island, and David was only seven years older than Seinfeld. But they saw the world differently, as well as their own place in it. Jerry was *Seinfeld*: He wrote it and starred in every episode—he has an estimated net worth now of $800 million. But once *Seinfeld* ended, Jerry lost some hair and gained some weight. He does things still, though he sometimes seems like a bobblehead version of himself. He has only created one other show, a game show, that came and vanished.

Whereas, David shifted to the West Coast and created *Curb Your Enthusiasm* for HBO. It is said that the show is one you have to develop a taste for—a lot of people don't like it. One reason for that is David's own naggy wish to come off awkward, unpleasant, tactless, selfish, and blind to all his own faults. But still, in *Curb Your Enthusiasm* (which might be a warning to audiences) he plays a semi-fictional version of himself, and we are left to decide whether he is just a clever creator or a rather Asperger's-like person. *Curb Your Enthusiasm* has a devoted following, but on cable that is still far smaller than the *Seinfeld* numbers. Comedy of embarrassment does less well than amused fellowship. David is said to have a net worth half that of Seinfeld, and I suspect he keeps score. David has as confused an attitude to the public as Charlie Chaplin had. But like Charlie he has found release and self-love in performing. He is maybe the most fascinating awful person on television—and a welcome sign that the medium doesn't have to be monopolized by likeability. At times, he seems a self-haunted misanthrope such as Dickens might have written.

||||||||||||||||||||||||||||

BUT THAT IS NOT the whole story. Larry David does have a predecessor—his name was Basil Fawlty, as played by John Cleese. And that takes us into the rich fields of comic insurrection coming out of Britain. We must begin with a show that might have been called *A Horse, a Spoon and a Basin* or *Owl Stretching Time*. Those were possible titles put forward by a group of young men who wandered around the BBC Television Centre, looking for an opportunity. They were Terry Jones and Michael Palin (from Oxford University), and Graham Chapman, Eric Idle, and John Cleese (who had been at Cambridge). There was a sixth man, an American, Terry Gilliam, who would contribute unprecedented and often toxic and violent animated sequences to a flagrantly elitist show that was eventually called *Monty Python's Flying Circus* and had 45 casual yet momentous episodes from 1969 to 1974.

It is still beyond belief that this happened, and that it later took America by storm, too. It was commissioned by the inspiring but probably unwitting David Attenborough. The team that made the show all joined in the creation and the performance, but they had the assertive mood of the French surrealists of the 1920s, cut with the superiority of an Oxbridge common room for those reading

PYTHON WAS SELF-CONSCIOUSLY MAD, BUT IT FOUND AN AUDIENCE IMMEDIATELY.

Wittgenstein and Kafka. The show was aggressively male (and adolescent), and Carol Cleveland, a voluptuous young actress, was usually the one woman allowed (though she was given little to say). On the other hand, some of the boys (Terry Jones in particular) developed a line of raving, grotesque women closer to Punch's Judy than to some of the real women in Britain of that era (Mary Quant, Jean Shrimpton, Julie Christie, Shirley Williams, Barbara Castle, Dusty Springfield, Iris Murdoch, and Margaret Thatcher, who was already Secretary for Education by 1970).

The show had what might have been called sketches—the Cheese Shop Without Cheese, the Ministry of Funny Walks, and the Dead Parrot routine were celebrated examples, learned by heart and reenacted by some viewers. The show had no budget that one could see, and a lot of amateur acting. It also had a habit of spilling out into the evening. In those days, the BBC had a prim and pious transition shot (of a globe revolving), after which, with suitable pause, a new program would commence. The globe had been a sign of control and overview, but sometimes *Python* ran the globe and then did another sketch. This had the liberating effect of letting some antique British shows later on in the evening seem included in Python's derision.

Many wise men and women would have predicted disaster for the show. But the established and trusted role of wisdom was drawing to a close. It was an underlying suggestion in *Laugh-In* that the institu-

tional forces in television had abandoned ship, leaving an asylum play-
ground for the rogue inmates. *Python* was self-consciously mad (and
not really politically aligned), but it found an audience immediately. It
was natural to suppose that the viewers were from the Oxbridge chat-
tering classes and the few people who had a grasp of surrealist history.
But the show played on BBC1 (the mainstream channel) and it was
evident that—just like university education—the humor was reaching
well beyond the upper intellectual levels.

There would be movies and full careers to follow—and this very
private vein of comedy went to America, where it succeeded again and
was informing people like Jerry Seinfeld and Larry David. In the first
instance, the BBC's attitude had been casual and even whimsical. No
one had reckoned on a hit; many had anticipated showers of complaint. But the tradition of straight-faced nonsense was richer in Britain than complainers knew. It was there in Laurence Sterne and Lewis

Carroll, in Wodehouse and Waugh, in cricket, seaside holidays, and the way the voice of comedian Kenneth Williams could go through three or four characters in a sentence, desperate not to be himself. The role of "Monty" in the title was a dig at Field Marshal Montgomery, a complacent hero from the Second World War (he had beaten Rommel in the North African desert) and an admired idiot. In the modern history of the giving up on pomp and circumstance in Britain, and the creeping onset of respectable madness, *Monty Python* is one of the most influential of TV programs. It had many messages, all jumbled together, but one was, "Don't trust it if it's on television."

There were only two series and twelve episodes of *Fawlty Towers*, playing in 1975 and 1979. It was prompted by a visit made by John Cleese and his then wife, Connie Booth, to a country hotel owned by the rudest man Cleese had ever encountered. He and Booth invented a show based on that man, to be set in a hotel in Torquay, in Devon. The BBC found the scripts unfunny, and advised that the action get outside the hotel as much as possible. But Cleese and Booth knew that the hotel was the necessary prison for those who ran it. And they may have asked why anyone assumed the show was a comedy just because Cleese was in it.

BASIL FAWLTY IS A DESPERATE MAN, SO ANXIOUS HE COULD TURN FASCIST.

So the BBC trusted Cleese and built a complicated set in which the tight spaces, the kinks in staircases, and the chance of tripping illustrated Basil's tragic awareness that his pride and joy, Fawlty Towers, was hell. His disapproving but stately wife Sybil was played by the magnificent Prunella Scales (in 1988 she would play the reigning queen on stage in *A Question of Attribution*, written by Alan Bennett). Connie Booth was the dogged chambermaid Polly, and Andrew Sachs was the constantly frustrated, linguistically impaired, and demented Spanish waiter, Manuel.

The show was painfully funny: not because the laughing hurt physically but because the jokes grew out of humiliation. The British Film Institute would vote it the best-ever British television show. But it was also a nightmare in which the authoritarian yet neurotic Basil became almost Hitlerian in all the plots and bad breaks made to prevent him from running an orderly establishment. Marriage was invariably painful at the hotel—and Cleese and Booth were divorced between the two series.

Basil Fawlty is a desperate man, so anxious he could turn fascist, an effect heightened by Cleese's own rampant and angry uneasiness. He longs for control and dreads disorder. In the episode "The Kipper and the Corpse," Basil has to deliver breakfast in bed to a guest, Mr. Leeman. He is punctual, but obsessed, and so he does not notice that Leeman, though sitting up in bed, is dead:

> BASIL: Breakfast! (*He puts the tray down.*) Here we are. (*He looks at the newspaper that accompanies breakfast.*) Another car strike. Marvellous, isn't it. Taxpayers pay 'em millions each year, they get the money, go on strike. It's called Socialism. I mean if they don't like making cars, why don't they get themselves another bloody job designing cathedrals or composing viola concertos? The British Leyland Concerto in four movements, all of 'em slow, with a four-hour tea break in between. I'll tell you why, 'cos they're not interested in anything except lounging about on conveyor belts stuffing themselves with my money. (*Leeman never responds, so Basil leaves the room.*) Unbelievable. Unbe-lievable. Not a single bloody word. You get up at five thirty so they can lounge around in bed till midday and do you get so much as a word of thanks?

Only the dead listen to Basil's rant. Sybil cuts him off short. The whole *Fawlty Towers* is six hours, so it's like a long play or movie—it reminds me of a darker version of Alan Ayckbourn's trilogy of plays, *The Norman Conquests*, which opened in 1973. Not that *Fawlty Towers* ever reached its begged-for conclusion, an act of murder (you can choose your own participants). Still, it benefits from its limited arc and the mercy that it did not have to go on and on repeating itself just because that was the alleged nature of television.

But there was a show that surely influenced the two John Cleese programs. Alas, it hardly survives because the BBC wiped most of the tapes of *Not Only…But Also*. Peter Cook and Dudley Moore met in the making of *Beyond the Fringe*, a stage revue, satirical and mocking, that began at the Edinburgh Festival in 1960 and then moved on to London and Broadway. The other members of the university quartet were Jonathan Miller and Alan Bennett. Theirs is one of the most unexpected and exciting gatherings of talent in English show business, and all four of the players would make idiosyncratic contributions to television.

Not Only began as a showcase for Dudley Moore, a facile pianist across a range from jazz to classical. But he was nervous of all that exposure on television, so he asked if Peter Cook could join him. I know that details of origins can seem dull and formal, but I have to share this information: Cook was born in Torquay in 1937, the son of a civil servant who expected Peter to become a diplomat. Peter Cook was never anyone's obedient envoy. He went to Cambridge and started writing sketches for the Footlights Club. He was tall and handsome, and he cultivated a superior manner that suggested he could dominate anyone. Dudley Moore was five feet three, and born with a club foot.

PETER COOK WAS NEVER ANYONE'S OBEDIENT ENVOY.

He was raised in Dagenham, in east London, a working-class suburb known for making cars. His father was a railway electrician. But Dudley's unusual musical talent won him a scholarship to Oxford. And so the two met on *Beyond the Fringe*, that corollary of the Beatles.

Not Only was a bit of a ragbag. Moore played the piano, often with a guest singer. Cook did his monologues in the persona of E. L. Wisty, a raincoat-wearing neo-derelict on a park bench, monotonously voicing the grievances of his drab life. The core of the show was Dud and Pete together, in raincoats and flat caps, lugubrious, ill-educated, but helpless chums as much as Vladimir and Estragon in Samuel Beckett's *Waiting for Godot*. They would start to talk about inconsequential but vaguely sinister things—like the way in an art gallery the eyes in some portraits seemed to follow you around the room. Cook wrote the bases of these "Dagenham dialogues," and it was Cook who would sometimes improvise in a spirit of languid mischief. He had a goal, to make Dud crack up and start to giggle. That sounds schoolboyish and unprofessional (lasting strains in British comedy), but their friendship turned the challenge into something lyrical and affectionate.

They were their characters, "Dud" and "Pete," but those stooges were watched and overheard by Mr. Cook and Mr. Moore. The duality was essential yet mysterious, and it was a forerunner of Seinfeld and David (and Louis C.K.) playing themselves. These routines were elegant, touching, fond, and hilarious; they often diced with fun and fatality. The audience didn't need to laugh—and that can be the acme of our highest comedy. The chat could sound very local, until you felt its poetry, with desolate pals muttering as the wasteland and the night drew in. Every great city deserves an underground that sings and sighs with noir romance:

> DUD: A lady is peppered from head to foot with erogenous
> zones.
> PETE: Have you seen this diagram?
> DUD: I daren't look.
> PETE: It's like a map of the Underground.
> DUD: I mean, a man is very hard put to know where to
> start his sexual voyage.
> PETE: Well, not the Northern Line. You end up in
> Crouch End.

In fact, you don't. There *is* a Crouch End in north London, a no-man's-land between other unlikely spots, but it's not on the Tube. In 1993, no less than Stephen King wrote a story called "Crouch End"; it was published in his book *Nightmares & Dreamscapes*, and it saw Crouch End as a place, or a zone, not just where surface activities disappeared below ground, but where reality nudged against fantasy in the darkness. The London Underground is littered with real stations with forlorn innuendo names—like Mornington Crescent (in the 1990s, that was closed; nothing stopped there anymore, except in your imagination; trains hurried through the empty place as if spirits lurked there). There are also Limehouse, Cockfosters, Snaresbrook, Burnt Oak, Tooting Bec—I could go on. (I'm not going to say this out loud, but there is even a station called Elephant & Castle.)

There is something else to say about television over the decades: It has been a place where generally young people gathered in an effort to make us laugh, when bemused laughter was maybe as sane a response to the wide world as we could muster. The embodiment of that disenchanted collegial gaiety was *Saturday Night Live*, in which the stress on "now," year after year, newcomer after newcomer, has often diverted us from the awareness that everything is passing by in a blur of inconsequence and absurdity. The mood of a frat party has lasted over four decades.

Saturday Night, as it was then, began in 1975 at NBC, and it is still there as *Saturday Night Live*. The show was created by Lorne Michaels and Dick Ebersol. The format has hardly varied: Lively comics would gather to have fun—if a public showed up in response so much the better. There would be a studio audience to stand in for us, not just live but maybe the best studio audience TV has ever had. There is still a surge of excitement at NBC when the announcer—for thirty-nine seasons it was Don Pardo—roars out renewal and some putatively timely guest host strides forward to challenge us and the camera.

As Lorne Michaels said at the outset:

> So much of what *Saturday Night Live* wanted to be, or I wanted it to be when it began, was cool. Which was something television wasn't, except in a retro way. Not that there weren't cool TV shows, but this was taking the sensibilities that were in music, stage, and the movies and bringing them to television.

Laugh-In seems like a precursor of *SNL*, but that great show was canned, it was pledged to maintain showbiz shtick, and it was LA. As soon as *SNL* appeared, the novelty and exuberance of *Laugh-In* felt fabricated and Hollywoodesque, when the rumor of Hollywood's death was gaining ground. 1975 was an apt moment for launching: The departure of Nixon and the end of Vietnam could not hide the devastation that had overtaken the American Dream. And the place, New York, was tottering: Seemingly in terminal debt, it was rife with drugs, criminal violence, homelessness and the deadpan attitude of

Warholian celebrity. It was a frightening backdrop, but it was the place for staying cool in the face of chaos and disbelief. And really there is no excuse for New York unless it's frightening. Who really thinks *Law and Order* will take care of us?

Lorne Michaels was Canadian, born in 1944, a bit of a writer, something of an actor but, as it turned out, a beguiling coach who could keep so many jittery egos and talents in line, and let bench-players feel they were stars. No one on the show has ever doubted the authority Michaels had. He launched the show. He left it in the early eighties, but only to prove that he was essential and bored elsewhere, so that he had to come back. He had exceptional judgment over talent and material; he could bring a turbulent setup into being a show at 11:30, Eastern time; he managed to pay people very little; and he has kept it going for decades (when seventy-two is no longer cool). It's not just that he is a creative figure himself, but he is a producer, one of the best show business has ever offered. As Candice Bergen put it—and she was there at first, long before *Murphy Brown* —"I remember the

terror. You know, the total exhilaration of it. I just didn't know you could have that much fun after thirty. It was like the inmates taking over the asylum. Totally."

The "asylum" could be explained away as studio space at NBC, but in truth, and without stressing, that attitude was a metaphor for the world at large and the mocking thought that expanding entropy could be controlled by a medium like television. More to the point, we could begin to see that TV was a replacement for a world that was passing beyond order and experience long before "virtualness" appeared.

The show had grievous shortcomings: It was entirely juvenile—as in a college fraternity (think *Animal House*—1978, too), the notion of adult perspectives, of melancholy, of family torment such as *Fawlty Towers* recounted, of the Beckett-like surrealism in Dud and Pete—those things were smothered by sheer American energy and the turmoil of written skit material, screwing up, improvising and just letting laughter wrap it all together. It was based on wicked impersonation, instant take-off, insolence, and the certainty that there was no dignity or purpose in public life. It would go from Sinead O'Connor cutting up a picture of a pope to Tina Fey ripping off Sarah Palin. Without any plan, it promoted the insight that anyone running for anything (including O. J. Simpson) was a bad actor in crude disguise.

The show produced its comic geniuses, it dumped them or let them fall off their own brinks, and it replaced them. In a book that has had to learn to be unafraid of leaving people out, I will only offer a quick cast of attractions before being cut off: Gilda Radner, John Belushi, Chevy Chase, Bill Murray, Jane Curtin, Eddie Murphy, Steve

Martin, Dana Carvey, Norm Macdonald, Phil Hartman… There were many movies spun off from the cast, but I'm not sure how much any of them mattered. I don't know if there were any geniuses on the team—but that doesn't matter on a team. *SNL* said most kids are pretty funny for a few minutes—and now, on cable, streaming, here, there, everywhere and nowhere, no one dares be serious any longer. (Look at William Buckley now and he seems eighteenth century— perhaps he always did. Trump's own trump is his bad-boy urge to be comic.) That is the real cool of today, and it has its desperate side.

The show was a triumph for NBC at first. In 1978–79, it had a 12.6 rating and a 39 share—39 percent of the TV sets on in America were watching *SNL*, or doing something else while it was on. That meant huge revenue for the network when NBC ruled late-night already, Monday to Friday, with Carson. Nothing lasts. In the new century, the numbers were 5.4 and 15—more than enough to stay on, even if "Saturday," "Night," and "Live" are now dubious concepts. In November 2015, for a night, the figures rallied: The show had a 6.6 rating and maybe 10 million viewers. "Why not?" asked the guest host that night. "I get the best ratings." Of course, it was Donald Trump, hot to the point of explosion, but cool, too, just because this scoundrel madman could go from *The Apprentice* to being the apprentice's sorcerer in one blithe insult.

21 ETERNALLY ON

IT WAS LABOR DAY 1975 when I watched my first American television in America. I had heard in England that the muscular dystrophy

telethon was a wonder of the electronic world, as inescapable as it was relentless. So I watched the show and realized that, while America grew tomatoes the size of Hulk fists and had lately disposed of a troubling president without bloodshed, it might be a wild and dangerous place.

This weird telethon contained nearly everything the box had to offer: It was live, with constant glee at the mounting sum of money being raised; in being about money prompted by suffering, it was a religious or redemptive gesture; it was also a commercial, though it was hard to decide whether for health or illness; it was comedy and variety, and for sure it had a talking head— that of Jerry Lewis, sometimes so moved, or so persuaded that he was moved, that his rubbery face seemed to pick up its own symptoms of dystrophy. Long before the term became current, this was a reality show, a breakthrough that actually separated it from most relevant traces of reality. Its impulse was gross sentimentality; you felt you must be a lost soul to be carping at it—or even laughing. As for drama...wouldn't it have Jerry reuniting with Dean in 1976? And wasn't it Frank bringing them back together?

It was schmaltz up to your gag reflex, bland yet fevered, monstrous but passive. Like humidity and 3,000-mile highways, it might go on forever, unless one stretch of 21.5 hours a year was enough to stand for perpetuity. The show lasted, with Lewis, from 1966 to 2010, and it is alleged to have raised $2.5 billion. Perhaps the money went on wheelchairs, poster campaigns, summer camps, and the telethon itself. Jerry was emotionally and physically exhausted, always; he did exhausted so well, and it is said he was not paid. So he did it for the kids and to be on? There's still no cure for that urge, or for MD.

It seemed a new idea— a telethon—until we realized that television was already and always a telethon. It went on forever, if you didn't pay attention.

Television has also been a terrain of mundane joy, of familial togetherness and a jaunty air of pleasure. How can we forget gathering in our living room before so many enticing windows on the world? The being there felt cozy. One hundred and fifty years ago, such windows were as formal as early photographs and descriptive prose. But now the windows are instantaneous, and so profuse as to make choice redundant. In his 1993 essay on television, "E Unibus Pluram," David Foster Wallace reckoned that one great benefit of television was that it was the window where fiction writers could get a proper sense of the range of life and the genres of vitality. He understood the irony in that distancing, but he guessed that many classic novelists had learned about life…from reading novels. So let's enjoy our screens, for a few days an hour.

I can hear arguments that say *Friends* was fun yet not really that "good" or "true to life." But did we have a good time with it! We most of us like what we like on television and tell the critics and the ratings to get lost. There are no guilty pleasures with TV—guilt has gone. So television is remembered and rejoiced in when its on-ness unites a household, just like Mom's fussy chandelier

THE BEING THERE FELT COZY.

dropping its wan light on all of us. Criticism turns insignificant because there is too much TV for us to catch it all. We sometimes meet people who never watched *60 Minutes* ("we played bridge Sunday evenings") or *I Love Lucy* ("she made me nervous").

Not that *Friends* produced anxiety. Or it didn't for our family. And what other "our" matters so much? Our nation? Our constitution? Our standard of living? Our future? Those stalwart clichés are available now as brands, subject to suspicion and distrust. A large burden of "entertainment," or distraction, is helping us forget that unease. My family loved *Friends* because of our luck in timing and a feeling that the title of the show applied to us. That's a staple in feeling "good" or at ease. And television can be as close to ease as the favorite chair from which we watched it. "Couch potato" is a derisory term acquired from our TV habit, but it doesn't impede the pleasure of sinking into something warm and soft that has our shape. (It may even remind you of making love.) "Television" was always a rather forbidding word with a hint of science fiction. An adman as sharp as Don Draper might have had a brainwave: "No. Let's call it 'The Friendly!'"

Friends played on NBC for ten seasons, from September 1994 to May 2004, in 236 22-minute episodes. It seemed as essential and flimsy as tissue paper, with a perishable immediacy like that of ice cream short of melting. My wife, Lucy, and I watched *Friends* with our two sons, when it was already in syndication, playing on some local station at 6:30 in the evening. The boys were maybe twelve and seven when we began, often with ice cream on our laps. We felt obliged to watch it, or not to miss it; it was a family occasion. We took the boys to Paris, Venice, and London, where they grumbled. With *Friends* they smiled before it started.

The show had been an immediate success, averaging 23–24 million viewers at a time, and never falling out of the top 10. It and its players were nominated for many Emmys, and it won once as best comedy (2002), yet only Jennifer Aniston and Lisa Kudrow ever won individual Emmys. Was the lack of prizes because it seemed such an ensemble piece? It was shot at the NBC studios in Burbank, and each episode required about six hours with a multi-camera setup. (*Friends* was still Freund—*sound of an elephant groaning.*) The show had been created by David Crane and Marta Kauffman, who were themselves old friends, and they kept close control of the scripts. But *Friends* was product rolling off the assembly line and a tribute to what prime-time television could be. After half a dozen episodes you knew what was coming. It was the promise fulfilled that made it so gratifying.

The team included the show's creators, some executives at Warners (Les Moonves) and NBC (Warren Littlefield), as well as Wendy Knoller, Todd Stevens, and director Kevin Bright—on fifty-four of the episodes. Gary Halvorson directed another fifty-five, and Mikel Neiers and Nick McLean did most of the photography. James Burrows, a co-creator of *Cheers*, was also a key force on the show. Anyone from a long-running show knows **FRIENDS SEEMED AS ESSENTIAL AND FLIMSY AS TISSUE PAPER.** the spirit of the unit and the reverence felt for its standing sets. A new home has been created and on *Friends* it was the two New York apartments (West Village) and the coffee shop, Central Perk, where so many meetings occurred. We recall those sets, but not the credit names I listed. We remember the room where *we* watched, and we know Rachel, Ross, Chandler, Phoebe, Monica, and Joey. They were all six of them "perfect" or axiomatic, and a tribute to very shrewd casting. Yet our sense of television does not abandon the thought that *Friends* might have been six other actors, and done just as well.

As the show began, there were some fears at Warner Bros. about the coffee shop seeming elitist. Should the site be a diner, as had served so well on *Seinfeld*? But the creators held to their instinct that these characters preferred a latte to a burger. The era of *Friends* saw the coffee shop become a hangout for young, upwardly mobile, diet-conscious urban Americans seeking romance, sex, a big job, or security (and being uncertain what order to give those options). These were kids not long out of college, away from home, and anxious for company. Some of those coffee shops were named Starbucks, but the chain could have been called Friends. That worldwide franchise, started in Seattle in 1971, was into profit and expansion by 1991, three years before *Friends* appeared. That was

THE ABSENCE OF SCREENS FOSTERED THE ROMANTIC SINCERITY . . .

when the franchise moved into California, on its way to over 12,000 outlets in the United States. Starbucks made an early association with music in its stores, and it produced CDs on its own. There was a time when Starbucks seemed to be brewing Madeleine Peyroux as well as fresh coffee. But try finding a television set in its outlets. The screens there are all for the Internet, and often those machines are our best friends. We now carry iPads in the way hospital dwellers have an IV drip.

Seen again ten years after it closed, *Friends* can seem dated just because its intense pulse lasted only a moment. It was natural to suppose that *Friends* was playing to the demographic of its six lead characters, but that empire was waning. *Two and a Half Men*, on CBS, began a year before *Friends* ended. It was a hit show that ran twelve seasons, but it seldom had an audience beyond 14–15 million. In part that was because friends were no longer sitting at home at 8:30 on a Thursday waiting for a new episode. They were attached to their own screens, their smartphones, a way of life notably missing from *Friends*. The absence of screens fostered the romantic sincerity of the six characters, and their concentrating on a conversation. They truly wanted friends, and did not grasp yet how all the smaller versions of a TV screen muddled that quest. That potent nostalgia lingers: There are stories of young people doing binge weekends on boxed-set *Friends*—just to be together?

More than a thousand actors were considered for its six lead roles, and maybe 10 percent of them would have done a good job. The roles were not deeply conceived or searchingly written. The kids had hang-ups and neurotic traits, but not a neurotic personality. They were going to be all right; they seemed to be paid-up members of the advertising pact that framed the show. Their oddities were comic shtick, like catchphrases and repetitious routines. What deepened the show was our trust and our familiarity with them, and the confidence that they cared for each other with family loyalty. The writers and the actors got to know the characters, in the way of all situation television. The ensemble spent so much time together (and so much effort in getting a better financial deal), it was inevitable that they became "friends."

This served us, too: The longer we stayed faithful, the richer the texture of the show became, and the quicker the cross-reference to events going back over the years.

... OF THE SIX CHARACTERS AND THEIR CONCENTRATING ON A CONVERSATION.

We and they were wired together. Sometimes a word or a glance reopened the rooms of the past, producing whoops of delight from us.

This is not complaint, but the group of friends became more like a company of actors—attractive, egotistical but amiable, alert to every nuance and cue, and so confident with their characters that they may have felt they were making the talk up as they went along.

David Schwimmer, Matt LeBlanc, Matthew Perry, Jennifer Aniston, Courteney Cox, and Lisa Kudrow became rich. They were more lifelike than the figures on *The Muppets* or *The Simpsons*. Their characters were delivered with the same vivid, cursory depiction. Being animated, or watchable, was their DNA. By the time the show ended, each actor was earning $1 million an episode (they had started at $22,500), as well as a cut in the residuals. Their lives have not been the same since *Friends* stopped. Jennifer Aniston has been a cheerful marvel of discipline, Matt LeBlanc has had other series, *Joey* and *Episodes*, but the identity of the six was that of an ensemble. In isolation they feel a tad lonely.

Saying the actors could have been replaced, or swapped roles (Aniston and Cox did exchange parts in preproduction), is a tribute to their family style. As the concept required, they were very pretty (like perfect, in an ordinary next-door way), funny, foolish, and touching. But they could have been the grandchildren of Donna Reed. No one got out of line or plunged into depression, mania, or self-destructive

behavior—conditions that can occur in young American lives. In television shows people intensify their own brand or type as the seasons pass. In the self-service of any show, actors begin to play themselves as dramatic potential ebbs away. One message from that is that life itself might abandon triumph or tragedy and settle for being a placid, ongoing show. It was as if the kids were saying to themselves, "Sure, I lost X or Y, and I was upset for a moment, until I realized the show had to go on." They were parent-friendly.

Looking back, I see the moods in which our family watched *Friends* more clearly. For people who might have been parents to the six (caught between the memory of Donna the Madonna and Phoebe the nut), it was reassuring. Yes, we could trust that our kids would stay this stable, tossed about by life and romance, jobs and disappointments, but resilient in their collegiality. "They have good friends!" you hear one parent tell another, when often the kids see themselves and their fellows as ships passing in a frightening night. The six were growing older (Aniston was thirty-five by 2004, and about to end her marriage to Brad Pitt; Cox was forty and Kudrow was forty-one) but remaining like children. They had their ups and downs, but no one went rogue or launched into private orbit, away from the group. None of them was truly "difficult" (they looked neat and clean and spoke their funny lines, and they were buoyed by studio laughter). It was the cleverness of the show to offer a few parent types—Elliott Gould, Christina Pickles, Bruce Willis, and Kathleen Turner—and make them the wacky ones!

So Lucy and I enjoyed the four of us being there for the on, and the humor of the show, and were inclined to hope for the best when our sons got to New York or wherever. The older son may have felt he was watching and learning from older siblings, while the younger was dazzled to see such youthful "grown-ups." It was a precious moment.

But I suspect the boys (both of them living in Brooklyn now) might look back on the moment with some disdain. They might take pity on *Friends* now because it had no iPhones—and no overt sex.

You see, it was a network sitcom, determined to believe in love and marriage, as if unaware of how unlimited spectator sex has reassessed those older institutions and made watching a basic erotic experience. This is a tricky point, when any kid knows where to get day after day of porn, lessons in anatomy and its variations, but also instruction in degrees of sexual aggression, the abuse of women, and the lack of feeling or memory in the transactions. Our handheld screens do those things, but the official screen of television is still frightened of the reality of numb or selfie sex. What it amounts to is that the situation in real life is obliterating the fond romantic sit of so much television entertainment. All in a medium that says you can watch as much sexual action as you wish for, with every taste catered to, but don't expect to understand what the experience feels like. After all, kids take it for granted that the people in porn are simulating joy (it's their job and protection). Acting or pretending rival "sincerity" in our culture.

There could be room for a new television series (long form probably, but imagine it working at 8:30), in which friendship is treated as a shifting system made out of chance, convenience, friction, betrayal, and pretense (as well as all the golden-oldie things like kissing, shared silences, and nostalgia). That series could begin with a packed city street where smart people are always knocking into one another because they are intent on screens in their hands. It might push on into a time when friends lose or forget one another.

|||||||||||||||||||||||||||||

I TURN TO *FRIENDS* because a friend read my first draft and suggested I might be neglecting the ordinary, casual pleasure to be felt with television. I knew he was right. I hope this book recalls and draws your attention to exceptional and pleasurable television, some of which you may have missed or never heard of; but the same survey is tinged with unease at what the medium has done to us. That sort of conflict is common these days: It's easy to enjoy the daily warmth and clear skies here in California while realizing that balmy climate is drying us out to a point of peril. It's picnic

FRIENDS EXISTED IN AN APOLITICAL CLIMATE, AS WELL AS A NON-CLIMATIC CLIMATE.

weather, but the grass is burnt brown in May. There are coyotes in our hills desperate for drink and more reckless because of that. The derelict on my street sometimes throws a fiercer glance than I expect, as if he had had to fight a coyote at dawn.

The young people on *Friends* were attractive and fun—surely we deserved 22 minutes of them some nights when our own lives lacked those qualities. But our contract with television was growing strained. The media stress on being positive couldn't protect the West Village apartments from being close to Ground Zero. In the aftermath of 9/11, *Friends* picked up larger audiences; for its finale it had over 50 million viewers. Not that 9/11 and its backstory were talked about on the show. Was that because the friendliness of the show (and its medium) reached out to us like a silent, apolitical comforter? For a century, disasters in the real world had been countered by the assurances offered by movies and television, a part of which said, "We will not talk of strife and the things that are causing it." That mollifying principle had as its rock the theory that the ongoing, nonpartisan American party of purchase and profit would let us overcome, or forget, strife. After all, the United States was the greatest nation on earth. It was hardly realized at the time, but the thawing that officially ended the Cold War had not settled the debate over rights and equality, even if Communism on the Soviet model had been knocked out.

In its merry swell of romantic intrigue and love's follies, *Friends* omitted many things (even if some of them got a brief nod from conscientious writers). The ideas, the issues, could not compete with the "she loves me/she loves me not" puzzles. So *Friends* existed in an apolitical climate, as well as a non-climatic climate. Weather was not included; the show stayed very white, and just as committed to attractiveness. There was an engaging mess in the characters waiting to be explored, but that risk was tidied away by their looks, their chat, and the cosmetic armory that hoped they were not actually aging. Political or religious allegiances were elided. None of the friends quite noticed the millennium, terrorism, increasing economic uncertainty, or the changes in marriage as an institution. In a curious way, their incessant togetherness left them little private life. It's hard to think of scenes of them alone.

That's why I raised the matter of sexual activity earlier. Any analysis of story structure (and why we kept watching) showed the emphasis in *Friends* on love and marriage. The action was frenzied and "up-to-date" but the concentration was not so distant from that of Jane Austen. *Friends* was a *ronde* offering nearly every possible arrangement—except for authentic gay interaction. In 1994, for certain, and just as likely in 2004, a *Friends* with gay action, or hesitation over sexual choice, would have been wiped away as a ratings leader. But in the real world that seemed to support *Friends*, that enquiry was growing bolder. Attitudes to same-sex marriage, or love (they don't have to be the same), shifted from outright majority denial (and horror) to conflict and then a spreading estimate that people should be permitted to do what they want. But that liberty could easily undermine the regular advertising stress on conventional attractiveness, or the social transaction of looking cute for the "opposite" sex.

Of course, network television would say, "Oh, we can't *do* sex— we suggest it." In truth, cable television has not been much more liberated, even if its suggestiveness allows more nudity (female as a rule), franker language, while confronting the hopeless task of actually conveying sexual experience in cinematic or friendly form. That means that sexuality is always suggestive and a screened performance, and that can be a debilitating pressure on how we think and behave.

Moreover, instead of the narrow quandary of "Are we in love?" some young people were bypassing the question simply by having sex. In that lay the realization that many of us might have made lyrics on love—in poetry, in music, in our own heads—because getting sex was once so constrained and difficult. But that was less the case from about 1960 onward. Another possibility arose behind the move for same-sex marriage—it was that marriage no longer mattered as much in the ways recommended by romantic literature and movies.

Perhaps my picture of our family watching *Friends* was at risk of being idealistic and sentimental. Did we all feel good in the same way, or was it just that I felt good watching us and the show? Did the boys sometimes fret over having to watch *Friends* one more time? Did they chuckle and smile at their parents to signal happiness or contentment? Did they regard the TV and its shows as tricks to keep them calm and better behaved?

I don't mean to say that beneath the surface laughter we were unhappy. But if a marriage has only tranquility, it may not be alive long. The boys left home (in the advised ways) and they discovered their own difficulties. These problems were not exceptional, but parents and children find it hard to discuss such things. My wife remembered that her mother had looked like Donna Reed, but she felt dismay if she watched *The Donna Reed Show* again.

PERHAPS MY PICTURE OF OUR FAMILY WATCHING *FRIENDS* WAS AT RISK OF BEING IDEALISTIC AND SENTIMENTAL.

To some extent, in young lives today, sex has become a more frequent anchor than love—and I use "anchor" because it has a TV meaning. Thus Brian Williams was striving to be an anchor, without noticing that the ship had sunk. Our sons talked about politics, Islam, terrorism, the economy, the future, and sexual patterns that might have driven Donna frantic. But that talk had an unnerving undertone of dismay—what can we do about such things? What can we do to make the United States the idea that Alistair Cooke once rhapsodized over in his dry way?

So our boys tried to be American: decent, good sons, and emerging men. And they are doing well at it. But an overcast of futility seldom goes away. It is the irony that is sometimes called "cool," requiring real thought, intellectual courage, and a gambler's instinct for tomorrow. This tone can lead not just to watching television, a medium built on choices, but to walking past our screens the way we go past windows, noting without choosing. And it has silly highlights: Just yesterday you could see Tina Fey whipping off her blue cocktail dress for David Letterman, because she vowed she was never going to dress up for TV again; or you could exult in Jon Stewart taking the compromised Tom Brady apart—while guessing that the disgrace didn't matter, except as today's gossip. After all, Stewart and Letterman had handed in their own resignations months earlier, which meant that television was losing two of its smartest, funniest commentators with the most lively surreal instincts. Is it going to matter?

||||||||||||||||||||||||

IN THE LATE SEVENTIES, I wrote a book called *America in the Dark: Hollywood and the Gift of Unreality*. It was barely noticed. But that was a long time ago. Video was only just appearing. The computer and the smartphone were unknown as the universal possessions that now identify us and give us entrance to the world. Of course, it was also long before the technological transformations we don't know or can't imagine yet (the 2030 breakthrough?).

That pretentious subtitle—"the gift of unreality"—alluded to a prospect that film had already detached us from many realities and helped guide us into a substitute dream. I didn't exactly understand that condition, but I felt it coming. Decades later, on May 20, 2015, in the *New York Times*, the Thomas Friedman column quoted a remark by Tom Goodwin put up on TechCrunch.com on March 3 that was a more precise description of a loss of reality:

> Uber, the world's largest taxi company, owns no vehicles. Facebook, the world's most popular media owner, creates no content. Alibaba, the most valuable retailer, has no inventory. And Airbnb, the world's largest accommodation provider, owns no real estate. Something interesting is happening.

Nothing in that was new, or beyond challenge. But the summary of virtual life was startling. There was much more in the same issue of the *Times*. Another article reported on the curious status of Edward Snowden. He was then in a kind of isolation in Russia, because he was under threat of arrest if he returned to the United States. But the article, by Scott Shane, observed how academic that "exile" was:

May has been another month of virtual globe-hopping for
Mr. Snowden, the former National Security Agency con-
tractor, with video appearances so far at Princeton, in a
"distinguished speakers" series at Stanford and at conferences in Norway and Australia. Before the month is out, he
is scheduled to speak by video to audiences in Italy, and also
in Ecuador, where there will be a screening of *Citizenfour*,
the Oscar-winning documentary about him.

There was an accompanying picture in the paper of the Swedish
Parliament in Stockholm, where the audience was intent on a large
streaming video screen of Snowden speaking to them. I was reminded
of being at AT&T Park for a baseball game where 41,000 people have
not just the game to watch but the "Jumbotron" screen that shows a
montage of the baseball, statistics, diverting video games, and, of
course, the crowd, the people who come for the game but enjoy the
sidebar of being seen on TV. Every ticket sold has a small-print dis-
claimer where the spectator consents to his or her image and likeness
being used in any way the San Francisco Giants deem fit.

But the *Times* went further than Edward Snowden. May 20 was
the day of David Letterman's last appearance on his show after thirty-
three years and over 6,000 episodes. And no one has been better at
celebrating the innate silliness of television. There was a story about
the events honoring Letterman's reign, and a photograph of Dave with
Julia Roberts, who had been his guest on air twenty-six times over the
years. There was a TV chemistry between them, the story said. The
Web was playing a collection of their moments, put together by the
Letterman show, in which they both aged (gracefully) and seemed
sustained by their rapport, fits of shared laughter, by kisses and
hand-holding, televisual intimacy and commonality, and the larger
sense of friends having a good time. I like Roberts and Letterman, so
I was a willing audience, reminded of that moment long ago when
Angie Dickinson laughed at a Carson joke on *The Tonight Show*.

But the story that went with the picture had a ruinous truth. The
performance of comradeship and fondness was a myth and a scene.

Julia rejoiced in how she would pick up Dave's beat on the show and just go with it. But the story (by John Koblin) admitted that she "had never once seen him away from his studios. Other than an occasional phone call or a brief chat during commercial breaks, the whole of their relationship has played out on television."

For the moment, that kind of relationship sounds like an aberration, or sci-fi. So, think back to the calm of fifty years ago (it seemed heady and unstable at the time), and just wonder how many relationships will have become screen functions, or apps. Maybe "app" is already the new word for "relationship." Didn't the latter always seem vague and hopeful?

‖‖‖‖‖‖‖‖‖‖‖‖‖‖‖‖‖‖‖‖‖‖‖

WE REMEMBER THE SURGE IN TV OWNERSHIP IN THE 1950S. In just a few years, the medium, the service, and the plaything became an essential household resource, a piece of furniture. Only the very poor, the remote, or the intransigent lived without it. Many houses had several receivers. But then, around 2010, the percentage of American households possessing at least one television set began to drop.

We can't say yet how reliable a trend this is, but our sons in Brooklyn do not have television sets. They cannot afford to buy them, let alone sustain the cable packages, the streaming possibilities, the fine-tuned remote that their parents labor with—because we pay a lot for that deal every month without knowing enough about how it works. But our sons are not cut adrift or out of the stream. They have other screens—their computer, a laptop, or a smartphone—on which, one way or another, they can get a lot of what they want, on HBO Go, Hulu Plus, or Netflix. A lot of people, young and old, watch on the computer, using "shared" passwords. It is piracy, but the pirated system wants their attention and their eyes on ads, and it doesn't quite know how to catch them, or

OUR SONS IN BROOKLYN DO NOT HAVE TELEVISION SETS.

whether to bother. I wonder if even the prosperity we wish for our sons, or the solvency, will persuade them to get a black plasma screen screwed to the wall, with all the necessary attachments. When analog television gave way to digital, there were press pictures of defunct sets lined up like mothballed bombers on a Mojave Desert airfield. The debris of yesterday's crazes is technology's offhand poetry.

In some homes now, the TV sets recently known as "home theaters" can seem cumbersome invasions of domestic space that few of us would tolerate if they were introduced by the police (or Big Brother). Increasingly, the machinery we have for amusement scans our habits and reports them back to the marketplace—or might it be some other security system? But the equipment is only one matter. For

THERE WERE PRESS PICTURES OF DEFUNCT SETS LINED UP LIKE MOTHBALLED BOMBERS.

several years now, television prophets have been warning that cable—that liberating novelty—will not last. Cable had seemed like a providential arrival; we regarded it as the force that carried long-form shows and some of the most innovative comedy. Moreover, cable just about kept faith with the principle of watching *Sex and the City* or *Game of Thrones* at an appointed time. Instead, we hear that we are an ever-present audience for streaming, tapping into the multiplicity of offerings as and when we want them. With *House of Cards* on Netflix, we got the whole pack at once. This sounds like a natural development: Let the people see what they want when they want. That is a weird assignment of power to us that does not ameliorate the loss of community or society or the increase of loneliness in watching.

The sheer volume of things that can be streamed may be confounding. Who can keep up and still leave the house? Kevin Spacey has predicted *House of Cards* will go twelve seasons. But Netflix has altered in its brief history. Once it offered a rich selection of DVDs that could be ordered through the mail, with return envelopes—a method that now resembles the Pony Express. But its library for streaming is already reduced so that, in the matter of seeing old movies (my archaic hobby), a lot of titles are reverting to their prior status of unavailable (*not on*) that lasted for decades before the arrival of home video. It is either that or collect a large library of DVDs that could be stranded if the system simply declined to keep making or repairing DVD players. It has done such things before.

Let's say I have 4,000 books, their shelves rising above me like rose windows in a cathedral. I came to that word because my books are a testament to faith or respect. I love them because of the culture of literacy they represent. Yet there are many volumes that I have not read and can hardly expect to read or read again at my age. So the cathedral is a monument where I wait without quite doing anything. My library represents the idea of love itself, and the hope that books can alter the world. If all my books vanished save for one—it might be Elena Ferrante or Conan Doyle—I would fall upon it with the force of lust and desperation. But with all the books there, ready and patient, I often watch television instead, in the vague assurance that I know what love is. I think television has always partaken of that casual sense of need. That's why we still watch it "now" and resent tape delays. Grant that everything could become available on streaming— every movie, every episode of every series, every ad, newscast, and live event—would the habit of watching decline? At the very least the automatic linkage to ads with everything might shrivel—if the system ever permitted that.

So I'm at a point of considering where television is "going," a challenge that can slip from technological or business forecast to science fiction in a sentence. Two basic conditions underlie the question, one simple, the other historically demanding. The short point is to note that asking where television is going is not the same as wondering where we are taking it, or guiding it. We are not in charge. We cannot reform the system or harness its mechanical energy. However potent or absurd they might seem in outline, technological changes will sweep over and through us, teaching us how insignificant we are. Sometimes we tell ourselves that these changes can promote adjustment. So it is asserted that in discovering or freeing nuclear weapons we set up an equation of intimidation and deterrence in which they would not be used. World war might be stopped, but the safer world has been so industrious with local wars. Is it only when you have the Bomb that you realize you shouldn't use it?

Isn't it pretty to think so, especially when deterrence seemed to work for a few decades? But balances shift, knowledge is shared or traded, and we are still only a few minutes short of midnight on the Doomsday Clock. We are so ingenious, so headstrong, such gamblers with ourselves. Perhaps our only way of lasting will be to remove all those dangerous human urges. Some simpler, pain-free, cost-effective dehumanizing process might serve, especially one that could tranquilize "belief." "Just believe" we were urged once, but belief can now seem our greatest danger.

The larger point—still neglected—is to admit that this process began a long time ago. We have to give credit to the pioneering distraction of the photograph. I know, photographs are fantastic fun, so beautiful, so endearing, whether from the eyes of Eadweard Muybridge or Josef Koudelka. We

THAT BEING SAID, I WOULD RATHER LIVE IN A WORLD BEFORE SCREENS.

love photographs: They shine and feel like skins; we keep them in our wallets; we regard them as "art" as well as a universal scheme of identity and recognition—though that faith is already so fanciful it only exposes the frivolity of solemn security systems.

The photograph was lifelike, so in an instant life had a rival, the more serious for seeming casual and charming. That thin end of the wedge became more seductive when it reached out for movie, then movie with sound, then television, then all our tiny smart screens and even an entrancing toy like Oculus Rift where, by putting on a clever mask, you can be living in a virtual world that is complete, intoxicating, and unsettling. A friend of mine in movies said of Oculus, "It's like heroin," as if having experienced a miracle.

It was easy to assume that these versions of movie were giving us information, news, entertainment, story, and art. So the enterprise seemed as large and improving as many other revolutions in technology. But in time, we realized that some of the information was unsound, that the news might be a press release or a sly fictional genre, that the entertainment could grow stale so fast it had to be thrown in the trash. The stories were endless and so monotonous that we learned to view story as a trick, not a unique link to life. Some of the most intriguing new art is a way of saying story no longer functions. Picking a narrative thread out of duration and context may be sentimental. We may be in a crucial battle now between experience/meaning and some such thing as mere, indifferent duration. Long ago (actually only 1927) Heisenberg (I mean Werner, not the *nom de meth* for Walter

White in *Breaking Bad*) saw a problem in separating particles and flow in matter. Television has always nagged at the same question in our attentiveness, but "particles" are a hope for isolation and meaning, while flow says, forget that.

Is "art" left? Well, if that makes you more comfortable, so be it. But art has been so commercialized and commodified lately that it hardly bears examination, or faith. Once we thought art was "sublime," "life-enhancing," and "profoundly penetrating"—you know the language of art appreciation; you can still find its addled idiom in movie ads. Art could be held up against every horseman the apocalypse might enlist. But the life allegedly enhanced moves on, uninterested in being appreciated, preoccupied with its own impetus. Some impresario may play the big bang against Beethoven's Ninth Symphony, but it will be up to us to determine whether that conjunction is deeply moving or a grisly joke. It won't matter.

And the not mattering is a serious influence of movie, a playing with life (and shaping it as a series of plays) to distract us from doing nothing about what we are seeing—so we contemplate outrages we might not tolerate in life. We have been converted from participants to observers, aware—like the first movie audiences—that the great *Wow!* we are seeing is something in which we cannot intervene, so we are not expected to try, which leaves it problematic whether we exist. That has fed political futility as the threats to continuing life become so concentrated that gallows humor may be the last respectable response.

So it's not a matter of how streaming will alter the medium and its content; of Verizon buying AOL; of whether long-form series can "last"; is Kardashiana a dynasty, about to buy out Rupert Murdoch; will there be a TV verdict on Bill Cosby; or will Ricky Gervais ever get to host the Oscars? It's more the wondering when the intimate electronic monitoring of ourselves will make us virtual figures, statistics but not quite individuals. I am thinking of the enhancement of a kind of GPS: a way of registering where we are, what we're doing, what our blood pressure is, our credit scores, our passwords, whether we are close to a stroke, whether we are worth saving, in plus/minus terms, or whether control of us is so significant statistically that it cannot be left to us.

I mean a set of systems, pregnant already in our screens, where we can watch ourselves (if we have the nerve), but where the decision-making is out of our hands—because of our incurable traits of unreason, emotional attachment, and "feeling." In sci-fi terms you can protest that this is "a very bad thing," like the pod-dom in *Invasion of the Body Snatchers* and other urban legends. But many advanced minds studying human psychology, social engineering, and the wiring of the brain will say those tendencies are not central to existence, an area in which drastic decisions wait to be taken, most of which cannot be trusted to the whims of individualism. The technology is the only force cool enough to have a chance at surviving, even if that evolutionary process turns us into tightly wired cockroaches.

We thought we were watching Chaplin, Garbo, Brando, and Mickey Mouse, and no one denies the appeal of those ghosts. But we were also watching screens, and beginning to recognize our own diminished necessity in the process. So whether the human race "survives" (a touchingly self-dramatizing concept—the cult of the particle after 13.8 billion years of duration) may depend on how the race can eradicate its own human tendencies toward love and hate, differences spiked by passion and rivalry, and the brief era in which the cult of the individual flared up like a sunspot.

Of course, the sun is watching us, as always, but long ago it knew we were just a screen, so it gave up on being involved or identifying with us. Is that why deep space ignores the radio signals we keep sending? Why bother with a world stuck in radio and television?

||||||||||||||||||||||||||||

YOU MAY BE AS CONFLICTED READING THAT AS I WAS WRITING IT. It describes a future so bad…yet if you think about it long enough, the melodrama of "bad" burns off in the sun, along with the pomp of "good." A duration of 13.8 billion years, give or take, is more than long form. So we might as well watch *Friends*, or whatever your preferred fun has been. It's not quite that there is an elephant *in* the room—by now the elephant has *become* the room. And television is not simply a means of fun, education, and art for the world. Our being wired to and by screens is the world we have. Throw your set away—you're still "on." Smart as we like to think ourselves, we never saw that coming, and only now realize that the thing we call technology is simply time and destiny, oblivious to our affection for meaning, sentiment, and the good or the bad.

But we are renegades to our own prophecies. We have to be. For most of my life I have watched movies, rejoiced in them, and tried to share those feelings as an encouragement. So in writing this book, have I really believed that television is a dead end in which we surrendered so many of the best things about us? No, I couldn't write in that dank spirit, and I live with hope that wiser futures will find ways ahead. Television may be the medium that leads us away from our most perilously "human" impulses—even if that makes us duller or rather less than the people in Velázquez or Henry James, or the minds listening to Mozart or Mahler.

There I go again, as someone taught by a student of F. R. Leavis and raised to honor the pantheon of movie directors laid down by Andrew Sarris (or most of it). That old-fashioned hero-worshipper has tried to win you over to *The Singing Detective* and *Fawlty Towers* as much as *Breaking Bad* or *The Gong Show*. But he knows enough to heed Chuck Barris's profound lesson: Being gonged doesn't matter. Everything on TV is miraculous and ridiculous, and it will still be on after we are off.

Still, I cannot forsake that familial history with *Friends*, even if I misunderstood it at the time. I was in conversation recently with my son Nicholas, three thousand miles away (precious e-mail screens—where would we be without them?). I asked him in his busy life how many hours a day he lived in touch with screens. He is a writer; he works for a publishing house. He did some estimates. Take away an hour and a half for his commute, an hour for eating, two more for reading printed books…"So let's say I am awake for sixteen hours a day, I'm on a screen for about eleven of them." So much for "no more than seven" thirty-five years ago.

Then I asked him, "Suppose all your screens were removed, leaving you with people, sleep, books, exercise, and so on. Would that be plus or minus?"

He answered:

Very hard to say, but something I think about a lot. There are two ways of reading your question. One: Only I am deprived of screens. Everyone else gets them. This option is horrible. Possibly worse than death. Two: No one has them anymore. This is much discussed in op-ed pieces. There are probably pros and cons to this (world seems more democratic now, writers and public figures are held to greater accountability). That being said, I would rather live in a world before screens.

I assumed the elephant had given up reading my e-mails a long time ago, but something or other now caught his attention. (I know, that stress on attention is sentimental.) His trunk went up to scan my screen—elephants have learned to act out their part for us. *That your son?* he sent. He didn't actually speak, but with elephants the knowledge pulse just enters our system. We'll get this app soon.

He tossed his enveloping ears to cool himself. He nuzzled the foliage at the ceiling. *Don't go away*, he said.

"I'll try not to. You're staying?"

Buddy, he sighed. *I have no choice. I'm the room.*

We can get used to something as immense and imponderable as an elephant in our room. We can adjust to the gentle disquiet and the nagging inconvenience. We can learn to tolerate the smell, our crushed sofa, and the larger unease of being on the edge of the veldt. We can manage. But do not fall for any simple assurance that this enormous, unflappable creature can fix the TV if it goes "wrong," and do not suppose that he is of very much use when that vacant question arises, "Well, what are we going to watch tonight?" He'll sit through anything. He says it doesn't matter.

I T IS OCULUS NOW; it will have rivals and other names. Perhaps it is just the latest big thing, soon to be surpassed. But it may be a radical reappraisal of movie and TV so far. So big a thing, it makes us forget the past.

Meanwhile, just look at it. Isn't it the best evidence that we are becoming screens—plastic, masked, anonymous, isolated?

A NOTE ON SOURCES

FRONT COVER

This is an image from the 1982 movie *Poltergeist*, which, even though it was credited as "directed by Tobe Hooper," was produced, co-written, and pre-designed by Steven Spielberg. The doubt over credit matters less than that it is an astonishing and very imaginative film, in which a child (played by Heather O'Rourke) is actually sucked into a television set inhabited by malign spirits. As is so often the case, the best movies made about television are filled with awe, fear, and envy.

EPIGRAPHS

The Mark Lawson quote is from "Splitting Hares," *Guardian,* May 2, 1999, about the original TV production of Hare's play, *Licking Hitler*. Over the years, Hare has written and directed movies (*Wetherby, Paris by Night, Strapless*) and television "plays" (*Saigon: Year of the Cat, Salting the Battlefield*, and *Turks & Caicos*) that are not really distinguishable as separate forms or media.

The David Foster Wallace piece comes from his essay "E Unibus Pluram: Television and U.S. Fiction," originally published in *Review of Contemporary Fiction* in 1993, and collected in *A Supposedly Fun Thing I'll Never Do Again* (1997). This is an essential essay, among the best things ever written about television, and testament to how Wallace resorted to the sofa again and again.

INTRODUCTION: THE ELEPHANT IN THE ROOM?

Jerry Mander's *Four Arguments for the Elimination for Television* was published in 1977, and it was one of the first books that saw how far television was victimized not just by crass commercial instincts and poor program content but by its own technology. Mander had worked fifteen years in the advertising business, and he began by saying that that experience had taught him that "it is possible to speak through media directly into people's heads and then, like some otherworldly magician, leave images inside that can cause people to do what they might otherwise never have thought to do." The novelty of his book was appreciated in review attention and good sales. Wise people nodded over its insights and resolved that others should watch less television. Ashley Montagu said, "The case against TV has never been made more effectively. It should

⊙

be read by all addicts and anyone contemplating participation in the desertification of the mind to which TV leads." People did read the book—and the desert is here.

Experimenter (2015) is a movie made by Michael Almereyda, starring Peter Sarsgaard as Stanley Milgram. It was one of the most intelligent films of its year and it did not do well. The elephant is just one of its surprises, along with a subterranean interest in how people watch each other, that did not arise in the days of movie. The furtive regularity and its absence of motive or hope comes from TV. I reviewed *Experimenter* in *Film Comment*, September–October 2015.

The illustration on p. 26 is one of a series by Lee Friedlander (b. 1934), begun in the 1960s, in which he photographed screens and their images as items in our domestic interiors and everyday experience, and helped us see that they could be seeds or tumors, decorations or primal essences that reappraised the nature of our household. He is not the only photographer to have noticed this phenomenon, but he seems the most persistent and elegant, and the most disconcerting. Another Friedlander, *Philadelphia, 1961* on p. 4, appealed to me because it is gentle and calm, and because the woman— I don't know who she is; I don't want to know—is some suburban Madonna who embodies the vague, tolerant affection between us and our TV. Even if our chair is empty.

Chapter 1
BUY THE NUMBERS

This is the place to list a number of books—histories of television, or of aspects of the medium—that helped in this book: The first and most influential, and the book I chose as a text for my television course at Dartmouth, was Erik Barnouw, *Tube of Plenty: The Evolution of American Television* (1976; with a revised second edition in 1992). It speaks of a different world, new and vivid in its time, now past—but it does so with a prescience of what was still to come. The other books on the first era of TV that I value are Les Brown, *Television: The Business Behind the Box* (1971); *Television: The Critical View*, ed. Horace Newcomb (1976); Martin Mayer, *About Television* (1972); *Watching Television*, ed. Todd Gitlin (1986); Wilbur Schramm, Jack Lyle, and Edwin B. Parker, *Television in the Lives of Our Children* (1961); Gitlin, *Inside Prime Time* (2000).

Chapter 2
WHERE ARE YOU GOING, FUGITIVE?

See Mel Proctor, *The Official Fan's Guide to The Fugitive* (1995); Ed Robertson, *The Fugitive Recaptured: The 30th Anniversary Companion to a*

Television Classic, with an introduction by Stephen King (1993). The entire series is on DVD, and the episode examined here, "Brass Ring," is on YouTube. There is an interview with Roy Huggins at the Archive of American Television. Ellie Janssen and J. D. Michael Phelps wrote a biography, *David Janssen—My Fugitive* (1994). See also, on Angie Dickinson (there seems to be no biography), Sam Kashner, "A Legend with Legs," *Vanity Fair,* January 2008.

Chapter 3

NORMA'S SESSIONS

Many of the sources repeat those for Chapter 3. On Loretta Young, see Joe Morella and Edward Z. Epstein, *Loretta Young: An Extraordinary Life* (1986). "What do we have to sell here?..." is p. 227 of that book. On Ms. Dickinson, see also Wilmer Ames, "Angie Keeps On Going," *People,* November 27, 1978. On Johnny Carson, see Henry Bushkin, *Johnny Carson* (2013); Kenneth Tynan, "Fifteen Years of the Salto Mortale," *New Yorker,* February 20, 1978, collected in KT, *Show People* (1980); Nora Ephron, *And Now Here's Johnny!* (1968).

Chapter 4

OH, DONNA!

See Jay Fultz, *In Search of Donna Reed* (1998); donnareed.org; Tom Gilbert, "Donna Reed's Show Reflects an Era When Mother, Too, Knew Best," *Pittsburgh Post-Gazette,* December 27, 2011.

Chapter 5

GENTLY "ON":
A NEW AGE OF TELEVISION PEOPLE

On Karl Freund, Lucille Ball, and Desi Arnaz, see Stefan Kanfer, *Ball of Fire: The Tumultuous Life and Comic Art of Lucille Ball* (2003), but take a look at a few Freund films—like *The Last Laugh, Metropolis,* and *Dracula*—to measure how a visionary of Expressionist dread found his lasting subject in bright American interiors. On Milton Berle, see Berle and Haskel Frankel, *Milton Berle, An Autobiography* (1975); Gerald Nachman, *Seriously Funny: The Rebel Comedians of the 1950s and 1960s* (2003). On John Wayne and *Gunsmoke,* see Scott Eyman, *John Wayne: The Life and Legend* (2014). On James Garner, see Garner and Jon Winokur, *The Garner Files: A Memoir* (2011).

Chapter 6

THE SIT AND THE SITUATION

On the idea of two facing boxes posed in television-watching, see Raymond Williams, *Television: Technology and Cultural Form* (1975), in which, on p. 59, Williams marveled that people might be watching two or three hours of TV drama a day, and admits (from what was a height of academic survey—the universities of Cambridge and Stanford), "The implications of this have scarcely begun to be considered." He was correct about that, even if he was way off on the hours. But I fear he was in error in thinking that sturdy consideration could affect the phenomenon.

On situation television, see Gerard Jones, *Honey, I'm Home: Sitcoms Selling the American Dream* (1992). On *M*A*S*H*, see Larry Gelbart, *Laughing Matters* (1998); James Wittebols, *Watching M*A*S*H, Watching America: A Social History of the 1972–1983 Television Series* (1998). Kenneth Tynan's "Nobody—on TV..." is p. 219 of *The Diaries of Kenneth Tynan*, ed. John Lahr (2001).

Chapter 7

COMMERCIALS

On Britain's development of television, see Asa Briggs, *The History of Broadcasting in the United Kingdom*, 5 vols. (1961–95); volume 4 is *Sound and Vision* (1979); I. McIntyre, *The Expense of Glory: A Life of John Reith* (1993); Marista Leishman, *My Father—Reith of the BBC* (2008); Joe Moran, *Armchair Nation: An Intimate History of Britain in Front of the TV* (2013).

On *Mad Men*, see Dave Itzkoff, "Mad Men is Gone, but its Characters Live On," *New York Times*, May 20, 2015; Ken Tucker, "The Mad Men Series Finale: A Sweet, Self-Conscious Kiss-Off," May 18, 2015, https://www.yahoo.com/tv/mad-men-finale-review-119272140530.html, accessed April 18, 2016; Jon Blistein, "Matthew Weiner on Mad Men Finale: 'I Don't Owe Anybody Anything,'" May 14, 2015, http://www.rollingstone.com/tv/news/matthew-weiner-on-mad-men-finale-i-don-t-owe-anybody-anything-20150514, accessed April 18, 2016, and Blistein, "Jon Hamm Weighs in on Mad Men Finale," May 19, 2015, http://www.rollingstone.com/tv/news/jon-hamm-weighs-in-on-mad-men-finale-20150519, accessed April 18, 2016. On Bill Backer, see Sydney Ember, "Behind a '71 Coke Jingle, A Man Who Wasn't Mad," *New York Times*, May 19, 2015.

John Berger's *Ways of Seeing* was a BBC program, a critical exploration, done in four 30-minute episodes, written or created by Berger and Mike Dibb. It aired in 1972, and it is one of the great achievements of television. Berger's influence hangs over this book and over the lives of so many people who were affected by *Ways of Seeing*. See also Emily Nussbaum, "The Price is Right," *New Yorker*, October 12, 2015.

Chapter 8
WASTELAND

On Jerry Springer, see Rebecca Johnson and Kathleen Powers, "Jerry Springer Under Siege," *Good Housekeeping*, September 1998; Sharon Waxman, "King of the Trash Heap: Jerry Springer Digs the Dirt on Television," *Washington Post*, January 20, 1998.

On Newton Minow, see Minow, "Television and the Public Interest," address to the National Association of Broadcasters, May 9, 1961, and Minow, *Abandoned in the Wasteland: Children, Television & the First Amendment* (1996).

On Chuck Barris, see Barris, *Confessions of a Dangerous Mind* (1984) and *The Game Show King* (1998).

Chapter 9
IS THAT AN OASIS?

See Barry Dornfeld, *Producing Public Television, Producing Public Culture* (1998); James Ledbetter, *Made Possible By: The Death of Public Broadcasting in the United States* (1998); Robert Saudek, "Experiment in Video Programming," *New York Times*, November 9, 1952; Nick Clarke, *Alistair Cooke: The Biography* (1999), Cooke on Saudek is p. 282. See also, Cooke, *America—A Personal History of the United States*, shown in 1972 and published in book form as *Alistair Cooke's America* (1973).

Chapter 10
A PLAY, FOR TODAY?

On Paddy Chayefsky, see Shaun Considine, *Mad as Hell: The Life and Work of Paddy Chayefsky* (1995); Chayefsky interview in John Brady, *The Craft of the Screenwriter* (1981). On Rod Serling, see Joel Engel, *Rod Serling: The Dreams and Nightmares of Life in the Twilight Zone* (1989). On Charlton Heston, see Heston, *In the Arena: An Autobiography* (1995), the passage I quote is on p. 88.

On Britain, see Shaun Sutton, *The Largest Theatre in the World—Thirty Years of Television Drama* (1982); Lez Cooke, *British Television Drama: A History* (2003); Andy Murray, *Into the Unknown: The Fantastic Life of Nigel Kneale* (2006); and on Rudolph Cartier, see Tobias Hochscherf, "From Refugee to the BBC," *Journal of British Cinema and Television* (2010); Yvonne Mitchell, *Actress* (1957).

See also, Alan Rosenthal, *The New Documentary in Action: A Casebook on Filmmaking* (1972); Peter Watkins, *Media Crisis* (2004); *Loach on Loach*, ed. Graham Fuller (1998); W. Stephen Gilbert, *The Life and Work of Dennis Potter* (1998); *Potter on Potter*, ed. Graham Fuller (1994); Michael Billington, *Harold Pinter* (1996).

Chapter 11
TALKING HEADS

For the Gielgud story, see Jonathan Croall, *John Gielgud: Matinee Idol to Movie Star* (2011). On Edward R. Murrow, see A. M. Sperber, *Murrow: His Life and Times* (1998). On Nixon and the Checkers speech, see *Nixon, Six Crises* (1962); Stephen Ambrose, *Nixon: The Education of a Politician,* 1913–1962 (1988); Mark Feeney, *Nixon at the Movies* (2004); and a play, *Checkers* (2012), by Douglas McGrath.

On Johnny Carson and *Tonight*, see notes for Chapter 4.

On *Face to Face*, see Hugh Purcell, *A Very Private Celebrity: The Nine Lives of John Freeman* (2015).

On Dick Cavett, see Cavett and Christopher Porterfield, *Cavett* (1974); Cavett, *Brief Encounters, Magic Moments, and Assorted Hijinks* (2014); on Jed Harris on the Cavett show, see Martin Gottfried, *Jed Harris: The Curse of Genius* (1984).

On. A. J. P. Taylor, see Adam Sisman, *A. J. P. Taylor: A Biography* (1994), the passage I quote is on p. 381, as printed in *The Listener*, November 27, 1980.

On Colonel Sanders, see Jason Brow, "Darrell Hammond Replaced by Norm Macdonald as Colonel Sanders in Hilarious KFC Ads," *Hollywoodlife*, August 18, 2015.

Chapter 12
POLICEMAN, SAVE MY LIFE

There are good books that deal with cop shows on television—like Robert J. Thompson, *Television's Second Golden Age: From Hill Street Blues to ER* (1996), and books that deal with their creators, like Brett Martin's *Difficult Men: Behind the Scenes of a Creative Revolution: From* The Sopranos *and* The Wire *to* Mad Men *and* Breaking Bad (2013), and there are books that have prompted series, like David Simon's *Homicide: A Year on the Killing Streets* (1991). And there are books that pay tribute to particular series, with detailed, fanzine knowledge. But the best commentary on crime and police, murder and justice, still exists in works of fiction that reach from Dickens and Dostoyevsky to Norman Mailer and James Ellroy, from *Oliver Twist* or *Crime and Punishment* to *An American Dream* or *American Tabloid*. (There is a sense of crime as a vital thread in America, not quite defined in the Constitution or the Bill of Rights, but given room to play.) In Britain, there are the David Peace novels that are the basis for *Red Riding* (1999–2002). I would also recommend Steven Pinker, *The Better Angels of Our Nature: Why Violence Has Declined* (2011), a brilliantly researched and argued history of the abatement in actual violence, which still does not account for or tame the vast increase in its role in our imagination. Still, the source that most affected me is Erik Larson, *The Devil in the White City: Murder, Magic and Madness at the Fair That Changed America* (2003). Every time I read it, I say, well, it's not exactly a great book—every time.

Chapter 13
THE NEWS, OR ISN'T THERE ANYONE?

Still not surpassed as a study on this subject is Edward Jay Epstein, *News from Nowhere* (1973); Frank Reuven, *Out of Thin Air: The Brief Wonderful Life of Network News* (1991); Michael J. Arlen, *The View from Highway 1* (1974). On Cronkite, see Douglas Brinkley, *Cronkite* (2012); Louis Menand, "Seeing It Now: Walter Cronkite and the Legend of CBS News," *New Yorker*, July 9, 2012. On Bob Hope, see Richard Zoglin, *Hope: Entertainer of the Century* (2014). On Brinkley, see Richard Severo, obituary, *New York Times*, June 12, 2003. The extract from *The War of the Worlds* is from Howard Koch, *The Panic Broadcast* (1970). On Brian Williams, see Erik Sherman, "NBC's Brian Williams Signs New Long-Term Deal with Network," *aol.com*, December 15, 2014; Jonathan Mahler, Ravi Somaiya, and Emily Steel, "With Apology, Williams Digs Himself Deeper," *New York Times*, February 6, 2015; Dylan Stableford, "Brian Williams Returns to Air to Anchor MSNBC's Coverage of Pope's Arrival," *Yahoo News*, September 22, 2015.

Chapter 14
WOMEN, WIVES, AND WONDERERS

On *I Love Lucy*, see Kanfer, *Ball of Fire*. The Jess Oppenheimer passage I quote is pp. 122–23. The Susan Sontag quote is p. 308. On Mary Tyler Moore, see Moore, *After All* (1995); *MTM: "Quality Television,"* ed. Jane Feuer, Paul Kerr, and Tise Vahimagi (1985). On Grant Tinker, see Tinker and Bud Rukeyser, *Tinker in Television* (1994). On Kenneth Tynan and "fuck," see Kathleen Tynan, *The Life of Kenneth Tynan* (1987), pp. 311–14. On *All in the*

Family, see Donna McCrohan, *Archie & Edith, Mike & Gloria: The Tumultuous History of* All in the Family (1988). On Norman Lear, see Lear, *Even* This *I Get to Experience* (2014).

Chapter 15
THE LONELINESS OF THE ROLE MODEL

On Bill Cosby, see Mark Whitaker, *Cosby: His Life and Times* (2014); Rebecca Traister, "No One Wanted to Talk About Bill Cosby's Alleged Crimes Because He Made America Feel Good About Race," *New Republic*, November 20, 2014. On Alex Haley, see Haley, *Roots: The Saga of an American Family* (1976). On O. J. Simpson: How can books—mere self-contained collections of pages—compete with or convey the thousands of hours of Simpson as a running back, as some kind of movie actor, and then as the silent lead figure in his immense and inept trial? Even in prison, in Nevada, he must have had to endure seeing (or being told about) the 2016 mini-series, *The People v. O. J. Simpson: American Crime Story* (note that insecure stress on "American" again), with the forlorn Cuba Gooding Jr. standing around nearly as numb and helpless as Simpson at his trial. On Clarence Thomas and Anita Hill, see Jane Mayer and Jill Abramson, *Strange Justice: The Selling of Clarence Thomas* (1994), and the HBO biopic *Confirmation* (2016).

Chapter 16
MR. PRESIDENT

On Ronald Reagan, see Anne Edwards, *Early Reagan: The Rise to Power* (1987); Dan E. Moldea, *Dark Victory: Ronald Reagan, MCA and the Mob* (1986); Edmund Morris, *Dutch: A Memoir of Ronald Reagan* (1999). On Richard Nixon, see Mark Feeney, *Nixon at the Movies* (2004). Eisenhower on Nixon, see http://www.presidency.ucsb.edu/ws/index.php?pid=11915, accessed April 18, 2016. On the Kennedy-Nixon debates, see Theodore H. White, *The Making of the President 1960* (1961); Sidney Kraus, *The Great Debates: Kennedy vs Nixon (1977)*; Gary A. Donaldson, *The First Modern Campaign: Kennedy, Nixon and the Election of 1960* (2007). On *The Manchurian Candidate*, see Greil Marcus, *The Manchurian Candidate* (2002). Newton Minow on the presidency, see Minow and Craig L. LaMay, *Inside the Presidential Debates: Their Improbable Past and Promising Future* (2008). On Nixon at Disney World, see Feeney, p. 41. On Frost-Nixon interview, see David Frost and Bob Zelnick, *Frost/Nixon: Behind the Scenes of the Nixon Interviews* (2007); Feeney, p. 45.

Chapter 17
LIVE?

On Ed Sabol, see Douglas Martin, "Ed Sabol, NFL Films Founder, Dies at 98," *New York Times*, February 10, 2015. On Hillsborough disaster, see author, "Sport and Tragedy," *New Republic*, May 26, 2014. On Oscar Levant, see Sam Kashner and Nancy Schoenberger, *A Talent for Genius: The Life and Times of Oscar Levant* (1994), p. 366.

Chapter 18
DOCUMENTARY?

See Erik Barnouw, *Documentary: A History of the Non-Fiction Film* (1993); David Attenborough, *Life on Air* (2002). On BBC series, see Kenneth Clark, *Civilisation: A Personal View* (1969); Jacob Bronowski, *The Ascent of Man* (1973); Alistair Cooke, *Alistair Cooke's America* (1973). On *60 Minutes*, see Don Hewitt, *Minute by Minute* (1985), and *Tell Me a Story: Fifty Years on 60 Minutes* (2002); Frank Coffey, *60 Minutes: 25 Years of Television's Finest Hour* (1993). On the Robert Durst case, see Jonathan Mahler, "Irresistible TV, But Durst Film Tests Ethics, Too," *New York Times*, March 17, 2015. On Adam Curtis, see Curtis, "The Medium and the Message," his personal blog at BBC Online. On Ken Burns, see Burns and Geoffrey C. Ward, *The Civil War* (1990) and *Baseball: An Illustrated History* (1994); author, interview with Burns, *Projections 4* (1995). On Fredrick Wiseman, see Thomas W. Benson and Carolyn Anderson, *Reality Fictions: The Films of Frederick Wiseman* (2002); interview with Wiseman, *Sight & Sound*, February 2015.

Chapter 19
LONG FORM

See Brett Martin, *Difficult Men*; Rafael Alvarez, *The Wire: Truth Be Told* (2009); David Chase, *The Sopranos Scriptbook* (2001); David Simon and Tamar Love, *Tony Soprano's America: The Criminal Side of the American Dream* (2004); Maurice Yacowar, *The Sopranos On the Couch: Analyzing Television's Greatest Series* (2003); *Breaking Bad: The Official Book*, ed. David Thomson (2015), which includes an interview with Vince Gilligan; Clive James, *Play All* (2016).

Chapter 20
LAUGH ON/LAUGH OFF

See William A. Henry III, *The Great One: The Life and Legend of Jackie Gleason* (1992). On Jon Stewart, see John Koblin, "A Sarcastic Critic of Politics and

Media, Signing Off," *New York Times*, August 6, 2015; Anita Bennett, "Jon Stewart Says 'Dissatisfaction,' Presidential Politics Caused Him to Quit *Daily Show*," *The Wrap*, April 19, 2015. On Ernie Kovacs, see Diana Rico, *Kovacsland: A Biography of Ernie Kovacs* (1990). On Ricky Gervais, see Kimberly Nordyke, "Ricky Gervais' 10 Bawdiest Jokes at the Golden Globes," *Hollywood Reporter*, January 16, 2011. On *Seinfeld*, see Jerry Seinfeld, *Sein Language* (1993); *Seinfeld and Philosophy: A Book About Everything and Nothing*, ed. William Irwin (1999); Josh Levine, *Pretty, Pretty, Pretty Good: Larry David and the Making of* Seinfeld *and* Curb Your Enthusiasm (2010). On *Monty Python's Flying Circus* and John Cleese, see Marcia Landy, *Monty Python's Flying Circus* (2005); John Cleese and Connie Booth, *The Complete Fawlty Towers* (1988). On Peter Cook and Dudley Moore, see Harry Thompson, *Peter Cook: A Biography* (1997). On *Saturday Night Live*, see Tom Shales and James Andrew Miller, *Live from New York: An Uncensored History of* Saturday Night Live (2002)

Chapter 21
ETERNALLY ON

On Jerry Lewis and the Telethon, see Nick Tosches, *Dino: Living High in the Dirty Business of Dreams* (1992); Shawn Anthony Levy, *King of Comedy: The Life and Art of Jerry Lewis* (1997). On *Friends*, see David Wild, *Friends 'Til the End: The Official Celebration of All Ten Years* (2004). On David Letterman, see John Koblin, "A Prickly Innovator Counts Down His Exit from Late-Night TV," *New York Times*, May 29, 2015. On Edward Snowden, see Scott Shane, "Snowden Sees Some Victories from a Distance," *New York Times*, May 20, 2015. The quote from Nicholas Thomson was a personal communication to the author, May 8, 2015.

INDEX

ACKNOWLEDGMENTS

THIS BOOK OWES SO MUCH to its editor, Will Balliett. He saw the possibility of a single book on television's history and achievement, and encouraged me even if my first drafts were not always what he had expected. He applied himself to the editing with patience, intelligence, and a tireless sense of detail. He then discussed ideas on how the book should look and turned them into reality—with the special skill and sensitivity of designer Beth Tondreau, aided by picture researcher Jennifer Berry. I don't think I've done another book on which the inspiration of an editor has meant so much.

In all of this, Will and I benefited from the tact and expertise of his associate managing editor, Elizabeth Keene. I also owe thanks to Rick Ball who did an outstanding job as copy editor. I felt very lucky to be working with him, and he was of huge benefit to the book, as was proofreader Neil Mann. And I am also grateful for the understanding and enthusiasm of my agent, Steve Wasserman, and for the support of Tom Luddy and Michael Barker.

Beyond that, I had generous advice from Elizabeth Farnsworth, a filmmaker and once an anchor on the PBS *NewsHour*. Her advice on the book was of enormous value and it was offered with the encouragement of friendship. The book is dedicated to one of my best friends, Mark Feeney, who read early versions and could not have been more astute or wise in his comments and suggestions.

I am grateful to the Dartmouth students in the first TV course I taught—one of whom, Holly Goldberg, is still a close friend.

But television is the medium we watch at home with families and I know that this book has drawn from experience with grandparents and parents, with Anne, Kate, Mathew, and Rachel, with Nicholas and Zachary, and above all with Lucy Gray who has watched over this project and its sometimes desperate author with her unique love and insight. She and I discussed so much of this book together, frequently while watching television, or while it was on. People often watch TV alone, and the medium does cater to solitude, but we should do all we can to resist that.

PHOTO CREDITS

Cover: MGM/UA/Photofest

Page 1: Jgroup/CanStockPhoto; Page 2–3: Bill Romerhaus/Photolibrary/Getty Images; Page 5: Francis Miller/Time Life Pictures/Getty Images; Page 6: Lee Friedlander, *Philadelphia*, 1961. © Lee Friedlander, Courtesy Fraenkel Gallery, San Francisco; Page 10: Bert Hardy Advertising Archive/Hulton Archive/Getty Images; Page 17: Harold M. Lambert/Lambert/Getty Images; Page 26: Lee Friedlander, *Florida*, 1963. © Lee Friedlander, Courtesy Fraenkel Gallery, San Francisco; Page 28–29: Nick Koudis/Photodisc/Getty Images; Page 30: V. Prazak/FPG/Hulton Archive/Getty Images; Page 31: GraphicaArtis/Hulton Archive/Getty Images; Page 35: GraphicaArtis/Hulton Archive/Getty Images; Page 40: ABC/Photofest; Page 43: ABC/Photofest; Page 46: ABC/Photofest; Page 53–54: NBC/Photofest (2); Page 55: ABC/Photofest; Page 58: ABC/Photofest; Page 59: Showtime Networks/Photofest; Page 61: CBS/Photofest; Page 64–67: CBS/Photofest (4); Page 70: CBS/Photofest; Page 71: NBC/Photofest; Page 79–80: CBS/Photofest (2); Page 85: CBS/Photofest; Page 92: AMC/Photofest; Page 97: Central Press/Hulton Archive/Getty Images; Page 98: PBS/Photofest; Page 109: AMC/Photofest; Page 112: Pete Ryan/National Geographic/Getty Images; Page 121–22: AMC/Photofest (2); Page 125: Pete Ryan/National Geographic/Getty Images; Page 127: PBS/Photofest; Page 130: CBS/Photofest; Page 135: PBS/Photofest; Page 138–39: Thomas J. Peterson/Photographer's Choice RF/Getty Images; Page 140: CBS/Photofest; Page 141: NBC/Photofest; Page 146–47: CBS/Photofest (2); Page 148: NBC/Photofest; Page 149: HBO/Photofest; Page 156: BBC/The Everett Collection; Page 160: Top: ABC/BBC/Photofest; Bottom: ITV/REX/Shutterstock; Page 162: ABC/Photofest; Page 164: CBS/Photofest; Page 168–69: NBC/Photofest (2); Page 176: John Chillingworth/Picture Post/Getty Images; Page 177: NBC/Photofest; Page 182: Popperfoto/Getty Images; Page 186: Popperfoto/Getty Images; Page 187: NBC/Photofest; Page 193: NBC/Photofest; Page 195: NBC/Photofest; Page 196: ABC/Photofest; Page 202: NBC/Photofest; Page 205: NBC/Photofest; Page 206: MSNBC/Photofest; Page 209: CBS Photo Archive/Getty Images; Page 210: United Artists/Photofest; Page 219: MSNBC/Photofest; Page 228: CBS/Photofest; Page 229: ABC/Photofest; Page 232: CBS/Photofest; Page 236: Frank Romeo/123RF; Page 237: HBO/Photofest; Page 241: CBS/Photofest; Page 245–47: NBC/Photofest (3); Page 250: ABC/Photofest; Page 255: NBC/Photofest; Page 258: POOL/AFP/Getty Images; Page 259: ABC/Photofest; Page 267: CBS/The Everett Collection; Page 272: CBS/The Everett Collection; Page 273: The Ronald Reagan Presidential Foundation and Library, C3695–18; Page 277: John Bryson/The LIFE Images Collection/Getty Images; Page 285: Jim Watson/AFP/Getty Images; Page 286: MGM/UA/Photofest; Page 291: Jim Davis/The Boston Globe via Getty Images; Page 295: MGM/UA/Photofest; Page 298: NASA Photo/DAST Project; Page 301: Popperfoto/Getty Images; Page 304: Popperfoto/Getty Images; Page 305: Ron Tom/NBC/NBCU Photo Bank via Getty Images; Page 315: Carolita Johnson/The New Yorker Collection/The Cartoon Bank; Page 319: AMC/Photofest; Page 323–24: HBO/Photofest (2); Page 330: AMC/Photofest; Page 337: NBC Television/Getty Images; Page 339: CBS/Photofest; Page 346: Hollywood Foreign Press/Photofest; Page 349: NBC/Photofest; Page 351–52: NBC/Photofest (2); Page 355: BBC/Photofest; Page 361: NBC Television/Getty Images; Page 362: Al Levine/NBC/NBCU Photo Bank via Getty Images; Page 364: Warner Bros/Photofest; Page 365: Ethan Miller/Getty Images; Page 370: Warner Bros/Photofest; Page 371: Chris Hondros/Getty Images; Page 385: Harold M. Lambert/Lambert/Getty Images; Page 387: David Paul Morris/Bloomberg via Getty Images; Page 416: James Whitaker/Getty Images